OUTLINES OF

HISTORICAL JURISPRUDENCE

VOLUME II

JURISPRUDENCE OF THE GREEK CITY

In preparation:

VOLUME III: THE MEDIAEVAL JURISPRUDENCE
OF WESTERN CHRISTENDOM

OUTLINES

OF

HISTORICAL
JURISPRUDENCE

BY

SIR PAUL VINOGRADOFF, F.B.A.

CORPUS PROFESSOR OF JURISPRUDENCE IN
THE UNIVERSITY OF OXFORD

Volume Two

The Jurisprudence of the Greek City

OXFORD UNIVERSITY PRESS

LONDON   EDINBURGH   GLASGOW   COPENHAGEN

NEW YORK   TORONTO   MELBOURNE   CAPE TOWN

BOMBAY   CALCUTTA   MADRAS   SHANGHAI

HUMPHREY MILFORD

1922

Printed in England

TO THE MEMORY

OF

RODOLPHE DARESTE

PREFACE

IT may not be amiss to state from the outset what will be attempted in this volume and what remains outside its scope. The subject treated is not Greek positive law in all its bearings, but the Greek jurisprudence of the epoch when democracy prevailed in the leading cities.

One of the Nestors of Hellenic studies, Dareste, had this distinction in view when he dedicated a book to the Science of law in Greece (*La Science du droit en Grèce*). But instead of tracing, as he might well have done, the application of juridical doctrines in the institutes of positive law, he contented himself with presenting a sketch of the teaching of Plato, Aristotle, and Theophrastos.

And yet it might be said that we actually possess in a fragmentary form the elements of Greek jurisprudence. They are set out in the writings of Aristotle and of his school—not so completely as the comparative politics of the period, but with sufficient definiteness and clearness. The well-known chapters of the *Ethics*, the *Rhetoric*, the *Politics*, the treatise on the *Athenian Constitution*, supply precious indications as to the way in which the various rules of substantive law and of procedure, illustrated by inscriptions and speeches, were connected in the minds of philosophers of the fourth century into a system of city-law. Some of the rules have disappeared, some of the applications appear problematical or contradictory, but on the whole the Aristotelian teaching on Political Science makes it possible to treat the details of Greek law as the ramifications of philosophical and juridical principles conditioned by the development of City-commonwealths. Greek juridical theory was undoubtedly connected with actual practice of Courts and Assemblies. There is no lack of books on general jurisprudence nowadays: why should we not try to reconstitute the general jurisprudence of the fourth century B.C.?

Another preliminary warning is suggested to me by some of the criticisms—generally kind and pertinent— called forth by the first volume of the *Outlines*. In that volume I restricted my field of observation as much as possible to a comparative study of Indo-European legal antiquities, called for the sake of brevity Aryan antiquities. The only exception allowed was the use of ethnological materials from various racial surroundings to characterize the elements of the family, for which Aryan culture does not provide sufficiently primitive examples. But I purposely avoided including within the range of comparison the data of Semitic or Babylonian history, not because I ignored the importance of Hammurabi's legislation or of Babylonian inscriptions, but because I did not want to lose my way in the maze of extremely different Social situations. The Aryan group seemed wide enough for a more or less definite statement of tribal institutions. In the same manner in this volume I have abstained from plunging into the immense sources of materials opened up for the Hellenistic period in papyri and inscriptions. It is with the City of the fifth and fourth centuries that I have to deal, and not with the equally interesting manifestations of Greek genius in Egypt and Hellenistic Asia. By way of exception I have referred to a few inscriptions of the third and second centuries B.C. because they presented some characteristic institutions with particular clearness, but I have renounced with regret any idea of following in the footsteps of Grenfell and Mitteis.

The fact that I refer seldom to Roman law will be easily understood ; the subject has been treated so often and so well that any one who wants to institute comparisons can easily do so by turning to the works of the well-known masters of the study.

It remains for me to acknowledge with sincere gratitude the advice and assistance of kind friends—Prof. J. A. Smith, Prof. J. L. Myres, Prof. De Zulueta, Mr. C. K. Allen, of University College, and Miss M. F. Moor, of Somerville College, Oxford. I am indebted to Miss Moor for the compilation of the Index.

TABLE OF CONTENTS

THE JURISPRUDENCE OF
THE GREEK CITY

CHAPTER I

INTRODUCTION

1. *Unity of Greek Law.*

ANCIENT writers have often called attention to the great
change effected in the history of civilization by the advance
from tribal conditions to city organization. Plato summarizes in the *Laws*[1] the received view as to tribal lordships (δυναστεῖαι) which still existed in backward countries,
and had sprung from patriarchal communities like the one
described by Homer in his account of the Kyklopes. " Did
not such States arise out of single settlements and kindreds
scattered and weakened by destructive misfortunes in the
course of which the eldest became the ruler ? With them
government originated in the authority of a father and
a mother, whom, like a flock of birds, they followed, forming
one troop under the patriarchal rule and sovereignty of their
parents." Thukydides in his introductory chapters describes
the contrast between the migrations of Greek tribes during
the early period and the final settlement in cities. "The
country which is now called Hellas was not regularly
settled in ancient times. The people were migratory, and
readily left their homes whenever they were overpowered
by numbers. There was no commerce, and they could not
safely hold intercourse with one another by land or by sea.
The several tribes cultivated their own soil just enough to
obtain a maintenance from it. But they had no accumula-
tions of wealth, and did not plant the ground permanently ;
for, being without walls, they were never sure that an

---

[1] *Laws* III, 680 b d e δοκοῦσί μοι πάντες τὴν ἐν τούτῳ τῷ χρόνῳ
πολιτείαν δυναστείαν καλεῖν, ἣ καὶ νῦν ἔτι πολλαχοῦ καὶ ἐν Ἕλλησι καὶ κατὰ
βαρβάρους ἐστίν· λέγει δ᾽ αὐτήν που καὶ Ὅμηρος γεγονέναι περὶ τὴν τῶν
Κυκλώπων οἴκησιν . . . μῶν οὖν οὐκ ἐκ τούτων τῶν κατὰ μίαν οἴκησιν
καὶ κατὰ γένος διεσπαρμένων ὑπὸ ἀπορίας τῆς ἐν ταῖς φθοραῖς, ἐν αἷς τὸ πρε-
σβύτατον ἄρχει διὰ τὸ τὴν ἀρχὴν αὐτοῖς ἐκ πατρὸς καὶ μητρὸς γεγονέναι, οἷς
ἑπόμενοι καθάπερ ὄρνιθες ἀγέλην μίαν ποιήσουσι, πατρονομούμενοι καὶ βασι-
λείαν πασῶν δικαιοτάτην βασιλευόμενοι ;

B

invader might not come and despoil them. Living in this
manner and knowing that they could obtain a bare subsistence anywhere, they were always ready to emigrate;
so that they had neither great cities nor any considerable
resources."[1]

Political thinkers laid stress on the immense advantages
of constant intercourse and close co-operation, which induced citizens to forgo the superficial greatness arising
from huge numbers and extensive territory.   Aristotle
emphasizes the transition from tribal villages to cities, as
a necessary condition of welfare.   " When several households are united and the association aims at something
more than the supply of daily needs, then the village comes
into existence.   And the most natural form of the village
appears to be that of a colony of the household. . . .   When
several villages are united in a single community perfect
and large enough to be nearly or quite self-sufficing, the
State comes into existence—originally for the sake of mere
life, but continuing in existence for the sake of good life."[2]

" It is further asked : When are men, living in the same
place, to be regarded as a single city—what is the limit?
Certainly not the wall of the city, for you might surround
all Peloponnesos with a wall. But a city, having such
a vast circuit, would contain a nation rather than a State,
like Babylon, which, it is said, had been taken for three
days before some part of the inhabitants became aware of
the fact."[3]

The older *jus civile* of Rome as well as the law of Greek
States presents combinations of legal rules which depend on
one dominant fact—the nature of the city commonwealth
(πόλις) ; let us try to determine the balance of juridical

[1] THUK. I, 2.
[2] AR. *Pol.* I, 2, 1252 b 15 ἡ δ' ἐκ πλειόνων οἰκιῶν κοινωνία πρώτη
χρήσεως ἕνεκεν μὴ ἐφημέρου κώμη.   μάλιστα δὲ κατὰ φύσιν ἔοικεν ἡ κώμη
ἀποικία οἰκίας εἶναι. . . .   ἡ δ' ἐκ πλειόνων κωμῶν κοινωνία τέλειος πόλις, ἤδη
πάσης ἔχουσα πέρας τῆς αὐταρκείας ὡς ἔπος εἰπεῖν, γινομένη μὲν οὖν τοῦ ζῆν
ἕνεκεν, οὖσα δὲ τοῦ εὖ ζῆν.   (Cf. Jowett.)
[3] *Ibid.* III, 3, 1276 a 24 ὁμοίως δὲ καὶ τῶν τὸν αὐτὸν τόπον κατοικούντων
ἀνθρώπων πότε δεῖ νομίζειν μίαν εἶναι τὴν πόλιν.   οὐ γὰρ δὴ τοῖς τείχεσιν·
εἴη γὰρ ἂν Πελοποννήσῳ περιβαλεῖν ἐν τεῖχος.   τοιαύτη δ' ἴσως ἐστὶ καὶ
Βαβυλὼν καὶ πᾶσα ἥτις ἔχει περιγραφὴν μᾶλλον ἔθνους ἢ πόλεως· ἧς γέ
φασιν ἑαλωκυίας τρίτην ἡμέραν οὐκ αἰσθέσθαι τι μέρος τῆς πόλεως.   (Cf.
Jowett.)

principles in this stage of development, taking as our text
not the much studied *jus Quiritium* but the less familiar
law of Greek States. In spite of many drawbacks, the
latter has the great advantage that it can be more clearly
imagined as existing on one plane, namely, in the stage of
the City Commonwealth, while the law of Rome gradually
becomes the law of an Empire, and loses its municipal
complexion.

A perplexing problem presents itself at the very outset :
are we justified in speaking of Greek law ? Does such
a thing exist ? In other words, can Greek law be treated
as a unity in spite of the fact that there were more than
a hundred independent cities, each with its own laws ?
Had we not better speak of Athenian, Lakedaimonian,
Kretan, Boiotian, Korinthian law ? The contrast between
centralized Roman jurisdiction and the autonomous law-
building commonwealths of Hellas seems to involve the
hopeless task of inquiring into countless local varieties of
jurisprudence. No very wide acquaintance with the
material is needed, however, in order to perceive that, in
a general sense, there is good reason to treat of Greek law
as such, and to analyse the contents of this great unity.
The Greeks themselves were conscious of a number of
institutions and customs which were peculiar to them and
bound them together in contrast with the barbarians.

Consciousness of national unity.

When citizens of divers Greek states met abroad, and
were obliged to stand together against foreigners, they
established common legal arrangements without difficulty ;
consider, for instance, the evidence from Naukratis in
Lower Egypt. We are told that in the seventh century B.C.
members of many different Greek States recognized and
appreciated common ties and common institutions.

Naukratis was originally a Milesian colony,[1] founded
about 650 B.C. ; it was reconstituted in 570 B.C. by Amasis,
who, as Herodotos tells us, was a "philhellene," and gave
the town to the Greeks for their use as a trading dépôt.[2]
The site contained a sanctuary dedicated to "the Gods of

[1] STRABO XVII, p. 801.
[2] D. G. HOGARTH, *Journal of Hellenic Studies* XXV, "*Naukratis*",
pp. 105 ff ; H. PRINZ in *Klio, Suppl.* VII (*Funde aus Naukratis*).

the Hellenes" as well as temples of individual deities, such as Aphrodite, Artemis, and others. One building, called the Hellenion, was the common sanctuary of nine Greek cities, both Ionian and Dorian ; their names are given by Herodotos, who also informs us that these nine cities elected the overseers of the mart.[1] There were also sanctuaries of Apollo, Hera, and Zeus belonging respectively to the Milesians, Samians, and Aiginetans. Judging by the types of pottery found on the spot, it is probable that the Greek settlement was in existence in the seventh century, but the finds from the Hellenion are less archaic, and the evidence goes to show that this was built when the town was re-settled by Amasis in 570 B.C. The development of this colony is a striking instance of the common action of Greeks of different races and cities in the early period in regard to religious, commercial, and legal custom.

The "common law" of Greece. In the fifth century B.C. the numerous treaty-arrangements as to reciprocity in the administration of justice (σύμβολα), and the levelling practice of Athenian courts during the sway of the first Athenian League, did much to produce uniformity of legal procedure and of substantive law in the Hellenic world. The Athenians were by no means solely responsible for the growth of a common system. In the fourth century we find that as regards contracts and commercial relations the Greeks came to look upon the laws of the various cities as fundamentally similar, so that Demosthenes could say : " Have we not all the same laws and the same justice as regards commercial cases? "[2] Isokrates' Aiginetic speech deals with a case of disputed succession, and shows that the law of three separate States

---

[1] HERODOTOS II, 178 φιλέλλην δὲ γενόμενος ὁ Ἄμασις . . . τοῖσι ἀπικνευμένοισι ἐς Αἴγυπτον ἔδωκε Ναύκρατιν πόλιν ἐνοικῆσαι· τοῖσι δὲ μὴ βουλομένοισι αὐτῶν οἰκέειν, αὐτοῦ δὲ ναυτιλλομένοισι, ἔδωκε χώρους ἐνιδρύσασθαι βωμοὺς καὶ τεμένεα θεοῖσι. τὸ μέν νυν μέγιστον αὐτῶν τέμενος, καὶ ὀνομαστότατον ἐὸν καὶ χρησιμώτατον, καλεύμενον δὲ Ἑλλήνιον, αἵδε πόλιές εἰσι αἱ ἱδρυμέναι κοινῇ· Ἰώνων μὲν Χίος καὶ Τέως καὶ Φώκαια καὶ Κλαζομεναί· Δωριέων δὲ Ῥόδος καὶ Κνίδος καὶ Ἁλικαρνησσὸς καὶ Φάσηλις· Αἰολέων δὲ ἡ Μυτιληναίων μούνη. τούτων μέν ἐστι τοῦτο τὸ τέμενος, καὶ προστάτας τοῦ ἐμπορίου αὗται αἱ πόλιές εἰσι αἱ παρέχουσαι· ὅσαι δὲ ἄλλαι πόλιες μεταποιεῦνται, οὐδέν σφι μετεὸν μεταποιεῦνται. χωρὶς δὲ, Αἰγινῆται ἐπὶ ἑωυτῶν ἱδρύσαντο τέμενος Διός, καὶ ἄλλο Σάμιοι Ἥρης καὶ Μιλήσιοι Ἀπόλλωνος. Cf. THUK. IV, 97.

[2] DEM. XXXV, c. 45 οὐχ ἅπασιν ἡμῖν οἱ αὐτοὶ νόμοι γεγραμμένοι εἰσὶ καὶ τὸ αὐτὸ δίκαιον περὶ τῶν ἐμπορικῶν δικῶν;

was substantially identical in this connexion. A native of
Siphnos in Keos, dying without issue, had adopted as his
heir a fellow-countryman whom he had known all his life.
Both men were residents at Aigina, and the trial took
place in the court there. The will was disputed by a party
belonging to a third city (unnamed). It was assumed that
the law as to wills was identical in all three places.[1]

In the Hellenistic period initiated by the conquests
of Alexander the common institutions and doctrines of
Greek law form a kind of "κοινή" in keeping with the
common Greek language of the period.[2] The documents
which give us an insight into this process are the
inscriptions of Asia Minor and the Egyptian papyri. It
is out of the question for us to go into details in this
respect, but I should like to cite as an example the
decree of Antigonos which directs the inhabitants of Teos
to remodel their law on the pattern of a neighbouring
State.[3] Such a procedure could only be adopted in the case
of institutions very similar in their essence. Another
example may be taken from Egypt: the recently discovered
collection of juridical notes prepared for an Alexandrian
lawyer of the second century B.C. contains among other
things a textual quotation from the municipal law of
Alexandria as to the rights and duties of neighbouring
owners of land. The law in question is borrowed literally
from one of the ἄξονες of Solon.[4]

The directing fact in the formation of all the more Common
important varieties of Greek law was the existence of the principles.
small, closely-united City-State, and this fundamental condition produced similar results in Ionic as well as in Doric
and Aiolic surroundings, in the Peloponnesos and in Attika

---

[1] ISOKRATES (XIX), §§ 12–15. § 13 κατὰ τουτονὶ τὸν νόμον, . . . υἱόν
μ' ἐποιήσατο Θρασύλοχος, πολίτην μὲν αὐτοῦ καὶ φίλον ὄντα, γεγονότα δ'
οὐδενὸς χεῖρον Σιφνίων, πεπαιδευμένον δ' ὁμοίως αὐτῷ καὶ τεθραμμένον.
ὥστ' οὐκ οἶδ' ὅπως ἂν μᾶλλον κατὰ τὸν νόμον ἔπραξεν, ὃς . . . κελεύει παῖδας
εἰσποιεῖσθαι. λαβὲ δή μοι καὶ τὸν Κείων νόμον, καθ' ὃν ἡμεῖς ἐπολιτευόμεθα.
εἰ μὲν τοίνυν . . . τούτοις μὲν τοῖς νόμοις ἠναντιοῦντο, τὸν δὲ παρ' αὐτοῖς κεί-
μενον σύνδικον εἶχον, ἧττον ἄξιον ἦν θαυμάζειν αὐτῶν· νῦν δὲ κἀκεῖνος ὁμοίως
τοῖς ἀνεγνωσμένοις κεῖται.
[2] DIO CHRYSOSTOM, quoted by MITTEIS, Römisches Privatrecht, I,
61.
[3] DITT. Syll.³ I. 344.
[4] Dikaiomata, ed. by the Univ. of Halle (Graeca Halensis), pp. 64 ff.

as well as in Sicily or Asia Minor. In spite of the differences of political organization, the fact made itself felt that
these City-States were welded out of federations of agnatic
clans and that agnatic relationship continued to exert its
influence even when the autonomy of the clans had given
way before the requirements of the city-union. Besides,
apart from certain wilfully backward cities like Sparta,
the Greek world was a world of adventure, migration,
commercial intercourse; the psychology of the race was
marked by definite and ever-recurring traits—by a highly
sensitive, artistic spirit, by eager exploration both on the
theoretical and on the practical side, by a sense of harmony
and measure. Starting from common family arrangements,
the various cities carried out the process of law-making on
analogous lines. When Hermione in Euripides' play wishes
to sting her rival Andromache to the quick, she opposes
the purity of Greek monogamy to the disgusting habits of
barbarians accustomed to unions between the nearest relations.[1] "Such is the whole of the barbarian race; father
cohabits with daughter, son with mother, sister with
brother; the nearest and dearest die at one another's
hands, and law in no wise keeps them from these crimes.
Bring not these practices among us; for it is not right that
one man should control two women; but having due regard
for one marriage tie they are content,—unless one consents
to an evil life." The connexion between family law and
family religion, the efforts to keep up the material households centred around ancestral cults, the peculiar value of
adoption, the treatment of the heiress as a link in the
transmission of family property to the next of kin,[2] the
conception of the κλῆρος as the normal allotment of a citizen family, the restrictions imposed on testamentary power

---

[1] EURIPIDES, *Andromache*, 173 ff. :

> τοιοῦτον πᾶν τὸ βάρβαρον γένος·
> πατήρ τε θυγατρὶ παῖς τε μητρὶ μίγνυται
> κόρη τ' ἀδελφῷ, διὰ φόνου δ' οἱ φίλτατοι
> χωροῦσι, καὶ τῶνδ' οὐδὲν ἐξείργει νόμος·
> ἃ μὴ παρ' ἡμᾶς εἴσφερ'· οὐδὲ γὰρ καλὸν
> δυοῖν γυναικοῖν ἄνδρ' ἕν' ἡνίας ἔχειν,
> ἀλλ' εἰς μίαν βλέποντες εὐναίαν Κύπριν
> στέργουσιν, ὅστις μὴ κακῶς οἰκεῖν θέλει.

[2] HERODOTOS, VI, 57.

in favour of legitimate children—all these features recur over and over again and evidently go back to an archaic association of kinsmen common to all Greeks.[1] On the other hand, the humanizing strain of Greek psychology and the early influence of commercial intercourse make themselves felt in such constant traits as the weakness of *patria potestas*, a feature noticed by Dionysios of Halikarnassos in contrast with Roman legal notions. The early development of the property rights of married women, the facilities for divorce, the emancipation of sons, the early disappearance of formalism in contracts, may also be referred to the humane tendencies of Greek life. On all these points the rules of the Kretan city of Gortyn are quite as characteristic as those of Athens, in spite of the fact that the Doric cities of Krete framed their law without being influenced in any way from Athens.[2]

Once the fundamental unity of Greek law has been recognized, we are, I think, at liberty to notice the more important variations within this comprehensive whole. Differences of race must have affected legislation as they have affected dialects, but it would be impossible in the present state of our knowledge to attempt any general inferences as to Doric or Ionic rules beyond such contrasts in racial character as have been noticed by the Greeks themselves—the rougher, coarser ways of the Dorians, the bent of Ionians towards exuberance and a freedom bordering sometimes on licence. What modern writers have tried to do in tracing such general characteristics in detail has not been very convincing. One must not forget that Argos and Syrakuse were quite as Doric as Sparta, and yet in government and legal arrangements these cities had certainly more in common with Miletos or Athens than with Lakedaimon. The most conspicuous monument of Doric law, the code of Gortyn, shows features of very progressive legal thought (e.g. the treatment of daughters as to succession, the law of divorce, &c.). Customs as to

Racial characteristics.

---

[1] MITTEIS, *Röm. Privatr.*, I, pp. 11 f. Cf. e. g. the dispositions of the law of Gortyn as to the πατρωιῶκος (I. J. G., I, xvii §§ 43-48, p. 375), with the Athenian law as to the ἐπίκληρος (DAR. *et* S. s.v. ἐπίκληρος).

[2] See e. g. *Law of Gortyn*, §§ 9, 14, 20, 31 (I. J. G. pp. 359 ff.).

common meals, and the military clubs which gave a peculiar
stamp to Kretan cities as well as to Sparta, were the result
of a life in camp which was not essentially Doric, but was
rather brought about by preparation for war on land, as
was clearly perceived and well expressed by Plato.[1] Neither
Korinth, nor Syrakuse, nor Argos had anything of the sort.

Constitu-
tional
contrasts.
On the other hand, a promising line of inquiry leads to a
comparison between variations of juridical treatment conditioned by differences of constitutional systems. Democracies did not shape their law in the same way as
oligarchies, and monarchies or tyrannies were also bound
to influence legal arrangements in a peculiar manner. To
mention one characteristic fact of this kind, in Isokrates'
speech ascribed to Nikokles, King of Salamis in Cyprus, it
is laid down as a consequence of the monarchical principle
that citizens are not allowed to form associations without
the leave of the government: this doctrine runs counter to
the ordinary law of Greek republics, and is evidently a
consequence of the fact that citizens of Salamis were subjects of a personal ruler, and that monarchs are jealous of
combinations which might gather political importance and
become a menace to their power.[2] Aristotle has some
interesting remarks as to legislation desirable and actually
obtaining in oligarchies and democracies. In discussing
Spartan institutions he notices the tendency to equalize the
members of the ruling minority in respect of property.
The Lakedaimonian ruling class was composed of ὁμοῖοι,
meant to be equals in social standing as well as in political
rights. One of the means of securing such equality was to
prohibit the alienation of land. But Aristotle is careful to
add that the Spartan legislators were not consistent in this
respect. They forbade sales, but allowed donations and
bequests. The result was a rapid growth of inequality of

---

[1] *Laws* I, 633 a τὰ ξυσσίτιά φαμεν καὶ τὰ γυμνάσια πρὸς τὸν πόλεμον
ἐξευρῆσθαι τῷ νομοθέτῃ; Ναί.

[2] ISOKRATES III, 54, p. 38 a b :
"Do not form clubs and associations without my sanction; for combinations of this kind may be profitable in other kinds of States, but
in monarchies they are dangerous. Keep yourselves not only from
crimes, but from practices of this kind, as to which it is inevitable
that suspicion should arise."

fortunes, and more especially the concentration of wealth in land through marriages.[1]

Those observations of the defects and inconsistencies of the Spartan legal system lead on to a scheme of legislation on property recommended to oligarchies, if they want to maintain the rule of a minority.[2]

Plato's well-known legislative plan in the *Laws* is dictated by similar considerations. In this case an *aristocracy*, a government of specially educated citizens, is aimed at. The corner-stone of the system is the formation of 5,040 indivisible and inalienable shares or holdings.[3] The prescriptions of Aristotle and Plato were not followed to the letter in any one State, but in Sparta and elsewhere drastic measures were occasionally taken to preserve or to renew compulsory equality between holdings: witness the reforms in the reigns of Agis III and Kleomenes III, when attempts were made to re-enact the legendary distribution of holdings by Lykurgos.

Democracy had a natural bent towards loosening the strictness of social ties, and it inclined therefore to great indulgence in the treatment of women, children, and slaves.[4] In commenting on Kleisthenes' reform Aristotle explains how important it was for the establishment of democracy to break the influence of ancient clans, and to introduce a reform of social law by reducing the number of private cults, and transferring their privileges to public bodies.[5] There are also many hints as to a policy by which the mass of the poor citizens, once they have acquired political sway, subject the rich to exactions of all kinds, and ruin them by burdening them with λειτουργίαι.[6] This view is

---

[1] AR. *Pol.* II, p. 1270 a, 19:
"Although the legislator rightly holds up to shame the sale or purchase of an inheritance, he allows anybody who likes to give and bequeath it."

[2] *Ibid.* VII (V), 1309 a, 14 ff.

[3] PLATO, *Laws*, V, 737 e and 740 b.

[4] NEWMAN, *Politics of Aristotle*, Vol. IV, p. 460. (*Pol.* 1313 b and 1319 b.)

[5] AR. *Pol.* VIII (VI), p. 1319 b 23 φυλαί τε γὰρ ἕτεραι ποιητέαι πλείους καὶ φρατρίαι, καὶ τὰ τῶν ἰδίων ἱερῶν συνακτέον.

[6] *Ibid.* VII (V), p. 1305 a 3 ὁτὲ μὲν γάρ, ἵνα χαρίζωνται, ἀδικοῦντες τοὺς γνωρίμους συνιστᾶσιν, ἢ τὰς οὐσίας ἀναδάστους ποιοῦντες ἢ τὰς προσόδους ταῖς λειτουργίαις· ὁτὲ δὲ διαβάλλοντες, ἵν' ἔχωσι δημεύειν τὰ κτήματα τῶν πλουσίων.

expressed in a blunt and cynical way in the oligarchic pamphlet on the Athenian constitution ascribed to Xenophon.[1]

Limits of inquiry.

In describing the way in which legal systems arise in the course of European development, our aim ought to be to strike averages and to discover the balance of forces, not to trace the innumerable fluctuations of the growth and decay of actual laws. The latter task belongs to legal history, while historical jurisprudence has to deal with the relation between the legal rules and the institutions of an epoch in their doctrinal connexion. This means that we shall have to concentrate on certain periods and abstain from an attempt to account for all details. We are not concerned either with the tribal beginnings of Greek law, or with its exuberant growth in Hellenistic times, although now and then a principle established in the fifth and fourth centuries B. C. may be well illustrated from late inscriptions or papyri. But we must renounce all systematic exposition of the complex legal currents of Hellenistic civilization, and as for the institutions of ancient Greece, they have already been referred to on some occasions in the volume on Tribal Law.[2] It is the inscriptions, the speeches, the historical and philosophical writings of the sixth, fifth, and fourth centuries B.C. that form the main basis for our study.

Another limitation is imposed by the fragmentary state of our data. The materials bearing on Athenian legal institutions are much more copious than the evidence from

---

[1] [XEN.] *Resp. Ath.*, I, 3 and 4 ἔπειτα ὁπόσαι μὲν σωτηρίαν φέρουσι τῶν ἀρχῶν, χρησταὶ οὖσαι καὶ μὴ χρησταὶ κίνδυνον τῷ δήμῳ ἅπαντι, τούτων μὲν τῶν ἀρχῶν οὐδὲν δεῖται ὁ δῆμος μετεῖναι (οὔτε τῶν στρατηγιῶν κλήρῳ οἴονται σφίσι χρῆναι μετεῖναι οὔτε τῶν ἱππαρχιῶν)· γιγνώσκει γὰρ ὁ δῆμος ὅτι πλείω ὠφελεῖται ἐν τῷ μὴ αὐτὸς ἄρχειν ταύτας τὰς ἀρχάς, ἀλλ᾽ ἐὰν τοὺς δυνατωτάτους ἄρχειν· ὁπόσαι δ᾽ εἰσὶν ἀρχαὶ μισθοφορίας ἕνεκα καὶ ὠφελείας εἰς τὸν οἶκον, ταύτας ζητεῖ ὁ δῆμος ἄρχειν. ἔπειτα δέ, ὃ ἔνιοι θαυμάζουσιν ὅτι πανταχοῦ πλέον νέμουσι τοῖς πονηροῖς καὶ πένησι καὶ δημοτικοῖς ἢ τοῖς χρηστοῖς, ἐν αὐτῷ τούτῳ φανοῦνται τὴν δημοκρατίαν διασῴζοντες. οἱ μὲν γὰρ πένητες καὶ οἱ δημόται καὶ οἱ χείρους εὖ πράττοντες, καὶ πολλοὶ οἱ τοιοῦτοι γιγνόμενοι τὴν δημοκρατίαν αὔξουσιν· ἐὰν δὲ εὖ πράττωσιν οἱ πλούσιοι καὶ οἱ χρηστοί, ἰσχυρὸν τὸ ἐναντίον σφίσιν αὐτοῖς καθιστᾶσιν οἱ δημοτικοί.

It was by tracing the connexion between constitutions and ordinary laws that Montesquieu came to plan his famous *Esprit des Lois*. Ancient materials, sometimes misunderstood and sometimes analysed with considerable acumen, served to a great extent as the basis for his generalizations.

[2] *Historical Jurisprudence*, Vol. I, pp. 243, 303, 326, etc.

all other cities of the Greek world taken together. Therefore every attempt to state Greek juridical doctrines is bound to assume an Athenian colouring. If we had possessed an approximately equal number of ascertained facts in respect of the laws of Sparta, Argos, Thebes, Korinth, we might have been able perhaps to notice more or less fully the interesting variations brought in by the difference of race and the contrasts of political organization. As it happens, nothing complete can be achieved with the help of the materials at hand, and although peculiarities of the law of Gortyn, or of the laws of Ionian cities, will be noticed whenever possible, it is the common law of Greece, the κοινή of the classical period, that will have to be reconstituted as far as possible by the help chiefly of Athenian materials.

The Greeks did not allow their law to lapse into abstruse Public technicality and to become a tool of professional jurists. opinion. Greek law in its application was meant to be a frame for public opinion. In Athens, at any rate, the remarkable experiment was made of handing over the administration of justice and the application of legal rules to batches of 201, 401, 1,001 jurors. The principle on which heliasts were called to decide cases was the same as that which has made the institution of the jury the usual device for deciding questions of fact in modern criminal procedure. It is the view that justice should be administered to the members of a community in accordance with the standards of morality and common sense prevailing in this community. But the Greeks went much further than we do, and entrusted to their many-headed juries not only questions of fact and responsibility, but questions of law which affected the distribution and enforcement of rights. It is most instructive to watch the results of this experiment on a large scale. Opinions differed among the experimenters themselves. We need not lay much stress on the contemptuous estimate of Plato, for he condemns all the democratic institutions of Athens, and yet Athenian democracy had formed the background for the greatest achievements of Greek genius. The extant speeches of pleaders indeed show that the experiment led to a somewhat

capricious application of the law, opened the door for senti-
mentalism, prejudice, and sophistry.[1] The heliasts were
often circumvented, "bamboozled" by crafty pleaders, as
Wyse, one of our authorities on the subject, has irreverently
expressed it.[2] But, on the whole, I confess that the wonder
seems to be not that the heliasts should have been sometimes led astray or that they proved unable to analyse
doctrine in the same way as this was done by Roman
jurists, but rather that they should have grappled with
their task as well as they did. These large tribunals were
admittedly free from corruption, and, what is more, they
were well able to appreciate the acute dialectics of Isaios
or the refined literary skill of Hypereides. Apart from
that, although learned jurisprudence in the sense of the
Romans could not arise on such soil, the courts succeeded
in treating problems of property, possession, obligation,
association, etc., in the light of advanced notions of justice,
fairness, and social expediency. This explains why Greek
legal rules, instead of disappearing before the more strict
and technical doctrines of Roman jurists, came to modify
the latter in many ways : the more we study Roman Law,
the larger is the share we have to assign to the influence of
Greek custom and Greek legislation.

2. *The Social Type.*

The *polis*.   In considering the Greek *polis* and its institutions four
features appear to be of special importance from the outset.

1. The Greeks recognized a close analogy between the
organization of the State and the organism of the individual
human being. They thought that the two elements of body
and mind, the former guided and governed by the latter,
had a parallel in two constitutive elements of the State, the
rulers and the ruled. As Aristotle puts it in the *Politics*:

---

[1] Cf. ISOKRATES, XVIII, 9, 10 . . . ὡς πολλὰ παρὰ γνώμην ἐν τοῖς δικαστηρίοις ἀποβαίνει, καὶ ὅτι τύχῃ μᾶλλον ἢ τῷ δικαίῳ κρίνεται τὰ παρ' ὑμῖν.
And LYKURGOS, *in Leokr.* §§ 11, 12 οἱ . . . πλεῖστοι τῶν εἰς ὑμᾶς εἰσιόντων
πάντων ἀτοπώτατον ποιοῦσιν· ἢ γὰρ συμβουλεύουσιν ἐνταῦθα περὶ τῶν κοινῶν
πραγμάτων, ἢ κατηγοροῦσι καὶ διαβάλλουσι πάντα μᾶλλον ἢ περὶ οὗ μέλλετε
τὴν ψῆφον φέρειν. . . . τούτων δὲ αἴτιοι ὑμεῖς ἐστέ, ὦ ἄνδρες· τὴν γὰρ
ἐξουσίαν ταύτην δεδώκατε τοῖς ἐνθάδ' εἰσιοῦσιν.

[2] WYSE, *Speeches of Isaeus*, p. 483.

" he who can foresee with his mind is by nature intended
to be lord and master, and he who can work with his body
is a subject, and by nature a servant." [1]

2. The second point to notice is the restriction in size of
the Greek State; in contrast with the modern State the
πόλις may be described as a political club, endowed with
powers of government and legislation, and requiring a close
connexion in thought and action between all its members.
Aristotle in the *Ethics* compares the number constituting
a circle of friendship with that of a city, saying that there
must be a definite limit: " for a city could not consist either
of ten persons or of a hundred thousand." [2]   And again in
the *Politics*: " the most natural limit of the population of
a State is said to be the largest number which suffices for
the purposes of life, and can be easily surveyed." [3]

3. The political association practised in the Greek States The
may be regarded as the very opposite of the restricted pursuit of welfare.
State organization recommended by modern individualists.
In order to discover anything analogous to the *laissez-faire*
doctrine one would have to go down in Greek political
development to the views of Epicurus, suggested by the
decay of the Hellenic polity. [4]   In the classical period the
State was not conceived as a kind of necessary evil to be
tolerated for the sake of order and security.   On the contrary, the Greeks attributed a positive aim to the State;
it exists not merely to facilitate association, but to shape
it : to help reasonable and strong-minded men in the pursuit of *welfare*.   This is the proper sphere of the State,
because the task of finding true welfare is out of the range

---

[1] *Pol.* I, 1252 a 31 τὸ . . . δυνάμενον τῇ διανοίᾳ προορᾶν ἄρχον φύσει
καὶ δεσπόζον φύσει, τὸ δὲ δυνάμενον τῷ σώματι ταῦτα ποιεῖν ἀρχόμενον καὶ
φύσει δοῦλον.   Cf. *ibid.* I, 1254 a ; III, 1287 a ; IV (VII), 1332 b.

[2] *Eth. Nik.* IX, 1170 b ἔστι τι μέτρον καὶ φιλικοῦ πλήθους, ὥσπερ πόλεως·
οὔτε γὰρ ἐκ δέκα ἀνθρώπων γένοιτ᾽ ἂν πόλις, οὔτ᾽ ἐκ δέκα μυριάδων ἔτι πόλις
ἐστίν.

[3] *Pol.* IV (VII), 1326 b 23 οὗτός ἐστι πόλεως ὅρος ἄριστος, ἡ μεγίστη τοῦ
πλήθους ὑπερβολὴ πρὸς αὐτάρκειαν ζωῆς εὐσύνοπτος.   We know from the
statement of Philochoros (*Schol. in Aristoph. Vesp.* v. 718) that in
445 B.C. the number of citizens of Athens was reduced from 21,000
to about 15,000. Cf. FRAENKEL, *Die attische Geschworenengerichte*,
pp. 13 ff.

[4] MAX WUNDT, *Geschichte der griechischen Ethik*, II, pp. 195 f. Cf.
ZELLER, *Outlines of the History of Greek Philosophy* (Eng. trans. 1901),
pp. 266 f.

of individual effort, but within the range and power of
a political association. The State exists οὐ μόνον τοῦ ζῆν
ἕνεκα, ἀλλὰ τοῦ εὖ ζῆν.

But what is meant by " welfare "?   How did the Greeks
conceive a " good life " (εὖ ζῆν)?   Without going into the
details of philosophical doctrines on this subject, let us consider some of the common interpretations which were given
of the notion of welfare.   In the following passage of his
Rhetoric[1] Aristotle collects some of the current definitions
of εὐδαιμονία: ἔστω δὴ εὐδαιμονία εὐπραξία μετ᾽ ἀρετῆς,
ἢ αὐτάρκεια ζωῆς, ἢ ὁ βίος ὁ μετ᾽ ἀσφαλείας ἥδιστος, ἢ
εὐθηνία κτημάτων καὶ σωμάτων μετὰ δυνάμεως φυλακτικῆς
τε καὶ πρακτικῆς τούτων· σχεδὸν γὰρ τούτων ἐν ἢ πλείω τὴν
εὐδαιμονίαν ὁμολογοῦσιν εἶναι ἅπαντες.   In point of interest
these definitions may be examined in inverted order.   The
thought expressed in the words βίος μετ᾽ ἀσφαλείας ἥδιστος
presents a kind of naïve Epicurean view which does not
require very close examination.   Nor again does the last.
More important are the other two.   The second definition
summarizes in two words a principle which is insisted on
from the very beginning of Aristotle's *Politics* to the end,
namely that the aim of society is to enable men to be self-
sufficient.   Again, welfare is said to consist in " well-
doing combined with virtue."   Virtue in the abstract is not
sufficient : it must be accompanied by εὐπραξία, virtue in
action.   This is characteristic of popular ideals in Greece.
The conception of active virtue is fundamental in the
idealistic philosophy of the fourth century.   Aristotle
refers to it several times; in the *Politics* he puts it for
example in the following way : " happiness is . . . a realization and perfect practice of virtue ", εὐδαιμονία . . . ἀρετῆς
ἐνέργεια καὶ χρῆσίς τις τέλειος.[2]

[1] AR. *Rhet.*, I, 5. 3, p. 1360 b.   "Take Happiness to be either well-
doing, through the exercise of virtue or self-sufficiency of life; or
that existence which combines safety with pleasure ; or a flourishing
state of wealth and health, with the power of guarding and producing
it ; for it may be said that all men allow Happiness to be one or more
of these things."   Cf. *Pol.* IV (VII), p. 1325 b 14 ἀλλ᾽ εἰ . . . τὴν εὐδαιμονίαν εὐπραγίαν θετέον, καὶ κοινῇ πάσης πόλεως ἂν εἴη καὶ καθ᾽ ἕκαστον
ἄριστος βίος ὁ πρακτικός.

[2] *Pol.* IV (VII), 1328 a 38 ; cf. 1332 a 9 ; cf. PLATO, *Republic*, VII,
p. 540.   A kindred notion is expressed by Thukydides in the famous
sentence: φιλοκαλοῦμέν τε γὰρ μετ᾽ εὐτελείας καὶ φιλοσοφοῦμεν ἄνευ μαλακίας.

As it was on these lines that the State aimed at providing for the attainment of welfare, the initial problem clearly was to decide what kinds of things it could actually guarantee. Of course the State could not promise that it would achieve an absolutely favourable result: however careful the organization may be, human life is surrounded with possibilities favourable or unfavourable, as the case may be, which may upset all calculations by the impact of blind forces of nature. What can be attempted is similar to the activity of mariners, who, though unable to eliminate rocks and bad weather, try to use the winds and to overcome dangers by courage and skilful management. Aristotle holds fast to the conclusion that in spite of the element of chance in human affairs, it is possible to direct political life in such a way that wise and virtuous men may reasonably expect the maximum of human happiness.[1] " He who would duly inquire about the best form of a State ought first to determine which is the most eligible life; while this remains uncertain the best form of the State must also be uncertain; for in the natural order of things, those may be expected to lead the best life who are governed in the best manner of which their circumstances admit." To this end the individual must endeavour to combine the four cardinal virtues—courage, justice, moderation, and wisdom.

4. The practical question remains: What means are to be employed to construct the ship in such a way that it may provide the desired help for withstanding peril? The utmost care must be taken in regard to the component parts. The individual is a component part of the whole, and therefore the direct action of the State upon the individual in Greece was much greater than that contemplated in any modern society.

In the case of the military socialism of Sparta this is obvious; in Athens there was of course a good deal of room for individual development, as is insisted upon, for

Educational rule.

---

[1] AR. *Pol.* IV (VII), p. 1323 a 14 ἀνάγκη δὴ τὸν μέλλοντα περὶ αὐτῆς ποιήσασθαι τὴν προσήκουσαν σκέψιν διορίσασθαι πρῶτον τίς αἱρετώτατος βίος. ἀδήλου γὰρ ὄντος τούτου καὶ τὴν ἀρίστην ἀναγκαῖον ἄδηλον εἶναι πολιτείαν· ἄριστα γὰρ πράττειν προσήκει τοὺς ἄριστα πολιτευομένους ἐκ τῶν ὑπαρχόντων αὐτοῖς, ἐὰν μή τι γίγνηται παράλογον.

instance, in Thukydides' account of the Funeral Oration of Perikles. In fact, according to Aristotle, democracy tended generally towards the emancipation of the individual: "the basis of a democratic state is liberty", he says, and liberty with the sense of doing what one likes (ὅπως ἂν βούληταί τις)[1]; but he feels that this tendency is a dangerous one, "for where absolute freedom is allowed there is nothing to restrain the evil which is inherent in every man."[2] As a matter of fact Aristotle mentions a number of measures contemplated or adopted in democratic communities for the purpose of regulating property and its uses.

In any case, from the point of view of present-day individualists, Greek citizens were subject to frequent interference by the City. The State was an educational institution, and it was its duty to take the citizens at as early an age as possible and to keep them under the beneficial influence of laws throughout life. Thus in the *Ethics* Aristotle says: "the factors which tend to produce virtue in general are those regulations which are prescribed with reference to the education of man as a citizen."[3] A socialistic point of view is expressed with exaggeration by Plato in the *Laws*: "O my friends, we will say to them, hard is it for you, who are creatures of a day, to know what is yours,—hard, too, to know yourselves, as the Delphic oracle says, at this hour. Now I, as the legislator, regard you and your possessions, not as belonging to yourselves, but as belonging to your whole family, both past and future, and yet more do I regard both family and possessions as belonging to the State."[4] Being creatures of a moment, we cannot profess to understand what we

---

[1] *Pol.* VIII (VI) 1317 a 40. Cf. ZIMMERN, *The Greek Commonwealth*, pp. 195 ff.

[2] *Ib.* 1318 b 39 ἡ γὰρ ἐξουσία τοῦ πράττειν ὅ τι ἂν ἐθέλῃ τις οὐ δύναται φυλάττειν τὸ ἐν ἑκάστῳ τῶν ἀνθρώπων φαῦλον.

[3] *Eth. Nik.* V, 2, 11, 1130 b 25 τὰ ποιητικὰ τῆς ὅλης ἀρετῆς ἐστι τῶν νομίμων ὅσα νενομοθέτηται περὶ παιδείαν τὴν πρὸς τὸ κοινόν. Cf. PÖHLMANN, *Geschichte der sozialen Frage und der Sozialismus in der antiken Welt*, I, pp. 152 ff.

[4] *Laws*, XI, 923 a ᾿Ω φίλοι, φήσομεν, καὶ ἀτεχνῶς ἐφήμεροι, χαλεπὸν ὑμῖν ἐστιν γιγνώσκειν τὰ ὑμέτερ' αὐτῶν χρήματα καὶ πρός γε ὑμᾶς αὐτούς, ὥσπερ καὶ τὸ τῆς Πυθίας γράμμα φράζει, τὰ νῦν. ἔγωγ' οὖν νομοθέτης ὢν οὔθ' ὑμᾶς ὑμῶν αὐτῶν εἶναι τίθημι οὔτε τὴν οὐσίαν ταύτην, σύμπαντος δὲ τοῦ γένους ὑμῶν τοῦ τε ἔμπροσθεν καὶ τοῦ ἔπειτα ἐσομένου, καὶ ἔτι μᾶλλον τῆς πόλεως εἶναι τό τε γένος πᾶν καὶ τὴν οὐσίαν.

are, nor what belongs to us, nor what our real function is for ourselves and for the State.

Such were the aims of the Greek State—enunciated sometimes in a moderate and sometimes in an exaggerated manner. In spite of the well-known contrasts in life and character between Sparta and Athens, the philosophers assumed a fundamental similarity between them as regards the educational task of the State. As Aristotle put it, although the conceptions of Sparta may be narrow, the way in which they are brought to bear upon the individual should serve as a model for all States. The ideal of social existence is attained when every man lives as an equal of his fellow-citizens, an ὅμοιος, and is thoroughly imbued with devotion to the corporate life of the city.[1] Commonplace notions in this respect were formulated, e. g. by Isokrates, an orator not conspicuous for originality and power, but a characteristic representative of public opinion in his time. In his *Areiopageitikos* he declares that those who have means should be taught horsemanship, athletics, and philosophy in order to be able to live the higher life.[2]

---

[1] Cf. WILAMOWITZ-MOELLENDORFF, in HINNEBERG, *Kultur der Gegenwart*, II, 4, 1, pp. 114 f.

[2] ISOKRATES, VII, 45 τοὺς δὲ βίον ἱκανὸν κεκτημένους περί τε τὴν ἱππικὴν καὶ τὰ γυμνάσια καὶ τὰ κυνηγέσια καὶ τὴν φιλοσοφίαν ἠνάγκασαν διατρίβειν, ὁρῶντες ἐκ τούτων τοὺς μὲν διαφέροντας γιγνομένους, τοὺς δὲ τῶν πλείστων κακῶν ἀπεχομένους.

CHAPTER II

THE CONCEPT OF LAW

1. *Popular notions.*

Defini-
tions of
law.

THE precepts concerning a welfare achieved by means of civic virtue are, of course, all counsels of perfection. In their bearing on juridical issues they culminate in the notion of *justice*. The abstract qualities of courage and wisdom cannot be directly governed by law, but justice (δικαιοσύνη) is a conception which is of the utmost importance in the whole Greek theory of law, and leads to the particular domain of νόμος which it is our purpose to investigate.

In order to determine the nature of νόμος let us again notice some popular definitions which will serve as a guide. In the *Digest* (I. 3. 2) we find a passage which has been taken over by the Romans in the original Greek—it comes from the first speech of Demosthenes against Aristogeiton.[1]

Aristogeiton is treated by Demosthenes as a typical lawbreaker, and the speaker lays stress on the idea that it is only in accordance with the established laws that healthy social life is possible. The concrete points mentioned are: that law is sacred in its origin, being a gift of the gods; that it is instituted by wise men; that its function is to redress and correct mistakes and failures, whether they be the result of deliberate intention or of negligence; and finally that it is a compact (συνθήκη) entered into by the members of the city. These attributes are clearly set forth, and indicate the direction which the Greek mind took in considering the social functions of law.

---

[1] DEM. XXV, § 16, p. 774. The original text has been remodelled slightly by Tribonian's commission. οἱ δὲ νόμοι τὸ δίκαιον καὶ τὸ καλὸν καὶ τὸ συμφέρον βούλονται, καὶ τοῦτο ζητοῦσι, καὶ ἐπειδὰν εὑρεθῇ, κοινὸν τοῦτο πρόσταγμ᾽ ἀπεδείχθη, πᾶσιν ἴσον καὶ ὅμοιον, καὶ τοῦτ᾽ ἔστι νόμος. ᾧ πάντας πείθεσθαι προσήκει διὰ πολλά, καὶ μάλισθ᾽ ὅτι πᾶς ἐστι νόμος εὕρημα μὲν καὶ δῶρον θεῶν, δόγμα δ᾽ ἀνθρώπων φρονίμων, ἐπανόρθωμα δὲ τῶν ἑκουσίων καὶ ἀκουσίων ἁμαρτημάτων, πόλεως δὲ συνθήκη κοινή, καθ᾽ ἣν πᾶσι προσήκει ζῆν τοῖς ἐν τῇ πόλει. (Text of Butcher's ed., S.C B.O.)

These general expressions received particular meaning in the popular mind, and indicated certain characteristics which were far from being commonplace. They are expressed in one or two typical definitions. Aristotle, in the *Rhetoric*, thus defines δικαιοσύνη : ἔστι δὲ δικαιοσύνη μὲν ἀρετὴ δι' ἣν τὰ αὐτῶν ἕκαστοι ἔχουσι, καὶ ὡς ὁ νόμος, ἀδικία δὲ δι' ἣν τὰ ἀλλότρια, οὐχ ὡς ὁ νόμος.[1] The characteristic point here is that positive legality is introduced as a substantive element of justice. It is not sufficient to accept the principle of justice in the abstract, because it is vague and ambiguous; the question arises: "What is my own, and what is somebody else's?" and although from the pleader's point of view this is a matter of subjective appreciation, the city is called upon to give definite and objective directions in its laws.

There is nothing in the Greek language exactly corresponding to the Latin *jus*. The Roman term cannot be translated by νόμος, which is mainly used for statutory law—*lex*. Nor is τὸ δίκαιον an equivalent, for it signifies "the just," and is so employed, for instance, by Cicero, who does not even attempt to translate the term. These phraseological peculiarities point to the highly important fact that the Greeks regarded law primarily as the embodiment of justice— it is τὸ δίκαιον as interpreted by the city. Again, take such a word as τὸ νόμιμον : in its etymological origin it is connected with νομίζειν, and connotes the currently accepted notions of morality and justice (ἃ νομίζεται).[2]

All these indications point towards a traditional view of law in general as a complex of ethical rules. To the Greek philosophers of the older schools law was a sacred and fundamental institution. Herakleitos declared that citizens ought to defend their laws as they defend the walls of their city,—μάχεσθαι χρὴ τὸν δῆμον ὑπὲρ τοῦ νόμου ὅκωσπερ τείχεος [3]; and again, he tells us that the law is

Varieties of custom.

---

[1] *Rhet.* I, 9, 1366 b 9. "Now justice is a virtue, through which every set of men have their own under the law; injustice is a vice, through which men have —not under the law—what is *not* their own." (Cf. Jebb, p. 37.)

[2] See article by WILAMOWITZ-MOELLENDORFF in *Zum ältesten Strafrecht der Kulturvölker*, p. 22, ed. K. BINDING, Leipzig, 1905.

[3] DIELS, *Fragmente der Vorsokratiker*, I, 3, p. 86, fr. 44. BYWATER, Fr. 100.

a divine creation—τρέφονται γὰρ πάντες οἱ ἀνθρώπειοι νόμοι ὑπὸ ἑνὸς τοῦ θείου.[1] It is evident, however, that there is a certain contradiction between these two asser-tions. Is it possible to claim a divine origin for law and at the same time to localize it within the walls of a particular city? The force of this objection was brought home to the Greeks by their experiences in the discovery of varied customs and legal rules. It is out of the question to think of Greek cities as if they were isolated: they were self-sufficient to some extent, but not isolated. A German economist, von Tühnen, has written about what he calls the "isolated State," and has drawn many deductions from a consideration of the State as an isolated economic unit of social organization. It is impossible to regard the Greek States in this way; they were inextricably bound up with each other, and the traveller had only to cross some arm of the sea to find himself among barbarians whose institutions were very different from those of his own home.

This is one of the starting-points in the consideration of Greek social institutions. We cannot understand the Sophists or Plato without taking into account that they lived at the close of an age of discovery. Travellers from Greece were penetrating into Persia, Italy, Gaul, Africa. The book which best represents this spirit of discovery and curiosity is the work of Herodotos. His history is in a sense a general survey of the *Mirabilia Mundi*. It is interesting to note how the comparative view of law asserts itself in his narrative. He realizes that the customs of different countries exhibit remarkable differences, and that it is impossible to apply the same standards to all. Take a curious tale in the third book of his history.[2] Certain Greeks were being entertained by King Dareios at a ban-quet, and Dareios asked them for what price they would eat the bodies of their dead parents. They repudiated the suggestion with horror. The king then called up men from an Indian tribe who happened to be at the court at

[1] *Ibid.* p. 100, Fr. 114. BYWATER, Fr. 91 b. Cf. ISOKRATES XV, 82 τῶν μὲν νόμων ἐπαινεῖσθαι τοὺς ἀρχαιοτάτους, τῶν δὲ λόγων τοὺς καινοτάτους.

[2] HERODOTOS, III, 38. Cf. GOMPERZ, *Greek Thinkers*, trans. L. Magnus, I, p. 403.

the same time, and among whom such a custom actually prevailed. These Indians were asked to say what price they would take for burning their dead, and they repudiated such an idea with as much indignation as the Greeks had shown in regard to eating human flesh. Herodotos evidently notes this as an example of how widely peoples differ in their fundamental notions of morals and right. In a dialogue ascribed to Plato, and probably written by some anonymous contemporary of his, there occurs a passage of some interest in this connexion:[1] "Whereas for ourselves human sacrifices are not customary, but are unrighteous, the Carthaginians do make such sacrifices as being righteous and customary for them; some even sacrificing their own sons to Kronos ... Moreover, you have probably been told of the customs which we ourselves practised in former days in connexion with the dead, slaying victims before the funeral procession started and sending for women to gather up the bones. And still earlier generations used even to bury the dead in their houses. But we ourselves do none of these things." Thus the intercourse between cities and some knowledge of comparative institutions enabled the Greeks to take up the comparative point of view in jurisprudence and political science. These national divergences were in themselves enough to show that law could not be regarded as something universal and immutable. How then was it possible to ascribe a divine origin to it? This could evidently apply only to the process of lawmaking in general, and not to the particular results in each single case. Perhaps it were better to say, as Herakleitos had said, that the laws should be defended as resolutely as the walls of the city.

There was yet another reason for social unrest. The close of the fifth century was a time of terrible catastrophes; all the fundamental notions of men were shaken and disturbed: throughout Greece parties were in conflict and

---

[1] PLATO, *Minos*, 315 b c ἐπεὶ αὐτίκα ἡμῖν μὲν οὐ νόμος ἐστὶν ἀνθρώπους θύειν ἀλλ' ἀνόσιον, Καρχηδόνιοι δὲ θύουσιν ὡς ὅσιον ὂν καὶ νόμιμον αὐτοῖς, καὶ ταῦτα ἔνιοι αὐτῶν καὶ τοὺς αὐτῶν υἱεῖς τῷ Κρόνῳ ... ὥσπερ καὶ ἡμᾶς αὐτοὺς οἶσθά που καὶ αὐτὸς ἀκούων οἵοις νόμοις ἐχρώμεθα πρὸ τοῦ περὶ τοὺς ἀποθανόντας, ἱερεῖά τε προσφάττοντες πρὸ τῆς ἐκφορᾶς τοῦ νεκροῦ καὶ ἐγχυτιστρίας μεταπεμπόμενοι· οἱ δ' αὖ ἐκείνων ἔτι πρότεροι αὐτοῦ καὶ ἔθαπτον ἐν τῇ οἰκίᾳ τοὺς ἀποθανόντας· ἡμεῖς δὲ τούτων οὐδὲν ποιοῦμεν.

strife prevailed everywhere. The situation was summed
up by Thukydides in his third book (c. 82) when he said:
"Men believe nothing but that nothing is secure."

Legal con-
ceptions
in the
plays of
Aischylos.

With regard to law—as indeed in all other subjects of
public importance—the evolution of the Greek drama
throws a strong light on the movements of public opinion.
The intense strain of dramatic literature at this period
may be traced to a great extent to the influence of
the tremendous social and political conflicts which were
taking place in actual life. If we consider the historical
features of this time, we cannot help being forcibly struck
by its dramatic framework and by the irreconcilable contrast between its elements. Take, for example, the *Supplices*. There has been considerable controversy in connexion
with this play. The plot is well known. The Danaids fly
from the sons of Aigyptos because they revolt with horror
from the idea of a marriage with their first cousins. Now
the marriage of first cousins was an every-day occurrence
in Athens, and it is asked as a problem of criticism, how
could an Athenian audience listen with patience to a drama
which is founded upon the idea that a union between
cousins is a form of loathsome incest? The explanation
seems to be that the extant play emphasizes one of the
points of view in the dramatic conflict; that it is part of
a trilogy, and, no doubt, if we had the complete trilogy, we
should see the point of view of the bridegrooms as strongly
represented as that of the brides. This means that Aischylos and the Athenians who followed the play with interest
were fully able to appreciate the tragic greatness of con-
flicting opinions, even when they did not coincide with
their own. Take again the *Oresteia*: once more Aischylos
puts before us the conflict of views and moral duties. The
central problem of the play cannot be solved without a
disturbance of moral equilibrium; and it is significant that
the poet is not only concerned with the tumult in the soul
of Orestes, but with the fact, emphasized by the Erinyes,
that the most sacred commandment—the filial duty of a
son towards his mother—had been broken. The liberating
crisis comes through the intervention of Apollo and Athena,
who represent a new current in thought and law. As they

recognize the claim of the father to filial piety as being as great as that of the mother, they open the way to atonement for the unfortunate man who had to avenge his father on his own mother. One can hardly doubt that the legend which forms the subject of the play had been suggested by a conflict between matriarchal and patriarchal ideas. This does not mean that just before the time of Aischylos Athens had been living under matriarchal rule; but there were many traces of matriarchal customs in early Greece, and in writing this fifth-century drama the poet was able to assume that the audience would follow the thread of folk-lore with understanding and interest. In process of time dramatic authors concern themselves more and more with the problems of individual conscience and political struggle. Sophokles, for instance, dealt primarily with the problem of *fate* in relation to the life of individuals.

The most copious and interesting materials illustrating the fermentation of popular ideas as to law are presented by Euripides. He subjects individual rights and ideas to the most searching and unsparing criticism. Two plays are especially striking in this connexion, the *Medeia* and the *Phoinissai*. It can hardly be doubted that in the first of these plays the principal character is intended to enlist the sympathy of the audience as against the hypocritical assertion of a national superiority of Greeks in matters of law and justice.

Contrasts in the plays of Euripides.

The story is well known: Jason wins the love of Medeia, a barbarian princess, who betrays and deserts her country and her parents for his sake. She follows him to Korinth, but there, in the hope of making a good match, he abandons her and woos a Korinthian maiden. The pathos of Medeia's position is beautifully rendered by Euripides; in defending himself against her claims Jason appears in a very unfavourable light; he tries to turn the tables against his accuser and to prove that he has in truth conferred benefits upon her. " But indeed you have received more than you have granted, something greater than my safety, as I will tell. In the first place you have come to dwell in Hellas instead of a barbarian country, and you are learning to know justice and to live by laws whose sanction is not force." [1] There is a pungent irony in the fact that the betrayer, the faithless man, is made to boast of the national sense of justice—justice for its own sake, not as an outcome of force.

In the *Phoinissai* the scene is laid in the city of Thebes. After the death of Oidipus the two brothers Eteokles and Polyneikes are struggling for the throne of Thebes. They have made a compact which both have sworn to recognize; their rights are supposed to be equal, and it is agreed that they shall rule in turn, the one in odd, the other in even years. But when Eteokles' year is out, he refuses to surrender the throne to his brother, breaks the convention, and indeed scorns the idea of observing obligations imposed by morality or law. His mother exhorts him not to persist in this attitude, but to yield to the commands of justice (δικαιοσύνη); he refuses, saying: "If for all alike the same thing were both noble and wise, there would not have been fierce strife among mankind; but as things are, there is no likeness or equality for men except in name; it is otherwise in fact." [2] And again, "If one is bound to act unjustly, it is most noble to do so for the sake of power; as regards other things one ought to act righteously." [3]

This is an emphatic repudiation of legal obligation; agreements, according to this view, are mere words; they do not express any realities: this is the key to the dramatic conflict and its tragic solution. The quest for something enduring and fundamental could not, however, be sup-

---

[1] *Medeia* 534 ff. :

μείζω γε μέντοι τῆς ἐμῆς σωτηρίας
εἴληφας ἢ δέδωκας, ὡς ἐγὼ φράσω.
πρῶτον μὲν Ἑλλάδ᾽ ἀντὶ βαρβάρου χθονὸς
γαῖαν κατοικεῖς καὶ δίκην ἐπίστασαι
νόμοις τε χρῆσθαι μὴ πρὸς ἰσχύος χάριν.

[2] EUR. *Phoin.* 499 ff. :

εἰ πᾶσι ταὐτὸν καλὸν ἔφυ σοφόν θ᾽ ἅμα,
οὐκ ἦν ἂν ἀμφίλεκτος ἀνθρώποις ἔρις·
νῦν δ᾽ οὔθ᾽ ὅμοιον οὐδὲν οὔτ᾽ ἴσον βροτοῖς,
πλὴν ὀνόμασαι· τὸ δ᾽ ἔργον οὐκ ἔστιν τόδε.

[3] *Ibid.* 524 f. :

εἴπερ γὰρ ἀδικεῖν χρή, τυραννίδος πέρι
κάλλιστον ἀδικεῖν, τἄλλα δ᾽ εὐσεβεῖν χρεών.

pressed: in spite of perplexing doubts men sought to justify and explain the binding force of law.

In a well-known passage of Sophokles we find expressed another view of law as understood by the Greeks. Law may appear in a sense as a command of nature, as an absolute obligation distinct from the technical requirements of the State. Antigone is defending herself against the charge of having wilfully disobeyed the king's orders; she says to King Kreon: " It was not Zeus that had published that edict; not such are the laws set among men by the Justice who dwells with the gods below; nor deemed I that thy decrees were of such force, that a mortal could override the unwritten and unfailing statutes of heaven. For their life is not of to-day or yesterday, but from all time, and no man knows when they were first put forth." [1]

2. *The Critical Analysis of the Sophists.*

Reference has been made to the Sophistic views presented in the plays of Euripides: indeed the Sophists devoted most attention and ingenuity to problems of conduct and to the criticism of received opinions on which conduct was based. They were keen to inquire and examine into everything, and the more they examined the more they became convinced that absolute notions were groundless. Plato describes the chaos which resulted from their subversive dialectics: " These, my friends, are the sayings of clever men . . . which find a way into the minds of youth. They are told by them that the highest right is might, and in this way the young fall into impiety and entertain the idea that the gods are not such as the law bids them imagine them; and hence arise contentions—the philosophers inviting them to lead a true life according to nature,

---

[1] SOPH., *Antigone*, 450 ff. :

οὐ γάρ τί μοι Ζεὺς ἦν ὁ κηρύξας τάδε,
οὐδ᾽ ἡ ξύνοικος τῶν κάτω θεῶν Δίκη
τοιούσδ᾽ ἐν ἀνθρώποισιν ὥρισεν νόμους·
οὐδὲ σθένειν τοσοῦτον ᾠόμην τὰ σὰ
κηρύγμαθ᾽, ὥστ᾽ ἄγραπτα κἀσφαλῆ θεῶν
νόμιμα δύνασθαι θνητὸν ὄνθ᾽ ὑπερδραμεῖν·
οὐ γάρ τι νῦν γε κἀχθές, ἀλλ᾽ ἀεί ποτε
ζῇ ταῦτα, κοὐδεὶς οἶδεν ἐξ ὅτου ᾽φάνη.

that is, to live as masters of others, and not in legal subjection to them."[1]

One cannot help being struck by the double aspect of a movement which was unquestionably progressive in the philosophical sense and which at the same time tended to the dissolution of manners, customs, and laws. Ideas which constituted an advance in the domain of thought appeared as a solvent in the social life of the time. The principal problem examined by the Sophists in regard to jurisprudence was how far the basic laws of society can be regarded as ingrained in the nature of things, and how far they are merely artificial establishment. The latter view did not originate with the Sophists themselves, but made its appearance at a much earlier date. In fact its point of departure may be found in a political atmosphere which has nothing to do with the catastrophes of the fifth century. It seems to me that the contrast between φύσις and νόμος may be traced to Demokritos, and was therefore a product of thought contemporaneous with the Persian War. This philosopher said: "νόμῳ γλυκύ, νόμῳ πικρόν, νόμῳ θερμόν, νόμῳ ψυχρόν, νόμῳ χροιή, ἐτεῇ (v.l. φύσει) ἄτομα καὶ κενόν."[2] It is not easy to interpret this passage, and almost impossible to translate it without explanations. Νόμος cannot be simply rendered "law"; stress is laid on its opposition to ἐτεῇ (φύσει) and therefore a connexion with νομίζειν seems inevitable. An approximate translation would be: "Things are [deemed] sweet and bitter, hot and cold, and have colour by conventional rule; in reality (or in nature) they are atoms and void." The peculiar use of the word νόμος in this fragment is suggested, as it seems to me, by a perception of the difference between things as they are and things as we take them to be. But it implies at the same time that our formal rules also exist as phenomena, in contrast with φύσις.

[1] Laws X, 890 a ταῦτ' ἐστίν, ὦ φίλοι, ἅπαντα ἀνδρῶν σοφῶν παρὰ νέοις ἀνθρώποις . . . φασκόντων εἶναι τὸ δικαιότατον ὅτι τις ἂν νικᾷ βιαζόμενος· ὅθεν ἀσέβειαί τε ἀνθρώποις ἐμπίπτουσι νέοις, ὡς οὐκ ὄντων θεῶν οἵους ὁ νόμος προστάττει διανοεῖσθαι δεῖν, στάσεις τε διὰ ταῦτα ἑλκόντων πρὸς τὸν κατὰ φύσιν ὀρθὸν βίον, ὅς ἐστιν τῇ ἀληθείᾳ κρατοῦντα ζῆν τῶν ἄλλων καὶ μὴ δουλεύοντα ἑτέροισι κατὰ νόμον.

[2] DIELS, Fragmente der Vorsokratiker, II, 3, p. 60, Fr. 9.

A kind of scientific investigation was attempted on this basis in the school of Anaxagoras. We read about an interesting work of one of his pupils, Archelaos: ἔλεγε (Ἀρχέλαος) τὸ δίκαιον εἶναι καὶ τὸ αἰσχρὸν οὐ φύσει ἀλλὰ νόμωι,[1] "He said that right and wrong existed not by nature but by opinion." The saying appears in connexion with a theory of what we should call transformism. Briefly stated it amounted to this: all things are developed from indistinct matter and the products of matter. They become slowly differentiated, and in the process the initial contrast is that between the warm lower parts and the cold upper parts of the universe. In the warm lower parts, organisms arose out of a kind of protoplasm. They gradually shaped themselves into different forms, and eventually the highest shape was reached in man himself. The next stage was the setting up of leaders, laws, and social rules.[2] This being so, it is idle to think of any fundamental and permanent justice, and Archelaos says this in as many words. His doctrine may be regarded, in short, as a development of the idea of Demokritos, and amounts to the distinction between νόμος and φύσις. For Archelaos, law resolves itself into a set of historical rules created by gradual evolution.

Such a view allies itself naturally with the teaching of relativism, which occupied so much place in the philosophy of the Sophists. In the conflict of ideas, people came to the conclusion that everything was in a state of flux, and the first thing to be done in order to arrive at the truth was to take stock of purely subjective notions. This was what Protagoras meant when he said: "Man is the measure of all things." Undoubtedly Protagoras achieved a great stride in philosophy, and many of his views are still considered with respect; but he gave a dangerous instrument to those who wished to misunderstand and misuse his teaching. One of the results of the notions which he advanced was

Relativism.

[1] DIELS, *op. cit.*, I, p. 410, Fr. 1.
[2] DIELS, I, p. 412 περὶ δὲ ζῴων (Ἀρχέλαος) φησίν ὅτι θερμαινομένης τῆς γῆς τὸ πρῶτον ἐν τῷ κάτω μέρει, ὅπου τὸ θερμὸν καὶ τὸ ψυχρὸν ἐμίσγετο, ἀνεφαίνετο τά τε ἄλλα ζῷα πολλὰ καὶ οἱ ἄνθρωποι . . . καὶ διεκρίθησαν ἄνθρωποι ἀπὸ τῶν ἄλλων καὶ ἡγεμόνας καὶ νόμους καὶ τέχνας καὶ πόλεις καὶ τὰ ἄλλα συνέστησαν.

that, in one at least of its ramifications, concrete individuals
were substituted for the abstract conception of man as a
psychological unit.[1] Gorgias is the chief representative of
this extreme subjectivism. In his philosophy every man
has the right to set up his own standard of truth. Of
course, if this were so, there would be no general and
ultimate truth at all. Logic would have no meaning; and
indeed it came to be slighted in the school of Gorgias.
This particular group of Sophists sought to develop *Rhetoric*
as a substitute for *Logic*, and used "suggestion"—the
ἐνθύμημα—instead of logical deduction. Too often the object
of such Sophists was simply to make the weaker cause
appear as the stronger, τὰ ἐλάττω κρείττω ποιεῖν.

Even apart from special pleading, it was not difficult
for ingenious persons to attack many positive institutions
of the Greek commonwealths. For instance, it was not
difficult for Archidamos to show that slavery is no part of
the law of nature; or for Lykophron to show that in the
natural order of things there is no virtue in mere nobility
of birth. It was easy to show that men were not bound to
particular spots on the earth, and therefore if a man should
happen to find himself in disagreement with the laws or
the ideas of his country, he was under no obligation of
loyalty to that country. This is what Hippias of Elis meant
when he called himself a citizen of the world.[2] Such
sceptics might have appealed to the authority of Demokritos himself, for it was Demokritos who had said: "For
the wise man, the whole world lies open."[3]

In this way relativism came to be a political and social
solvent. If then it was impossible to speak of an eternal
or immutable law, how were particular forms of law to be
regarded? The most important discussion of this problem is
to be found in Plato. What was the legal basis of sovereignty
in particular States? The view put forward by Sophists
(as represented by Plato repeatedly) is that force is the
ultima ratio. In the view of Thrasymachos, as shown in
the *Republic*, if people would only speak without hypo-

---

[1] Cf. H. RIKKERT, *System der Philosophie*, I, p. 27.

[2] Cf. K. HILDENBRAND, *Geschichte der Rechtsphilosophie*, I, p. 73.

[3] DIELS, II, p. 110, Fr. 247 ἀνδρὶ σοφῶι πᾶσα γῆ βατή· ψυχῆς γὰρ
ἀγαθῆς πατρὶς ὁ ξύμπας κόσμος.

critical pretences, they would say frankly that the law-
givers imposed laws which are really in their own interest.
Law is therefore nothing more or less than a confirmation
of the selfish interests of the rulers. Another view of law
is represented by Glaukon, according to whom law is essentially a combination of the weak against the strong. In
other words it arises not only because the strong wish
to enforce their wills upon the weak, but because the
weak combine in order that the strong shall not have
everything their own way. Kallikles in the *Gorgias* goes
even further than this. He assumes the existence of a
league of the weak against the strong, but adds that if an
opportunity presents itself, the strong should burst all
bonds and do practically what he likes. "Lust and self-
will and licence, if they can be indulged in with security,
are happiness and virtue." [1] This is, of course, a caricature,
but, like all Plato's caricatures, it is suggested by a vivid
sense of reality.

A papyrus recently discovered in Egypt throws a strong Antiphon
light on the mixture of acute analysis and moral licence the
which characterizes the Sophistic movement of the period. [2] Sophist.
"Justice," says the writer, "consists in not transgressing
any of the ordinances of the State of which one is a citizen.
A man would therefore exercise justice with most advantage to himself if in the presence of witnesses he held in
esteem the laws, but, in the absence of witnesses, the
precepts of nature. For the precepts of the laws are
adventitious, while those of nature are necessary; the rules
of the laws are the product of agreement, not of growth,
while those of nature are the product of growth, not of
agreement ... Most of what is just according to law stands
in opposition to nature. The law has laid down for the
eyes what they ought and what they ought not to see, for
the ears what they ought and what they ought not to hear,
for the tongue what it ought and what it ought not to say,

---

[1] PLATO, *Gorgias*, 492 c τρυφὴ καὶ ἀκολασία καὶ ἐλευθερία, ἐὰν ἐπι-
κουρίαν ἔχῃ, τοῦτ' ἐστὶν ἀρετή τε καὶ εὐδαιμονία. Cf. NETTLESHIP,
Lectures on the *Republic*; PÖHLMANN, *Gesch. der sozialen Frage*, I,
pp. 557 ff.

[2] *Oxyrhynchus Papyri*, XI, 1364. ANTIPHON the Sophist. See
appendix to chapter, p. 42.

for the hands what they ought and what they ought not to do, for the feet whither they ought and whither they ought not to go, and for the mind what it ought and what it ought not to desire . . . Much of what has been mentioned would be found to be in opposition to nature; greater pain is produced by it when less might be forthcoming, or, on the other hand, less pleasure when more is possible, or injury when injury might be avoided. Now if those who adopted such courses as these had any protection from the laws, whereas those who did not adopt them but opposed them incurred loss, obedience to the laws would not be without advantage; but as it happens, legal justice is found inadequate to protect those who follow legal rules. First of all it allows the injury of the injured and the aggression of the aggressor, and besides the fact that it does not prevent the injured from being injured, nor the aggressor from making aggression, being held over until punishment is inflicted, it is no more favourable to the injured than to the aggressor." The cynicism of this declaration can hardly be surpassed.

Alkibiades and Perikles. The bearing of Sophistic theories on political thought may be illustrated by a story related in the *Memorabilia* of Xenophon,[1] which may possibly be derived from Antisthenes. Perikles, the great statesman and wise man, is said to have been questioned by the irreverent youth, Alkibiades. Asked for his definition of law, Perikles declares it to be "the command of the mass of the people (τὸ πλῆθος)." What then is to be said of an oligarchy? If the sovereign power

[1] Xen. *Mem.* I, ii. 42 Πάντες γὰρ οὗτοι νόμοι εἰσίν, οὓς τὸ πλῆθος συνελθὸν καὶ δοκιμάσαν ἔγραψε, φράζον, ἅ τε δεῖ ποιεῖν καὶ ἃ μή. . . . . Ἐὰν δὲ μὴ τὸ πλῆθος, ἀλλ', ὥσπερ ὅπου ὀλιγαρχία ἐστίν, ὀλίγοι συνελθόντες γράψωσιν ὅ τι χρὴ ποιεῖν, ταῦτα τί ἐστι; Πάντα, φάναι, ὅσα ἂν τὸ κρατοῦν τῆς πόλεως βουλευσάμενον, ἃ χρὴ ποιεῖν, γράψῃ, νόμος καλεῖται. Κᾂν τύραννος οὖν κρατῶν τῆς πόλεως γράψῃ τοῖς πολίταις ἃ χρὴ ποιεῖν, καὶ ταῦτα νόμος ἐστί; Καὶ ὅσα τύραννος ἄρχων, φάναι, γράφει, καὶ ταῦτα νόμος καλεῖται. Βία δέ, φάναι, καὶ ἀνομία τί ἐστιν, ὦ Περίκλεις; ἆρ' οὐχ ὅταν ὁ κρείττων τὸν ἥττω μὴ πείσας, ἀλλὰ βιασάμενος, ἀναγκάσῃ ποιεῖν ὅ τι ἂν αὐτῷ δοκῇ; Ἔμοιγε δοκεῖ, φάναι τὸν Περικλέα. Καὶ ὅσα ἄρα τύραννος μὴ πείσας τοὺς πολίτας ἀναγκάζει ποιεῖν γράφων, ἀνομία ἐστί; Δοκεῖ μοι, φάναι τὸν Περικλέα. (κτλ.) Cf. Plato, *Laws*, IV, 714 c d Τίθεται δήπου, φασίν, τοὺς νόμους ἐν τῇ πόλει ἑκάστοτε τὸ κρατοῦν. . . . Ἆρ' οὖν οἴει, φασίν, ποτὲ δῆμον νικήσαντα, ἤ τινα πολιτείαν ἄλλην, ἢ καὶ τύραννον, θήσεσθαι ἑκόντα πρὸς ἄλλο τι πρῶτον νόμους ἢ τὸ συμφέρον ἑαυτῷ τῆς ἀρχῆς τοῦ μένειν; . . . Οὐκοῦν καὶ ὃς ἂν ταῦτα τὰ τεθέντα παραβαίνῃ, κολάσει ὁ θέμενος ὡς ἀδικοῦντα , δίκαια εἶναι ταῦτ' ἐπονομάζων;

is in the hands of a few, will not their enactments have the force of law? Perikles admits that they will. What then if the sovereign power is in the hands of one man only? Perikles admits that in this case also the command of the sovereign would have the force of law, although it be imposed by a tyrant. The cross-examination is resumed in the reverse order, beginning with an inquiry as to the imposition of rules by the violence of a tyrant, and proceeding with the analysis of violence (βία) in oligarchies and democracies. Eventually Perikles comes to the disappointing conclusion that he cannot offer a satisfactory solution of these embarrassing contradictions!

The difficulty arose, of course, from the fact that States do not rely in practice on law only, but also on force. But the converse is also true: they do not rule merely by force, but also by law. It must be admitted that there is some other power behind the law, but the problem is: What is this power? What is the difference between power (τὸ κρατοῦν) and violence (βία)? We should answer now that the distinction cannot lie in the mere mechanical arrangement of society, but rather in the recognition of certain extra-legal, moral ties; but it is highly significant that in the Sophistic discussion reported by Xenophon this conclusion is not reached, and the problem remains open in a disconcerting manner.

3. *The Justification of Law.*

The Greek world of the fifth century was full of stir and ferment. But men naturally could not remain content with this confusion, and they addressed themselves to the task of finding some way out of it. They attempted, in short, to justify the existing moral and legal order. After considering the critical point of view in regard to these problems we have now to ask: How was positive law justified as against the doubts and objections of critics and sceptics?

After all, people had to make up their minds not only to solve such problems in practice, but to explain how, in spite of all the factors making for disintegration, society did exist and hold together. The life of society continues

The political psychology of Protagoras.

in spite of selfishness and conflict, and there must be
some kind of harmony and organization to keep it up.
The attempt to justify positive law and to reconstruct
the ideas of right and duty comes originally from the
same school of searching criticism which had introduced
so many elements of dissolution. This side of its activity
has not been sufficiently noticed, as it seems to me, but
it is interesting in itself and fraught with important
consequences in the course of subsequent development.
It was a Sophist, Protagoras, who initiated a considered
justification of positive law. He was the principal ad-
vocate of the theory of relativism, and it may be said
of him that he was in a truer sense than either Sokrates
or Plato the originator of a definite theory of jurisprudence.
In the dialogue [1] bearing his name Protagoras is asked
to explain why people live in States and obey the laws, and
why when men are obviously actuated by selfish interests,
they still consent to some kind of social regulation; he gives
his answer in the form of a myth. His theory is a fiction,
but it is the expression of a psychological truth. He tells
his interlocutors that the first men were quite helpless and
threatened with extermination by wild animals. Prometheus
brought them intelligence in order to protect them against
this danger. They gathered in cities, but it soon became
apparent that intelligence was not sufficient in itself to hold
people together in harmony, because they were all selfish,
and their interests clashed: they began to fight among
themselves instead of fighting the animals. Zeus made a
second attempt to save human kind by sending Hermes to

---

[1] We are met here by a problem of literary criticism : How can we
reconstruct the teaching of Protagoras ? Only fragments have come
down in the works of Plato, who was professedly an opponent of his,
and there is therefore considerable difficulty in ascertaining what
Protagoras actually did say. There seems, however, to exist a sufficient foundation for reconstructing his main principles. To begin
with, whatever liberties Plato may have taken with his references,
still he was a great literary artist, and we have no reason to suppose
that he reduced things to a mere parody. He always managed to
make his people live, and represented them as real characters.
Secondly, there is no reason to suppose that Plato disagreed with all
the doctrines which he attributed to Protagoras, and he seems to have
accepted some of his statements. The doctrine analysed in the text
is of this kind, and in any case Plato states it not as a matter of
controversy, but merely as a matter of fact.

men with αἰδώς and δίκη.[1] The word αἰδώς, which is sometimes translated "reverence," seems rather to connote "sense of shame," or "conscience."[2] In a fragment of Demokritos we find the verb αἰδεῖσθαι used in this sense: "One ought not to feel ashamed (αἰδεῖσθαι) before others more than before oneself, nor should one do evil any the more if no one is likely to know of it than if every one will; but one should respect (αἰδεῖσθαι) oneself most and set before one's soul as a principle to do nothing unseemly."[3] There is also a remarkable passage in Plato's Laws, which describes the transition from αἰδώς as "sense of shame," to ἀναισχυντία (shamelessness). Plato dwells on the deplorable results of the abuse of freedom: "Men fancying that they knew what they did not know, had no longer any fear (conscience?), and the absence of conscience begets shamelessness (ἀναισχυντία). For what is shamelessness but the insolent refusal to regard the opinion of one's betters by reason of an over-daring sort of liberty?"[4]

In addition to self-consciousness and the conscience produced by it, man came to possess henceforth the faculty of judging himself in his relation to others (δίκη). These might be described as the social instincts which render possible political union. One of the fundamental ideas of all philosophy and sociology was thus elaborated: the affectus socialis, which in later theory was chiefly insisted on by Grotius in contrast with Hobbes. Protagoras discerned in this social instinct two elements—αἰδώς, shame or conscience (cf. the Biblical narrative of the Fall of Man), and

---

[1] PLATO, Protagoras, 322 b c ἐζήτουν δὴ ἀθροίζεσθαι καὶ σῴζεσθαι, κτίζοντες πόλεις· ὅτ᾽ οὖν ἀθροισθεῖεν ἠδίκουν ἀλλήλους ἅτε οὐκ ἔχοντες τὴν πολιτικὴν τέχνην, ὥστε πάλιν σκεδαννύμενοι διεφθείροντο. Ζεὺς οὖν δείσας περὶ τῷ γένει ἡμῶν, μὴ ἀπόλοιτο πᾶν, Ἑρμῆν πέμπει ἄγοντα εἰς ἀνθρώπους αἰδῶ τε καὶ δίκην, ἵν᾽ εἶεν πόλεων κόσμοι τε καὶ δεσμοὶ φιλίας συναγωγοί.
[2] Cf. BURNET, Nic. Eth. IV, c. 9, p. 200.
[3] DIELS, op. cit. p. 114, fr. 264 μηδέν τι μᾶλλον τοὺς ἀνθρώπους αἰδεῖσθαι ἑωυτοῦ μηδέ τι μᾶλλον ἐξεργάζεσθαι κακόν, εἰ μέλλει μηδεὶς εἰδήσειν, ἢ ⟨εἰ⟩ οἱ πάντες ἄνθρωποι· ἀλλ᾽ ἑωυτὸν μάλιστα αἰδεῖσθαι, καὶ τοῦτον νόμον τῇ ψυχῇ καθεστάναι, ὥστε μηδὲν ποιεῖν ἀνεπιτήδειον. Cf. PLATO, Laws, IV, 713 e for a similar use of αἰδώς.
[4] Laws, III, 701 a b συνεφέσπετο δὲ ἐλευθερία· ἄφοβοι γὰρ ἐγίγνοντο ὡς εἰδότες, ἡ δὲ ἄδεια ἀναισχυντίαν ἐνέτεκεν· τὸ γὰρ τὴν τοῦ βελτίονος δόξαν μὴ φοβεῖσθαι διὰ θράσος, τοῦτ᾽ αὐτό ἐστιν σχεδὸν ἡ πονηρὰ ἀναισχυντία, διὰ δή τινος ἐλευθερίας λίαν ἀποτετολμημένης.

δίκη, or the capacity for judging the actions of man in his relations to others.

How does that agree with the principle *homo omnium mensura*? In the *Theaitetos* this question is actually put: If there is no standard of objective truth—if, in other words, every man is his own standard of truth, how can any means be found for men to join together and to live harmoniously in cities and States? In a striking passage [1] Protagoras' solution of this difficulty is presented. It amounts to this: with regard to truth in the abstract, nobody can speak with absolute certainty, and therefore no city can say that its laws are better than those of any other. But while this is undeniable, there is another definite standard which can be ascertained, namely that of *utility*. According to this positive standard, some cities will achieve success, others arrive at deplorable results. Thus in practice the consequences may be taken as a definite and ascertainable standard of reasonable action. This reads like an early example of *pragmatism*. The position, reduced to its simplest elements, is that truth cannot be discovered, but utility can.

Obvious objections may be advanced against this view. As a matter of theory, the standard of utility is as difficult to discover as that of truth. In fact it is much more difficult to arrive at it. When we are dealing with problems of truth, we can at least base ourselves upon logical processes, but when we attempt to discover utility, every one has the right to ask: in what does this utility consist? For whom does it exist? Does it exist for the majority, as Bentham held, or for the "best people," as Aristotle held, or for the superman, as Nietzsche held? And besides all these varying considerations, how is the standard of utility to be applied to States? For instance, in the case of the Peloponnesian war, have we to conclude that

---

[1] PLATO, *Theaitetos*, 172 a b οὐκοῦν καὶ περὶ πολιτικῶν, καλὰ μὲν καὶ αἰσχρὰ καὶ δίκαια καὶ ἄδικα καὶ ὅσια καὶ μή, οἷα ἂν ἑκάστη πόλις οἰηθεῖσα θῆται νόμιμα αὑτῇ, ταῦτα καὶ εἶναι τῇ ἀληθείᾳ ἑκάστῃ, καὶ ἐν τούτοις μὲν οὐδὲν σοφώτερον οὔτε ἰδιώτην ἰδιώτου οὔτε πόλιν πόλεως εἶναι· ἐν δὴ τῷ συμφέροντα ἑαυτῇ ἢ μὴ συμφέροντα τίθεσθαι, ἐνταῦθ', εἴπερ που, αὖ ὁμολογήσει σύμβουλόν τε συμβούλου διαφέρειν καὶ πόλεως δόξαν ἑτέραν ἑτέρας πρὸς ἀλήθειαν, καὶ οὐκ ἂν πάνυ τολμήσειε φῆσαι, ἃ ἂν θῆται πόλις συμφέροντα οἰηθεῖσα αὑτῇ, παντὸς μᾶλλον ταῦτα καὶ συνοίσειν.

because Sparta happened to win, her institutions were
necessarily better than those of Athens? Anyhow, the
pragmatic standard of utility was set up by Protagoras
in connexion with his theory of relativism. Each State,
according to him, sets up its own principles of justice
(δόξα τῆς πόλεως), and it is in the competition of practical
life that these principles are tried and either approved or
found wanting.

What means could be employed to arrive at practical
results on this basis? Protagoras considered this question
especially in relation to criminal law. The aim of criminal
law, he said, is least of all punishment in the sense of
retribution. What is done cannot be undone; why then add
more evils to those which have already happened? Punishment therefore should be primarily a deterrent, and punitive law is worthless unless it contains some reformatory
element.[1] Punishment in the scheme of Protagoras is
a measure of social utility. We can discover something
of the same kind in modern theories of penology.

Thus we see that there was an attempt on the part of
a leading Sophist to explain the working of society and the
function of law on the basis of relativism.

Protagoras had laid down that justice is the result of
certain social instincts regulated by each State according to
its own standard. This view was partly accepted and
partly rejected by Sokrates.[2] He held that each State

Sokrates and the δόξα τῆς πόλεως.

---

[1] PLATO, *Protag.* 324 a b οὐδεὶς γὰρ κολάζει τοὺς ἀδικοῦντας πρὸς τούτῳ
τὸν νοῦν ἔχων καὶ τούτου ἕνεκα, ὅτι ἠδίκησεν, ὅστις μὴ ὥσπερ θηρίον ἀλογίστως
τιμωρεῖται· ὁ δὲ μετὰ λόγου ἐπιχειρῶν κολάζειν οὐ τοῦ παρεληλυθότος ἕνεκα
ἀδικήματος τιμωρεῖται—οὐ γὰρ ἂν τό γε πραχθὲν ἀγένητον θείη—ἀλλὰ τοῦ
μέλλοντος χάριν, ἵνα μὴ αὖθις ἀδικήσῃ μήτε αὐτὸς οὗτος μήτε ἄλλος ὁ τοῦτον
ἰδὼν κολασθέντα.

[2] In Sokrates' teaching there are difficulties similar to those
which met us in the case of the Sophists. Our chief information
comes from Plato, who referred to Sokrates as an exponent not only
of the latter's personal teaching, but of his own views. It is therefore
impossible to distinguish absolutely between the Platonic and the
historic Sokrates; but in spite of this, and of many vexed questions
of detail, it is to be remarked that there are points which can be
ascertained with considerable confidence in this respect. In some
cases the account given by Plato coincides with evidence from other
sources. In the particular case which I am about to consider we are
able to corroborate Plato's evidence by the statements in Xenophon's
Memorabilia. Cf. ZELLER, *Socrates*, Chap. V.

should be autonomous in formulating its principles of law, but he based this view not only on the suggestion of social instincts and utility, but also on the requirements of knowledge and thought.   In Sokrates' view there is no inherent opposition between natural justice and what is laid down by every State as law ; in any case the individual is not called upon to act as an umpire in possible conflicts between these two elements.   This was the cardinal view which is emphasized in the *Krito*, and corroborated by the evidence of Xenophon concerning the facts of the trial and condemnation of Sokrates.   These facts were, substantially, that when Sokrates had been accused of corrupting the youth, had been found guilty and condemned to death, an attempt was made by his friends to rescue him from prison. It was in connexion with this attempt that Sokrates said emphatically that the State may require from the citizen absolute obedience to its positive laws.   Sokrates refused to fly.   He did not think it right for a citizen who disagreed with the government of his native land to rebel against its positive enactments.   The law of the Commonwealth, he is made to say, is higher than that of father, mother, or ancestors ; the right of the city is immeasurably greater than any private right.[1]   What the individual has obtained as a kind of unearned increment from the State cannot be balanced by anything else but absolute submission to the laws of the city.

How then was Sokrates' own action to be justified ?   For it was he above all others who had taught the citizens to differ from received views.   Does his teaching, as represented in the *Krito*, mean that the individual is to cease to think for himself ?   No ; the individual has the right to think for himself, and to seek his own way towards right life.   Sokrates had been urging all along that he had tried to lead Athens to a better management of her affairs than her ordinary statesmen could devise for her.   He said in fact

---

[1] PLATO, *Krito*, 51 a b ἢ οὕτως εἶ σοφὸς ὥστε λέληθέν σε, ὅτι μητρός τε καὶ πατρὸς καὶ τῶν ἄλλων προγόνων ἁπάντων τιμιώτερόν ἐστιν ἡ πατρὶς καὶ σεμνότερον καὶ ἁγιώτερον καὶ ἐν μείζονι μοίρᾳ καὶ παρὰ θεοῖς καὶ παρ' ἀνθρώποις τοῖς νοῦν ἔχουσι, καὶ σέβεσθαι δεῖ καὶ μᾶλλον ὑπείκειν καὶ θωπεύειν πατρίδα χαλεπαίνουσαν ἢ πατέρα;

that in teaching and speaking as he did, he was performing
a public duty. If then he was now condemned by the very
State which he had attempted to serve, how was this conflict to be explained?

Thought is free; no restriction can be placed upon a
man's own subjective ideas. But in regard to external
conduct, every citizen has entered into an implied contract
with the State in which he lives, and on the strength of
that contract, if for no other reason, he must submit to the
laws which are imposed upon him. He must not only bow
to the immense weight of historical tradition, but also
recognize the fact that he has enjoyed the protection of the
State, and having accepted benefits from it, he must
accept unpleasant consequences as well. The State has
a right to say to him: If you do not like my ways, you can
leave the country. The implied contract therefore is agreed
upon as soon as the citizen settles permanently in a city;
the counterpart of this is the possibility for him to leave
the State.[1] This seems a very harsh view; but at least it
was consistent, and moreover it was not only theory, for
every day people all over Greece were leaving their native
cities because they found themselves in disagreement with
social ordinances.

This theory of the implied contract and of the supremacy
of State law is supplemented by a less vague and arbitrary
doctrine than that of social instinct which culminated in
the appeal to $a i\delta \omega s$ and $\delta i \kappa \eta$. Sokrates' whole teaching is
based on a kind of idealistic intellectualism. His chief
position was that we have in the human mind a force
which makes for combination and unity. This force is
reason governed by logic. There is a striking contrast
between Sokrates as the artist of dialectics derived from
universal logic and Gorgias, the teacher of impressionist
rhetoric. The one operated with deductions, the other with
suggestions ($\epsilon \nu \theta \upsilon \mu \eta \mu \alpha \tau \alpha$), and we all remember the con-

The intellectualism of Sokrates.

---

[1] *Krito*, 51 d ἡμεῖς γάρ σε γεννήσαντες, ἐκθρέψαντες, παιδεύσαντες, μετα-
δόντες ἁπάντων ὧν οἷοί τ' ἦμεν καλῶν σοὶ καὶ τοῖς ἄλλοις πᾶσιν πολίταις,
ὅμως προαγορεύομεν τῷ ἐξουσίαν πεποιηκέναι Ἀθηναίων τῷ βουλομένῳ,
ἐπειδὰν δοκιμασθῇ καὶ ἴδῃ τὰ ἐν τῇ πόλει πράγματα καὶ ἡμᾶς τοὺς νόμους,
ᾧ ἂν μὴ ἀρέσκωμεν ἡμεῖς, ἐξεῖναι λαβόντα τὰ αὑτοῦ ἀπιέναι ὅποι ἂν
βούληται.

temptuous way in which Sokrates refers in Plato's *Apology* to the art of making weak things look strong, τὰ ἐλάττονα κρείττονα ποιεῖν, τὸν ἥττω λόγον κρείττω ποιεῖν.[1]

As regards law, logic gave a convenient clue to the universal elements underlying local variations. Men communicate their ideas to one another and reflect in common because they possess means of mutual understanding and agreement: there must be some mutual understanding of this kind if we merely wish to avoid quarrels: and this makes it possible to arrive at general results in jurisprudence. For Sokrates, any problem may be solved by conscientious analysis, and the process of searching for admissions and inferences is the key to his eristic method. The implication in regard to jurisprudence is clear. If we can subject evidence to definite logical principles, then even locally different centres of juridical work will eventually produce similar juridical results as regards fundamental problems.

Such are the two main points in Sokrates' doctrine: on the one hand the recognition of the δόξα τῆς πόλεως, in the sense that every State has the right to set up its own legal standards[2]; and on the other hand the assertion that moral and legal duties are connected primarily with the logical framework of human understanding.

Plato's solution.

What was Plato's own contribution to the solution of the problem? We need not dwell long on his juridical position, because in spite of Plato's aesthetic power and philosophical depth, his conclusions appear only as an extension of Sokrates' views. There is a most emphatic adherence to the δόξα τῆς πόλεως principle. Why did Plato regard his scheme of the threefold division of society not merely as a device of political wisdom, but as the result of jurisprudential requirements? In his quest of justice, after having tried to derive definitions from individual conduct, he comes to the conclusion that in order to solve the problem it is essential to determine the purpose of the State. Justice, he says, is writ large in the State and writ small in the individual, and if we wish to understand the smaller type,

---

[1] Cf. GOMPERZ, *Greek Thinkers*, II, iv, pp. 66 ff., and ZELLER, *Socrates*, pp. 87–88 (of Eng. Trans.) (German, Vol. II, pp. 92–3). Cf. p. 28 above.   [2] Cf. above, p. 34.

we must first understand the larger.[1] Justice cannot be
embodied in any single individual: it depends on the har-
monization of elements in the State, and all attempts to
reconcile individual interests with justice apart from the
State are absurd. We must take up the problem, therefore, as being one of political harmony. This view is very
emphatically stated in the *Republic*. For Plato the problem hinges entirely on public and not on private law. He
dwells on the insufficiency of popular definitions of justice
based on the distinction between what is due to a person
and what is due to others, and shows that the notion of
" due," ὀφειλόμενον, as regards any private individual is
purely relative.[2] The measure of rights and claims ought
to correspond with the measure of duties, as imposed by the
State. Therefore justice is rooted in the wise and permanent distribution of obligations between the classes of
citizens. These duties are ranged under the well-known
rubrics of *reflection* of philosophers, of *courage* of the
defenders, and *industry* of the workers in the State. It
would be absurd for the industrial workers to ask for
the same range of power as the philosophers, and to grant
it to them would not be an act of justice. The rights and
duties of the individual must be assigned according to the
δόξα τῆς πόλεως, and "justice consists in doing one's own
business and not being a busybody."[3]

Let us notice in this connexion a very characteristic
passage in the VIIth book of the *Republic*:[4] "There is
a necessary inference from what has preceded, that neither
the uneducated and uninformed of truth, nor yet those who
never make an end of their education, will be able ministers
of State; not the former, because they have no single aim
of duty which is the rule of all their actions, private as
well as public; nor the latter, because they will not act at
all except upon compulsion, fancying that they are already
dwelling apart in the Islands of the Blest." Plato here
advances the view that the different classes of the people
should not only be assigned to their relative places, but

---

[1] *Republic*, II, 368. [2] *Ibid*. I, 332 c.

[3] *Ibid*. IV, 433 a τὸ τὰ αὑτοῦ πράττειν καὶ μὴ πολυπραγμονεῖν δικαιοσύνη
ἐστί.

[4] *Ibid*. VII, 519. Cf. *ibid*. 540 a b.

should be obliged to engage in some form of activity useful to the State.   For example, philosophers should not be allowed to lead an entirely contemplative life, but should be made to concern themselves with practical affairs.   If they remove themselves entirely from the practical sphere, they are infringing the principle of justice, because the State requires their service, and has a right to demand it. On the other hand, the man in the street ought not to try to thrust himself forward and claim the same privileges as the philosophers.   This is the net result of the whole teaching; it was partly inspired by Plato's own bitter experiences in the world of decadent democracy.

Law of
Nature.
In the perplexity which prevailed concerning the basis of morals and law, there was only one way out of the fundamental difficulties, and that was to leave the interpretation of the main problems to the State.   But what was the Ideal State which was to act as arbitrator in these differences?   Certainly it was not the city as it existed in Plato's own time, and Plato was acutely conscious of the fact.   The tragic position of philosophy in the fourth century is that the philosophers proclaimed the doctrine of the δόξα τῆς πόλεως at the same time as they found that the πόλις, called upon to enunciate this δόξα, was bankrupt. In order to steer through these rocks it was necessary to appeal to a universal principle, independent of historical variations and the arbitrary establishments of lócal laws. All the philosophical schools admit so much, and all turn to *nature* (φύσις) as the counterpart of law.   But while the representatives of subjectivism and relativism regard the dictates of nature as opposed to the conventional rules decreed by the tyrant νόμος (Antiphon, Hippias) and concede to the latter only the value of cunning devices and fictions (Gorgias, Kritias), the idealistic thinkers seek to connect positive laws with an immutable background of natural justice.   One may notice the idea already in Demokritos' teaching: "The good and the true (goodness and truth) are the same for all men, but sweetness is different for different people."[1]   Fragment 2 shows that Demokritos

---

[1] Diels, *Fragmente der Vorsokratiker*, II, p. 77, Fr. 69 ἀνθρώποις πᾶσι τωὐτὸν ἀγαθὸν καὶ ἀληθές· ἡδὺ δὲ ἄλλωι ἄλλο.   Cf. p. 26 above.

looked to reason as the source of universal truth and justice.[1]

Speculation on these lines is, however, much more prominent in Herakleitos' philosophy. While he underlines the contrast between the absolute character of the good as conceived by God with the forms of justice established by men,[2] he lays stress on the derivation of the latter from the former. There is a common element in justice as well as particular elements, and this common element (τὸ ξυνόν) should be defended or contended for (ἰσχυρίζεσθαι) with even greater vigour than in the case of cities defending their laws. And this because all justice comes from God, and value is imparted to all laws from that one source.[3] The ground for this belief is found in the universality of human reason.[4]

Thus appears the germ of the idealistic intellectualism which may be regarded as the characteristic feature of Sokrates' teaching, and for which his eristic method provided the dialectical complement. Φρόνησις, τὸ φρονεῖν, provided the possibility of evolving certain general principles of justice which may be regarded as commandments of human nature and are therefore superior to the δόξα τῆς πόλεως. Sokrates argued on these lines against Hippias according to Xenophon's account in the Memorabilia.[5] With Plato the notion is enlarged in the famous teaching as to "ideas," which, however, is too transcendental to form part of our juridical discussion. In Aristotle's Encyclopaedia the conception of the νόμος κοινός as opposed to νόμοι ἴδιοι reappears again.[6] It is, however, characteristic

[1] Ibid., p. 56, Fr. 2 γίνεται δὲ ἐκ τοῦ φρονεῖν τρία ταῦτα· βουλεύεσθαι καλῶς, λέγειν ἀναμαρτήτως καὶ πράττειν ἃ δεῖ.

[2] Ibid., I, p. 98, Fr. 102. BYWATER, Heracliti Reliquiae, 61 τῶι μὲν θεῶι καλὰ πάντα καὶ ἀγαθὰ καὶ δίκαια, ἄνθρωποι δὲ ἃ μὲν ἄδικα ὑπειλήφασι ἃ δὲ δίκαια.

[3] DIELS, Fr. 114. (BYWATER, 91 b) ξὺν νόωι λέγοντας ἰσχυρίζεσθαι χρὴ τῶι ξυνῶι πάντων, ὅκωσπερ νόμωι πόλις, καὶ πολὺ ἰσχυροτέρως. τρέφονται γὰρ πάντες οἱ ἀνθρώπειοι νόμοι ὑπὸ ἑνὸς τοῦ θείου· κρατεῖ γὰρ τοσοῦτον ὁκόσον ἐθέλει καὶ ἐξαρκεῖ πᾶσι καὶ περιγίνεται. Cf. J. L. MYRES, The Background of Greek Science, in California Chronicle, XVI, no. 4.

[4] DIELS, Fr. 113. (BYWATER, 91) ξυνόν ἐστι πᾶσι τὸ φρονέειν.

[5] Mem. IV, iv.

[6] AR. Rhet. I, x. 1368 b 7 νόμος δ' ἐστὶν ὁ μὲν ἴδιος ὁ δὲ κοινός. λέγω δὲ ἴδιον μὲν καθ' ὃν γεγραμμένον πολιτεύονται, κοινὸν δὲ ὅσα ἄγραφα παρὰ πᾶσιν ὁμολογεῖσθαι δοκεῖ. And I, xiii, 1373 b 4 λέγω δὲ νόμον τὸν μὲν

of the development of Greek juridical ideas that the "law
of nature," though appealed to as a philosophical explanation of existing facts, does not serve as a means for concrete
juridical deductions. It is at a later stage—with the advent
of Stoicism, especially in its Roman form—that the law
of nature began to be considered as a source of law in the
practical sense of the term. The explanation of this fact
may be found, I think, in the powerful development of
equity in the jurisdiction of the democratic courts of the
classical period, which left to the popular juries great latitude in the interpretation and application of positive law.

APPENDIX TO CHAPTER II

Antiphon the Sophist. *Oxyrh. Pap.* XI. 1364. pp. 96 ff.

Δικαιοσύνη πάντα τῆς πόλεως νόμιμα· ἐν ᾗ ἂν πολιτεύηταί
τις μὴ παραβαίνειν· χρῷτ᾽ ἂν οὖν ἄνθρωπος μάλιστα ἑαυτῷ
ξυμφερόντως δικαιοσύνῃ, εἰ μετὰ μὲν μαρτύρων τοὺς νόμους
μεγάλους ἄγοι, μονούμενος δὲ μαρτύρων τὰ τῆς φύσεως· τὰ
μὲν γὰρ τῶν νόμων ἐπίθετα, τὰ δὲ τῆς φύσεως ἀναγκαῖα·
καὶ τὰ μὲν τῶν νόμων ὁμολογηθέντα οὐ φύντ᾽ ἐστίν, τὰ δὲ
τῆς φύσεως φυντὰ οὐχ ὁμολογη[θέν]τα . . . τὰ πολλὰ τῶν
κατὰ νόμον δικαίων πολεμίως τῇ φύσει κεῖται· νενομοθέτηται
γὰρ ἐπί τε τοῖς ὀφθαλμοῖς ἃ δεῖ αὐτοὺς ὁρᾶν καὶ ἃ οὐ δεῖ·
καὶ ἐπὶ τοῖς ὠσιν ἃ δεῖ αὐτὰ ἀκούειν καὶ ἃ οὐ δεῖ· καὶ ἐπὶ
τῇ γλώττῃ ἅ τε δεῖ αὐτὴν λέγειν καὶ ἃ οὐ δεῖ· καὶ ἐπὶ
ταῖς χερσὶν ἅ τε δεῖ αὐτὰς δρᾶν καὶ ἃ οὐ δεῖ· καὶ ἐπὶ τοῖς
ποσὶν ἐφ᾽ ἅ τε δεῖ αὐτοὺς ἰέναι καὶ ἐφ᾽ ἃ οὐ δεῖ· καὶ ἐπὶ τῷ
νῷ ὦν τε δεῖ αὐτὸν ἐπιθυμεῖν καὶ ὦν μή . . . καὶ τούτων τῶν
εἰρημένων πόλλ᾽ ἄν τις εὕροι πολέμια τῇ φύσει· ἔνι τε αὐτοῖς
ἀλγύνεσθαί τε μᾶλλον ἐξὸν ἥττω. καὶ ἐλάττω ἥδεσθαι ἐξὸν
πλείω, καὶ κακῶς πάσχειν ἐξὸν μὴ πάσχειν· εἰ μὲν οὖν τις
τοῖς τοιαῦτα προϊεμένοις ἐπικούρησις ἐγίγνετο παρὰ τῶν
νόμων, τοῖς δὲ μὴ προϊεμένοις ἀλλ᾽ ἐναντιουμένοις ἐλάττωσις,
οὐκ ἀνωφελὲς ἂν ἦν τοῖς νόμοις πείθεσθαι· νῦν δὲ φαίνεται
τοῖς προϊεμένοις τὰ τοιαῦτα τὸ ἐκ νόμου δίκαιον οὐχ ἱκανὸν
ἐπικουρεῖν· ὅ γε πρῶτον μὲν ἐπιτρέπει τῷ πάσχοντι παθεῖν
καὶ τῷ δρῶντι δρᾶσαι, καὶ οὔτε ἐνταῦθα διεκώλυε τὸν πά-
σχοντα μὴ παθεῖν, οὐδὲ τὸν δρῶντα δρᾶσαι· εἴς τε τὴν τιμωρίαν ἀναφερόμενον οὐδὲν ἰδιώτερον ἐπὶ τῷ πεπονθότι ἢ τῷ
δεδρακότι.

ἴδιον τὸν δὲ κοινόν, ἴδιον μὲν τὸν ἑκάστοις ὡρισμένον πρὸς αὐτούς, καὶ τοῦτον
τὸν μὲν ἄγραφον τὸν δὲ γεγραμμένον, κοινὸν δὲ τὸν κατὰ φύσιν κτλ.
I cannot help thinking that the exposition of the matter by Salomon
in the *Z. SS. Roman. Abth.* XXXIII does not distinguish sufficiently
between the various periods.

CHAPTER III

THE LEGAL SYSTEM

1. *Preliminary Notions.*

THE Encyclopaedia of Greek life and thought worked Aristotle's terminology. out by Aristotle and his school at the end of the classical period supplies us with invaluable material for connecting philosophical doctrines with actual politics and law. The immense accumulation of data preserved by these encyclopaedists has certain drawbacks. The work was collective, not individual, and therefore not equally sustained even in its most important parts; it was not carefully edited or published as a whole. It consists to a great extent of lectures and surveys, taken down, no doubt, with care, but presenting obscurities and contradictions such as are inevitable when *viva voce* instruction and discussion are reported by listeners. We must not attempt to make everything fit precisely, but have to allow for gaps, misunderstandings, repetitions, and obscure passages, some of which were probably not very clear when the master delivered his lectures.[1]

Another important question concerns the terms used by Aristotle: their meaning is not to be established simply by reference to the dictionary. The copious information supplied by Bonitz or by Liddell and Scott has to be sifted and classified from the special point of view of the jurist.

---

[1] A preliminary remark on a literary question may be of some use. An important part of our material comes from the ethical writings. These are not of equal value in themselves, and therefore cannot be of equal authority. The *Nikomacheian Ethics* (Book V) is the most important source, but for terminology and for the clearing up of difficulties we have to turn to the other works. The *Eudemian Ethics,* written by Aristotle's pupil Eudemos, is not parallel to Aristotle's fifth book, but often contains expressions which help to interpret passages of doubtful meaning in the Nikomacheian text. The 'Ηθικὰ Μεγάλα, or *Magna Moralia*, is apparently a report of earlier lectures, and therefore the statements contained in it represent Aristotelian doctrine in a preparatory stage of its development. So much for the general perspective in which I propose to consider the ethical works.

The three terms to be noticed from the very beginning are δίκαιον, νόμιμον, and ἴσον ; of these νόμιμον is the easiest to translate, as its meaning does not vary : it always stands for the legal (or the lawful), that which is in conformity with law. The other two terms are ambiguous, and Aristotle sometimes gives explanations as to his use of them. In the *Magna Moralia* [1] we find that δίκαιον is used in two senses :

1. It is justice as a virtue enjoined by the community and formulated in its laws. Justice therefore covers a wide field ; it embraces the conduct of every single citizen in the State, and may be concerned with the most intimate details of his life ; for example, under a " paternal " government justice may enjoin us to be temperate ; in other words, there may be a law against drunkenness or incontinency. This kind of justice concerns the individual in his relation to the State of which he is a citizen.

2. The second kind of justice is termed " civic " (πολιτικὸν δίκαιον) [2] and is specifically directed towards regulating the relations between citizens ; it is justice not between self and the State, but between self and others.

In the *Nikomacheian Ethics* there is a more precise use of terms. Justice as a general conception has to be subdivided into two classes ; it is obedience to laws or equitable treatment of neighbours.[3] "There is a division of injustice into the illegal and the unequal, and of justice into the legal (or lawful) and the equal (or equitable)." It must be observed that our expression "equitable" should not be used without qualification, because, though it corresponds in part to ἴσον in Aristotle's writings, it also

---

[1] *Magna Moralia*, I, 1193 b ἔστι δὴ διττὸν τὸ δίκαιον, ὧν τὸ μέν ἐστι κατὰ νόμον· δίκαια γάρ φασιν εἶναι ἃ ὁ νόμος προστάττει. ὁ δὲ νόμος κελεύει ... ἁπλῶς ἅπαντα ὅσα κατὰ τὰς ἀρετὰς λέγεται ... ἀλλὰ τὸ δίκαιον τὸ πρὸς ἕτερον ἄλλο ... ἐστίν. The term τὸ πολιτικὸν δίκαιον for justice of the first kind occurs later on p. 1194 b.

[2] Cf. *Eth. N.* V, 6, § 4.

[3] *Eth. Nik.* V, 2, 1130 b, 8 ff. διώρισται δὴ τὸ ἄδικον τό τε παράνομον καὶ τὸ ἄνισον, τὸ δὲ δίκαιον τό τε νόμιμον καὶ τὸ ἴσον. ... ἐπεὶ δὲ τὸ ἄνισον καὶ τὸ παράνομον οὐ ταὐτὸν ἀλλ᾽ ἕτερον ὡς μέρος πρὸς ὅλον. ... καὶ περὶ τῆς ἐν μέρει δικαιοσύνης καὶ περὶ τῆς ἐν μέρει ἀδικίας λεκτέον. ... τῆς δὲ κατὰ μέρος δικαιοσύνης καὶ τοῦ κατ᾽ αὐτὴν δικαίου ἐν μέν ἐστιν εἶδος τὸ ἐν ταῖς διανομαῖς τιμῆς ἢ χρημάτων ἢ τῶν ἄλλων ὅσα μεριστὰ τοῖς κοινωνοῦσι τῆς πολιτείας ..., ἐν δὲ τὸ ἐν τοῖς συναλλάγμασι διορθωτικόν.

covers the term ἐπιείκεια to which we shall come later on. Thus Justice is qualified on the one hand as satisfying the law, on the other as fairness or equality in dealings with others.

In Aristotle's classification of the kinds of justice,[1] we find— (1) General Justice (τὸ καθόλου δίκαιον), and (2) Justice as a particular or specific virtue (τὸ ἐν μέρει δίκαιον). The first is a complex of all the rules formulated by the State as legally obligatory for the members of the community; the second is the set of rules which govern relations *between* the members of the community. The latter falls into two classes (*a*) Distributive justice (διανεμητικόν), and (*b*) Corrective justice (διορθωτικόν) or legal redress: (*a*) covers all cases in which an answer is given to the question as to what one person can claim on the ground of just distribution as against others; (*b*) covers all functions of justice directed towards redressing wrongs as between members of the State.

This is the main scheme: by the side of this stands an "annex," which Aristotle calls ἐπιείκεια, fairness or equity, not to be distinguished as specific or general, but acting as the correction of both according to circumstances. Another digression occurs in connexion with retaliation or retribution (τὸ ἀντιπεπονθός),[2] a doctrine originating with the Pythagoreans; by considering this doctrine Aristotle is diverted from the main thread of the discussion to the subject of exchange; thus the clear scheme with its three parts—General, Distributive, Corrective—becomes disturbed in exposition.

2. *Corrective Justice.*

We need not follow Aristotle's arrangement, but let us take the simplest part first, reserving the more difficult departments for a later stage. The part which admits of the easiest interpretation is the one relating to corrective justice (διορθωτικόν). Here Aristotle proceeds on lines similar to the modern classification, whereas in dealing with the distributive and the general departments he takes up peculiar points of view.

Conventions.

---

[1] *Loc. cit.*   [2] *Eth. Nik.* V, 5 1132 b 21, see below, p. 69.

Legal Redress or Corrective Justice falls into two sub-divisions; (a) Obligations which are the result of voluntary agreements (συναλλάγματα ἑκούσια), and (β) obligations which are not voluntary, but arise from delicts or torts (συναλλάγματα ἀκούσια). For example, a man who has inflicted an injury on another is charged with an obligation to make the damage good. This is plain, but the question arises, in what sense contractual obligations can be treated under the heading of *legal redress*. In the case of "breach of contract" the connexion is obvious. One party suffers by the breach, and the Court is asked to give redress. But Aristotle's treatment is wider: he takes the whole range of contract, enumerating sale, loans, security, lease and hire, bailment, deposit.[1]

Corrective Justice, in his view, covers not only breaches of conventions, but also their execution. Contractual obligations may remain unfulfilled because one of the parties has misinterpreted the terms of a contract, and thus the question of fitting redress involves the interpretation of the convention.

In enumerating the various forms of agreement, Aristotle does not mention expressly the type of the contract of service, although such conventions occurred in Greece.[2] They were not, however, very frequent, and we cannot expect an exhaustive enumeration of juridical subdivisions in a philosophical treatise.

Torts.

These relations are treated very much on the same lines as in Roman and modern law: the case is different in regard to delicts. Aristotle's words are worth considering with attention, especially as some commentators seem to have gone astray in their interpretation. He gives examples of the principal kinds of delicts creating obligations.[3] They form two groups; (1) those characterized by fraud

---

[1] *Eth. Nik.* V, 2, 1131 a 2 πρᾶσις ὠνὴ δανεισμὸς ἐγγύη χρῆσις παρακατα-θήκη μίσθωσις.

[2] In Roman law they belong mainly to the group of innominate contracts (according to the formulae *facio ut facias, facio ut des,* and *do ut facias*). They might also come under *locatio operarum*. See on the subject BEAUCHET, *Droit privé*, IV, 221 ff.

[3] *Eth. Nik.* V, 2, 1131 a 5 τῶν δ' ἀκουσίων τὰ μὲν λαθραῖα, οἷον κλοπὴ μοιχεία φαρμακεία προαγωγεία δουλαπατία δολοφονία ψευδομαρτυρία, τὰ δὲ βίαια, οἷον αἰκία δεσμὸς θάνατος ἁρπαγὴ πήρωσις κακηγορία προπηλακισμός.

(λαθραῖα), and (2) those characterized by violence (βίαια). To the first group belong theft, adultery, poisoning, procuring for immoral purposes, enticing of slaves from their masters, causing death by fraud, and false witness. Some exceedingly "criminal" items have found their way into this category, and the list makes an odd impression on a modern reader. The Greek law of tort is based on principles different from ours; for example, murder was not primarily considered as a crime against the community, but as a private tort to be avenged by the nearest kinsman. Therefore crimes like poisoning, or causing death by fraud, come under this head, and are considered here from the point of view of the damages to be exacted by the injured party. This does not mean, of course, that poisoning, manslaughter, and murder are treated exclusively as private wrongs; the public side is apparent, e.g. in the jurisdiction of the Areiopagos. But the injury to private interests gives rise to claims of the same kind as those against thieves or adulterers. In the second group we find assault, imprisonment, homicide, rape, maiming, slander, contumelious treatment. All these give the injured persons the right to seek compensation.

The treatment of compensation is also peculiar. Aristotle explains the situation by referring to certain mathematical processes [1]: disputes covered by distributive justice are to be settled according to geometrical proportion (κατ᾽ ἀναλογίαν), whereas compensation in disputes arising out of corrective justice is to be adjudged according to arithmetical proportion (κατὰ τὴν ἀριθμητικήν).[2] This means that, as regards obligations from delicts, the personal factor does not come in; it is the same if a good man robs a bad man or if a bad man robs a good one; they are equal—the unit being the citizen or man. The points to be considered are the act and the fact, not the person.

It is quite different in the case of distributive justice, because that should be determined in consideration of

---

[1] *Eth. Nik.* V, 4, 1131 b 32 τὸ δ᾽ ἐν τοῖς συναλλάγμασι δίκαιον ἐστὶ μὲν ἴσον τι, καὶ τὸ ἄδικον ἄνισον, ἀλλ᾽ οὐ κατὰ τὴν ἀναλογίαν ἐκείνην ἀλλὰ κατὰ τὴν ἀριθμητικήν. οὐδὲν γὰρ διαφέρει, εἰ ἐπιεικὴς φαῦλον ἀπεστέρησεν ἢ φαῦλος ἐπιεικῆ.

[2] See below, p. 56.

personal values. Advantage ought to stand to advantage
in quantity as man stands to man in quality.

The case of corrective justice may be made clear by an
example. Suppose that some furniture has been stolen;
the fact of the theft sets in motion a process of restitution
and compensation: a certain quantity of goods has been
carried away from the legal sphere of one individual to the
legal sphere of another. Justice must first restore the
things to their original owner; but this is not enough;
compensation goes further than restitution. Besides the
material damage suffered by the aggrieved party, there is
a moral element to be accounted for; the disturbance of
economic order, the feeling of humiliation, the sense of loss
and indignity, have to be estimated, and the moral injury
must be made good as well as the material one. The point
may be well illustrated by a reference to the speech of
Isokrates against Lochites.[1] He says: "If there had been
no contumely attached to my opponent's action, I should
not have come before you; but as it is I come to obtain
redress from him, not merely for the damage arising out of
the blows, but for the assault and dishonour, for which it
is right that free men should feel the greatest indignation
and should obtain the highest reparation. I see that when
you convict a man of temple robbery or theft you do not
assess the penalty in proportion to the amount stolen, but
you condemn all alike to death, and consider it just for
those who attempt the same crimes to be punished by the
same penalties. You ought then to hold the same view as
regards those guilty of contumelious aggression, and not to
ask whether the blow was very severe, but whether the
law was broken, and to exact redress not for the particular
circumstance only, but for the conduct of the aggressors as
a whole."

Moreover, the penalty ($\zeta\eta\mu\iota\alpha$) must be made commen-
surate with the advantage ($\kappa\epsilon\rho\delta\sigma$) which the thief had in
mind when he committed his crime.[2] In the case of crimes
of violence it is especially obvious that the moral damages

---

[1] Isokrates, XX, 396 c.

[2] *Eth. N.* V, 4, 1132 a πειρᾶται τῇ ζημίᾳ ἰσάζειν, ἀφαιρῶν τοῦ κέρδους.
. . . ὥστε τὸ ἐπανορθωτικὸν δίκαιον ἂν εἴη τὸ μέσον ζημίας καὶ κέρδους.

have to be considered, but in all cases the estimation of
these damages presents problems which are sometimes very
complex. Modern illustrations of the view that moral injury
should be considered in assessing damages may be found in
cases of breach of promise of marriage, or of seduction.

The necessity of restoring the disturbed equilibrium by The
bringing the goods back to their owner and appreciating assess-
the moral loss is clear; but the question is, how is this to damages.
be done? The Athenian courts had recourse to the process
called τίμησις, assessment. When the person had been
found guilty, then came the question of damages. In the
so-called ἀγῶνες ἀτίμητοι the amount of the fine was determined beforehand by law; in the ἀγῶνες τιμητοί, on the
contrary, the assessment was left to the jury. The procedure about which we hear most is the competitive proposal
of assessment made by plaintiff and defendant. The jury
had to choose between the two, and usually it was impossible for them to vary the estimates. If the court had
consisted of a few expert judges it would have been comparatively easy to do so; even with the numbers constituting a modern jury, the assessment can be left to their
deliberation and verdict; but in the huge Heliastic Courts,
consisting at least of 201, often of 401, sometimes even of
1,001 members, nothing like systematic discussion could be
allowed. The defects of the competitive procedure were
recognized, and Aristotle tells us of a different method of
voting advocated by Hippodamos of Miletos,[1] who suggested
that jurors, instead of receiving only the voting-counters
(ψῆφοι), should be provided with tablets (πινάκια) on which
every one could note what he thought best. Aristotle criticizes this suggestion in some detail.[2] "Neither is the law
to be commended which says that the judges, when a

---

[1] *Pol.* II, 1268 a.
[2] *Ibid.* 1268 b οὐ καλῶς δ' οὐδ' ὁ περὶ τῆς κρίσεως ἔχει νόμος, τὸ κρίνειν
ἀξιοῦν διαιροῦντα τῆς κρίσεως ἁπλῶς γεγραμμένης, καὶ γίνεσθαι τὸν δικαστὴν
διαιτητήν. τοῦτο δ' ἐν μὲν τῇ διαίτῃ καὶ πλείοσιν ἐνδέχεται (κοινολογοῦνται
γὰρ ἀλλήλοις περὶ τῆς κρίσεως), ἐν δὲ τοῖς δικαστηρίοις οὐκ ἔστιν, ἀλλὰ καὶ
τοὐναντίον τούτῳ τῶν νομοθετῶν οἱ πολλοὶ παρασκευάζουσιν ὅπως οἱ δικασταὶ
μὴ κοινολογῶνται πρὸς ἀλλήλους. ἔπειτα πῶς οὐκ ἔσται ταραχώδης ἡ κρίσις,
ὅταν ὀφείλειν μὲν ὁ δικαστὴς οἴηται, μὴ τοσοῦτον δ' ὅσον ὁ δικαζόμενος; . . .
δῆλον ὅτι μεριοῦσιν (οἱ δικασταί). . . . τίς οὖν ὁ τρόπος ἔσται τῆς διαλογῆς τῶν
ψήφων;

simple issue is laid before them, should make distinctions
in their judgement; for the judge is thus converted into
an arbitrator. Now, in an arbitration, although the arbitrators are many, they confer with one another about the
decision, and therefore they can draw distinctions; but in
courts of law this is impossible, and, indeed, most legislators
take pains to prevent the judges from holding any com-
munication with one another. Again, will there not be
confusion if the judge thinks that damages should be given,
but not so much as the suitor demands? The latter asks,
say, for twenty minae, and the judge allows him ten minae,
or one judge more and another less; one five, another four
minae. In this way if they will go on apportioning the
damages, and some will grant the whole and others nothing,
how is the final reckoning to be made? Indeed, no one
who votes for a simple acquittal or condemnation is compelled to perjure himself, if the indictment is quite simple
and in right form; for the judge who acquits does not
decide that the defendant owes nothing, but that he does
not owe the twenty minae. He only is guilty of perjury
who thinks that the defendant ought not to pay twenty
minae, and yet condemns him."

This concluding remark implies that it was in the
interest of the plaintiff not to put up his claim too high,
because he endangered his case thereby before the jury.

The procedure in the first instance evidently took place
in most cases before the arbitrators ($\delta\iota\alpha\iota\tau\eta\tau\alpha\iota$), and even in
those cases which were submitted to Heliastic tribunals
various magistrates had the preliminary investigation ($\dot{\alpha}\nu\dot{\alpha}$-
$\kappa\rho\iota\sigma\iota\varsigma$), which must have included proposals as to assessment.[1] We have some evidence that it was possible for a
court to adjudicate a supplementary assessment by some
process which is unfortunately not described in detail;
a case in point is referred to in the speech of Demosthenes
against Meidias.[2] "The people resolved that Evander the
Thespian was guilty of a contempt of the Mysteries, upon
a complaint brought against him by Menippos, a Karian.

---

[1] Plato has something of the same kind in view when he is treating
of agrarian disputes in *Laws*, VIII, 844.
[2] DEM. XXI, 175, 6, p. 571, 2 (cf. Kennedy's translation).

He had obtained a verdict against Menippos in a mercantile cause, and being unable (as he said) to catch him before, he seized his person while staying here at the Mysteries. When he (Evander) came into court, you were disposed to punish him with death, but, the complainant coming to terms, you compelled him to forgo the whole of the judgement which he had formerly recovered, amounting to two talents, and to pay such damages as the man computed he had sustained by stopping to prosecute."

We know that the case arose out of a προβολή [1] introduced before a Heliastic commission by the θεσμοθέται, and the punishment inflicted by the tribunal must have been the result not of a proposal by the accuser, but of a προστίμησις. Thus the courts were not absolutely bound by the proposals of plaintiff and defendant as to the assessment.

3. *Distributive Justice.*

If we turn now to Distributive Justice, a clear definition of it is supplied in the chapter of the *Ethics* referred to above [2]; " it is concerned with the distribution or division of honours or of property or of other things which may have to be divided between the members of a community." We have to reckon, therefore, with either the simple case of property coming up for division (e. g. an inheritance), or the more complex case of the distribution of honours or dignities (τιμαί). Occasions for a division of property arise under any system. In the treatise on the Athenian Constitution [3] there is a reference to the duty of the First Archon to receive claims in the process of so-called δατητῶν αἵρεσις, the granting of umpires to distribute property among heirs who could not agree as to respective shares. According to Harpokration, δατητῶν αἵρεσις also took place in the case of any kind of distribution of κοινά (*communia*); these proceedings correspond in Roman law to actions *familiae erciscundae* and *communi dividundo*.

Distribution of property.

---

[1] See below, p. 63.
[2] *Eth. Nik.* V, 2, 12, 1130 b. See above, p. 44. Cf. *Pol.* IV (VII), 1326 b 15, and 1330 a 2 ff.; also *Top.* VI, 143 a, 145 b.
[3] *Ath. Const.* 56 εἰσάγει ... εἰς δατητῶν αἵρεσιν, ἐάν τις μὴ θέλῃ κοινὰ τὰ ὄντα νέμεσθαι.

Another occasion on which distributive justice is seen in practice is the foundation of a colony. We have the evidence of inscriptions to show us what was done. For example, there is the document relating to the foundation of Brea about the year 444 B. C.[1] Ten men were to be chosen, one from each tribe, to divide the land; in this way κλῆροι, allotments, or family holdings, were formed. The conception of the κλῆρος is an ancient and universal one in Greek law. The κλῆρος is a plot of land intended to form the basis of subsistence for a household, and corresponding to the standard of a citizen family. The principle obviously required equal distribution in the course of colonization, and even in Athens an effort was made to keep up the tradition of the old κλῆροι; according to the testimony of Aristotle a law of Solon prohibited the accumulation of property in land.[2] It was the special duty of the Archon Eponymos to watch over the preservation of families (οἶκοι) in the sense of units of property.[3]

Distribution of honours and profits.

Thus, as regards the division of property, the meaning of the term "distributive justice" is sufficiently clear; but it applies also to the division of offices, honours, and privileges (τιμαί). Here we enter on a subject treated in a very peculiar manner by the Greeks. On account of the intimate connexion between politics and law all the Greeks recognized that there must be a correspondence between the duties and the rights of the members of a community. In the *Ethics* Aristotle says: "He who does not do any good to the community does not get honoured; the community is assigned to him who benefits the community; dignities are of the community."[4] People disagreed, however, as to the principle on which such a distribution should be effected. To quote again from the *Ethics*: "In distribution all men agree that what is just must be in accordance with a value of some kind, but they do not all adopt

---

[1] DITT. *Syll.*[3] I. 67, p. 83 γεονόμος δὲ ἑλέσθαι δέκα ἄνδρας ἕνα ἐχ φυλῆς. οὗτοι δὲ νεμάντον τὲν γὲν.

[2] *Pol.* II, 7, 1267 b.

[3] *Ath. Const.* c. 56.

[4] *Eth. Nik.* VIII, 14, 1163 b 6 οὐ γὰρ τιμᾶται ὁ μηδὲν ἀγαθὸν τῷ κοινῷ πορίζων· τὸ κοινὸν γὰρ δίδοται τῷ τὸ κοινὸν εὐεργετοῦντι, ἡ τιμὴ δὲ κοινόν. Cf. *Pol.* II, 1266 b, and III, 1278 a.

the same standard of value; in democratic States they take free birth as the standard, in oligarchic States wealth, or nobility of birth, in aristocracies virtue." [1] This discussion as to justice is, of course, closely connected with political theory, and the clearest embodiment of the principle is to be found in timocratic constitutions, where rights and duties were graduated according to classes determined by relative wealth. In general the right to hold office was brought into relation to the performance of civic functions, and in case of doubt the ultimate decision rested with the courts.

In order to make this point clear, and to show the working of the principle in practice, a few simple cases may be cited.

1. Election to a public office or dignity (ἀρχή). After the election by lot a procedure of "estimation" (δοκιμασία) had to be gone through, by which the fitness of the candidate was tested. Stress was laid on the question whether the person who aspired to be a member of the government had served the city by contributing to its expenses and sharing in its burdens. As to this process we have e. g. the evidence of three speeches of Lysias,[2] making it clear that there was an actual distribution (διανομή) of offices. On behalf of a defendant Lysias tried to prove that his client claimed the dignity by right, because he had done good service to the commonwealth; on the other hand, as an accuser he contested elections on the ground that the candidate did not come up to the standard in respect of services to the State.

2. Privileges of citizenship. Besides the actual offices of the State, there were special rights and privileges attached to the possession of citizenship. In Athens, which was for some time at the head of an Empire, citizens drew all sorts of benefits from their position in the city. In the twenty-fourth chapter of the *Athenian Constitution* we find a list

---

[1] *Eth. Nik.* V, 3, 1131 a 25 τὸ γὰρ δίκαιον ἐν ταῖς νομαῖς ὁμολογοῦσι πάντες κατ' ἀξίαν τινὰ δεῖν εἶναι, τὴν μέντοι ἀξίαν οὐ τὴν αὐτὴν λέγουσι πάντες ὑπάρχειν, ἀλλ' οἱ μὲν δημοκρατικοὶ ἐλευθερίαν, οἱ δ' ὀλιγαρχικοὶ πλοῦτον, οἱ δ' εὐγένειαν, οἱ δ' ἀριστοκρατικοὶ ἀρετήν.

[2] XVI, XXVI, XXXI.

of the advantages which could be claimed in this way[1];
we are told that more than 20,000 Athenians possessed
rights which materialized in the form of various payments
and bonuses. At the head of the list stand the Heliasts,
the jurymen in the Courts, then come the members of the
Council, archers, horsemen, citizens performing garrison
service, city police, etc.

Public
assist-
ance. This condition of affairs was not one of purely political
exploitation; it was the result of the performance of
administrative and judicial duties. Again, Athens, wealthy
city as she was, had introduced a system of doles or pen-
sions for citizens disabled by wounds, sickness, and old age.
It amounted in some cases only to an obol a day, but for
the poor it was an important matter, as is shown by
a speech of Lysias delivered before the Council.[2] The
speaker's plea is that he is destitute, and would be lost if
he were deprived of the daily obol. The man was accused
of having cheated the State, inasmuch as he was possessed
of some means, while he had been exempted from public
dues, and was receiving public assistance. He defended
himself against the charges made: "My adversary maintains that I am sufficiently strong and well-off, that I can
afford to ride horses, and that I make money by my craft,
that I am seen in the company of rich men." He denies

---

[1] *Ath. Const.* c. 24 . . . κατέστησαν δὲ καὶ τοῖς πολλοῖς εὐπορίαν τροφῆς,
ὥσπερ Ἀριστείδης εἰσηγήσατο. συνέβαινεν γὰρ ἀπὸ τῶν φόρων καὶ τῶν τελῶν
καὶ τῶν συμμάχων πλείους ἢ δισμυρίους ἄνδρας τρέφεσθαι. δικασταὶ μὲν γὰρ
ἦσαν ἑξακισχίλιοι, τοξόται δ' ἑξακόσιοι καὶ χίλιοι, καὶ πρὸς τούτοις ἱππεῖς
χίλιοι καὶ διακόσιοι, βουλὴ δὲ πεντακόσιοι, καὶ φρουροὶ νεωρίων πεντακόσιοι,
καὶ πρὸς τούτοις ἐν τῇ πόλει φρουροὶ ν̄, ἀρχαὶ δ' ἔνδημοι μὲν εἰς ἑπτακοσίους
ἄνδρας, ὑπερόριοι δ' εἰς ἑπτακοσίους· πρὸς δὲ τούτοις ἐπεὶ συνεστήσαντο τὸν
πόλεμον ὕστερον, ὁπλῖται μὲν δισχίλιοι καὶ πεντακόσιοι, νῆες δὲ φρουρίδες
εἴκοσι, ἄλλαι δὲ νῆες αἱ τοὺς φόρους ἄγουσαι τοὺς ἀπὸ τοῦ κυάμου δισχιλίους
ἄνδρας, ἔτι δὲ πρυτανεῖον καὶ ὀρφανοὶ καὶ δεσμωτῶν φύλακες· ἅπασι γὰρ
τούτοις ἀπὸ τῶν κοινῶν ἡ διοίκησις ἦν.

[2] LYSIAS, XXIV, 4 φησὶ γὰρ ὁ κατήγορος οὐ δικαίως με λαμβάνειν τὸ
παρὰ τῆς πόλεως ἀργύριον· καὶ γὰρ τῷ σώματι δύνασθαι καὶ οὐκ εἶναι τῶν
ἀδυνάτων, καὶ τέχνην ἐπίστασθαι τοιαύτην ὥστε καὶ ἄνευ τοῦ διδομένου τούτου
ζῆν. καὶ τεκμηρίοις χρῆται τῆς μὲν τοῦ σώματος ῥώμης, ὅτι ἐπὶ τοὺς ἵππους
ἀναβαίνω, τῆς δ' ἐν τῇ τέχνῃ εὐπορίας, ὅτι δύναμαι συνεῖναι δυναμένοις ἀνθρώποις ἀναλίσκειν. . . . πρόσοδος δέ μοι οὐκ ἔστιν ἄλλη πλὴν ταύτης, ἣν ἂν
ἀφέλησθέ με, κινδυνεύσαιμ' ἂν ὑπὸ τῇ δυσχερεστάτῃ γενέσθαι τύχῃ. μὴ
τοίνυν, ἐπειδή γε ἔστιν, ὦ βουλή, σῶσαί με δικαίως, ἀπολέσητε ἀδίκως· . . .
μηδ' ἐμὲ τολμήσαντες ἀδικῆσαι καὶ τοὺς ἄλλους τοὺς ὁμοίως ἐμοὶ διακειμένους
ἀθυμῆσαι ποιήσητε.

that these are really indications of wealth, and claims that he is truly entitled to the scanty help which he enjoys.

Aristotle's remark has been quoted above, that the principle of distribution in a democracy is ἐλευθερία, freedom (of birth). This could on occasion be made a very stringent test; for example, in 445 B.C., an incident [1] occurred which led to a considerable decrease in the number of free citizens. A fleet from Egypt arrived, bringing a supply of corn to Athens, and the problem of the distribution of the corn had to be solved. A revision in the Demoi followed (διαψήφισις), and in consequence about 5,000 persons lost their status as free citizens (ἐλευθερία).

3. Public burdens (λειτουργίαι), in the shape of heavy expenses undertaken by citizens in fitting out ships, equipping embassies, providing dramatic choruses, etc. The result of the principle of correspondence between needs, services, and dignities was that an exchange of property (ἀντίδοσις) might be demanded by the overtaxed party. The procedure is foreign to modern ideas, but very characteristic of Greek politics. Isokrates pretends to have made use of it in his defence against charges of bad citizenship. It was said of him that he was so rich that he ought to be on the roll of persons liable to contributions, and as a result of legal proceedings his name was entered on the roll. The extant speech on the Ἀντίδοσις is not the one actually delivered at the time, but a literary version published afterwards; the arguments, however, are no less significant. The speech of Demosthenes on the same subject [2] is probably genuine, and certainly forensic. A citizen challenged another on the ground that he was richer than himself, and ought to be on the roll of the λειτουργίαι, as the division of burdens ought to be proportioned to wealth. Accordingly both households were put under seal, and watchmen guarded the property until the valuation could be made. The complaint made in the speech is that Phainippos had broken the seals and removed a portion of his goods.

Public burdens.

---

[1] This incident is mentioned by Plutarch in his Life of Perikles (c. 37), and also by a scholiast on Aristophanes' *Wasps* (v. 718). Both derived their information from the antiquarian Philochoros.

[2] Dem. XLII.

Propor-
tionate
standards.

The general conclusion arrived at by Aristotle points
to a correspondence in accordance with geometrical proportion between a man's social value and his claims to
honour. He draws a distinction between equality in number
(ἀριθμῷ) and equality in proportion (λόγῳ).[1] Thus citizen
A should lay claim to certain advantages m according to
his general qualifications or status, against citizen B, whose
claims may be estimated at n. The symbols may represent
any amount, and the advantages so represented may take
any form; the point is that the relations between A and B
and between m and n must be the same. Taking an illustration from actual numbers, one might say that the relation
of 20 to 10 is the same as that of 6 to 3, although 20 and 6,
10 and 3, represent different quantities.

That this is not merely a personal theory of Aristotle's
is clear from a passage in Isokrates' *Areiopageitikos*; he
refers to the earlier timocratic form of government as the
best, and extols the Athenians of that age for recognizing
an equality which was not absolute, but proportionate.
He says: "A very important factor in the good government of the city at that time was that of the two kinds
of equality recognized—the one giving the same to all, and
the other giving each his due: they were well aware which
was the more profitable. That kind which considers the
good and the bad worthy of the same rewards they rejected
as not just; that which honours each man according to his
worth they adopted, and in accordance with it they governed
the city, not electing magistrates by lot from the whole people,
but choosing out the best and the most competent for each
function."[2]

In Aristotle's view the standard of distribution ought to
be civic virtue; and our whole reading of his work must
be determined by the fact that he starts with a political
ideal of this kind. We may ask what a democratic states-

---

[1] AR., *Eudemian Ethics*, VII, 1242 b ὁτὲ μὲν γὰρ ἀριθμῷ τοῦ ἴσου
μετέχουσιν, ὁτὲ δὲ λόγῳ. εἰ μὲν γὰρ ἴσον ἀριθμῷ εἰσήνεγκεν ἀργύριον, ἴσον
καὶ τῷ ἴσῳ ἀριθμῷ διαλαμβάνουσιν, εἰ δὲ μὴ ἴσον, ἀνάλογον· ... δεῖ ἄρα τινὶ
ἑτέρῳ ἀνισάσαι καὶ ποιῆσαι ἀνάλογον. τοῦτο δ' ἐστὶν ἡ τιμή, ... δεῖ δὲ ἰσασθῆναι τὸ κέρδος πρὸς τὴν τιμήν. Cf. *Pol.* III, 1281 a 31 τιμὰς γὰρ λέγομεν εἶναι τὰς ἀρχάς. Cf. also *Magn. Mor.* I, 1195 b; see below, p. 57.

[2] ISOKRATES, VII, 21, 22.

man of the type of Kleon—one who had broken with the old tradition of timocracy and aristocracy—would say about such a conception. He would, no doubt, disagree as to virtue being the standard, but would certainly have insisted on ἐλευθερία, and worked out the other aspect of the doctrine, viz., that the rich and influential should be made to pay for their advantages by being burdened with heavier duties and expenses.[1]

Does Distributive Justice cover not only the distribution of property, but also its protection? Supposing some one claims to have a better right to certain goods than their actual possessor—is that a case for distributive justice? There is no reason for treating the case under that head, as claims to things depend in this case on title and not on estimates; the proper place for it in the system described by Aristotle is under the heading of General Justice.

4. Justice in General (ἡ καθόλου δικαιοσύνη).

In comparison with the modern classification, Aristotle's general justice covers two great divisions— public law and the law of things (jus in rem)—and a large part of a third, namely, of the law of persons. We read in the fifth book of the Ethics: "The acts which manifest complete virtue form, we may say, the bulk of the acts which are in accordance with law; for the law orders us to display all the virtues and none of the vices in our lives. But the acts which tend to produce virtue are those legal acts which are prescribed with reference to the education of man as a citizen."[2] In positive legislation, the principle of equality does not hold good as a leading requirement; inequalities may be necessary for the sake of public utility. The inequalities between citizens, denizens (μέτοικοι), freedmen

---

[1] Eth. Nik. VIII, 14, 1163 b 10 τῷ δὴ περὶ χρήματα ἐλαττουμένῳ τιμὴν ἀπονέμουσι καὶ τῷ δωροδόκῳ χρήματα. Cf. above, p. 52. Cf. Magn. Mor. I, 1195 b πάντες γὰρ οἱ ἔλαττον λαμβάνοντες ἀντικαταλλάττονται ἢ τιμὴν ἢ ἔπαινον ἢ δόξαν ἢ φιλίαν ἢ ἄλλο τι τῶν τοιούτων.

[2] Eth. Nik. V, 2, 1130 b 22 σχεδὸν γὰρ τὰ πολλὰ τῶν νομίμων τὰ ἀπὸ τῆς ὅλης ἀρετῆς πραττόμενά ἐστιν· καθ᾽ ἑκάστην γὰρ ἀρετὴν προστάττει ζῆν καὶ καθ᾽ ἑκάστην μοχθηρίαν κωλύει ὁ νόμος. τὰ δὲ ποιητικὰ τῆς ὅλης ἀρετῆς ἐστι τῶν νομίμων ὅσα νενομοθέτηται περὶ παιδείαν τὴν πρὸς τὸ κοινόν.

and slaves are of this kind. Positive enactments may be independent of our moral conceptions; take, for example, the case of the attitude of the citizens of Amphipolis in relation to the cult of Brasidas;[1] there was nothing immoral in not wanting to join in this worship, but the enactment was binding for them, it was part of the religion of their State.

Thus in the field of General Justice the State maintains by legislation its standards of compulsory morality and political expediency; duties correspond to virtues, crimes to vices. Accordingly it is under this heading that we have to look for criminal justice. It is not to be found under the head of Corrective Justice, although the Greeks certainly realized that theft, rape, murder, etc. were crimes affecting the city (δημόσια) and not mere private wrongs. Accordingly laws inflicted punishments in a number of cases apart from any compensation.

Contro-
versies as
to rights.

The second class of rights which are to be derived from General Justice, as expressed in positive enactments, are the rights of property and possession. They give rise primarily to so-called ἀμφισβητήσεις, disputes; these are characterized by the fact that there is no plaintiff and no defendant in them; the parties stand both in the same position in the trial, both seeking to ascertain their right, and to have it declared. This variety is represented in procedure by the form of process called διαδικασία, a special kind of trial arising in cases where no one asserts that there is any wrong on the side of the opponent, but each party insists on his supposed right. The process was chiefly used for the protection of those rights which might be called rights of *tenure* or property.[2] The fact that διαδικασία treats of rights of tenure protected by the State as long as no better title has been produced is shown by the definition given, e.g. in the *Lexica Segueriana*;[3] the aim of the action is only to establish and maintain the strongest claim. Thus there is a clear contrast with the Roman *rei vindicatio*.[4]

[1] *Eth. Nik.* V, 7, 1134 b, 23.   [2] See below, Chap. X, p. 221.
[3] *Lexica Segueriana*, ed. Bekker οὐχ ἁπλῶς πᾶσα δίκη διαδικασία καλεῖται, ἀλλ' ἐν αἷς περί τινος ἀμφισβήτησίς ἐστιν ὅτῳ προσήκει μᾶλλον.
[4] LIPSIUS, *Att. Recht und Rechtsverfahren*, p.463, is of a different opinion.

Turning to the actual material for the study of the process in the extant forensic speeches we find nothing treating of rights to property derived from purchase, but several speeches on rights derived from inheritance. Very conspicuous instances are presented by Isaios' speech on the estate of Hagnias,[1] and those of Demosthenes against Makartatos and Leochares;[2] in the last there is a discussion of a very difficult point of Athenian law, namely, the relative standing of a person claiming kinship as against a posthumously adopted son of the last owner. Other examples of διαδικασία concern religious offices, which were of importance, naturally, as sources of income.

If we compare these cases with those of Roman, English, or French law, we find that under the latter systems it was advisable to try to get possession before urging one's claim to the title. The historical explanation of this consists in the fact that Praetorian law developed as a system working against the principle of "self-help" by means of interdicts, e.g. *uti possidetis* or *utrubi*. The introduction of interdicts was intended as a substitute for juridical self-help, which was one of the most powerful agents in the archaic process of securing right. While the executive power of the State was weak, it had to let people make their claims good on their own initiative, e.g. by *pignoris capio* or *manus injectio*. As the authority of the State developed, these methods became obsolete and undesirable—in fact dangerous to society—and the State began to assert its judicial monopoly. The gradual restriction of self-help led also in French and English law to a procedure aiming first of all at protecting or securing possession and relegating the trial as to rights to a subsequent stage.

Restriction of self-help.

It may be asked whether there was in Greek law anything similar to that procedural relation between possession and title.[3] It may seem that lawful possession was protected in accordance with a passage in the *Athenian Constitution* containing a notice of a proclamation by the First

---

[1] ISAIOS XI.   [2] DEM. XLIII and XLIV.
[3] HERMANN-THALHEIM, *Rechtsalterthümer*, p. 113.

Archon, made upon entering office for the year.[1] He gave
out that every one would be entitled during his archonship
to hold all land and movable property which he held when
the Archon entered office, and should remain in possession up
to the end of his term of office. It might be argued that
this constitutes protection, and would form the ground
for an action if the proclamation were infringed. But this
idea can hardly stand when we consider the existing evidence;
there is no speech on such a theme, and although the
argument *a silentio* is not always a very sound one, it
is pretty strong in this case, because so many forensic
speeches have survived, and we are informed as to
the general contents of many lost orations. The truth
probably is that the proclamation was an archaic survival
from the time when the First Archon was really a very
important magistrate, a kind of President of the Republic.
The proclamation has great historical significance, but it is
not the foundation of any process in law. It was meant to
guarantee the rule of law in connexion with every right of
property as well as of possession.

Yet in a community so highly developed as the Athenian
State protection against dispossession by violence had to be
provided in some way, and we do find certain forms of
procedure intended to meet the need. The principal remedy
was the δίκη ἐξούλης, employed against those who ousted
other people from their possessions. The name was derived, according to Harpokration, from the verb ἐξίλλειν
meaning "to push out."[2] This is so clear that the only
doubt as to the bearing of the action arose from additional
remarks of Harpokration on various cases when it was
applied. These remarks have been interpreted to mean
that the action was directed towards the execution of a
judgement. But these cases mentioned by Harpokration
concern particular applications, and the fundamental idea
remains the defence of possession.[3]

---

[1] *Ath. Const.* c. 56 ὅσα τις εἶχεν πρὶν αὐτὸν εἰσελθεῖν εἰς τὴν ἀρχήν,
ταῦτ' ἔχειν καὶ κρατεῖν μέχρι ἀρχῆς τέλους.

[2] HARPOKR. δίκη ἐξούλης (LIPSIUS, 665); see below, p. 225.

[3] As to the other statements contained in Harpokration's fragment
see the controversy between RABEL and LIPSIUS in *Z. SS. Roman.
Abth.* 1915 to 1918.

Instances of the process are found in several speeches of
the Attic Orators ; Demosthenes used it in a trial arising
from his suit against his guardian Aphobos. The latter
had been convicted of mismanaging Demosthenes' property
during his minority, and was condemned to pay both fine
and compensation ; but when Demosthenes tried to get the
money, a certain Onetor came forward saying that that
part of Aphobos' property was pledged as the dowry of his
wife. Demosthenes had the right to remove this obstruction by means of the δίκη ἐξούλης.[1]

A second process, δίκη βιαίων, applies to dispossession by
violence as regards chattels.

We now turn to the question of the protection of public Public
rights and interests.   This was secured in two ways : wrongs.
through individual and through State action.

1. The private accusation, which under the name of
συκοφαντία became the scourge of Greek public life, was
based on the principle that every citizen was called upon
to defend and enforce public rights by actions which involved personal profit. The point of view that there is a
fundamental difference between public and private, or between criminal and civil law is modern ; while recognizing
the distinction, the Greeks admitted it only in an attenuated
form.   An illustration is provided by the typical case of
Demosthenes' prosecution of Meidias.[2] The quarrel was
a personal one ; Meidias tried to humiliate Demosthenes in
every possible way, and even took advantage of the fact
that Demosthenes had undertaken a State service as Choragos—he was providing the chorus and appurtenances for a
dramatic performance—to insult him publicly. The crown
and vestments worn by Demosthenes in his official capacity
were torn and cast in the dirt : Meidias actually slapped
his enemy in the face.

In bringing his action against Meidias Demosthenes had
ample material for enlarging on the personal aspect of the
case and the insult to himself, but he went further than
this, insisting that in his person as Choragos, the Commonwealth had been insulted. In his speech he brought out

---

[1] DEM. XXX.   [2] DEM. XXI.

the point of view that when a man's action includes violence, the effect is public; "what a man does with violence constitutes an injustice against the community." [1] Aristotle in the *Rhetoric* remarks on the contrast between an action for assault (αἰκίας), a private wrong, and an action for military desertion (ἀστρατείας, λιποταξίας), which entirely concerns the κοινόν; "he who commits adultery or assault infringes the rights of a single citizen, but he who fails to perform military duties breaks the law and commits injustice against the commonwealth." [2]   Greek law presented in this way what seems to us a peculiar mixture of civil and criminal procedure.

2. There were also cases in which it was considered that the public offence was so grievous or the public danger so great that the city itself came forward and acted, as it were, personally against the offender. Such a process was called εἰσαγγελία, to which a corresponding process is presented under the English system by the Bill of Attainder. This was a political trial in the Council or in the Assembly. The proceedings against the unfortunate commanders who had fought at Arginusae were conducted by εἰσαγγελία. Right through the fifth century the Council wielded extensive powers, and was not obliged to wait for the lengthy procedure involved in actions before the Assembly. We read in the *Athenian Constitution* that it was possible and usual for the Council to arrest, imprison, and even put to death people accused of what we should call high treason; [3] Aristotle describes with approval the action of one Archinos, who persuaded the Council to inflict punishment without trial on persons who had broken one of the principal conventions for the return of exiles after the downfall of the Thirty. [4] A resolution of the people,

---

[1] DEM. XXI, c. 45 πάνθ᾽, ὅσα τις βιαζόμενος πράττει, κοίν᾽ ἀδικήματα καὶ κατὰ τῶν ἔξω τοῦ πράγματος ὄντων ἡγεῖθ᾽ ὁ νομοθέτης.

[2] AR. *Rhet.* I, 13, 3 διὸ καὶ τἀδικήματα καὶ τὰ δικαιώματα διχῶς ἔστιν ἀδικεῖν καὶ δικαιοπραγεῖν· ἢ γὰρ πρὸς ἕνα καὶ ὡρισμένον ἢ πρὸς τὸ κοινόν· ὁ γὰρ μοιχεύων καὶ τύπτων ἀδικεῖ τινα τῶν ὡρισμένων, ὁ δὲ μὴ στρατευόμενος τὸ κοινόν.   Cf. COPE's *Commentary*, Vol. I, p. 248.

[3] *Ath. Const.* c. 45 ἡ δὲ βουλὴ πρότερον μὲν ἦν κυρία καὶ χρήμασιν ζημιῶσαι καὶ δῆσαι καὶ ἀποκτεῖναι.

[4] *Ibid.* c. 40 δοκεῖ ... πολιτεύσασθαι καλῶς Ἀρχῖνος ... ἐπεί τις ἤρξατο τῶν κατεληλυθότων μνησικακεῖν, ἀπαγαγὼν τοῦτον ἐπὶ τὴν βουλὴν καὶ πείσας ἄκριτον ἀποκτεῖναι.

(ψήφισμα) which afterwards obtained force of law (νόμος), put a stop to this use of power by the Council. One Eumelides prevented the execution of a certain Lysimachos by summary process, and a law was passed that no Athenian citizen could be sentenced to death, imprisonment, or confiscation without a decision of the People.[1] This kind of justice appears as the spontaneous action of the political body.

One more variety of procedure must be mentioned in this connexion, namely, the action called προβολή.[2] This was a form of procedure in which a private accuser brought a case before the Assembly and obtained a prejudicial verdict as to the guilt of the accused, but had to bring the case before the Heliastic tribunal afterwards for regular trial. The Court was not bound by the previous decision, but a general atmosphere unfavourable to the accused was obviously created, and an acquittal became improbable, though not impossible. By a curious inconsistency the accuser was allowed to drop the action if he wished.

These were the principal means for the protection of public safety: they can all be traced in modern law, though in different combinations.

5. Fairness.

Aristotle adds one more chapter on a kind of justice Ἐπιείκεια. which he describes as justice outside legality. This is called ἐπιείκεια, in the sense of *fairness*; the English word "equity"—originally an equivalent—having assumed a technical connotation as a branch of English law, does not quite fit for our purpose.

The teaching on this department of justice forms one of the most instructive parts of Greek jurisprudence; it has had a long history and a great influence on modern developments of the theory of law. It is noticeable that the

---

[1] *Ibid.* c. 45 καὶ Λυσίμαχον αὐτῆς ἀγαγούσης ὡς τὸν δῆμον καθήμενον ἤδη μέλλοντα ἀποθνήσκειν Εὐμηλίδης . . . ἀφείλετο, οὐ φάσκων δεῖν ἄνευ δικαστηρίου γνώσεως οὐδένα τῶν πολιτῶν ἀποθνήσκειν· . . . ὁ δὲ δῆμος . . . νόμον ἔθετο, ἄν τινος ἀδικεῖν ἡ βουλὴ καταγνῷ ἢ ζημιώσῃ, τὰς καταγνώσεις καὶ τὰς ἐπιζημιώσεις εἰσάγειν τοὺς θεσμοθέτας εἰς τὸ δικαστήριον, καὶ ὅ τι ἂν οἱ δικασταὶ ψηφίσωνται, τοῦτο κύριον εἶναι. Cf. P. CLOCHÉ, *Revue des études grecques*, XXXIII.   [2] See below, Chap. IX.

framers of the Code Napoléon in 1804 thought it necessary
to restate the doctrine of Aristotle on ἐπιείκεια in their
introductory chapter. The best and shortest way of
approaching the subject is to start with Plato's dialogue
called the *Statesman,* in which we read : " The law, in aiming at what is best or most just, cannot at once enjoin what
is best for all. The differences of men and actions, and the
endless irregular movements of things, do not admit of any
universal and simple rule. No art whatsoever can lay
down a rule which will last for ever."[1]   Compare with this
short statement the definition given by Aristotle in the
Ethics: " The nature of the equitable is the correction of
law, inasmuch as law falls short of what is required by the
universal terms in which it is expressed. This (deficiency)
is the reason why all things cannot be regulated by law, so
that decrees are required ; that which does not admit of
definition must be governed by indefinite rules."[2]   Thus
laws are general rules, and for this reason they sometimes
fail to do justice to the circumstances of particular cases.
There is often a wide gap between the abstract rule and
the concrete case, embedded, as it were, in circumstances ;
it would lead to great injustice if we applied such a rule
indiscriminately in all instances. In order to get something more than " book " righteousness, we must admit the
force of conceptions which go beyond the rule. Ἐπιείκεια
is the liberal application of rules to special sets of circumstances ; it forms a link between the general νόμος and the
single case in its complicated surroundings.

Treatment
in the
Rhetoric.

In the *Rhetoric*[3] Aristotle's treatment is more developed
than in the *Ethics* ; he says : " The equitable seems to be
just, and equity (fairness) is a kind of justice, but goes

[1] PLATO, *Politikos*, 294 a νόμος οὐκ ἄν ποτε δύναιτο τό τε ἄριστον καὶ
τὸ δικαιότατον ἀκριβῶς πᾶσιν ἅμα περιλαβὼν τὸ βέλτιστον ἐπιτάττειν· αἱ γὰρ
ἀνομοιότητες τῶν τε ἀνθρώπων καὶ τῶν πράξεων καὶ τὸ μηδέποτε μηδὲν ὡς
ἔπος εἰπεῖν ἡσυχίαν ἄγειν τῶν ἀνθρωπίνων οὐδὲν ἐῶσιν ἁπλοῦν ἐν οὐδενὶ περὶ
ἁπάντων καὶ ἐπὶ πάντα τὸν χρόνον ἀποφαίνεσθαι τέχνην οὐδ᾽ ἡντινοῦν.

[2] AR., *Eth. Nik.* V, 10, 3, 1137 b τὸ ἐπιεικὲς δίκαιον μέν ἐστιν, οὐ τὸ κατὰ
νόμον δέ, ἀλλ᾽ ἐπανόρθωμα νομίμου δικαίου . . . καὶ ἔστιν αὕτη ἡ φύσις ἡ τοῦ
ἐπιεικοῦς, ἐπανόρθωμα νόμου, ᾗ ἐλλείπει διὰ τὸ καθόλου. τοῦτο γὰρ αἴτιον
καὶ τοῦ μὴ πάντα κατὰ νόμον εἶναι, ὅτι περὶ ἐνίων ἀδύνατον θέσθαι νόμον,
ὥστε ψηφίσματος δεῖ. τοῦ γὰρ ἀορίστου ἀόριστος καὶ ὁ κανών ἐστιν.

[3] I, 13, 13–18. See appendix to this chapter, p. 71. Cf. JEBB,
Translation of Aristotle's Rhetoric.

beyond the written law. This margin is left by legislators, sometimes voluntarily, sometimes involuntarily; involuntarily when the point escapes their notice, voluntarily when they are unable to frame a definition, and yet it is necessary to lay down an absolute rule; also in cases which inexperience makes it hard to define,—such as the case of wounding with iron of a given size and kind; for life would not be long enough for a person who tried to enumerate the cases. If, then, it is impossible to be definite, yet necessary to legislate, one must speak generally; and so, if even the wearer of a ring lift his hand against another or strike him, he is guilty of a wrong under the written law, but not in reality; and here fairness comes in."

The treatment of all the cases which may arise cannot be completely planned beforehand; as Aristotle says, it would take an age merely to enumerate the possibilities; so the general rules must be supplemented by the use of reason and fairness in the application of them.[1]

In spite of various drawbacks in their procedure, the Athenians had a great reputation among the Greeks for this very side of their administration of justice; they were admired for their humanity ($\phi\iota\lambda\alpha\nu\theta\rho\omega\pi\iota\alpha$) and fairness ($\dot{\epsilon}\pi\iota\epsilon\iota\kappa\epsilon\iota\alpha$).

To illustrate the philosophical treatment of $\dot{\epsilon}\pi\iota\epsilon\iota\kappa\epsilon\iota\alpha$ by Aristotle let us turn to a few examples drawn from actual litigation. But first let us observe one fundamental limitation; in all these cases we have to deal with *pleadings* in the Courts. Now the essence of forensic pleading is to make one's own case as strong as possible, and to minimize as far as one can the arguments of one's opponent; in no system of law can pleaders be expected to be impartial. In Greek law, so far as it is concerned with the application of $\dot{\epsilon}\pi\iota\epsilon\iota\kappa\epsilon\iota\alpha$, the subjective element is very prominent; artificial devices and legal fencing are strongly represented in the speeches of the orators. Wyse, in his very valuable edition of the Speeches of Isaios, has been brought by his close study of his author to an altogether sceptical conclu-

---

[1] AR., *Rhet.* I, xiii, 13 ff., ed. COPE, pp. 255 ff. Cf. *Pol.* III, 1282 b 2; *Magn. Mor.* II, 1.

sion. He detects so many sophisms and flaws in statement
and argument that his final estimate is an absolutely nega-
tive one. To this extreme view we may, however, find an
antidote in the commentary on the text; for Wyse sometimes attempts to show that both sides are equally wrong,
and their arguments equally fallacious, thus leading up to
a *reductio ad absurdum* of his main position.

Let us be content with the fact that the general considerations presented by the pleaders usually had public
opinion behind them; no audience would stand pure non-
sense, and, least of all, a critical Athenian audience. The
orators employ every kind of ingenious artifice, but it is to
be remembered that they are seeking to persuade a large
number of average citizens that certain legal rules had to
be applied in a certain way; the Courts *were* influenced by
those subjective considerations, which sounded plausible,
and appealed to public opinion.

Testa-
ments.

In two departments of law the orators made particularly
great use of general considerations of fairness as against
exact and rigid legal rules: Testaments and Contracts
afforded an extensive field for the application of equitable
principles, and many speeches deal with these subjects.
That of Isaios on the estate of Nikostratos, though otherwise not very interesting, contains a general remark of
great weight.[1] He says that in trials concerning inheritance it is much more important to give heed to circumstantial evidence than to statements of witnesses; because
the principal witnesses are generally either dead, or—if the
will has been made abroad—absent, and therefore not
amenable to cross-examination; their depositions have to
be taken as they stand, and strict standards of criticism
cannot be applied.

In these testamentary cases there were two facts before
the Court; (1) under Solon's law every childless citizen
had the free right to make a will, but (2) his will was

---

[1] ISAIOS, IV, § 12 ἐν μόναις δὲ ταῖς τῶν κλήρων εἰσαγωγαῖς δοκεῖ μοι
προσήκειν τεκμηρίοις μᾶλλον ἢ μάρτυσιν πιστεύειν. περὶ μὲν γὰρ τῶν ἄλλων
συμβολαίων οὐ πάνυ χαλεπὸν τοὺς τὰ ψευδῆ μαρτυροῦντας ἐλέγχειν. ζῶντος
γὰρ καὶ παρόντος τοῦ πράξαντος καταμαρτυροῦσι· περὶ δὲ τῶν διαθηκῶν πῶς
ἄν τις γνοίη τοὺς μὴ τἀληθῆ λέγοντας, εἰ μὴ πάνυ μεγάλα τὰ διαφέροντα εἴη,
αὐτοῦ μὲν καθ᾽ οὗ μαρτυροῦσι τεθνεῶτος.

invalidated if made in extreme old age, or when the
testator was of unsound mind, or under the influence of
a woman.[1] Thus, if the actual will had been made in due
form, and under normal conditions as to age and mental
sanity, the only way to get it set aside was to prove undue
influence. Several instances of this occur in the speeches.
In Isaios' speech on the estate of Kleonymos the case is
somewhat different. The facts were that Kleonymos had
quarrelled with his nearest relations, and in a fit of temper
had excluded them from his will, and devised his whole
estate to strangers. Subsequently, however, as Isaios tries
to show, he became reconciled with his relations, and there
were some circumstances indicating that at the time of
his death he was actually on the best of terms with them.
During his last illness he sent for his will with the intention of altering it in favour of his kinsmen; but it
did not arrive in time, and the alteration was not made.
Isaios pleads that there was sufficient evidence that when
he made the will he was not in a normal state of mind,
since later on, upon calmer consideration, he came to regret
his hasty action, and wished to change the dispositions
of his will in favour of his own kin.[2] The pleadings are
based entirely on psychological surmises; the case would
be quite impossible to maintain at the present day. There
is no doubt, however, that an Athenian Court would
frequently listen to such considerations, nor are they
entirely foreign to modern practice. Even now, for
example, jurymen may sometimes extend leniency to
an accused person, not only on account of mitigating
circumstances, but also because they are satisfied that
he acted under abnormal conditions. Aristotle in the
Problemata[3] says expressly that the efforts of sophists
and sharp practitioners were largely directed towards in-
validating wills; they persuaded the Courts to attach
weight to this kind of psychological suggestions (cf. ἐνθυ-
μήματα).

[1] Cf. HYPEREIDES, III (V), § 17.
[2] Is. I, e.g. §§ 10–21.
[3] *Problemata*, 29, 3, 950 b 5 Διὰ τί ἐνίοις δικαστηρίοις τοῖς γένεσι μᾶλλον
ἢ ταῖς διαθήκαις ψηφιοῦνται; ἢ ὅτι γένους μὲν οὐκ ἔστι καταψεύσασθαι, ἀλλὰ
τὸ ὂν ἀποφαίνειν· διαθῆκαι δὲ πολλαὶ ψευδεῖς ἤδη ἐξηλέγχθησαν οὖσαι.

Contracts. As regards contracts there is a very wide opposition between legal rules and the arguments of pleaders. Hypereides calls attention to the contrast between the letter and the spirit of justice. A certain Athenogenes had persuaded Hypereides' client to buy a shop; he had induced a clever woman of more than doubtful character to serve as his agent in the matter. Under her influence the plaintiff had concluded the bargain. Later on he found that he had been grossly imposed upon, and wanted to rescind the sale. He does not deny that the contract was actually made, but he urges that he was gulled by the blandishments of the lady. This would serve for an argument even now, if fraudulent mis-representation could be proved, but our present standard is much stricter. Hypereides put the point in a most emphatic way. He forestalled the argument of his opponent, saying: "Athenogenes will tell you that, according to law, agreements made between parties are valid. Yes, if they are in accordance with justice; but when they are not, the law on the contrary forbids them to stand."[1]

Interpretation of archaic laws. It is clear that the administration of law in Athens de-manded wide discretion on the part of the Courts. In the first place, we are often told that the old laws—especially those of Solon, which in the fourth century were still recognized as the foundation of existing law—were archaic and obscure. But the clumsiness and difficulty of the legislative process made it hard to introduce amendments in good time; conse-quently they mostly retained their archaic form, and the best course open for amendment was to use wide discretion in interpreting and applying them. This is expressed in the oath taken by the Heliasts, in which they say that if there is a law covering the case, they will obey it, but if the application be doubtful they will judge "to the best of their belief" ($\gamma\nu\omega\mu\eta$ $\delta\iota\kappa\alpha\iota\sigma\tau\acute{\alpha}\tau\eta$).[2] It is evident from the speeches that the range of "considerations of justice" was very extensive, and was not really restricted to cases where there were no laws.

[1] HYPEREIDES, op. cit. § 13 ἐρεῖ δὲ πρὸς ὑμᾶς αὐτίκα μάλα ᾿Αθηνογένης ὡς ὁ νόμος λέγει, ὅσα ἂν ἕτερος ἑτέρῳ ὁμολογήσῃ κύρια εἶναι. τά γε δίκαια . . . τὰ δὲ μὴ τοὐναντίον ἀπαγορεύει μὴ κύρια εἶναι. Cf. AR., Rhet. I, xv. 9.
[2] POLLUX, VIII, 10 ὁ δ᾿ ὅρκος ἦν τῶν δικαστῶν περὶ μὲν ὧν νόμοι εἰσί, ψηφιεῖσθαι κατὰ τοὺς νόμους, περὶ δὲ ὧν μὴ εἰσί, γνώμῃ τῇ δικαιοτάτῃ. Cf. Cope's Rhetoric, I, p. 271.

Another reason for such a free treatment of the laws **Residuary** lies in the fact that the higher Courts (the Heliastic **justice of the** δικαστήρια) represented the Sovereign People. Therefore **people.** orators sometimes addressed juries as "you citizens of Athens." Thus the use of discretionary power by the Courts constitutes an appeal to what is termed *residuary justice*. There must be, as we see even in our own law, a margin beyond actual legality. "Grace" is nowadays a political prerogative concerned with cases of commutation of criminal sentences; but in the fourteenth century, for instance, the residuary justice vested in the King was a very serious element in the juridical system. The King was to some extent the safeguard and guarantor that there should be no gaps and no exaggerations in the administration of justice. He acted, through his Council or through Parliament, especially with regard to cases where no remedy could be found at law. In the Athenian juridical system Demos takes the place of King or Parliament. The Heliaea, though we are inclined to oppose it to the Ekklesia, is really a sovereign assembly of the same kind. The word "Halia," used in Doric Greece for the Assembly of the People, is the same as the "Heliaea" of Athens.

In this way the wide scope of the doctrine of ἐπιείκεια covered general fairness and humanity; and it is not to be wondered at that it did not form a separate class of legal rights and remedies as did general, corrective, and distributive justice, but transcended these divisions and found expression in practically every department of law. Modern juries act to some extent on similar lines when they are moved by appeals to unwritten law, by psychological suggestions, by pressure of public opinion.

Before leaving the legal system, let us consider briefly **Retribu-** two additional passages in Aristotle's *Ethics*, dealing with **tion.** Retaliation, and Exchange. We read in the fifth book:[1] "There are some who consider retaliation (τὸ ἀντιπεπονθὸς) as justice." The reference is to the Pythagorean conception

[1] *Eth. Nik.*, V, 5, 1132 b 21 δοκεῖ δέ τισι καὶ τὸ ἀντιπεπονθὸς εἶναι ἁπλῶς δίκαιον, ὥσπερ οἱ Πυθαγόρειοι ἔφασαν. . . . τὸ δ' ἀντιπεπονθὸς οὐκ ἐφαρμόττει οὔτ' ἐπὶ τὸ νεμητικὸν δίκαιον οὔτ' ἐπὶ τὸ διορθωτικόν . . . πολλαχοῦ γὰρ διαφωνεῖ· οἷον εἰ ἀρχὴν ἔχων ἐπάταξεν, οὐ δεῖ ἀντιπληγῆναι, καὶ εἰ ἄρχοντα ἐπάταξεν, οὐ πληγῆναι μόνον δεῖ ἀλλὰ καὶ κολασθῆναι.

that the root of justice is in retribution. Aristotle denies this, and criticizes sharply the view, and yet in some respects he accepts it. He says that, while τὸ ἀντιπεπονθός cannot be applied in criminal justice, it may be applied to some measure in civil law. This seems a contradiction, for retaliation does occur in connexion with delict, and this stands on the border between criminal and civil justice. He rejects the Pythagorean view, first because τὸ ἀντιπεπονθός does not fit in with either distributive or corrective justice, and secondly because it is impossible to apply the principle of proportion; "eye for eye and tooth for tooth" cannot be exacted if the persons concerned are differently situated; supposing one were a magistrate and the other an ordinary citizen, or one were a citizen, and the other a slave. In these cases the mere returning of a blow would by no means equalize matters.

Justice in exchange.

Aristotle does, however, recognize that, as regards exchanges, real justice would lie in the establishment of equivalents, and this idea, though not identical with that of retribution, is analogous to it. He examines the work of various crafts in relation to each other, e.g., the problem of equating boots with houses, a process which can be accomplished by estimating the demand for a commodity in the market [1] or the amount of work put into the product, and the use which is to be made of it.[2]

The question may be asked, especially in our days of profiteers and soaring prices, whether there is any indication of a policy directed towards the establishment of a "fair price." The treatment of the subject in Plato's *Laws* might lead one to suppose that the Greeks favoured the idea that prices should be regulated, e. g. in regard to land. There is one sentence, and that a very short and obscure one, which could be interpreted in this sense. "If you want to establish proportion, you should not do it when the exchange has been made, but when everybody has got his own." [3] This

---

[1] *Eth. Nik.* V. 5, § 8, 1133 a 8 δεῖ οὖν λαμβάνειν τὸν οἰκοδόμον παρὰ τοῦ σκυτοτόμου τὸ ἐκείνου ἔργον, καὶ αὐτὸν ἐκείνῳ μεταδιδόναι τὸ [τοῦ] αὐτοῦ. ἐὰν οὖν πρῶτον ᾖ τὸ κατὰ τὴν ἀναλογίαν ἴσον, εἶτα τὸ ἀντιπεπονθὸς γένηται, ἔσται τὸ λεγόμενον· εἰ δὲ μή, οὐκ ἴσον οὐδὲ συμμένει· οὐθὲν γὰρ κωλύει κρεῖττον εἶναι τὸ θατέρου ἔργον ἢ τὸ θατέρου· δεῖ οὖν ταῦτα ἰσασθῆναι. . . . δεῖ τοίνυν ὅπερ οἰκοδόμος πρὸς σκυτοτόμον, τοσαδὶ ὑποδήματα πρὸς οἰκίαν.

[2] *Magn. Mor.*, IX, 1194 a 2 ff.

[3] *Eth. Nik.*, *loc. cit.*, § 12, 1133 b 1 εἰς σχῆμα δ' ἀναλογίας οὐ δεῖ ἄγειν,

seems to indicate the establishment of a maximum or tariff of some kind, which ought to be set up before the exchange takes place.

We have now concluded our survey of the legal system with its three categories, Specific Justice, subdivided into Distributive and Corrective, and General Justice, covering rules as to civil rights and public law ; all these departments were affected by ἐπιείκεια, the principle of fairness or equity, which appears to be the most characteristic contribution of Greece to the treatment of legal problems.

APPENDIX TO CHAPTER III

AR. *Rhet.* I. xiii. §§ 13–18.　(Cope's text.)

Τὸ γὰρ ἐπιεικὲς δοκεῖ δίκαιον εἶναι, ἔστι δὲ ἐπιεικὲς τὸ παρὰ τὸν γεγραμμένον νόμον δίκαιον. συμβαίνει δὲ τοῦτο τὰ μὲν ἀκόντων τὰ δὲ ἑκόντων τῶν νομοθετῶν, ἀκόντων μὲν ὅταν λάθῃ, ἑκόντων δ' ὅταν μὴ δύνωνται διορίσαι, ἀλλ' ἀναγκαῖον μὲν ᾖ καθόλου εἰπεῖν, μὴ ᾖ δέ, ἀλλ' ὡς ἐπὶ τὸ πολύ. καὶ ὅσα μὴ ῥᾴδιον διορίσαι δι' ἀπειρίαν, οἷον τὸ τρῶσαι σιδήρῳ πηλίκῳ καὶ ποιῷ τινί. ὑπολείποι γὰρ ἂν ὁ αἰὼν διαριθμοῦντα. ἂν οὖν ᾖ ἀδιόριστον, δέῃ δὲ νομοθετῆσαι, ἀνάγκη ἁπλῶς εἰπεῖν, ὥστε κἂν δακτύλιον ἔχων ἐπάρηται τὴν χεῖρα ἢ πατάξῃ, κατὰ μὲν τὸν γεγραμμένον νόμον ἔνοχός ἐστι καὶ ἀδικεῖ, κατὰ δὲ τὸ ἀληθὲς οὐκ ἀδικεῖ, καὶ τὸ ἐπιεικὲς τοῦτο ἐστίν.... ἐφ' οἷς τε γὰρ δεῖ συγγνώμην ἔχειν, ἐπιεικῆ ταῦτα, καὶ τὸ τὰ ἁμαρτήματα καὶ τὰ ἀδικήματα μὴ τοῦ ἴσου ἀξιοῦν, μηδὲ δὲ ἁμαρτήματα καὶ τὰ ἀτυχήματα· ἔστι δ' ἀτυχήματα μὲν ὅσα παράλογα καὶ μὴ ἀπὸ μοχθηρίας, ἁμαρτήματα δὲ ὅσα μὴ παράλογα καὶ μὴ ἀπὸ πονηρίας, ἀδικήματα δὲ ὅσα μήτε παράλογα ἀπὸ πονηρίας τ' ἐστίν· τὰ γὰρ δι' ἐπιθυμίαν ἀπὸ πονηρίας. καὶ τὸ τοῖς ἀνθρωπίνοις συγγινώσκειν ἐπιεικές. καὶ τὸ μὴ πρὸς τὸν νόμον ἀλλὰ πρὸς τὸν νομοθέτην σκοπεῖν, καὶ μὴ πρὸς τὸν λόγον ἀλλὰ πρὸς τὴν διάνοιαν τοῦ νομοθέτου, καὶ μὴ πρὸς τὴν πρᾶξιν ἀλλὰ πρὸς τὴν προαίρεσιν, καὶ μὴ πρὸς τὸ μέρος ἀλλὰ πρὸς τὸ ὅλον, μηδὲ ποῖός τις νῦν, ἀλλὰ ποῖός τις ἦν ἀεὶ ἢ ὡς ἐπὶ τὸ πολύ. ... καὶ τὸ ἀνέχεσθαι ἀδικούμενον. καὶ τὸ μᾶλλον λόγῳ ἐθέλειν κρίνεσθαι ἢ ἔργῳ. καὶ τὸ εἰς δίαιταν μᾶλλον ἢ εἰς δίκην βούλεσθαι ἰέναι· ὁ γὰρ διαιτητὴς τὸ ἐπιεικὲς ὁρᾷ, ὁ δὲ δικαστὴς τὸν νόμον· καὶ τούτου ἕνεκα διαιτητὴς εὑρέθη, ὅπως τὸ ἐπιεικὲς ἰσχύῃ.

ὅταν ἀλλάξωνται (εἰ δὲ μή, ἀμφοτέρας ἕξει τὰς ὑπεροχὰς τὸ ἕτερον ἄκρον), ἀλλ' ὅταν ἔχωσι τὰ αὑτῶν.

CHAPTER IV

THE SOURCES OF LAW

1. *Enactments.*

The term "source." IN proceeding to consider the subject of sources of Greek law, we must be careful not to confuse historical with juridical sources; the former term refers to material for information, while the latter deals with authority. Of course, testimony in words and in writing is employed in order to argue a case and to prepare a decision; in this sense information assumes a specially juridical aspect, and gives rise to the law of evidence. Evidence deals, however, with facts and not with law, though its use is regulated by law. What we mean by source of law is the authority from which law is derived.

Now what were these sources for Greek law? At present we recognize: (1) Statutory law, enacted by Parliament or under the authority of Parliament by subordinate bodies such as County Councils, Borough Councils, etc.; (2) Common law, a body of rules abstracted from decisions given in particular cases: it may be therefore designated judge-made law; (3) Custom, rules of law arising out of the traditional local practice, apart from direct enactment or authoritative decision of the Courts. In Greece the relation between these categories differed from that obtaining nowadays. In the period covering the greater part of the fifth and the beginning of the fourth centuries Greek democracies, as represented by Athens, required that laws should be enacted. This principle usually holds good for that period, though it is not absolutely applicable even then; still, at that time νόμοι undoubtedly were the principal source of law. In the speech made by Andokides in his defence against the charge of having taken part in the profanation of the Eleusinian Mysteries, the strongest argument is that the sentence of ἀτιμία, defamatory dis-

Νόμος.

franchisement, passed on him, had been abrogated by the amnesty declared in the archonship of Eukleides[1]; mention is also made of a great revision of the laws made in 403 B.C.,[2] in consequence of an enactment by the people, on the reconstruction of the constitution, to the effect that (1) no unwritten law should have force, which means, apparently, that nothing but the written laws were to be regarded as binding; (2) that no decree of the Assembly or of the Council should overrule a law; (3) that no law should be enacted in regard to single individuals (ἐπ' ἀνδρί); (4) written laws were declared to be those received and confirmed at the revision under Eukleides.[3]

These rules, enumerated by Andokides, are very characteristic; if applied in their full force they would amount to absolute abrogation of customary law and to the recognition of statute law as the one source of legal authority. Such a principle is suggested by democratic doctrine; the People were the only legislative factor, and therefore every kind of law should have come expressly from the People. Custom was looked upon with disfavour, because it had its roots in antiquity, when privileged groups or families held sway. Such a view certainly prevailed in Athens, as may be gathered, for instance, from a passage in Euripides' *Supplices*.[4] In this play suppliants come to seek the protection of the Athenians against the Tyrant of Thebes, Kreon, whose heralds pursue them. The King of Athens, Theseus, in spite of the anachronism, appears as the spokesman of democracy and opposes the heralds. He expresses the view of law held by every right-minded citizen. "Nothing

---

[1] ANDOKIDES, I, 73-80.

[2] *Ibid.* 81 ff.

[3] *Ibid.* 89 . . . ἔδοξεν ὑμῖν δοκιμάσαι μὲν τοὺς νόμους, δοκιμάσαντες δὲ ἀναγράψαι, ἀγράφῳ δὲ νόμῳ τὰς ἀρχὰς μὴ χρῆσθαι μηδὲ περὶ ἑνός, ψήφισμα δὲ ⟨μηδὲν⟩ μήτε βουλῆς μήτε δήμου ⟨νόμου⟩ κυριώτερον εἶναι, μηδ' ἐπ' ἀνδρὶ νόμον ⟨ἐξεῖναι⟩ τιθέναι ἐὰν μὴ τὸν αὐτὸν ἐπὶ πᾶσιν 'Αθηναίοις, τοῖς δε νόμοις τοῖς κειμένοις χρῆσθαι ἀπ' Εὐκλείδου ἄρχοντος . . . Cf. DEM. XXIV, § 42.

[4] *Op. cit.* 429 ff. :

οὐδὲν τυράννου δυσμενέστερον πόλει,
ὅπου τὸ μὲν πρώτιστον οὐκ εἰσὶν νόμοι
κοινοί, κρατεῖ δ' εἷς τὸν νόμον κεκτημένος
αὐτὸς παρ' αὑτῷ· καὶ τόδ' οὐκέτ' ἔστ' ἴσον.
γεγραμμένων δὲ τῶν νόμων ὅ τ' ἀσθενὴς
ὁ πλούσιός τε τὴν δίκην ἴσην ἔχει.

is more deadly to a commonwealth than a tyranny, for then, to begin with, there are no common laws, but the single ruler himself holds sway over the law; this is not equitable. But when laws are written down, then both rich and poor can claim equal justice." Such a written law is νόμος; it is a measure carried through and promulgated according to the regular process of legislation.

Another term to be considered is θεσμός, which was properly applied to a declaration of customary law; the words "statement" or "establishment" would almost exactly render its meaning. It is not necessarily an act of the people as a whole, but rather of a college of magistrates or of a single lawgiver, declaring the law to the people. Thus Drakon is usually described as a θεσμοθέτης, Solon as a νομοθέτης[1]; but Solon himself uses both terms with no perceptible difference of meaning.[2]

Laws and decrees.

Let me revert again to the democratic principle that enacted law is the normal source of legal authority.

In his classification of democracies in the *Politics* Aristotle lays stress on the difference between constitutions and governments which follow strictly the legal rules of the Commonwealth, and those which, on the contrary, disregard these rules, and govern more or less according to the whims and fashions of the Demos. While explaining the contrast, he emphasizes the fact that in the first class law (νόμος) holds the chief place, while in the second it is the decree (ψήφισμα) which takes precedence of enacted law.[3] "This is a state of affairs brought about by the demagogues. For in democracies which are subject to law the best citizens are chosen as rulers, and there are no demagogues; but where the laws are not supreme, demagogues spring up. The people becomes practically a monarch. . . . And the people, which is now a monarch, and no longer under the control of law, seeks to exercise monarchical sway, and becomes a despot; the flatterer is held in honour; this sort of democracy being relatively to other democracies what tyranny is to other forms of monarchy.

[1] Cf. ANDOKIDES, I, § 81 χρῆσθαι τοῖς Σόλωνος νόμοις καὶ τοῖς Δράκοντος θεσμοῖς.   [2] Cf. however below, p. 129.
[3] AR., *Pol.* VI (IV), 4, 1292 a, 7 ff.

The spirit of both is the same, and they exercise alike a despotic rule over the better citizens. The decrees of the Demos correspond to the edicts of the tyrant. ... The demagogues make the decrees of the people override the laws, and refer all things to the popular assembly."

This theme is treated with many variations; Aristotle returns to it continually. It forms an important basis of his classification from the point of view of legality. For example, in Athens he notices systematic endeavours to keep up law-abiding democracy, as against the outbursts of passion and arbitrary rule towards the end of the Peloponnesian war, and in the course of the fourth century. Public law was maintained, on the whole, on the lines indicated by Aristotle, the central idea being that νόμος, enacted law, has to be guaranteed and fenced round by carefully-devised measures of a public character.

2. *Custom.*

Was the democratic ideal of a State governed by enacted law ever in force? Is it true that custom and juridical authority were not active as legal sources during the classical period? Even if there were no direct testimony to the contrary, it would be hard to believe that customary law did not exist, and in fact some evidence is available showing that there was a vast amount of customary and business rules in existence by the side of enacted law, and that Athens, in particular, was governed to a large extent by traditional law. *Interpreters of custom.*

In regard to sacral institutions, and in all cases where religion was concerned, the influence of traditional usage asserted itself emphatically. The Council of the Areiopagos had jurisdiction in cases of homicide, arson, and similar offences, and this body was guided in its decisions by custom not put down in writing, and not enacted by the people, but preserved by traditional jurisprudence as τὰ πάτρια, ancestral custom. There were professional representatives of legal lore from whom the ordinary Athenian had to seek instruction. These were termed ἐξηγηταί (interpreters), who, according to the lexicographers, were able to give authoritative interpretation of traditional law;

inscriptions record three kinds of interpreters: (1) *ἐξηγηταὶ Πυθόχρηστοι*, (2) *ἐξηγηταὶ τῶν Εὐμολπιδῶν*, (3) *ἐξηγηταὶ τῶν Εὐπατριδῶν*. The first title contains a reference to the oracle at Delphi, and the officials in question evidently dealt with legal customs assumed to have been derived from Delphi. In cases of purification, for example, when a stain or pollution had to be removed from a family, or from the people as a whole, the *Πυθόχρηστοι* probably prescribed the measures to be taken. The second kind were a consultative board for matters connected with the Eleusinian Mysteries, the family of the Eumolpidai being the most influential of the clans concerned with the celebration of these Mysteries. As to the third kind, our knowledge is less definite; not all the Eupatrid families are meant, but a special group of jurisconsults.[1]

As to the process of consultation, a speech of Demosthenes against Euergos and Mnesibulos[2] gives graphic information. This case arose out of an execution for debt. A former trierarch (i. e. one responsible for fitting out a ship) had not rendered satisfactory account of some material supplied to him by the State; he was called to account and sentenced, and his goods were to be confiscated in payment. One Theophemos was empowered to carry out the execution, and in doing so treated the household of the debtor with great harshness; an old woman—an emancipated slave who had been all her life in the family—was so roughly handled that she died. The question arose, who had the right to prosecute in connexion with her death? If she had been a *relative* of the family, Drakon's rules would have been applied; they declared who among the kindred should be the accuser, and who should support him; but as the dead woman had not been a relative, but only a member of the household, the matter was uncertain. The plaintiff in the case explains that, being in doubt, he went to the Interpreters, and asked for their advice.[3]

---

[1] *R.-Enc.* s. v. *ἐξηγηταί.*

[2] DEM., XLVII. Euergos and Mnesibulos were accused of having given false witness in the suit between Theophemos and the present plaintiff.

[3] DEM., *op. cit.*, §§ 68, 69 ἀκούσαντες δέ μου οἱ ἐξηγηταὶ ταῦτα, ἤροντό με πότερον ἐξηγήσωνταί μοι μόνον ἢ καὶ συμβουλεύσωσιν. ἀποκριναμένου δέ

" When they heard the facts they asked me whether I wanted them merely to interpret, or also to tell me what would be expedient in the matter." Thus it is clear that they did not only expound legal custom, τὰ νόμιμα, but also gave advice to those who consulted them, that is, their function was that of *juris periti*, specially versed in a certain branch of law.   When we reflect on the vital importance of religion and ritual in Greek public life, we obtain some idea of the influence of the ἐξηγηταί.

There is another connexion in which traditional law was still of great importance; there can be no possible doubt that the chief forms of procedure—the different kinds of δίκαι and γραφαί—had been settled long before the period of Ephialtes and Perikles, that is, before the middle of the fifth century.   We know, for instance, that the First Archon had a wide jurisdiction in family affairs; that cases of wrongs to parents, orphans, heirs, and minors under guardianship, all of which constantly occurred from early times, were within his competence.[1]   The only innovation carried out by Ephialtes in this respect consisted in widening the range of appeal to the Heliastic Courts. These Courts were a Solonian institution, but in the sixth century, before the life of Attika became centralized in the metropolis, the difficulty and cost of coming into the city from the country districts materially limited the scope of appeal (ἔφεσις) to the Heliaea, and these Courts cannot have sat often.   The necessity for the introduction of μισθοφορία towards the middle of the fifth century shows that before that time the jurors could be called up only on rare occasions.   Again, for jurisdiction in the country districts, Peisistratos was the first to institute δικασταὶ κατὰ δήμους, who were not Heliasts, but substitutes for the Archon.

In the city the Archon's jurisdiction was the chief means of securing justice; he sat originally as αὐτοκράτωρ, and the appeal to the Heliaea was reserved for the most important cases.   In fact, most of the judicial life of Athens before

Rules laid down by magistrates.

μου αὐτοῖς ἀμφότερα, εἶπόν μοι " ἡμεῖς τοίνυν σοι τὰ μὲν νόμιμα ἐξηγησόμεθα, τὰ δὲ σύμφορα παραινέσομεν."

[1] AR., *Ath. Const.* 56.

the second quarter of the fifth century was conducted by the magistrates, and not by the Heliaea. It was not until the League gave the Athenians hegemony in a great part of Greece that these Courts acquired the importance attributed to them, for example, in the *Wasps* of Aristophanes, and we have to be on our guard against a possible distortion of juridical perspective arising from too exclusive attention to this period of their history.

Many of the forms of action handed down from earlier times were not regulated by enacted law, but had been evolved by practice; these forms were elaborated gradually, starting, in some cases, from times before Drakon and Solon, and were in general use in the sixth century. Thus the law of procedure remained chiefly traditional, though in some cases there were new laws enacted to regulate it.

3. *Authority of Precedents.*

Pre-
cedents as
examples.
Was there anything in Greek law corresponding to what is called judicial authority? In English law this is a very important source of law, operating with "precedents," which, though not actual law, lend authority to decisions; when a number of decisions on the same point follow one another on the same lines, they crystallize, as it were, into a rule of Common Law.

As far as Athens and other Greek democracies are concerned there is nothing quite similar, because precedents were not formally binding.[1] In Greece a peculiar way of influencing law by authority is apparent in the practice of the Heliaea. A δικαστήριον of the Heliaea was unable to refer to what is termed the *ratio decidendi* based on precedent, but when decisions followed each other in the same sense, direction was given to professional opinion and cases came to be decided not under direct precedent, but on the ground of similarity of motive and of prevailing conditions.

An instance in point may be cited from Demosthenes' speech against Dionysodoros. The case arose out of a loan

---

[1] It should be noted that even in English law the hierarchy of authorities culminating in the House of Lords only became binding in the course of the nineteenth century. In the United States Common Law exists apart from a general hierarchy of decisions.

made by certain merchants resident in Athens (μέτοικοι)
to the skipper of a ship sailing to Egypt to buy corn.
The loan was made on condition that the skipper should
return to Athens with the corn and sell it there, because it
was expected that the corn would realize a large profit in
the Athenian market, and the calculations of interest, etc.,
were made on this basis. But the ship, instead of bringing
the corn to Athens, went from Egypt to Rhodos, and, the
corn having being sold there, came home without a cargo.
The skipper was prosecuted for breach of contract; he
pleaded *vis major* (a storm) in excuse, but this was held to
be insufficient, as the corn had been sold in Rhodos contrary to agreement. At the end of the plaintiff's speech
occurs the following appeal to the Court [1]: "Do not disregard the fact that now, while you are deciding a single
case, you are legislating for the whole of the market, and
that numbers of those whose business is by sea are standing
here awaiting your decision. If you maintain the validity
of these contracts and agreements, and show no mercy to
those who break them, the money-lenders will be more
ready to make advances, and your trade will be stimulated."
Thus the decision of a Court could be regarded as a symp-
tom of the views held by the tribunals.

On a number of points the decisions of the Heliaea pro- Influence
duced changes of the law. This might occur in cases where of Heli-
there had originally been a definite νόμος, which, however, cisions on
had not been applied for a long time; if then a case came up law.
for decision under conditions non-existent at the time when
the law was made, the Court might treat it as if it were
not binding. As regards wills, there was considerable freedom in the use and application of ancient rules. The
cumulative effect of such free application was that a foundation was laid for a remedy which in Roman law took
definite shape in the *querela inofficiosi testamenti*—a tendency prompted by the fact that there was a general
distrust of, and disinclination to grant probate in the case
of wills in which the claims of near relatives were disregarded. In Roman law eventually this produced a custom
of the Courts to treat wills as void in which one-fourth of

---

[1] Dem., LVI, § 48, p. 1297.

the property had not been left to near relatives. The same feeling is shown in Greek law in the attacks made on wills by relatives whose claims have been ignored by the testator.[1]

In some cases claims are urged that are not acknowledged by formal law, but creep in by the help of Heliastic decisions; for example, inheritance by the mother The mother was not an heiress at law in the fourth century, while in the second she occupies a place in succession: in the same way in Roman law she eventually obtained a standing in the table of statutory succession. For this point in Greek law we have evidence in the speech of Isaios about the estate of Hagnias,[2] a case of διαδικασία. In this trial the mother of one of the parties was admitted to present a claim, and she obtained some votes. It was the Archon who admitted her, and his action in doing so shows that he recognized a powerful tendency of public opinion in this direction.

Again, as regards bequests, a similar tendency is at work. Bequests were valid if the heir consented to them, and had to be paid through him; this made it very difficult to leave anything to outsiders, and the law of the fourth century shows a bent in favour of legatees, while in the next century an actual change in the law takes place.[3] This change was not brought about by legislation (νομοθεσία), but by the enlargement of the application of the law in the Courts. Similarly in the case of dowry, though it was not legally required, it became in practice a test of the legitimacy of marriage.[4] These instances may serve as examples of a judge-made method for completing, supplementing, and correcting the law.

---

[1] E. g. Isaios, I, §§ 33, 34, 35, ending: ὥστε τίς ἂν ὑμῶν ταύτας εἶναι κυρίας τὰς διαθήκας ψηφίσαιτο, ἃς ὁ μὲν διαθέμενος ὡς οὐκ ὀρθῶς ἐχούσας ἀπεδοκίμασεν.

[2] Isaios, XI, § 2 ἐὰν δὲ καὶ τοῦτ' ἐκλίπῃ τὸ γένος, . . . ποιεῖ τοὺς πρὸς μητρὸς τοῦ τελευτήσαντος κυρίους αὐτῶν. § 17. εἰς τοσαύτας δ' ἀπορίας κατέστησαν ὅ τι ἀντιγράψωνται περὶ τῆς ἀγχιστείας, ὥστε . . . ῥᾳδίως ὑπ' ἐμοῦ τότε ἐξηλέγχθησαν . . . οἱ δ' ὑπὲρ τῆς Ἀγνίου μητρὸς . . . νόμῳ ἀποκληρουμένης ὃς κελεύει κρατεῖν τοὺς ἄρρενας, τοῦτο μὲν εἴασαν, οἰόμενοι δ' ἐμοῦ πλεονεκτήσειν μητέρα εἶναι τοῦ τελευτήσαντος ἔγραψαν· ὃ συγγενέστατον μὲν ἦν φύσει πάντων, ἐν δὲ ταῖς ἀγχιστείαις ὁμολογουμένως οὐκ ἔστιν.

[3] Beauchet, Droit privé, III, 697 ff.; Wyse, op. cit., 325.

[4] Isaios, III, § 28.

4. *Voluntary Jurisdiction.*

It is often forgotten by those who are not brought into Business
contact with the legal profession that actual law is often agreements.
based on things never promulgated as formal rules, but
elaborated by business practice. The latter is not the same
thing as custom; it represents not traditional views as to
justice, but the cumulative effect of voluntary agreements.
This phase is very fully illustrated in Greek law; we have
evidence, especially for the later period, from inscriptions
and papyri. An example may be taken from an inscription which belongs to the beginning of the second century B.C. It refers to a loan made by a banker named
Alexandros to the town of Arkesine in the island of Amorgos. The terms are set forth, and one sentence runs as
follows:[1] "If the citizens do not pay the interest, the
execution shall be double, falling on private property
by every means, just as if there had been a conviction in
a trial for ejectment before a tribunal of arbitrators."
Thus the whole trial, which should lead to the issue of
a writ of execution, becomes unnecessary, and a stage
in its development is omitted, for the sake of summary
execution. Instead of going to a Court and getting an
order for arrest or execution, the injured party can proceed
by the method of self-help on the basis of the agreement
made. This is possible because the other party has voluntarily submitted to the terms of the contract. In French
law there is an equivalent process called *Exécution parée*.
This way of claiming money is shown by inscriptions to
have been quite common in Greek law.[2]

A further point to be noted is that in Greek legal practice a contract could be made in writing, and the writing
of it established and guaranteed the details.[3]

If we ask who it was that made these agreements valid

---

[1] *I. J. G.*, I, xv, B, § 3, p. 318 ἐὰν δὲ τὸν τόκον μὴ ἀποδῶσιν, πρακτοὶ
ἔστων Ἀλεξάνδρωι οἱ μὴ ἀποδόντες διπλάσιον τὸ ἀργύριον ἐκ τῶν ἰδίων πράξει
πάσηι καθάπερ δίκην ὠφληκότες ἐξούλης ἐν τῆι ἐκκλήτωι καὶ ὄντες ὑπερή-
μεροι . . .

[2] See also DEMOSTHENES, XXXV. The speech is a claim for the
repayment of a loan; the case arises out of an ἐμπορικὸν συμβόλαιον.

[3] See below, Chap. XI.

and authorized the tribunals to give verdicts with regard to them, we can only say that the practice was the result of voluntary action on the part of contracting parties. The law was based on constantly recurring business arrangements, and on the fact that the Courts accepted the documents as conclusive evidence.

In the *Digest* the law on shipwreck or jettison is traced to the law of Rhodos, that is, the maritime customs made in the third and second centuries B.C. By that time Athens had lost her supremacy, and Rhodos was the commercial centre of the Eastern Mediterranean. For the earlier practice we can refer, among other things, to the speeches of Demosthenes against Lakritos and against Zenothemis. Customs originating in agreements between skippers, merchants, bankers, and crews gathered force, and were supported by the tribunals.

Scribes.   Let us note in conclusion the influence of a professional class of scribes (γραμματεῖς) corresponding to our clerks and solicitors. The direct bearing of their practice on the law is not hard to see; they were armed with technical knowledge and skill, which made their assistance indispensable to the less instructed citizens, although the latter were politically the masters. The influence of the scribe, it may be added, was of far greater importance in the East than in the West.

It may be said without paradox that the most influential scribes belonged to the lower personnel of the profession. There was a number of high-standing secretaries who were elected by lot in fourth-century Athens from among citizens. Five of these officials are mentioned in the list of the Council of 335 B.C.; the γραμματεὺς κατὰ πρυτανείαν, the γραμματεὺς τῆς βουλῆς, the ἀναγραφεύς, the γραμματεὺς ἐπὶ τὰ ψηφίσματα, and the ἀντιγραφεύς. Aristotle, in the fifty-fourth chapter of the *Athenian Constitution*, gives a somewhat different enumeration, but in substance his account does not contradict the evidence of inscriptions. Now the fact that these officials, as well as the γραμματεὺς τῶν θεσμοθετῶν, are all chosen by lot, shows that no importance was attached to their learning. On the contrary, their numerous subordinates for the keeping of accounts, drawing up reports, formulating and publishing decisions and decrees, were required to possess knowledge and experience. One of the most prominent Athenian orators, Aischines, had made his way to a great extent thanks to his training as a clerk.[1] Even the standing of a State slave did not debar men from acquiring important positions as specialists in this line. Most of the Athenian accountants seem to have been δημόσιοι, i. e. slaves. In the most ancient reference to the status of a γραμματεύς—an inscription of Olympia of the year 580 B.C.—if we are to trust Blass's interpretation—a certain Patrias is granted protection as to his person, family, and property, although of foreign descent, because of his employment as a scribe.[2] Altogether, the most definite evidence concerning the importance of skilled clerks comes from minor cities. The inscriptions of Priene are especially instructive in this respect. A certain Hegepolis, for instance, was sent as secretary to a citizen of Priene who had to act as an umpire in deciding a case between foreign cities, and the same man has to accompany another embassy of three representatives of Priene on a similar errand.[3] Perhaps the most interesting example is that of a certain Apellis, son of Nikophon, who asks to be relieved from the office of a γραμματεύς, in which he had served for twenty years; out of these twenty years, for fourteen he performed his duties without pay, and had even taken charge of other clerkships, thus saving the city from considerable expenses.[4]

---

[1] DEMOSTHENES, XVIII, § 127.

[2] Gr. Dial. Inschr. I, 320, No. 1152.

[3] MICHEL, 468 (pp. 346 f.).

I ... ἵνα ἡ βουλὴ καὶ ὁ δῆμος βουλεύσηται τίσιν δεῖ τιμαῖς τιμηθῆναι τὸν δῆμον τὸν Πριηνέων καὶ τὸν παραγενόμενον πρὸς ἡμᾶς δικαστὴν ... καὶ τὸν γραμματέα Ἡγέπολιν Ἡγίου· ... ἐπαινέσαι δὲ καὶ τὸν συνεξαποσταλέντα μετ' αὐτοῦ γραμματέα Ἡγέπολιν Ἡγίου ... καὶ στεφανῶσαι τὸμ μὲν δικαστὴν χρυσῶι στεφάνωι ..., τὸν δὲ γραμματέα θαλλοῦ στεφάνωι. II ... καὶ ἐστεφανώκασι ... τὸν γραμματέα θαλλοῦ στεφάνωι.

and 543 (pp. 407 f.) ... ἐπηινῆσθαι δὲ καὶ τὸν ἀποσταλέντα αὐτοῖς γραμματέα Ἡγέπολιν Ἡγίου καὶ στεφανωθῆναι ἐν τοῖς Ἀντιοχείοις ἐλαίας στεφάνωι.

[4] HILLER VON GAERTRINGEN, Inschriften von Priene, 4, p. 7 ἐπειδὴ Ἀπελλις Νικοφῶντος γραμματεὺς αἱρεθεὶς ὑπὸ τοῦ δήμου ἔν τε ταῖς δίκαις καὶ ἐν τῆι τῶγ κοινῶγ γραμμάτων πίστει καὶ κυριείαι καὶ ἐν τοῖς ἄλλοις τοῖς κατὰ τὴμ πόλιμ πρασσομένοις ἅπασιν ἴσως καὶ δικαίως τὴγ χρείαμ παρέσχηται τῶμ πολιτῶν ἑκάστωι, καὶ περὶ τοὺς κοινοὺς τῆς πόλεως ἀγῶνας χρήσιμος καὶ πρόθυμος ὢν διατετέλεκεμ περὶ πλείστου ποιούμενος τὸ τὰ δίκαια φαίνεσθαι πράττων, νυνὶ δὲ παρελθὼν εἰς τὴν ἐκκλησίαν ἐμπεφάνικεν, ὅτι τὰ μὲμ πάντα ἔτη πεπραγμάτευται εἴκοσιν, τούτων δὲ δεκατέτταρα ἔτη τὴν

The cumulative effect of the ant-like work of the innumerable clerks and accountants on the formation of technical rules can hardly be overestimated.

NOTE

I should like to make a few remarks as to a curious and doubtful case reported by Andokides in the speech on the Mysteries. It bears on the trial of his father Leogoras, who, during the famous process about the destruction of the Hermae, had been denounced by a slave as having participated in the sacrilege, and had been included in the proposal of a certain Speusippos, a councillor (βουλεύων) among the persons charged of the crime.[1] Leogoras had thereupon brought against Speusippos a γραφὴ παρανόμων, as to the contents of which Andokides does not give explicit information. But he states that this γραφή was discussed before a tribunal of 6,000, and that Speusippos succeeded in collecting only a couple of hundred votes. The problem is: What kind of Court could this assembly of 6,000 have been? The number of persons seems to indicate the Assembly (ἐκκλησία), but the terms of the reference speak definitely of a sitting of judges (δικασταί), and the case was treated on the lines of a γραφὴ παρανόμων, that is, as a legal and not as a political trial. It seems[2] that the speaker deals with a case assimilated to the passing of a decree ἐπ᾽ ἀνδρί, of which proscription by ostracism presents the most conspicuous instance. It is certainly remarkable that Andokides speaks of δικασταί; this means that the ἐκκλησία was considered a δικαστήριον when performing judicial duties.[3]

τοῖς στρατηγοῖς γραμματείαν λελῃτούργηκε δωρεὰν καὶ τοῦ ἀναλώματος τοῦ γινομένου ἐκ τῶν νόμων τῶι τῶν νομοφυλάκων καὶ τιμούχων γραμματεῖ παραλέλυκε τὸν δῆμον . . .

δεδόχθαι . . . παραλελύσθαι τε ῎Απελλιν τῆς γραμματείας καθότι ἠξίωκεν καὶ ἐπαινεῖν αὐτόν, κτλ. Cf. DITT. Syll.[3] I. 353. On the whole subject see SCHULTHESS in R.-Enc. VII, s.v. γραμματεῖς.

[1] ANDOK. I, 17 Σπεύσιππος δὲ βουλεύων παραδίδωσιν αὐτοὺς τῷ δικαστηρίῳ. κἄπειτα ὁ πατὴρ . . . ἐγράψατο τὸν Σπεύσιππον παρανόμων, καὶ ἠγωνίσατο ἐν ἑξακισχιλίοις ᾿Αθηναίων, καὶ μετέλαβε δικαστῶν τοσούτων οὐδὲ διακοσίας ψήφους ὁ Σπεύσιππος.

[2] Cf. FRAENKEL, Die attischen Geschworenengerichte, pp. 89 ff.

[3] The Assembly is treated as a δικαστήριον in AISCHINES, I, 86 συνδεκάζειν τὴν ἐκκλησίαν καὶ τὰ ἀλλὰ δικαστήρια.

CHAPTER V

THE STRUCTURE OF THE CITY

1. *The Federation of Kindreds.*

MODERN democracies which have arisen in the course of the struggle against feudalism and absolutism bear a strongly individualistic stamp. In France after the Revolution, for example, all organizations and social groups likely to claim autonomous authority were suppressed as dangerous rivals of the commonwealth. This tendency to isolate the individual is conspicuously absent in the Greek City-state; it was not conceived as an aggregate of individuals, but consisted of clusters of kinsmen, strongly bound together by common interests and common religion. The earlier ages may be characterized as epochs of federation—the federation of kindreds (γένη).

According to the testimony of Aristotle,[1] the ancient social constitution of Athens was based on an arithmetical scheme; four phylae or tribes, each divided into three phratries, each of the latter again divided into thirty kindreds (γένη), and each kindred represented by thirty men (ἄνδρες), forming a beehive-like community consisting of ten thousand and eighty units.

Such a scheme seems quite unreal to us—in fact the result of artificial calculation, but it must after all contain an element of reality. The number thirty (τριακάς) is actually taken as an equivalent term for the γένος; those who were not γεννῆται were said to be ἔξω τριακάδος, " outside the thirty." Plato, too, in the ideal State described in the *Laws*, estimates the number of householders at exactly five thousand and forty, just half of Aristotle's total.[2] Inscrip-

---

[1] This testimony is preserved by the lexicographers, who quote from pages of the *Athenian Constitution* no longer extant. VALENTIN ROSE, *Aristoteles Pseudepigraphus*, Fr. 385[3] (*Ath. Const.* ed. KAIBEL u. WILAMOWITZ-MOELLENDORFF, Fr. 3).

[2] *Laws*, V, 745.

tions from Samos and Kos refer sometimes to units of an
arithmetical scheme. In a decree of 324 B.C., two strangers,
Gorgos and Minyon, on receiving permission from Alexander
the Great to return to their native town, were granted
Samian citizenship; they were to be reckoned as "born
Samians," and therefore had to enter some division of the
population. They obtain leave to join any tribe, any
thousand, any hundred, and any kindred.[1] Thus the
schematic arrangement has clearly some foundation in
fact requiring explanation.

In the case of Plato's 5,040, it is plain that he had in
view the number of κλῆροι or *holdings* taken as normal,
and this is probably suggested by some historical fact. In
saying this I do not affirm, of course, that the scheme was
always in being; war, poverty, and death must have caused
many inroads on the regularity of the numbers; but, as the
policy was directed towards keeping up the kindreds
(γένη),[2] the disruption of the scheme was not so great as
one might expect. The system aimed, no doubt, at a certain
equilibrium between the tribal elements of the population by
assigning to them evenly distributed shares of the territory.
We may then assume that, even if the numbers cited are
only approximate, ancient Athens was arranged as a federation of kindreds. And this original scheme was never
entirely broken up; Kleisthenes did not abolish the kindreds, but restricted the sphere of their religious, punitive,
and cultural activity.

The constitution of a phratry after the reform of Kleisthenes is well known[3]; there were two elements in it:
(1) the γένη, provided with pedigrees, cults, and a close
organization, the members of which are all full γεννῆται or
ὁμογάλακτες; (2) besides these there was a large number
of "plebeians," if one may use the expression: these also
had their religious organization, though not so strict or

---

[1] DITT. *Syll.* I³. 312, p. 531 καὶ ἐπικληρῶσαι αὐτοὺς ἐπὶ φυλὴν καὶ
χιλιαστὺν καὶ ἑκατοστὺν καὶ γένος. The word ἐπικληρῶσαι evidently
means no more than "choose." It is noteworthy that the system
here is decimal as at Rome, not duodecimal as at Athens.

[2] Cf. FRANCOTTE, *La polis grecque*, pp. 22 f.

[3] See e. g. SCHOEMANN-LIPSIUS, *Griechische Alterthümer*, II,
pp. 574 f.

extensive as that of the γένη; they were called ὀργεῶνες,
and formed groups called θίασοι. The latter term is used
in two senses; it may denote any religious association of
free growth, and in this sense it occurs in a law of Solon;[1]
in the second sense it points to a circle formed of men who
could not trace their origin to a kindred, but were united
by religious rites (ὄργια). An interesting decree of the
Deme of Peiraieus may serve as an illustration.[2] It was
intended to keep the element of ὀργεῶνες within limits.
We have no direct information about the internal life
of the γένος; but we have inscriptions made by phratries
which not only describe the arrangements of these bodies
but also refer to the γένη.

Let us take two such inscriptions, both of the fourth cen- The
tury, one from Chios, set up by the Klytidae, the other from Klytidae.
Delphi, set up by the Labyadae. The first[3] treats of the
construction by the Klytidae of a kind of chapel or shrine
for their holy objects, which were previously dispersed in
private houses. The first part of the inscription contains
the decree forbidding to keep holy objects in a private
house; the inscription then proceeds: "The Klytidae have
decreed that the sacred house of the Klytidae in which the
holy objects are deposited, and the place in front of the
house, shall be used by the Klytidae in common, and no
kindred (φατρίαν?) or private person shall use it. He who
uses the house (privately), or allows anybody else to use it,
shall pay to the Klytidae a fine of 1,000 drachmae sacred
to Zeus Patroos for each case of use or leave to use, and he
shall be cursed in accordance with the law." This decree
was passed in a regular assembly with the sanction of a
heavy fine and with the additional penalty of the curse.
It is clear from this fact that the phratry had power to

---

[1] *Digest*, XLVII, 22, 4. See below, p. 120, Chap. VI.
[2] *C. I. A.* II, 573 b (p. 421).
[3] MICHEL, 997, p. 786 ἔγνωσαν Κλυτίδαι τῶι ἱερῶι οἴκωι τῶν Κλυτιδῶν
ἐν ὧι τὰ πατρῶια ἱερὰ κάθηται καὶ τῶι χώρωι τῶι πρὸς τῶι οἴκωι χρῆσθαι
Κλυτίδας κοινῆι, φατρίαν δὲ μηδὲ ἰδιώτην μηθένα τῶι οἴκωι τούτωι χρῆσθαι
μηδὲ ἄλλωι δοῦναι χρήσασθαι μηθενί. ὃς δ᾽ ἂν παρὰ ταῦτα ἢ αὐτὸς χρήσεται
τῶι οἴκωι ἢ ἑτέρωι δῶι χρήσασθαι, ἀποδότω καθ᾽ ἑκάστην χρῆσιν ἢ δόσιν
Κλυτίδαις χιλίας δραχμὰς ἱερὰς τοῦ Διὸς τοῦ Πατρώιου, καὶ ταῖς ἐκ τῶν νόμων
ἀραῖς ἔνοχος ἔστω.

inflict punishment. It is probable that if a person would
not pay the fine an action would lie in the public Courts,
and the delinquent would be made to pay, because by taking
part in the religious rites of his group he had made himself
liable to penalties inflicted by it. The word φατρίαν must
evidently be taken here as an equivalent for πατριάν, and
not for φρατρίαν; as to the reading a fragment of Dikaiarchos supplies an appropriate comparison.[1] Φρατρίαν is
impossible; the sacred house was only to be used by the
φρατρία as a whole—not by an individual or by a division;
the division must be a kindred, that is, a γένος or πατριά.

The
Labyadae.
The Labyadae inscription gives further information; it
is in the Delphic dialect, and contains several unusual
words, the meaning of which is, however, not difficult to
guess.[2] "It has been decided by the Labyadae by 182
votes that the tagoi shall not receive offerings on the
occasion of marriages or births or victims on majority,
unless by consent of the kindreds (γένη). If they give an
order against the law, it shall be done at the peril of those
who give the order." In other paragraphs of the decree we
find besides the tagoi other officials referred to, for example,
the δημιουργός. A similar prohibition concerns judges
who take an oath; the case is parallel to the veto above
on the arbitrary taking of offerings. These judges are
analogous to the Heliasts at Athens, and the formula of their
oath contains a prayer to the gods to give them the best of
good things if they judge rightly, and to afflict them with
misery if they judge wrongly.

Infamy (ἀτιμία) and fines could be inflicted by the phratry,
but this declaration of ἀτιμία is not identical with that
pronounced by the commonwealth; it could only mean that
the phratry considered the person in question to be deprived
of his status in the corporation. The inscription contains
also an enactment about funerals; the corpse is not to have

---

[1] *Fragm. Hist. Graec.* (ed. MULLER), DICAEARCHI MESS. 9, p. 238.
[2] *I. J. G.* II, xxviii, pp. 180-2, .§ 3 (about 400 B.C.) ἔδοξε
Λαβυάδαις . . . ἐν τᾶι ἁλίαι σὺμ ψά[φ]οις ἑκατὸν ὀγδοήκοντα δυοῖν: Τοὺς
ταγοὺς μὴ δέκεσθαι μήτε δαράταν γάμελα μήτε παιδήϊα μήτ' ἀπελαῖα, αἰ μὴ
τᾶς πατριᾶς ἐπαινεούσας καὶ πληθυόσας, ἆς κα ἦι· αἰ δέ τί κα πὰρ νόμον
κελεύσωντι, τῶν κελευσάντων ὁ κίνδυνος ἔστω.

more than one carpet and one pillow beneath it as it lies on
the pyre; it is not to be carried about the streets by people
wailing aloud; it must not be deposited at cross-roads on
the way to the pyre or burial ground.   These sacral regulations were issued by the phratry concurrently with rules
made by cities.   The decree of the phratry is passed by a
large majority.

An inscription from Attika presents another side of the The Demo-
activity of a phratry, namely the relations between mem- tionidae.
bers of the corporate body.   The most important are those
dealing with διαψήφισις, the revision of lists of citizenship.
A general revision took place because the phratry had to
revise its composition in accordance with a law introduced
by Perikles.[1] The usual mode of proof was by reference to
the entry of the individual into the phratry at birth or at
adolescence (at the Apaturia).   The deme and the city
generally accepted this evidence.   There was, however, a
general revision soon after 396 B.C., to which an inscription
set up by the Demotionidae refers.[2]   It contains, among
other things, the following rules: "Every one of the excluded has leave to appeal to the Demotionidae.   In this
case the house of Dekeleia shall elect five men of more than
thirty years of age as public representatives (συνήγοροι),
and they shall be made by the phratriarch and the priest
to swear an oath that they will decide in accordance with
justice, and not allow any one who does not belong to the
phratry to be admitted to the phratry.   Any appellant rejected by the Demotionidae shall pay a fine of 1,000
drachmae sacred to Zeus Phratrios."   The house of Dekeleia
is evidently the premier kindred of the phratry, and takes
the lead in any case affecting that body.   We do not see
what the majority of the members of the phratry have to do
in the appeal; the case seems rather like that depicted on the
shield of Achilles, where a trial is being held in the agora,

---

[1] PLUTARCH, *Perikles*, c. 37.
[2] *I. J. G.* II, xxix, pp. 200 ff., § 3 ἐὰν δέ τις βόληται ἐφεῖναι ἐς
Δημοτιωνίδας ὦν ἂν ἀποψηφίσωνται, ἐξεῖναι αὐτῶι· ἑλέσθαι δὲ ἐπ' αὐτοῖς
συνηγόρος τὸν Δεκελειῶν οἶκον πέντε ἄνδρας ὑπὲρ τριάκοντα ἔτη γεγονότας,
τότος δὲ ἐξορκωσάτω ὁ φρατριάρχος καὶ ὁ ἱερεύς.   συνηγορήσεν τὰ δικαιότατα
καὶ ὀκ ἐάσεν ὀδένα μὴ ὄντα φράτερα φρατρίζεν.   ὅτο δ' ἂν τῶν ἐφέντων
ἀποψηφίσωνται Δημοτιωνίδαι, ὀφειλέτω χιλίας δραχμὰς ἱερὰς τῶι Διὶ τῶι
Φρατρίωι.   (396–350 B.C. ?)

and the people take sides, though the chiefs of the γένη, or βασιλεῖς, decide the case, giving their decisions in turn. Similarly here the decision is entrusted to five συνήγοροι under oath before the whole phratry. A second fragment[1] of the decree refers to the procedure in an extraordinary διαδικασία. "When the revision (διαδικασία) takes place, the phratriarch shall not let the members of the phratry vote as to the children until the members of the *thiasos* of each candidate have given their votes by secret ballot, and these votes are counted and declared by the phratriarch in the presence of all the members of the phratry present in the meeting (ἀγορᾷ)."

Prosecution by kinsmen.

Other evidence is supplied by the Drakonian law for manslaughter of 621 B. C., which was re-enacted in 409 B. C. after the collapse of the Four Hundred.   In cases of manslaughter (when a man kills another μὴ ἐκ προνοίας)[2] the slayer has to flee; the accusation must be brought by relatives of the deceased, relationship being reckoned in circles. The first circle comprises the members of the household. The relatives of this first circle have the duty of prosecuting the slayer. "The proclamation against the slayer shall be made in the market-place by the relatives nearer in degree than cousins.   Cousins and sons of cousins, fathers-in-law, brothers-in-law and members of the phratry shall join in the prosecution."[3]   With the same relatives rests the right to compromise—to let off the slayer. If these near relatives are not forthcoming, the right to prosecute falls to the phratry; there is no mention of the γένος; it is the ἀγχιστεία, that is, the near relatives and representatives of the phratry, who are to avenge. The absence of the γένος looks like the result of a change made in the course of a revision of the law; in any case, in spite of the omission,

---

[1] *I. J. G.* II, xxix, p. 204, § 9 Ὅταν δὲ ἦι ἡ διαδικασία, ὁ φρατρίαρχος μὴ πρότερον διδότω τὴν ψῆφον περὶ τῶν παίδων τοῖς ἅπασι φράτερσι πρὶν ἂν οἱ αὐτὸ τοῦ εἰσαγομένο θιασῶται κρύβδην ἀπὸ τῶ βωμῶ φέροντες τὴν ψῆφον διαψηφίσωνται, καὶ τὰς ψήφος τὰς τότων ἐναντίον τῶν ἀπάντων φρατέρων τῶν παρόντων ἐν τῆι ἀγοραῖ ὁ φρατρίαρχος διαριθμησάτω καὶ ἀναγορευέτω ὁπότερ' ἂν ψηφίσωνται.

[2] See below, Chap. IX, section 2.

[3] *I. J. G.* II, xxi, p. 2, § 4 προειπὲν δὲ τῶι κτέναντι ἐν ἀγοραῖ ἐντὸς ἀνεφσιότετος καὶ ἀνεφσιό· συνδιόκεν δὲ καὶ ἀνεφσιὸς καὶ ἀνεφσιόν παῖδας καὶ γαμβρὸς καὶ πενθερὸς καὶ φράτερας.

the line of *agnatic* relationship is kept up. In the order
of succession cognates are admitted after the agnates, but
in the order of avengers the agnatic group of the phratry
follows immediately on the narrower ἀγχιστεία.

2. *The Household.*

If the scheme of federation of kindreds could have been
upheld systematically, the κλῆρος and the οἶκος would have
been two aspects of the same institution—*holdings* in the
sphere of property would have corresponded to *families* in
the sphere of kinship. But owing to the development of
industrial and commercial conditions this correspondence
had to be abandoned. At Athens, in spite of certain efforts
made to maintain the holding, property in land was mobilized. Yet the principle that family property should be
the basis of a citizen's status was preserved, as may be seen
from the practice of Athenian law in the fourth century.

The case of the estate of Hagnias.

Let us take as an example the case dealt with in the
speeches of Demosthenes against Makartatos, and of Isaios
on the other side in defence of Makartatos' claim.[1] The
matter in dispute was the inheritance of one Hagnias; both
parties based their claim on relationship to the deceased,
but Demosthenes claimed that his client Eubulides was the
only person who could really inherit on grounds of kinship,
the others being outside the limit of the household (οἶκος).
Demosthenes, at the beginning of his speech, explains the
situation as regards the family. This is as follows:[2]
Buselos had five sons, each of whom married and had
children and grandchildren, five families (οἶκοι) being thus

'Αγχιστεία and οἶκος.

[1] [Dem.] XLIII. Isaios, XI.

[2]

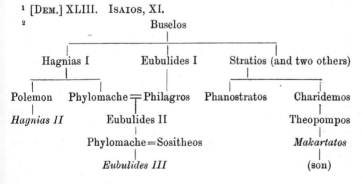

formed. Two of these sons have no connexion with the
case; the other three were Hagnias I, Eubulides I, and
Stratios. Hagnias had two children, Polemon and Phylomache, Polemon had a son *Hagnias II*, who died childless,
and whose inheritance (κλῆρος) is now in dispute. Phylomache, full sister to Polemon, was married to Philagros, the
son of Eubulides I, and therefore cousin to Polemon
(ἀνεψιός). Their son is Eubulides II, whose daughter gave
birth to *Eubulides III*, on whose behalf the claim to the
estate of Hagnias is being made by his father Sositheos,
the client of Demosthenes. Meantime Stratios, the third
son of Buselos, had a family consisting of two sons,
Phanostratos and Charidemos, of whom Charidemos had
a son Theopompos, whose son *Makartatos* is the other
claimant to the estate (κλῆρος) of Hagnias. Sositheos, in
the speech written for him by Demosthenes, rests the claim
of Eubulides III on the fact that the family (οἶκος) of
Hagnias was represented at the time only by Eubulides III,
whose grandfather was Hagnias' *first* cousin through
Phylomache, and whose great-grandfather was first cousin
to Polemon, the father of Hagnias. He maintained that
Theopompos and Makartatos were quite outside the family
(οἶκος), and could have no claim, Theopompos being only
second cousin to Hagnias. Makartatos, or Isaios on his
behalf, disputes Eubulides' claim on the ground that Phylomache (the elder) was not full sister to Polemon, and traces
his claim from Stratios as the brother of Hagnias' grandfather—Charidemos, grandfather of Makartatos, being first
cousin to Polemon, father of Hagnias, just as much as
Philagros was. That is, they go back a generation farther
and establish their claim as descendants of a common great-
grandfather, and not of a grandfather.

Thus the view that the οἶκος only included those descended
from one (common) grandfather (in this case the elder
Hagnias) was disputed, but it could not be contested that
the estate of Buselos had been divided among his five sons.
If it had remained undivided, the case might have been
considered differently. Anyhow, the discussion of the
question as to the οἶκος must be separated from that of the
ἀνεψιότης.

It would not do to restrict the issue to the question whether the expression μέχρι ἀνεψιαδῶν means " up to first cousins once removed "—as contended by Demosthenes—or, " up to second cousins "—as argued by Isaios. At first sight the right seems clearly to be on the side of the first interpretation, but it is impossible to go past the fact that in the previous trial a δικαστήριον had decided the case in favour of Theopompos, the father of Makartatos, and there-fore had pronounced in favour of the interpretation of Isaios. It would be too cheap an expedient to class this decision among the blunders of a democratic tribunal mis-led by crafty pleaders. The truth probably was that the Athenians were wavering between two conceptions of the ἀγχιστεία, a wider and a more narrow one. Theopompos succeeded on the strength of the latter. On the other hand, when the trial was resumed by Demosthenes on behalf of Sositheos against Theopompos' son, the new pleader sought to strengthen his client's argument by intro-ducing the notion of the οἶκος, as there could be no doubt that the unity of the household did not go higher up than the οἶκος of Hagnias.

The case helps to establish a point in the law of property descending by pedigree; the estate (κλῆρος) should remain compact, and could continue so for many generations, and the efforts of kindred were directed to this end, whoever the heir-at-law really was.

Nevertheless, property was much broken up, in spite of devices such as the marriage of the heiress (ἐπίκληρος) to the nearest agnate. On the religious and moral side, the notion of maintaining the family unity was more lasting; e. g. it was strongly felt that the family graves should be kept up by the elder line.

These points about kindred help to show how the Athenians drew the line between citizens and other classes of the population. The system of family holdings reacted on law, and courts had constantly to deal with the οἶκος and the phratry. *Restrictions as to citizenship.*

The result was the enforcement of stringent rules as to purity of descent. These were not mere devices of indi-vidual statesmen to prevent overcrowding by aliens; the

law regarding citizenship was connected with the main
principle of kinship, and was restored after any disturbance,
in order to keep up the principle of political privilege. The
laws against intrusion were very severe; at the time of
Kleisthenes many slaves and strangers had found their way
into the privileged circle,[1] but under Perikles citizenship was
again restricted to those whose parents on both sides were of
Athenian birth.[2]   Again, after the re-establishment of the
democracy in 403 B. C., in the archonship of Eukleides, the
law as to descent from citizens on both sides was re-enacted.
Towards the middle of the fourth century, in 364 B. C., a
third enactment of the same kind was made. The procedure and the penalties in connexion with it show how
much importance was attached to keeping up the barrier.
The demes as well as the families contributed to this end.
An illustration is given in the speech of Demosthenes
against Eubulides ;[3] as a result of the process of scrutiny
(διαψήφισις) in the deme of Halimus, one Euxitheos had
been deprived of citizenship; he took advantage of the fact
that he could appeal to the Courts, and accused the demarch
of unfair practices in carrying out the διαψήφισις. He
maintained that nearly every one had gone away before the
voting, and that, in spite of his request for an adjournment,
the demarch forced a vote, giving out more voting stones
than there were persons present. He admitted that his
family had become impoverished, but he pointed out that
this was no legal ground for disfranchisement. The fact
that the penalty for failure in such an appeal from the
decision of the deme to the popular Courts was the sale of
the appellant into slavery shows what importance was
attributed to the matter.

---

[1] See below, Chap. VI, p. 117.
[2] See above, p. 55.
[3] DEM. LVII, 3; cf. LIX, esp. § 13 ἐγὼ τοῦτον ἥκω ἐπιδείξων εἰς
ὑμᾶς, ξένῃ μὲν γυναικὶ συνοικοῦντα παρὰ τὸν νόμον, ἀλλοτρίους δὲ παῖδας
εἰσαγαγόντα εἴς τε τοὺς φράτερας καὶ εἰς τοὺς δημότας, ἐγγυῶντα δὲ τὰς
τῶν ἑταιρῶν θυγατέρας ὡς αὑτοῦ οὔσας, ἠσεβηκότα δ᾽ εἰς τοὺς θεούς, ἄκυρον
δὲ ποιοῦντα τὸν δῆμον τῶν αὑτοῦ, ἄν τινα βούληται πολίτην ποιήσασθαι· τίς γὰρ
ἂν ἔτι παρὰ τοῦ δήμου ζητήσειε λαβεῖν δωρειάν, μετὰ πολλῶν ἀναλωμάτων καὶ
πραγματείας πολίτης μέλλων ἔσεσθαι, ἐξὸν παρὰ Στεφάνου ἀπ᾽ ἐλάττονος
ἀναλώματος, εἴ γε τὸ αὐτὸ τοῦτο γενήσεται αὐτῷ;

We know, too, from the *Athenian Constitution*,[1] that
a scrutiny (δοκιμασία) as to the same point was obligatory
in the case of candidates for the archonship. Thus barriers
were set up against the intrusion of outsiders, and the
democracy of Athens when considered from a legal point
of view was a democracy by pedigree.

Citizenship in Greece was regarded in a different way
from that which developed later in the Roman Empire. It
was a political as well as a civil complex of rights; the fact
that a citizen was a potential ruler, and had actual access
in his turn to political power hampered the development
of forms of incomplete citizenship. Such an incomplete
form, similar to what the Romans called *civitas sine suf-
fragio*, existed, but arose in a peculiar way and in exceptional circumstances. In the fifth century those who did
not possess full rights were not regarded as citizens at all.
Usually when privileges were granted to benefactors of the
city they did not amount to citizenship. This is the
meaning of προξενία—the granting of rights to favoured
treatment as a specially protected visitor : quite a different
position from citizenship. In a case recorded by an inscription [2] full citizenship was granted by way of exception :
Thrasybulos of Kalydon, in consideration of his having
slain Phrynichos, one of the Four Hundred (in 411 B. C.)
was given full rights, and was admitted to the federation
of families, being allowed to select as his own any tribe,
deme, and phratry that he pleased. That is, he obtained
not only public and political rights, but also private family
rights : it was indeed a case of naturalization.

A lower class of the population of Athens clearly dis-
tinguishable from the foregoing are the denizens (μέτοικοι),
resident aliens not protected by any special decree, or by
any treaty between Athens and their own city. They live
on sufferance, are exploited by the State in taxation, and
liable to military service of a subordinate kind, such as
rowing in the fleet; we hear that some who had served in
this capacity at Arginusae were rewarded by promotion to

Marginal notes: Privileges of citizenship. Denizens.

[1] Chap. 55.
[2] DITT. *Syll.* I³. 108, p. 139.

citizenship.   Their situation is one of economic dependence
and legal sufferance.   They were kept strictly outside the
circle of active citizenship, and any attempt on their part
to get within that circle was punished by heavy penalties.
The unfavourable treatment of that class in fully-developed
democracies may be connected with the general view of
Greek political thinkers that handicraft and retail trade
were inferior occupations, and unworthy of free citizens.[1]

3. The City and Religion.

Psycho-
logical
unity of
the City.

No State has existed or can exist as an artificial and
mechanical arrangement; behind the constitution, the
magistrates, and the laws there always is a substratum of
group psychology, a conscious and subconscious unity, not
in itself political or juridical, but necessary for the vitality
of the political and juridical structure.   That is why the
term " organic " is used in speaking of States; they are
organized for common life and action, while nations are
social groups in which union is supposed to be derived from
common origin and breeding, as is shown by the very word.
It is immaterial whether the community of race can be
proved as a physical fact, or whether the term is extended
to cover an admixture of elements transformed and assimilated by civil intercourse.   It may seem doubtful whether
the word " nation " may apply to such small and simple
States as were the Dorians of Sparta or of Argos, offshoots
of one ethnographical stock.   But it seems appropriate to
use it also in their case, because each of those cities always
felt as a community of related people, very exclusive with
regard to outsiders.

As a result of this psychological fact, the law of Greece
cannot be understood unless we take stock of City-religion.
For in the religious domain the psychological substratum

[1] Cf. e.g. AR. Pol. IV (VII), 9, 1329 a 20 τὸ γὰρ βάναυσον οὐ μετέχει
τῆς πόλεως, οὐδ' ἄλλο οὐδὲν γένος ὃ μὴ τῆς ἀρετῆς δημιουργόν ἐστιν.   1328 b
37 φανερὸν ... ὡς ἐν τῇ κάλλιστα πολιτευομένῃ πόλει καὶ τῇ κεκτημένῃ δικαίους
ἄνδρας ἀπλῶς, ἀλλὰ μὴ πρὸς τὴν ὑπόθεσιν, οὔτε βάναυσον βίον οὔτ' ἀγοραῖον
δεῖ ζῆν τοὺς πολίτας (ἀγεννὴς γὰρ ὁ τοιοῦτος βίος καὶ πρὸς ἀρετὴν ὑπεναντίος),
οὐδὲ δὴ γεωργοὺς εἶναι τοὺς μέλλοντας ἔσεσθαι (δεῖ γὰρ σχολῆς καὶ πρὸς τὴν
γένεσιν τῆς ἀρετῆς καὶ πρὸς τὰς πράξεις τὰς πολιτικάς).   See, however,
ZIMMERN, Greek Commonwealth, pp. 270 f., and GLOTZ, Le travail en
Grèce, pp. 193 ff.

became personified. It is impossible to speak of the connexion, still less of the separation, of Church and State,
because there was no differentiation of the two; the City
was a religious as well as a political community. The
Greek commonwealths present themselves to our view as
households of the gods. Athens is the house of Athene,
Eleusis of Demeter Samos of Hera, Ephesos of Artemis,
&c. In the Athenian tradition Athene Polias appears as
the actual mistress of Athens, with her dwelling-place
beside that of Erechtheus, the Ἥρως of the soil.[1] In
illustration of this we read [2] that when Kleomenes occupied the Akropolis as an ally of Isagoras, and wanted to
enter the temple of Athene, he was met by the priestess
with the words: "Stranger from Lakedaimon, retire; enter
not the temple; for it is not lawfnl that Dorians should
pass therein."

The struggles between the cities were in a way struggles
for the supremacy of one or the other cult. In many
instances it was sought to weaken the political feeling of
a community by abolishing or modifying its cults. Thus
Kleisthenes of Sikyon got rid of the cult of Argive Adrastos,
substituting for him another Hero, from Thebes, Melanippos,
who had defeated Adrastos in war.[3] Dionysos probably
obtained participation in the patronage of the Apaturia in
connexion with a similar reform made by Kleisthenes of
Athens.

Cults provided centres of political grouping. It would
be a mistake to treat the matter in a rationalistic way. In
Aristotle's *Politics* [4] we have an interesting discussion about
the juridical nature of the State; he says that in one sense
the State was a continuous growth in which the elements
changed, but unity remained, in the same manner as in
a stream the water is always changing, while the river
remains one and the same. In a similar way it is possible
to conceive the State as a historical unit in which change of
form does not produce an essential difference of substance.

---

[1] HOMER, *Odyssey*, VII, 78 ff. Ἀθήνη . . . λίπε . . . Σχερίην ἐρατεινήν,
κετο δ' ἐς Μαραθῶνα καὶ εὐρυάγυιαν Ἀθήνην, δῦνε δ' Ἐρεχθῆος πυκινὸν δόμον.
[2] HEROD. V, 72. [3] *Ibid.* 67.
[4] *Pol.* III, 3, 6, 1276 b. See below, p. 105.

From another point of view, however, any profound change in "the constitution" starts a new era. Aristotle does not decide between these two views, though he seems to incline towards the second, and to hold that the State is comprised within the πολιτεία. In early Greece this problem could not arise, because the unity expressed in the cult was the accepted symbol and factor of union, and this idea persisted to some extent even in later times. If it be asked whether the Greeks conceived the State as a corporation, the reply should be, I think, that they did not think of a corporation in the modern sense of the word, but of a community whose life was connected with the immortal person of the god—Athens, for example, was as it were held in trust by Athene. Thus we have to deal in City-religion not only with a theological and psychological, but also with a juridical conception.

Religious obligations of citizens.

The fact of belonging to such a community imposed religious duties on the citizen. The order of procedure in public affairs shows the close connexion with religion ; in the πρυτανεῖον, τὰ ἱερὰ καὶ ὅσια have precedence over all other business.[1] The religious aspect of citizenship may be illustrated from Plato's *Euthyphron*, where the discussion turns on the meaning of religious obligation.[2] The belief in the gods of the city and the coincidence of religion and justice, it was argued by Plato in defence of Sokrates, do not go so far as Anytos and Meletos claimed. Yet from the general notion of justice as regards the gods, i.e. the duty of serving them in a particular way, there follow certain consequences. The importance attached to the oath of allegiance to the State is insisted upon, e. g. in Lykurgos' speech against Leokrates ; in accusing him of deserting the city in her hour of need, Lykurgos refers to that oath "The bond of democracy is the oath. The city is constituted of three elements—the magistrate, the judge, and the private citizen. Each one of these three tenders his fealty by right. . . . The oath-breaker cannot conceal himself from the gods, nor can he escape their punishment. If it

[1] SCHOEMANN-LIPSIUS, I. 414.
[2] *Op. cit. Euthyph.* 12 d εἰ γὰρ μέρος τὸ ὅσιον τοῦ δικαίου, δεῖ δὴ ἡμᾶς ὡς ἔοικεν, ἐξευρεῖν τὸ ποῖον μέρος ἂν εἴη τοῦ δικαίου τὸ ὅσιον.

is not he himself who succumbs to great misfortunes, then it is his children and the whole of his kindred." [1]

In dealing with the most important matters—legislation, judgement, conferment of privilege, even the enlightened democracy of the fifth and fourth centuries made a distinction between what was settled in the Assembly by an ordinary vote, and what was done under oath. Thus, in the case of νομοθεσία it was found necessary to entrust the most important part of the legislative function to sworn judicial commissioners. In correspondence with the public importance of the oaths taken by archons and dikasts, tending as it did to the establishment of confidence in political affairs, stands the fact that every Athenian when admitted to citizenship as an "ephebos" swore on oath to honour and worship the gods of the city.[2] Every now and then situations occurred in the history of Athens in which waves of religious reaction against frivolity in matters of religion rose high. Such was, for instance, the outbreak against Alkibiades and his companions in connexion with the mutilation of the Hermae.[3]

Scholars disagree as regards prosecutions for breach 'Ασέβεια. of the law as to religious duties. Some authorities, e.g. Schömann, hold that the Athenians never tried to impose a definite code of doctrine, and only insisted on outward respect and compliance with certain requirements of public ritual. Participation in the great festivals, e.g. the Panathenaic, was a duty prescribed by law; no one could refuse to take the part assigned to him. Even metoics had their place in the procession, and only slaves were *not* admitted to any festival except the Kronia, a Greek parallel to the Roman Saturnalia.[4] The highest expression of this participation was the public service (λειτουργίαι), the provision of choruses, and of religious embassies.

But it cannot be denied that the Athenians did now and then prosecute people for subversive teaching in matters

[1] LYK. *in Leokr.*, 79.
[2] SCHOEMANN-LIPSIUS, 379.
[3] THUK. VI, 60. Cf. I, 126.
[4] DAR. *et* S. s.v. *kronia*.

of religion. There was no special department of State to deal with religious thought, but every citizen had the right to bring an accusation of impiety against a neighbour. On some occasions special decrees were passed, e.g. that of Diopeithes, which served as a basis for the prosecution of Sokrates.[1] This case is the most familiar instance, but it is not the only one; Anaxagoras was condemned for teaching that the sun was a glowing mass of stone and not a deity.[2] One Hygiainon, in the course of a case of ἀντίδοσις, accused Euripides of impiety on account of a line in his *Hippolytos* (612): "My tongue it was that swore, my heart is free."[3] .

Thus the way was always open for accusation on the score of an offence against religion, but prosecution was not without danger for the accuser, and was not often resorted to. The Athenians treated these cases somewhat capriciously, but the juridicial basis for prosecutions for ἀσέβεια is apparent in the oath taken by ephebes (above, p. 99).

The hearth of the city. In a sense, the religion of the City-state was a family religion, although some cults, e.g. those of Zeus and Apollo, were represented in almost every city. The clearest form of ancestral worship is presented by the cult of Hestia at the central hearth of the city. Plato, in setting up his ideal State, orders that "the first step should be to found the temple of Hestia."[4] The interesting point about the holy hearth at Athens is that it was originally the centre of the government, and closely connected with the Prytaneion; it was not moved, however, from the old Prytaneion to the later place of meeting called the Tholos. It represented the ancient hearth established by Theseus at the time of the traditional union of Attika (συνοικισμός). As it had been the hearth of the royal household, a "king" was kept to preside over it; it was the function of the king archon (ἄρχων βασιλεύς) to direct all ceremonies connected with

---

[1] Plutarch, *Perikles*, c. 32.
[2] Thonissen, *Droit pénal*, pp. 178 ff.
[3] Ar. *Rhet.* III, 15, 8.
[4] *Laws*, V, 745 b μετὰ δὲ ταῦτα μέρη δώδεκα διελέσθαι, θέμενον Ἑστίας πρῶτον καὶ Διὸς καὶ Ἀθηνᾶς ἱερόν, Ἀκρόπολιν ὀνομάζοντα.

rites of purification. At Korinth it was usual to send out as leader of a colony a member of the ancient kingly line, the Bacchiadae, that he might carry over to the new city the fire from the mother hearth in Korinth. We read in Thukydides' story of the flight of Themistokles, that when he went to take refuge with Admetos of Thessaly, the king's wife, in her husband's absence, placed the fugitive beside the hearth, that is, under the protection of the gods of the house.[1]

All these religious and political forms of the personification of the city are connected with the idea of nativity, breeding, succession. They show that the restricted form of democracy characteristic of the Greek city was determined by the federation of kindreds which formed its structural framework.

[1] THUK. I, 136. See also AR. *Pol.* VIII (VI), 1322 b 28; also PAUSANIAS, V, 155, and HERODOTOS, I, 146, on the migration of the hearth. See on the social aspect of the Hestia-Vesta cult, B. W. Leist, *Alt-arisches Jus civile*, I, 80 ff.

CHAPTER VI

THE CITY AND THE CITIZEN

1. *The City as a juridical person.*

Peculiarity of Greek public law.

IT is strange that although the organization of the Greek States has been treated over and over again in all its minute details, no comprehensive attempt has been made to state the fundamental doctrines of Greek public law, if we except Aristotle's work on the *Politics*.[1] This is partly the result, of course, of the differentiation of the Greek people into many separate commonwealths; but yet as regards leading principles it is possible, and indeed necessary, to try to reconstruct the juridical concepts which governed public life. They inevitably group themselves round the idea of democracy, because even in the States ruled by the few the participation of the general body of citizens was admitted in some form or other, and exerted its influence on public law.

We have to start from an inquiry into the peculiar manner in which the Greeks understood the connexion between the commonwealth as a unity and the single citizens as members of the State. Of course the preponderance of the city over all private interests may be considered as an axiom; it is expressed, for instance, in Aristotle's *Politics*[2]: "The State is by nature clearly prior to the family and to the individual, since the whole is of necessity prior to the part; for example, if the whole body be destroyed, there will be no foot or hand. . . . The proof that the State is a creation of nature and prior to the individual is that the individual, when isolated, is not self-sufficing; and therefore he is like a part in relation to the whole." But, on the other hand, the commonwealth was

[1] SZANTO, *Das attische Bürgerrecht*, pp. 1 f.
[2] AR. *Pol.* I, 2, 12, 1253 a.

never thought of in abstract terms as separate from its concrete members; another passage of Aristotle[1] lays stress strongly on the fact that the properly constituted city may be defined as the sum of the citizens, that is, of those who have a share in the sovereign power over it. " He who has the power to take part in the deliberative or judicial administration of any State is said by us to be a citizen of that State; and, speaking generally, a State is a quantity of citizens sufficing for the purposes of life." This is more than a theoretical construction : the principle leads to some very significant inferences.

To begin with, it is difficult from this point of view to draw a rigid opposition between the commonwealth as a corporation and the citizens as individuals. The well-known problems which arise in our modern theory of legal personality as applied to the State appear in a peculiar light in Greek surroundings. What was the dominant doctrine in Greece in the fifth and fourth centuries B. C., concerning the juridical personality of the State? We are not now speaking of details of political organization and administration; but we have to inquire how far the Greek commonwealths were juridical persons or what we should call corporations of public law. The question whether the State is a corporation may be considered from two points of view; we may examine it in connexion with the working of positive law; in this sense there can be no objection to the assumption that the State in relation to the citizens is a corporate body—the greatest of them all, but still analogous to other corporations such as chartered companies. From another point of view we may consider the question in relation to the historic growth of particular communities; we have to look in this case chiefly at the matter-of-fact evolution which conditions the juridical formation of the State. What is really important here is not the vindication of certain rights as being corporate, but the actual

---

[1] *Ibid.* III, 1, 12, 1275 b ᾧ γὰρ ἐξουσία κοινωνεῖν ἀρχῆς βουλευτικῆς ἢ κριτικῆς, πολίτην ἤδη λέγομεν εἶναι ταύτης τῆς πόλεως, πόλιν δε τὸ τῶν τοιούτων πλῆθος ἱκανὸν πρὸς αὐτάρκειαν ζωῆς, ὡς ἁπλῶς εἰπεῖν. Cf. *Ibid.* 1, 6, 1275 a πολίτης δ' ἁπλῶς οὐδενὶ τῶν ἄλλων ὁρίζεται μᾶλλον ἢ τῷ μετέχειν κρίσεως καὶ ἀρχῆς. τῶν δ' ἀρχῶν αἱ μέν εἰσι διῃρημέναι κατὰ χρόνον, . . . ὁ δ' ἀόριστος, οἷον ὁ δικαστὴς καὶ ἐκκλησιαστής.

predominance of particular groups which assert their will in consonance and identity with that of the State.

Historical life of the City.   In a great measure the Greeks were keenly alive to the fact that every State possesses a moral and legal continuity distinct from the actual individuals who make up its population. It is a being with its own life, character, and historical identity. This historical and collective community of national life was perceived, and frequently discussed, in ancient Greece. In a passage in one of the minor dialogues ascribed to Plato [1] the author urges that Athens in the whole of its history was definitely one: " Then as now, and indeed always, from that time to this, speaking generally, our government was an aristocracy—a form of government which receives many names, according to the fancies of men, and is sometimes called democracy, being really an aristocracy of the many who love virtue . . ."

The author goes on to contradict the view that we must distinguish between several different kinds of Athens: that which existed under the kings, that which existed under the *régime* of democracy, and so forth. Athens, he declares, was never conquered; its kings still exist in democratic Athens as they did in former times, and on the whole it may be said that Athens is still governed by an aristocracy. This is obviously a fiction, but the point Plato tries to impress on his readers is that Athens lived a continuous constitutional life, and the history of the people is represented as one consecutive process. The point of view, however, is after all a cultural one; its juridical inferences are not definitely drawn. It may be regarded as the germ of the idea of an organic evolution of the State, but as yet the idea is expressed in a very incomplete manner.

Let us ask what term could be used by the Greeks to characterize the commonwealth of Athens considered as a moral personality. The word πόλις was an expression in

---

[1] *Menexenos*, 238 c d ἡ γὰρ αὐτὴ πολιτεία καὶ τότε ἦν καὶ νῦν, ἀριστο-κρατία, ἐν ᾗ νῦν τε πολιτευόμεθα καὶ τὸν ἀεὶ χρόνον ἐξ ἐκείνου ὡς τὰ πολλά. καλεῖ δὲ ὁ μὲν αὐτὴν δημοκρατίαν, ὁ δὲ ἄλλο, ᾧ ἂν χαίρῃ, ἔστι δὲ τῇ ἀληθείᾳ μετ' εὐδοξίας πλήθους ἀριστοκρατία· βασιλῆς μὲν γὰρ ἀεὶ ἡμῖν εἰσιν· οὗτοι δὲ τοτὲ μὲν ἐκ γένους, τοτὲ δὲ αἱρετοί· ἐγκρατὲς δὲ τῆς πόλεως τὰ πολλὰ τὸ πλῆθος, τὰς δὲ ἀρχὰς δίδωσι καὶ κράτος τοῖς ἀεὶ δόξασιν ἀρίστοις εἶναι.

very general use, but the term commonly used was δῆμος.
A third expression, κόσμος, is not used frequently.   It indicates rather the fact that the State does not consist in
a concourse of people, which constitute its population, but
that these people are organized in a certain order.[1]

This point of view is emphatically expressed by Aristotle Juridical
in the *Politics*:[2] "When the race of inhabitants as well as life of the
their place of abode remain the same, are we to say that City.
the commonwealth is also the same, although the citizens
are always dying and being born, as we are accustomed to
speak of rivers and fountains being the same, although the
water in them is constantly coming in and flowing away?
Or shall we say that the human population remains the
same for the above-mentioned reason, but the commonwealth is different?   For if a commonwealth is a union,
namely a union of citizens sharing in political life, it seems
necessary to maintain that the commonwealth is not the
same when the constitution is changed, in the same way as
we say of a chorus that it is a tragic one or a comic one,
although it may consist of the same persons. . . . And if this
is true, it is evident that the sameness of the State consists
chiefly in the sameness of the constitution, and may be
called by the same name, whether the inhabitants are the
same or entirely different."   Here Aristotle faces the problem in a very business-like manner ; to the question how
are we to consider the city as an organic unity, he replies
that we shall find it in the κοινωνία πολιτῶν πολιτείας.   It
is the fact that such a definite principle binds people together under a certain constitution that makes a commonwealth.   It is, in fact, the κοινωνία πολιτῶν πολιτείας which
represents the unity of State personality.

But this view was not accepted without qualifications.
Changes might occur in the actual policy of the State and
yet the national life would go on with a kind of organic
continuity nevertheless.   When the Thirty were overthrown
in Athens, after the short rule of oligarchy, they left

---

[1] See HIRZEL, *Themis*, &c , pp. 283 ff.
[2] *Pol.* III, 3, 6, 1276 b (ending) εἰ δὴ τοῦτον ἔχει τὸν τρόπον, φανερὸν
ὅτι μάλιστα λεκτέον τὴν αὐτὴν πόλιν εἰς τὴν πολιτείαν βλέποντας· ὄνομα δε
καλεῖν ἕτερον ἢ ταὐτὸν ἔξεστι καὶ τῶν αὐτῶν κατοικούντων αὐτὴν καὶ πάμπαν
ἑτέρων ἀνθρώπων.

behind them considerable debts. It is very remarkable
that although the rule of the Thirty was directly opposed
to the main principles of Athenian democracy, the δῆμος
took over and made itself responsible for the debts which
the oligarchs had incurred. This is, perhaps, the most
striking example in Athenian history of what Isokrates
calls the ἐπιείκεια of the Athenian people; but just because
it was often cited and admired, it can hardly be treated as
a normal case. As a rule, far-reaching political revolutions
put an end to the liabilities of commonwealths, and each
πολιτεία was supposed to embrace the life of a particular
collective being.

To sum up, Aristotle does not give us a definite solution
of the problem stated by him; he presents both sides, and
although he inclines towards the view that it is the unity
of the constitution which sets limits to the juridical existence of the commonwealth, he is willing to admit that from
a higher or "humane" point of view it would be fair to
consider the unity of a people's life historically rather than
juridically: wherever there is continuity of national life
the growth of one personality of public law might be
recognized.

The nearest approach to a conception of a corporate life
of the State distinct from that of the individuals composing
it was obtained in the idea of State religion. Every Greek
commonwealth had as it were representatives of its historical life in the gods protecting the State and revered as
its divine leaders.[1]

A second inference from the intimate connexion between
city and citizens in Greece consists in the fact that the city
is understood primarily as the complex of the individuals
who compose it. The element of territory does not play
a great part in the realization of its existence. Remarkable
and by no means uncommon cases occur in which the city
is separated, as it were, from its geographical basis and yet
continues to assert itself as an entity of public law. I mean
especially the cases when a great number of citizens had to
leave their home-land in consequence of disturbances or

---

[1] See above, p. 97. Cf. WIDE in GERCKE und NORDEN, *Einleitung*, II, pp. 217 ff.

conquests. A classical example is the building up of a
complete commonwealth by the Athenian fleet in Samos at
the time when the oligarchs overthrew the regular government in Athens.[1] In the same way the return of the exiles
after the collapse of the Thirty [2] was not regarded as a new
period in constitutional development, but merely as a re-
affirmation of a legal arrangement which had never ceased
to exist.

A third feature of the situation is disclosed by the
manner in which Greeks effected the representation of the
city on occasions when the commonwealth had to act as
a unit of public law. The case arose, to begin with, when
treaties had to be ratified and confirmed by oath. In the
inscription relating to the treaty of 446–5 B.C. between
Athens and Chalkis,[3] we find that the oath was to be taken
by "all the Chalkidians who had reached manhood;" but as
such a process is bound to be exceedingly cumbersome and
difficult to carry out in practice, the corresponding oath of
the Athenian Demos is restricted to "the members of the
Council and of the Heliaea." According to Aristotle's
definition, as we have seen above, these latter are to be
considered as the citizens exercising the supreme functions
of government. In the case of the treaty between Athens
and Eretria [4] the Athenian citizens are represented by "the
commanders, the Council, and the knights;" and in that
with Selymbria in 409 B.C.[5] by the commanders, the
trierarchs, the hoplites, and any other Athenians who
were there! In the case of smaller cities an attempt
was often made to call up all the citizens, although in
Athens, which was a comparatively large commonwealth,

*View of
the City
represen-
tation.*

---

[1] THUK. VIII, 75–77.
[2] *Ath. Const.* c. 41.
[3] DITT. *Syll.* I³, 64, p. 79 ὀμόσαι ᾿Αθεναίον τὲν βολὲν καὶ τὸς δικαστάς
. . . ὀμόσαι δὲ Χαλκιδέων τὸς ἐβõντας ἅπαντας.
[4] *Ibid.* I³. 123, p. 168 ὀμόσαι δὲ ᾿Αθηναίων μὲν τοὺς στρατηγοὺς καὶ
τὴν βουλὴν καὶ τοὺς ἱππέας.
[5] *Ibid.*, 112, p. 150 ὤμοσαν ᾿Αθεναίον οἱ στρατεγοὶ καὶ οἱ τριέραρχοι
καὶ οἱ ὁπλῖται καὶ εἴ τις ἄλλος ᾿Αθεναίον παρῆν, καὶ Σελυμβριανοὶ πάντες.
Cf. MICHEL, 19, and *ibid.*, 21, p. 26 κυρωθείσας δὲ τᾶς συνθήκας ἐλέσθω
ὁ δᾶμος παραχρῆμα ἄνδρας πέντε· τοὶ δὲ αἱρεθέντες μετὰ τῶν παραγεγενημένων
ἐξ ῾Ιεραπύτνας πρεσβευτᾶν ὁρκιξάντων τὸν νόμιμον ὅρκον ῾Ροδίους ἅπαντας
τοὺς ὄντας ἐν ἁλικίαι.

representation is restricted to some one or other group
of prominent citizens.   The fact, however, remains that
these prominent representatives appear in different combinations, and this shows that there was no standing organ
representing the city in its treaty-making capacity, but
that a certain number of influential citizens were acting for
the rest.

Another case in which the city materialized as a corporate unit is presented by the conclusion of city loans.
This was an occasion in which the distinction between the
property of the city and that of its individual members
arises in a most natural manner.   In a number of cases
such a distinction was actually drawn; take e.g. the inscription *C. I. G.* 1569: the πόλις as a whole incurred the obligation, and the pastureland of the πόλις was to be the security
in case of failure to pay.   There are, however, a number of
instances in which recourse is had to the private property
of individual citizens in order to guarantee the payment of
a loan and to provide material security for the execution.
The most remarkable case is that of Arkesine in the island
of Amorgos.   Inscriptions furnish details of two instances
in which bankers granted loans to the city; in both, the city
treasurers were responsible for the payment of the interest
due, and were liable to arrest and seizure of their goods in
the event of non-payment; as for the capital sum the
security was all the common property of the city as well as
the private possessions of the citizens.   If payment were
not made at the agreed term, the creditor in each case was
to recover the sum " by every means of execution on all the
common property of the citizens and their private property
wherever found." [1]

In another inscription [2] we find that instead of making
all the citizens liable in their private fortunes for the payment of a city debt, the creditor picked out the principal

---

[1] *I. J. G.* I, xv, A and B, pp. 313 ff., e.g. A, § 6 καὶ ἐξέστω πράξασθαι
Πραξικλεῖ ταῦτα τὰ χρήματα πράξει πάσηι ἔκ τε τῶγ κοινῶν ... καὶ ἐκ τῶν
ἰδίων τῶν ᾿Αρκεσινήωγ ... καὶ ἐξ ἑνὸς ἑκάστου ... καὶ ἐξ ἁπάντων.   In
the case of the city of Iulis (DITT. *Syll³.* I, 173 ; MICHEL, 95) execution
was also evidently directed towards all the property available within
the territory of the city.

[2] *I. J. G.* I, xiv, pp. 277 ff.

magistrates and the ten wealthiest citizens of the city contracting the loan. "Nikarete . . . made a loan (to certain
persons named, representing the city of Orchomenos). The
borrowers or the sureties shall pay back the money (on a
certain day). If not, execution shall be made upon the
borrowers (i. e. the magistrates), and the sureties alike,
singly, severally, or all at once, and upon their goods."[1]
The transaction was a complicated one, and there is some
controversy as to a point of detail. Was the city to reimburse Nikarete in the case of failure of payment in term
concurrently with the wealthy citizens selected as securities?
or was the latter's liability to come in only in case of the
insolvency of the city? If the first interpretation[2] is the
right one, then we should have a case of payment of the
double of the debt as a fine for failing to keep the term.
If the second interpretation[3] is preferred, we have simply
to do with a case of guarantors entering on their liability
in the place of the principal. There is something to be said
for both views, but it is not necessary for our purpose to
form a definite decision as to this point. What seems
material is the fact that private citizens were constrained
to come up with their property for the repayment of a debt
incurred by the city. In the case of Arkesine the enforced
liability fell on all the citizens; in the case of Orchomenos the
wealthiest were picked out according to the usual practice
of λειτουργίαι. Anyhow it would not do to consider the
arrangement merely from the point of view of the convenience to the creditor; it undoubtedly illustrates the
peculiar conception of Greek public law as regards the
political tie between the commonwealth and its members.

There is nothing in Greek law corresponding to the
notion of the *fiscus* as a separate subject of rights differentiated from the State. The obligations of the commonweath
in its fiscal affairs are intimately connected and mixed up
with the political life of the city. As a result the enforce-

Fiscal institutions.

---

[1] *Ibid.*, pp. 280–282, VI A ἡ δὲ πρᾶξις ἔστω ἔκ τε αὐτῶν τῶν δανεισα
μένων καὶ ἐκ τῶν ἐγγύων καὶ ἐξ ἑνὸς καὶ ἐκ πλειόνων καὶ ἐκ πάντων καὶ ἐκ τῶν
ὑπαρχόντων αὐτοῖς πραττούσηι ὃν ἂν τρόπον βούληται.
[2] Proposed by SZANTO, *Wiener Studien*, VII.
[3] The reading of the editors of *I. J. G.*

ment of liabilities falling on the city is dependent on the action of the Assembly, the Council, and the various financial officers. The only point on which we see a beginning of differentiation of the two spheres of private and public rights is the use of the judicial process to verify the proper carrying out of confiscations. When citizens deem themselves aggrieved by the arbitrary action of authorities in such a case they may claim a judicial inquiry, and a διαδικασία will take place. Lysias' speech on the Unjust Claim of State Funds[1] presents a good instance of the procedure. In this case one Eraton had incurred a debt, and had died without paying; his sons failed to pay the interest. The creditor obtained an order for the payment of the entire debt, principal and interest. Various complications ensued, and he then brought an action for the satisfaction of his claim; this action was brought against the Treasury because the State had confiscated the property from which the debtor was to make good the debt. In other respects the situation of the city as regards individual citizens in matters of pecuniary liabilities cannot be said to be based on reciprocal rights and obligations. While claims against the city can be enforced only with its good will, and are not made secure by coercive measures, apart from proceedings against officers, the claims of the city against its debtors are backed by exceedingly stringent measures, especially as regards those who failed to pay contributions or to deliver public money. A heavy fine of double the amount due was claimed after a very short respite; and the insolvent debtor could be eventually coerced by an execution directed not only against his property but also against his person.[2]

Consolidated funds.

On the other hand, there was no regular budget, and income and expenses were squared on the basis of laws and decrees passed from time to time by the community. Interesting attempts were made to create certain consolidated funds in order to meet the most important expenses. The first attempt of this kind was made on the initiative of

---

[1] LYS. XVII.
[2] PARTSCH, *Griechisches Bürgschaftsrecht*, pp. 312 f.

Themistokles when he persuaded the people to reserve
a hundred talents of the proceeds from the silver mines of
Laurion for the building of a fleet. The account of this
political measure is interesting in so far as the original
intention of the Athenians was to divide the money among
the citizens. In the time of the first Athenian League
a large fund was collected for war expenses, and although
eventually the people began to use part of it for the purpose
of embellishing the city (the building of the Parthenon,
Propylaea and so on),[1] the consolidated fund was still very
large towards the beginning of the Peloponnesian War.[2]
Out of this fund one thousand talents were kept as a special
reserve in case of extremity. The heavy expenses entailed
by the conflict with Sparta led, however, to the complete
exhaustion of this fund, and the collapse of Athens after
Aigospotamoi broke down the power which made such a
fiscal policy possible; the League had been destroyed, and
there were no more contributions to collect from the Allies
for the use of the city.

In a sense the subsequent fiscal history is even more
characteristic, because the resources of the city had to be
drawn chiefly from Athenian citizens themselves. The
main expedient was to ransom, as it were, the wealthier
people in order to keep the democratic majority in good
humour. In his second *Olynthiac* oration Demosthenes
refers to this policy of the Demos[3]: "If you assign to one
body of men the function of issuing orders to you, like
tyrants; to another, that of compulsory service as trierarchs or tax-payers or soldiers; and to another, only that
of voting their condemnation without taking any share in
the labour, nothing that ought to be done will be done in
time." By the help of such exactions the people made provision for securing a constant flow of money to the θεωρικόν,

---

[1] See PLUTARCH, *Perikles*, c. 12 and 13.
[2] According to THUKYDIDES, II, 13, the amount had been 9,700
talents, of which 6,000 talents remained in 431 B.C. As to the
reserve, see *ibid.*, c. 24.
[3] DEM. II, 30.   Cf. ISOKRATES, XII, 140 . . . ἐκ δὲ τῶν κοινῶν ταῖς
ἰδίαις ἀπορίαις βοηθεῖν ζητούντων, . . . καὶ πρὸς τούτοις ἐκείνους τοὺς τὰ μὲν
τῶν ἄλλων κτήματα τῆς πόλεως εἶναι φάσκοντας, τὰ δὲ ταύτης ἴδια κλέπτειν
καὶ διαρπάζειν τολμῶντας.

a consolidated fund destined to provide for payments in connexion with the attendance at the theatre on festal occasions. One of the most humiliating episodes of the political history of Athens in the fourth century is the struggle between public-spirited leaders like Apollodoros and Demosthenes, who insisted on the needs of the war equipment, as against demagogues like Agyrrhios and Eubulos, who cajoled the Demos by persuading it to ear-mark public money for popular amusements.

The treasuries of the gods.

A peculiar device of Greek political life for meeting permanent fiscal demands consisted in assigning large sums of money to the gods. The temple of Athene Polias was to some extent a treasury in which a reserve fund for the public administration of Athens was kept to meet emergency requirements.[1] The religion of the city was, as we shall often have to remark, a definite side of its political life, so that there was nothing strange in the fact that the Assembly passed decrees to direct the treasurers of the goddess to make certain payments in order to square the expenses of some expedition to Thrace or to the Islands, and for similar political purposes.[2] A decree published in the first volume of Dittenberger's collection gives detailed directions as to the disposal and management of the various monies kept in the temple of Athene ; some of these funds are public, and are managed by Hellenotamiae ; they are surplus revenue derived from the tribute (φόροι), and are to be kept apart from the treasure of the goddess.[3] The decree orders the repayment of a big loan which was made in critical circumstances by order of the people from the fund of the goddess. Three thousand talents were borrowed at a nominal rate of interest, and we know that such operations were constantly repeated during the great

---

[1] BOECKH-FRAENKEL, *Staatshaushaltung der Athener*, I, pp. 195 ff.

[2] DITT. *Syll.* I³. 94, pp. 123 ff. ταμίαι ἱερὸν χρεμάτον τὲς Ἀθεναίας . . . παρέδοσαν ἑελλενοταμίαις . . . ὅστε δôναι τοῖς τριεράρχοις ἐς Ἄργος τοῖς μετὰ Δεμοσθένος. ἔδοξεν τêι βολêι καὶ τôι δέμοι . . . ἀποδôναι τὸς ἑελλενοταμίας καὶ τὸς παρέδρος τοῖς ταμίαις τês θεό, . . . καὶ τὸς ταμίας τês θεοῦ πάλιν παραδôναι τοῖς ἑελλενοταμίαις καὶ τοῖς παρέδροις, τούτος δὲ δôναι στρατεγοῖς ἐπὶ Θράικες.

[3] *Ibid.* I³. 91 b, pp. 118 ff. ἐκ δὲ τôν φόρον κατατιθέναι κατὰ τὸν ἐνιαυτὸν τὰ ἑεκάστοτε περιόντα παρὰ τοῖς ταμίασι τôν τês Ἀθεναίας τὸς ἑλλενοταμίας.

war. Decrees ordering such loans could not be passed quite as easily as other measures; special permission of the people had to be asked in order to avoid the law which forbade orators to propose any decree tampering with the property of the goddess. But the necessary ἄδεια[1] was carried over and over again; so that the treasure of Athene could be considered as practically a reserve fund of the city.

All these peculiarities of Athenian fiscal administration are consequent on the main feature of Greek political life: the State was all-powerful as against the single citizen, but at the same time it was regarded not as a being separate from its live members, but as a complex of citizens (πλῆθος[2]), whose interests and rights are not differentiated from the interests of the "corporation." Hence, on the one hand, the use and abuse of political power for the satisfaction of personal needs and cravings; on the other hand, the ruthless exploitation of private property in the interests of the majority. One might almost say that with a slight change Bentham's idea of the aim of political union could be applied to this system; it was directed towards the greatest advantage of the greatest number of citizens.

2. The Rule of Law.

Apart from material profits, citizenship gave access to a highly privileged position in the legal domain. An Athenian citizen could claim rights which were refused to other classes of the population of Attika, and his legal standing corresponded in many ways to modern ideas of democratic freedom. The "rule of law" applied primarily to this privileged class.[3] *Personal security.*

The exercise by the magistrates of their powers as determined by law was carefully watched. The position of the magistrates was entirely different in Greece from what it was in Rome, where the magistrate's authority was based upon his *imperium*. In Greece, the principle was

---

[1] *Ibid.* 194.
[2] AR. *Pol.* III, 1, 12, 1275 b.   See above, p. 103.
[3] See DEMOSTHENES, XXIII.

rather to put the magistrates in such a position that they should always be subject to the superior authority of the community. We may take as an illustration of this view a passage from the speech of Lysias against the Corn-dealers. In this case certain persons were accused of having infringed the law forbidding any one to buy more than fifty measures of corn. The enactment was designed to prevent hoarding and monopoly. Referring to the policy of the law, Lysias describes one of the accused as having admitted that he bought more than the legal quantity, pleading, however, that it was at the bidding of the archons that he had done so. Then Lysias turning to the Court says: "If he shows that there is a law which bids corn-dealers buy up corn if the archons tell them to, acquit him; if not, justice demands condemnation. For we have put before you the law which forbids any one in the city to buy more than fifty measures of corn."[1]

On the other hand, the Roman rule as to appeal to the people, which provided the Roman citizen with a safeguard against any arbitrary action by a magistrate, cannot be said to have existed in that definite form in the Athens of the fifth century. It materialized, however, into a clear legal guarantee in connexion with a reform brought about by Eumelides at some date about 400 B.C. When a certain Lysimachos had been arrested and condemned to death by the Council, Eumelides rescued him, declaring that no citizen ought to be put to death without the verdict of a Court of law; a trial took place, and the Court acquitted Lysimachos. Thereupon a law was enacted providing that, in cases where the Council condemned or penalized a man, the Thesmothetae were to bring the verdicts and the penalties before the Courts, and whatever the Heliasts decided by their vote should stand.[2]

But the most usual means of keeping the magistrates in order was provided by the right of every citizen to attack and arraign a magistrate who had actually broken the law.

---

[1] Lys. XXII, 5, 6.

[2] *Ath. Const.* c. 45 ὁ δῆμος . . . νόμον ἔθετο ἄν τινος ἀδικεῖν ἡ βουλὴ καταγνῷ ἢ ζημιώσῃ, τὰς καταγνώσεις καὶ τὰς ἐπιζημιώσεις εἰσάγειν τοὺς θεσμοθέτας εἰς τὸ δικαστήριον, καὶ ὅ τι ἂν οἱ δικασταὶ ψηφίσωνται, τοῦτο κύριον εἶναι.

This was regarded as a most potent safeguard against abuses, although this rule certainly gave occasion for many unjust prosecutions by sykophants. In addition to this there were positive rules in Athens which imposed penalties upon magistrates for an improper use of their authority. Thus the archons were obliged to take an oath that they would not accept bribes or be guilty of any other form of corruption. The oath of the members of the Council of Five Hundred bound them not to imprison wantonly any Athenian citizen ;[1] they were obliged to allow bail on three securities. Now with regard to the oaths of the Council not to interfere with individual liberty, there is a curious contradiction in our authorities. Aristotle in the *Athenian Constitution*[2] tells us of the action of a certain Archinos, a leader of the restored democracy, who persuaded the Council to put to death without trial a citizen whom he suspected of treasonable designs. Aristotle makes much of this as a most important fact, for by it, he says, a large number of people were undoubtedly deterred from conspiracy.[3] It seems clear that the βουλή took upon itself the duties of the ἐκκλησία. In the fifth century such discretionary power undoubtedly existed, and in a time of political agitation an act of State of this kind might be resorted to, and certainly was sometimes used by the Areiopagos, or at a later time by the Five Hundred. It broke down, however, after the restoration of democracy ; and when the liberty of the individual is absolutely safeguarded, the rule of law is practically complete.

How could this rule of law be made effective ? We have seen already that the right of private citizens to prosecute offending officers kept the government within due limits. This right of accusation is one of the fundamental principles of the Athenian constitution, though it is difficult from the extant materials to put together a clear statement of the rules which governed it. But it is apparent throughout the whole Greek system that its importance was enormous.

Enforcement of legality.

---

[1] DEM. XXIV. 144.
[2] *Ath. Const.* c. 40.
[3] See the case of Lysimachos, p. 114 above, and a study by P. CLOCHÉ in the *Revue des études grecques*, XXXIII.

Hence it was sometimes said that the principal reform of Solon consisted in the fact that he gave every
citizen the right to take up the cause of a fellow-citizen
and help him to obtain justice. The following passage
from the speech of Hypereides for Euxenippos deserves
attention:[1] "Among the many splendid arrangements
that exist in the city, what is there better or more popular
(democratic) than the fact that, whenever a private person
standing trial and danger is unable to speak in his own
defence, any one of his fellow-citizens can if he likes come
forward to help him and instruct the jury as to the rights
of his case." Now what is said here with regard to the

Right of political accusation. defence of the weak by the strong applies, of course, as
much when an accusation is to be brought as when a de-
fence is to be maintained. The right of accusation, in
spite of all its defects and disadvantages, undoubtedly was
one of the greatest bulwarks of the constitution. In the
speech of Lykurgos against Leokrates the orator speaks of
the different elements of an action at law.[2] They are:
(1) the parties to the suit, (2) the law, (3) the judge. The
law must lay down what is allowable within the limits of
the action to be tried, the judges must find out whether the
acts put in issue are within the scope of the law; but neither
the one nor the other is of any avail unless somebody is
ready to come forward as an accuser and to deliver the
delinquent for judgement to the sovereign people. The
power of accusation was more than a mere private right.
Its essence was that it was political, and its value consisted
in the meting out of punishment to those who had violated
a law or exceeded their duty.

3. *The Privileges of Citizens.*

'Ελευθερία.   The status of a citizen assumed a particular importance
from the point of view of the close connexion between State
and individual interests; ἐλευθερία as a basis of citizenship
was a privilege in itself, inasmuch as it ensured a share in
the rights of the ruling class towering over a body of sub-

---

[1] Hyp. IV (III), 11.
[2] Lyk., *op. cit.*, 4.

jects.[1] The juridical inferences are well illustrated by the
history of citizenship in Athens. We need not trace the
process of its development further than the reforms of
Kleisthenes, which broke the political power of the ancient
clans. This crisis introduced a number of freedmen and
foreigners into the precincts of Athenian citizenship.[2] Pros-
perous democracy, however, took care to narrow the limits
of the conception.

The legal conditions of citizenship are very clearly set
down in cases when the right of citizenship was acquired
not by birth, but by a grant of the people. Such grants
were made on special occasions, and exact information about
them has been preserved in many inscriptions. They conferred the full right of taking part in all matters human and
divine—μετέχειν ἀνθρωπίνων καὶ θείων (ὁσίων). This meant
that the recipient acquired a position within the circle of the
ruling class, was eligible to offices, and was admitted to the
cults of the State religion. One of the first decrees of this
kind preserved for us—the inscription of Chaladria [3]—gives
the new citizen access to political office by describing him
as Ϝισοπρόξενος καὶ Ϝισοδαμιοργός. The inscription is interesting also inasmuch as it shows that the addition of ἴσος
to the notion of πολιτεία did not imply any special form of
grant of citizenship. Originally ἰσοπολιτεία and plain
πολιτεία are equivalent terms, and it is only gradually that
the idea of reciprocity between two States is brought into the
connotation of the term ἰσοπολιτεία.[4] One important consequence of the full admission to political rights by naturalization consists in the fact that the Greeks had no objection
to the cumulation of several citizenships in one person. In
this way they were less exclusive than the Romans.[5]

Such arrangements of συμπολιτεία shaded off gradually

*Ἰσοπολι-
τεία.*

*Συμπολι-
τεία.*

[1] AR. *Pol.* I, 2, 1252 a, on τὸ ἄρχον καὶ τὸ ἀρχόμενον.   See above,
p. 13.

[2] *Ibid.*, III, 2, 1275 b οἷον Ἀθήνησιν ἐποίησε Κλεισθένης μετὰ τὴν τῶν
τυράννων ἐκβολήν· πολλοὺς γὰρ ἐφυλέτευσε ξένους καὶ δούλους μετοίκους.

[3] MICHEL, 194, p. 179 ῾Α Ϝράτρα τοῖρ Χαλαδρίοιρ : καὶ Δευκαλίονι :
Χαλάδριον ἔμεν αὐτὸν καὶ γόνον : Ϝισοπρόξενον, Ϝισοδαμιοργόν : τὰν δὲ γᾶν
ἔχεν τὰν ἐν Πίσαι . . . Ϝισοπρόξενος is not taken in the sense of honorary
guest, but in that of a magistrate.

[4] SZANTO, *Griech. Bürgerrecht*, pp.67 ff.

[5] MICHEL, 285. *I. J. G.* I, xi, p. 180 ff.

into cases where the individuality of one of the States was merged into that of the other; in other words συμπολιτεία and συνοικισμός are connected by a variety of transitions. An interesting case is shown in the inscription recording the treaty of friendship made at the desire of King Seleukos between Smyrna and Magnesia about the middle of the third century B.C.[1] "The Smyrnaeans gave citizenship (πολιτείαν) to the dwellers in Magnesia ... The Magnesians shall share as citizens with the Smyrnaeans according to the laws of the city, without faction, having the same friends and enemies as the Smyrnaeans... To the dwellers in Magnesia citizenship in Smyrna to be given on the same terms as to the other citizens; and in like manner citizenship to be given to the rest of those dwelling in Magnesia who are of free birth and Hellenic race." A special case arose when a definite political tie was kept up between a metropolis and its colonies. In all cases religious intercourse was continued; we have evidence in regard to that in the inscription relating to the foundation of Brea by the Athenians,[2] and as regards the relations between Korinth and its colonies.[3]

These relations established by treaties form, as it were, a step towards the formation of federal governments, which are in Greece based on a wide autonomy of the component members and on their alliance for certain specified objects connected mainly with defence. It is well known that such federal governments came to play a very important part during the Hellenistic period, when single cities were in most cases too weak to maintain their political independence. But rudimentary forms of federation occurred already in earlier times. The best example is presented by the Boiotian League referred to by Thukydides.[4] He describes how the Boiotarchs planned an alliance with

---

[1] MICHEL, 19, p. 16 πολιτεύσονται δὲ μετὰ Σμυρναίων κατὰ τοὺς τῆς πόλεως νόμους ἀστασιάστως τὸν αὐτὸν ἐχθρὸν καὶ φίλον ἡγούμενοι Σμυρναίοις ... Δεδόσθαι δε τοῖς ἐμ Μαγνεσίαι κατοίκοις ... πολιτείαν ἐν Σμύρνηι ἐφ' ἴσηι καὶ ὁμοίαι τοῖς ἄλλοις πολίταις· ὁμοίως δὲ δεδόσθαι τὴμ πολιτείαν καὶ τοῖς ἄλλοις τοῖς οἰκοῦσιν ἐμ Μαγνησίαι ὅσοι ἂν ὦσιν ἐλεύθεροί τε καὶ Ἕλληνες. (HICKS, 176.)

[2] MICHEL, 72. HICKS, 29.

[3] GILBERT, *Staatsaltertümer*, II, p. 87.   [4] V. 38.

certain other cities and "communicated their intentions to the Four Councils of the Boiotians, whose sanction is always necessary."

4. *Societies and Unions.*

In considering the general relation between the State and the citizen we come across a problem of capital importance as regards the existence and the political treatment of intermediate combinations between individuals. There are cases when such combinations are prohibited, as for instance in France after the Revolution of 1789; in other cases social combinations are allowed on condition of an express recognition by the State, as in Rome; in yet another group of instances a marked juridical difference is made between various forms of societies, and special privileges are attached to corporations authorized by the State, as in English law. There are, lastly, examples of complete freedom as regards the formation of societies. This last category is represented by Greek jurisprudence.

It is true that at first glance our principal guide, Aristotle, appears to connect associations of all kinds with the State. We read in the *Ethics*,[1] "All associations appear to be parts of the political association." But it is evident on closer consideration that the philosopher did not want to lay down any rule as to the influence of the city on the formation, prohibition, or supervision of associations. The examples which he mentions in the same chapter,[2] and his way of grouping them according to aims, show conclusively that he is thinking primarily of voluntary associations. He cites partners of a shipping concern (πλωτῆρες) and soldiers (of fortune) who join in a military expedition; he contrasts companies formed for the sake of obtaining profits with societies which aim at pleasant pastimes in connexion with

Freedom of combines.

---

[1] *Eth. N.* VIII, ix, 1160 a, 28 πᾶσαι δὴ φαίνονται κοινωνίαι μόρια τῆς πολιτικῆς (κοινωνίας) εἶναι.

[2] *Ibid.* 1160 a, 14 ff. αἱ μὲν οὖν ἄλλαι κοινωνίαι κατὰ μέρη τοῦ συμφέροντος ἐφίενται, οἷον πλωτῆρες . . . συστρατιῶται . . . ὁμοίως δὲ καὶ φυλέται καὶ δημόται· ἔνιαι δὲ τῶν κοινωνιῶν δι' ἡδονὴν δοκοῦσι γίνεσθαι, θιασωτῶν καὶ ἐρανιστῶν. αὗται γὰρ θυσίας ἕνεκα καὶ συνουσίας.

sacrifices and common meals. His remark that all (private)
associations are part of the general political one is therefore
significant in so far as it shows that he did not make a distinction in principle between ties of friendship, common
interest, and social intercourse on the one hand, and the ties
of political union on the other. All these varieties were
considered by him from the point of view of the natural
tendency of men, acting as social beings (ζῷα πολιτικά) to
form combinations of various kinds and various degrees of
cohesion between their members. Thus, while he did not
pay attention to the contrast between temporary enter-
prises and associations for permanent ends, he laid stress
on the *reality* of all social combinations, from the lowest
to the highest, and traced them all to the political, or
rather social, tendency of human nature.

This general view is confirmed and developed on all
points by a consideration of the actual facts of Greek law.
To begin with, we have the rare advantage in this case of
possessing the text of a law by which Solon regulated the
relation between societies and their members. It has been
preserved in a fragment of Gaius inserted in the *Digest*.[1]
ἐὰν δὲ δῆμος ἢ φράτορες ἢ ἱερῶν ὀργίων ἢ ναῦται ἢ σύσσιτοι
ἢ ὁμόταφοι ἢ θιασῶται ἢ ἐπὶ λείαν οἰχόμενοι ἢ εἰς ἐμπορίαν,
ὅτι ἂν τούτων διαθῶνται πρὸς ἀλλήλους, κύριον εἶναι, ἐὰν
μὴ ἀπαγορεύσῃ δημόσια γράμματα. There are minor doubts
as to one or two points of the enumeration, but they have
no material importance for us. The general tenor of the
enactment is perfectly clear. The law of Athens, as stated
on one of Solon's ἄξονες, allowed all kinds of associations
to make rules or by-laws for their members provided that
these did not clash with existing laws of the State. The
enumeration of the societies is perhaps the most characteristic feature of the text. By the side of partnerships and
companies formed for the sake of trade (εἰς ἐμπορίαν) and
for the sake of privateering (ἐπὶ λείαν) stand sailors (ναῦται)
and associations for common meals (σύσσιτοι), and for the
use of common burial grounds (ὁμόταφοι), adepts of religious
societies (ὀργεῶνες, θιασῶται), and at the top of the list

---

[1] *Digest*, XLVII, 22, 4 Haec lex videtur ex lege Solonis tralata esse,
nam illuc ita est (GAIUS, *libro quarto ad legem duodecim tabularum*).

members of phratries and demes. In other words, no distinction is made in respect of the power to make decrees
obligatory for members between purely voluntary associations for temporary ends, societies whose object is the
satisfaction of some end permanent or at any rate enduring,
and, lastly, recognized subdivisions of the city. This does
not mean, of course, that there were no differences in fact
between these various species, but from a legal point of
view no sharp distinctions were drawn, and all varieties of
social combination were left to shift freely for themselves.

The next question to be examined concerns the distinction Moral
between casual combines and permanent unions. Even persons.
apart from State interference the juridical consequences of
these two kinds of associations are bound to be different,
but the contrast between them may be either strongly
insisted upon or, on the contrary, disguised by gradual
transitions. The latter was decidedly the case in Greece.
Apart from the way in which various combines are mixed
up both in Solon's law and in Aristotle's description, in
every group of associations mere partnerships pass over
imperceptibly into companies and into permanent unions.
A striking example is presented by the peculiar form of
combines termed ἔρανοι. The word is used to designate
the relations arising from a "friendly" loan—both between
the creditors and the debtor and between the creditors who
had contributed to raise the loan. The capital of the loan
seems as a rule to have been the result of a collection, and
no interest was charged on it, although conditions as to
liability and terms of repayment were stipulated as in the
case an ordinary loan. The wide extent of such transactions in ancient Greece seems to have been connected
with the frequent occasions when relatives and friends had
to render assistance in case of sudden misfortune, for instance, for raising a ransom, paying a heavy fine, &c. In
any case such ἔρανοι were obviously casual arrangements,
all traces of which disappeared on payment of the debt.[1]
And yet the same term ἔρανος is used currently for durable
associations formed with a view to common pastimes and

[1] LIPSIUS, *Attisches Recht und Rechtsverfahren*, 730 ff.

social intercourse. We may translate it "club" if we only keep in mind that most of these friendly circles were very small, consisting of a score of people who met on certain days to dine together and to offer certain sacrifices. Our dining and reading clubs are the nearest parallel to these associations. In this case the aim was neither casual nor transient, but, on the contrary, tended towards permanency. Thus the constitutive elements of a "moral person" were clearly at hand, and in a great number of instances a material basis was provided for the continuous existence of the "corporation" by the gift or the acquisition of a house, some land, the building of a shrine, &c.[1] The frequency and importance of this kind of social combination is attested by the fact that trials arising out of relations between members of ἔρανοι as well as between these corporations and outsiders (δίκαι ἐρανικαί) formed a special category ranged together with δίκαι κοινωνικαί, and were treated as commercial cases by summary procedure, so that the case had to come up before the Court in the course of a month after its inception.[2] I have called attention to this remarkable instance of affinity between a contractual transaction, a form of partnership, and a club because it throws a strong light on the gradual transition in Greek law from occasional association to the enduring life of moral persons. The element of super-individual personality is represented even more clearly in another class of association, namely in societies formed for the purpose of religious worship or, at any rate, for occupations connected with some cult. Our earliest recorded instances of corporative bodies in Greece belong to this class and, far from shrinking in course of time, they develop profusely in all directions. The corporation of ὀργεῶνες founded by Amynos in Attika in the fourth century B.C.,[3] the society founded by Epikteta in Thera[4] (end of third century B.C.), the θίασος of Poseidonios,[5] are remarkable instances of these religious corporations. The

---

[1] LIPSIUS, 770 ff.

[2] AR. *Ath. Const.* 52, 5.

[3] KOERTE, *Mitteilungen des deutschen archäologischen Instituts*, XXI, 1896, referred to by F. POLAND, *Gesch. des gr. Vereins*.

[4] *C. I. G.* 2448 (MICHEL, 1001).   [5] DITT. *Syll.*³, III, 1044.

story of the Epikteta foundation is known in detail from
a statute which has been preserved until our time. A
citizen of Thera, Phoinix, bequeathed land and a certain
capital to his widow, Epikteta, for the purpose of erecting
a shrine to the memory of their deceased son, on condition
that both he and the boy should be worshipped as heroes
at that shrine together with the nine Muses. Epikteta
added further funds of her own to the bequest, and founded
a society of worshippers composed originally of the relatives
with their wives and children, of husbands of married
daughters who had inherited property in their own right,
and of a few affiliated persons. In the act of foundation
she provided that she herself and her daughter should
enjoy the worship of the members of the corporation after
their death. In this way the family of Phoinix and of
Epikteta was raised to a semi-divine position as heroes to
be worshipped at the shrine of the Muses.

In this case and in many analogous ones the super-
individual element of corporative existence is provided
not by abstraction from the rights and liabilities of the
members, but by personification in the concrete form of
hero-worship. Phoinix and Epikteta continue to live in
their foundation, and their will remains active in the influence it exerts through the organization created in the
original statute. The statute of Epikteta is significant in
yet another direction: while it provides for the settlement
of all important questions by votes of the majority, it
forbids expressly any decision for dissolving the community.[1]
This means, of course, that the founders intended their
corporation to last for ever. And this is no singularity
on the part of the Epikteta document. Poland has rightly
drawn attention to the fact that the innumerable inscriptions treating of corporative arrangements never mention
the possibility of dissolution, which occurs constantly in
the statutes of modern companies of all kinds. As he

---

[1] ZIEBARTH thought that dissolution was possible in the abstract,
but rendered difficult by the prohibition of any proposal to that effect.
The matter is simpler, as $\pi\lambda|a|\nu$ has to be inserted between the two
clauses. See F. POLAND, *Geschichte des griechischen Vereinswesens*,
p. 275.

remarks, the Greeks who founded a shrine or a festival and a society connected with it never contemplated the possibility of its disappearance. It was to be alive for centuries (αἰώνιον) like the deity to which it was dedicated. It may be said that although moral persons were born of individual consent, they lived a real and concrete life for which the worship of a deity provided the spiritual tie. In this they were similar to the City which they imitated in their organization.

Organiza-
tion.

The link between the city and private associations was in Athens supplied by the tribal and local subdivisions, the phratries and the demes. They were officially recognized bodies of historical origin and at the same time they were considered in law to be a variety of the general class of associations. They were governed by assemblies and by elected magistrates—demarchs, phratriarchs, and subordinate employees. Apart from the γένη which represented the primordial nuclei of the tribal system of Attika, the component parts of the phratry were the *thiasoi*, or religious circles formed by what may be called the plebeian portion of the citizen class. They are called ὀργεῶνες on certain occasions, and there is no reason to doubt that the two designations—ὀργεών and θιασώτης—correspond to each other in the social terminology of Athens at least in the period between the sixth and the fourth centuries inclusive.[1] In these minor corporations government was also in the hands of assemblies of members and of elected magistrates. In connexion with the prominent part played by the religious element priests appear with a leading rôle. Altogether sacerdotal representatives of the organizations are more frequently mentioned in the inscriptions than purely civil or lay magistrates. The latter, however, are also mentioned as ἀρχερανισταί, ταμίαι, &c. In societies formed by women or for the worship of a female deity like the Meter in Athens, or Artemis, priestesses assumed important functions and exercised considerable influence.[2]

---

[1] ZIEBARTH, 33 ff.; cf., however, POLAND, *op. cit.*, 13 ff.
[2] POLAND, 290 f.

By-laws and regulations were made by the general body of members as νόμοι (sometimes ψηφίσματα). The assembly which makes them and also elects the magistrates and priests is called ἀγορά, even when it is composed only of a dozen or a score of members. On entering the corporation new members have to swear an oath which binds them to be faithful to the community and to obey its decrees.[1] Discipline was maintained in the societies by conventional fines: every infringement of the by-laws and rules was to be followed by the payment of a certain sum according to an established tariff. In extreme cases the culprit was excluded from the community. The enforcement of the payment was sometimes brought about by private execution (πρᾶξις, πράττειν) agreed upon in advance, but in the last resort the union might have recourse to the help of the city, and some of the ἐρανικαὶ δίκαι mentioned by Aristotle must have arisen from disputes as to fines and executive measures exercised by the corporations. Before matters came to this, however, influential unions tried cases in their own courts, as we may gather, for instance, from an interesting fragment informing us of a case in which the union of the Εἰκαδεῖς had tried certain members who had broken the oath of fidelity to the community by siding with its adversaries in a public suit and giving testimony against the corporation.[2] Apart from decisions of the tribunals of the city in the course of regular litigation, there was no interference of the State in the affairs of unions or corporations; as already indicated by Solon's laws, these affairs were considered as the results of voluntary agreement. A decree of the deme of Peiraieus has sometimes been cited in proof of the view that a deme could occasionally regulate and forbid the formation of new *religious* associations (θίασοι).[3] The decree in question need not, however, be interpreted in this manner. It does not express a general prohibition,

---

[1] ZIEBARTH, *op. cit.*, 141 f.
[2] *C. I. A.* II, 609 (324–323 B.C.) ἐπειδή τινες ἐναντίον τῷ ὅρκῳ ὃν ὤμοσαν . . . διατελοῦσι πράττοντες καὶ λέγοντες κατὰ Εἰκαδέων ἐπὶ βλάβει τῶν κοινῶν κτλ.
[3] *C. I. A.* II. 573 b. Cf. ZIEBARTH, *op. cit.*, 167 f.

but is directed against possible encroachments of private associations on the precincts of a temple belonging to the deme.

As members of the various combines we find in the earlier epoch (up to the third century B.C.) almost exclusively citizens. The opinion of Foucart,[1] one of the pioneers of the study of Greek associations, that the development started from the intrusion of foreign cults has been contested by Poland on the strength of an exhaustive study of the inscriptions. The oldest examples, like that of the Amynos *Orgeones*, testify indeed to religious motives in the formation of Colleges, but these motives are connected in Athens with the social reforms of the closing sixth century, leading to the recognition of new clusters of citizens gathered round traditional local cults similar to those of the *Lares compitales* in Rome.[2] The earliest appearances in Athens of a foreign cult and of a union connected with it is that of the Thracian goddess Bendis in the fifth century B.C. Later on foreigners appear chiefly as members of religious associations of a mystic character. Women are also mentioned only exceptionally in the older inscriptions; they appear naturally as members of cult-associations for the worship of female goddesses, but also in societies developing out of family relations. Slaves and freedmen appear very rarely in the early records; the most conspicuous instance is that of worshippers of *Men* which can be traced up to the third century. In *thiasoi* and *eranoi* with predominating citizen membership isolated slaves appear among the free, but these belong chiefly to the class of δημόσιοι, public slaves, who occupied an altogether privileged position, being independent of arbitrary control by private persons, and frequently holding important posts in the bureaucratic organization of the city. If I had to consider not only the classical, but also the Hellenistic period, I should have had to describe the remarkable growth of all sorts of combinations running across the established subdivisions and customary rules of city-organization. To mention only one point: in the

---

[1] *Des associations religieuses chez les Grecs*, 20 ff.
[2] POLAND, *op. cit.*, 515.

unions of the Pythagoreans and of Dionysiac artists the
combines stretched wide across the frontiers of States and
created international associations with authorities which
could not be derived from any single city nor subjected
to the law of any.   But these developments fall, as Poland
has rightly remarked, into a period when the city principle
was giving way and the Greeks were seeking new channels
for the satisfaction of their material and spiritual interests.
The facts of this momentous process lie beyond the scope
of the present work.   They have been to a great extent
collected and sifted in the excellent monographs of Ziebarth
and Poland.   Before concluding, I should, however, like to
formulate a protest against Poland's general contention
that the activity of associations was much restricted in
the time before Alexander the Great.[1]   It is true that we
do not possess anything like the profusion of documentary
material which confronts us for the third and subsequent
centuries, but it is impossible, I think, to make inscriptions
the exclusive test of the importance of a social development.   The clear statement of the law of Solon, the references given by Aristotle, and the use of special procedure
in trials of δίκαι κοινωνικαί and ἐρανικαί testify sufficiently
that already in the sixth, fifth, and fourth centuries social
combines were of common occurrence, and gave rise to
a considerable amount of litigation.   It is probable that
in many cases these combines would have turned out under
closer inspection to be more akin to the type of voluntary
association (*societas*) than to that of the corporation.   But
the latter variety was certainly represented not only
by tribal and local subdivisions (phratries and demes) but
also by the various religious bodies known as ὀργεῶνες and
θίασοι.   Altogether, although the Hellenistic epoch contributed powerfully to the diffusion and development of
unions and corporations, it did not introduce any new
principle in the law as shaped by city jurisprudence.   The
Greek "moral and juridical person" had reflected and continued to reflect the religious or quasi-religious personification of the social side of human life.

[1] See e.g. HEROD. V, 57, 61, 66.

CHAPTER VII

THE LAW OF THE CONSTITUTION

1. *The Deliberative Functions of the People.*

Division
of func-
tions.

In considering the fundamental principles of constitutional law in a democratic State, let us, to begin with,
notice a rather important difference between our own
current notions of the function of the State and those of
the Greeks. Our usual way of treating the subject is to
oppose three elements which since the time of Montesquieu
have been accepted as the factors of political life, *viz.* the
legislative, the judiciary, and the executive powers. For
purposes of convenience this is a good working classification,
but we must not lose sight of the fact that according to
Greek democratic thought supreme power was not distributed in equal shares between these three functions. The
Greeks regarded the ἀρχαί—the magistrates or the executive—as definite organs of the commonwealth, but they sub-
ordinated them to the people assembled for discussion and
decision. Thus supreme power did not really present three
aspects; it was twofold : (1) τὸ βουλευόμενον, the deliberative
aspect, and (2) τὸ δικάζον, the judicial.[1] One may go further
and say that even this twofold division is made only for
practical purposes; it is a division of functions, not of
powers. The latter would imply an opposition of forces,
whereas a division of functions only means that the same
body acts sometimes in one way and for certain purposes,
and sometimes in another way and for other purposes ; no
checks are intended by such a division.

This observation supplies the clue to the organization of

---

[1] Cf Ar. *Pol.* VI (IV), 14, 1298 a ἐν μὲν τί τὸ βουλευόμενον περὶ τῶν
κοινῶν, δεύτερον δὲ τὸ περὶ τὰς ἀρχάς, . . . τρίτον δὲ τί τὸ δικάζον. κύριον
δ᾽ ἐστὶ τὸ βουλευόμενον περὶ πολέμου καὶ εἰρήνης καὶ συμμαχίας καὶ διαλύσεως,
καὶ περὶ νόμων, καὶ περὶ θανάτου καὶ φυγῆς καὶ δημεύσεως, καὶ παρὶ ἀρχῶν
αἱρέσεως καὶ τῶν εὐθυνῶν. Cf. VIII (VI), 1, § 1, 1316 b. Cf. Hildenbrand, *Gesch. der Rechtsphil.* I, 464.

power in a Greek democratic State. Let us see how the deliberative function materialized at Athens for purposes of legislation. In the passage of the *Politics* referred to above [1] (1298 a) legislation is ascribed to the deliberative element (i. e. to the Assembly in conjunction with the Council). It is usually supposed that legislation belongs to the Heliaea, the δικασταί. This is true, however, only of one period, and of this only with certain reservations; the right of the dikasts was not really judicial in this case, though it assumed the forms of judicial procedure.

Before examining this question in detail, let us look at the various subjects which may come under the head of legislation. We find three groups: legal rules and enactments are described as θεσμοί, νόμοι, and ψηφίσματα. The difference between θεσμός and νόμος is one of epoch; [2] θεσμός belongs to the archaic period and does not occur in the age of Perikles or that of Demosthenes; Drakon was a θεσμοθέτης. The distinction is connected with the fact that θεσμός is a statement or declaration of customary law; customary law is *laid down*. The term was preserved in the title of the six minor archons, the θεσμοθέται. Their old legislative function gradually disappeared, and gave place to the judicial, but they were originally magistrates formulating law as well as enforcing it.

Classification of enactments.

Two forms persisted in the classical period, νόμος and ψήφισμα. This is a fundamental division not difficult to understand, as it is an equivalent to our own opposition between statute and decree. A statutory law is a general rule, and this is just what Aristotle says about νόμος—that it deals with τὰ καθόλου. A decree (ψήφισμα) is a rule or order laid down for a particular occasion, and may apply to definite persons or objects. This distinction seems indisputable: it is clearly indicated by Aristotle in the well-known passage in the fourth book of the *Politics* where he

---

[1] Page foregoing.
[2] Cf. above, pp. 74 f. Prof. J. A. Smith calls my attention to the fact that in Solon's Elegy quoted by Aristotle in *Ath. Const.* c. 12, l. 42–47, the terms νόμος and θεσμός are used one after the other, and the latter refers seemingly to rules of procedure. It would be hardly appropriate, however, to infer from this that νόμος stands in that passage for substantive law. It is opposed to βία, and points to law in contrast with violence or oppression.

is contrasting the legislation of normal and of degenerate democracies.[1] A democracy, he says, which forms general rules is normal and healthy, but there may come a time when a democracy ceases to take itself seriously,—trifles with the situation and legislates by decree. In this case a democracy is like a tyranny in that it acts arbitrarily, and its decrees (ψηφίσματα) are like the ukases (ἐπιτάγματα) of a despot. Aristotle refers to the same distinction in the Ethics.[2]

Objection has been raised to this general description: some modern writers[3] think that it is impossible to trace this opposition in the text; the distinction beween the two kinds is declared to be uncertain and fluid. We have a number of laws of the fifth century, passed (as these writers suppose) by ψήφισμα, e. g. the law of Ephialtes abolishing the rights of the Areiopagos was passed by the Assembly as a decree. The law establishing ostracism is regarded as the outcome of a decree and not of the ordinary procedure of legislation. But these instances are not convincing: we do not know in detail how these laws were passed, and if we did we might find that certain legislative forms were observed which would range them in the group of statutes. The decisive consideration for us in this matter is that it would be strange if a writer of the standing and qualifications of Aristotle should have fallen into a fundamental misconception. We may grant that he puts it down too dogmatically and does not allow sufficiently for the overlapping of boundaries and for intermediate links. The distinction was not so clearly realized in earlier times as it was in the fourth century, when political thought had been sharpened by analysis, but the general opposition between law and decree is a matter of common reasoning; and, what is more, the complicated process

---

[1] *Pol.* VI (IV), 4, 1292 a 15 ὁ δ' οὖν τοιοῦτος δῆμος, ἅτε μόναρχος ὤν, ζητεῖ μοναρχεῖν διὰ τὸ μὴ ἄρχεσθαι ὑπὸ νόμου, καὶ γίνεται δεσποτικός, . . . καὶ ἔστιν ὁ τοιοῦτος δῆμος ἀνάλογον τῶν μοναρχιῶν τῇ τυραννίδι. διὸ καὶ τὸ ἦθος τὸ αὐτό, καὶ ἄμφω δεσποτικὰ τῶν βελτιόνων, καὶ τὰ ψηφίσματα ὥσπερ ἐκεῖ τὰ ἐπιτάγματα.

[2] *Eth. Nik.* V, x, 1137 b ὁ μεν νόμος καθόλου πᾶς.

[3] B. KEIL in GERCKE und NORDEN, *Einleitung*, p. 351   Cf SWOBODA in K. F. HERMANN'S *Lehrbuch der griechischen Antiquitäten* III Th. (6te Aufl.), 122 f.

of νομοθεσία was certainly not introduced at random—it was a deliberate attempt on the part of the leaders of democracy to prevent hasty and contradictory legislation. If any corroboration were needed of Aristotle's remark that in bad democracies there was a tendency to confuse the two kinds of rule, it might be found in Demosthenes' speech against Leptines, where the orator says that the Athenians mixed up laws and decrees, and ceased to maintain even the general principle that laws should not be contradictory.[1]

A second rule to be noticed in this connexion is the requirement that no law should be made concerning single persons; if νόμος means a general rule, νόμος ἐπ' ἀνδρί is a contradiction in terms. But there were cases when the people had to exercise power in order to confer a privilege. Thus it is possible to make exceptionally a ψήφισμα ἐπ' ἀνδρί; the matter was, however, enacted in a manner different from ordinary legislation. A special assembly of not less than 6,000 was required, as in the case of ostracism, which was another special form of νόμος ἐπ' ἀνδρί. This constituted a guarantee against misuse.

In two other typical cases privileges may be conceded: for grants of citizenship the same procedure was employed, and again in the case where the people decided to liberate an intending legislator from a prohibition to legislate on some matter: this prohibition was added for the purpose of keeping law immutable. If changes, however, were considered necessary, an immunity (ἄδεια) was asked for and often granted.

How was legislation carried out, and what guarantee was there that the established views would be maintained in practice? What was done in Athens to keep the sovereign people within the bounds of legality? There being no appeal to any court of higher instance, certain forms were devised with a view of restricting its action.

The people was deprived of the initiative [2] in legislation;

Initiative in legislation.

---

[1] DEMOSTHENES, XX, 92, ψηφισμάτων δ' οὐδ' ὁτιοῦν διαφέρουσιν οἱ νόμοι ἀλλὰ νεώτεροι οἱ νόμοι καθ' οὓς τὰ ψηφίσματα δεῖ γράφεσθαι, τῶν ψηφισμάτων αὐτῶν ὑμῖν εἰσίν.
[2] HERMANN SWOBODA, III, 116.

it was supreme as to the decision, but impotent for initiation. For the latter purpose a preliminary draft (προβούλευμα) had to be received. This was necessary, indeed, because a large assembly had to start discussion from something definite. No law could be proposed without the προβούλευμα of the Council; no one but a citizen could attend the meeting; no one but a citizen could speak in the Assembly; and only a limited number of qualified persons could address it; only responsible men had the right *agere cum populo*. The Council (βουλή) must draw up the proposal, the generals (στρατηγοί) could summon an Assembly in addition to the ordinary ones which were fixed. Thus there could be no surprises.[1]

There is an additional point to be considered : when the people later on began to chafe at these restrictions, it found ways for circumventing them. The power of proposing amendment to bills was very wide ; an amendment might be quite opposed to the proposal made. We have an instance of this recorded in Plutarch's life of Perikles [2]; Perikles was attacked by his political enemies, who required him to produce his accounts. The original demand was drawn up by one Drakontides in a προβούλευμα giving Perikles the opportunity to vindicate his conduct. The proposal was that he should present his accounts to the Prytaneis (Πρυτανεῖς), and they should give judgement on oath. Hagnon entirely altered the proposal by introducing a general charge : Perikles should be judged by the usual tribunal, and the accusation should be for embezzlement and bribery, or for illegal practices. Thus the amendment went directly against the sense of the original προβούλευμα; material changes of the original proposals were, altogether, by no means an uncommon occurrence.[3] The result was greater elasticity and a good deal of confusion.

[1] AR. *Ath. Const.* 44, 45.

[2] PLUTARCH, *Perikles*, 32 Ἅγνων δὲ τοῦτο μὲν ἀφεῖλε τοῦ ψηφίσματος, κρίνεσθαι δὲ τὴν δίκην ἔγραψεν ἐν δικασταῖς χιλίοις καὶ πεντακοσίοις, εἴτε κλοπῆς καὶ δώρων εἴτ' ἀδικίου βούλοιτό τις ὀνομάζειν τὴν δίωξιν.

[3] Cf. DITT. *Syll.* I³. 64, ll. 70 ff. Ἀρχέστρατος εἶπε· τὰ μὲν ἄλλα καθάπερ Ἀντικλῆς· τὰς δὲ εὐθύνας Χαλκιδεῦσι κατὰ σφῶν αὐτὸν ἔναι ἐν Χαλκίδι καθάπερ Ἀθένεσιν Ἀθηναίοις, πλὲν φυγῆς καὶ θανάτο καὶ ἀτιμίας· περὶ δὲ τούτον ἔφεσιν ἔναι Ἀθέναζε ἐς τὲν ἐλιαίαν τὲν τὸν θεσμοθετῶν κατὰ τὸ ψέφισμα τῶ δήμο. περὶ δὲ φυλακῆς Εὐβοίας τὸς στρατεγὸς ἐπιμελέσθαι hος ἂν δύνωνται ἄριστα, hόπος ἂν ἔχει hος βέλτιστα Ἀθηναίοις. Cf. *ibid.* 116, ll. 33 ff

Any orator who made a proposal to the People was Responsibility for legislation.
responsible for the success or failure of the proposed line
of action. The People might act foolishly under stress of
passion, and afterwards repent and vent their rage on the
orator. This happened, for instance, after the battle of
Arginusae : the People regretted their action in condemning
the generals, and passed a decree that those who had
deceived the Demos should be subjected to a prejudicial
trial (προβολή), and then should be tried before the Courts.[1]
They were accused and condemned, and one of their
number, Kallixenos, who fled, but afterwards returned to
Athens, eventually died of starvation. Thus the People
might charge those whose proposals it had accepted, and
refuse to assume the responsibility for its own decisions.
Similarly in the case of the γραφὴ παρανόμων, impeachment
for illegal proposals, if a mistake was made it was the
proposer who was deemed guilty, not the People who had
passed the law. Under normal circumstances strict rules
were followed; in order to avoid surprises the various
assemblies of the Prytanies had to treat fixed subjects :
e.g. the first assembly of the first Prytany had to hold the
ἐπιχειροτονία τῶν νόμων, the first of the sixth had to deal
with the responsibility of officers, etc.

The process of legislation assumed about 450 B.C. a very Νομοθεσία.
peculiar and intricate character, presenting a great contrast
to our own system.[2] A person wishing to introduce a new
law had first to obtain permission to submit a bill in the
first Assembly of the first Prytany of the year. If this
were approved, the proposal took a more definite form ;
certain of the old laws were criticized as obsolete or otherwise defective, and the bill embodying the proposed changes
was posted up in the market-place. Then followed a discussion in the fourth Assembly of the first Prytany as to
whether definite schemes should be presented to the Courts.
If the decision was in the affirmative, advocates (συνήγοροι)
were appointed to defend the old law against the accusations brought forward by the author of the new project.

---

[1] XEN. *Hell.* I, 7. See below, p. 151.
[2] SCHOEMANN-LIPSIUS, I, pp. 415 ff.

A judicial commission of νομοθέται had to decide whether the old law was to be abrogated; all existing measures contradictory of the proposed new law had to be annulled before the latter could be passed.[1]

In all this the principle is clear that particulars of legislation should not be decided on in the Ekklesia or general Assembly, but in a Heliastic Court. *Decrees* (ψηφίσματα) were passed both by the Council and by the Assembly, but a law (νόμος) could only be introduced in the Assembly; its actual enactment was in the hands of the νομοθέται, who formed a Heliastic Commission. This latter thus acted as a kind of Second Chamber, but was not, as modern Second Chambers are, mainly conservative in its action; it must be added that the discussion as to the new law is not presented with the same clearness of details as the abrogation of the old one.

In the speech of Demosthenes against Timokrates the extracts purporting to be taken from actual laws may not be literally genuine, but there can be no doubt that in substance they correspond to facts.   Indirectly the process is referred to in inscriptions, which corroborate the evidence from speeches.   For example, there is an inscription[2] of the middle of the fourth century containing a decree in favour of one Peisitheides. After the statement of the usual privileges granted to this man come the words : "That the treasurer of the Demos should pay to Peisitheides a drachma a day, and that this should be authorized by an ordinance of the νομοθέται that the πρόεδροι in office at the time and the chairman (ἐπιστάτης) should draw up a special enactment that the ἀποδέκται should assign this money to the treasurer of the Demos year by year." Thus the Commission acted in regard to the passing of a financial measure.

---

[1] Dem. XXIV, § 33 ἐναντίον δὲ νόμον μὴ ἐξεῖναι τιθέναι τῶν νόμων τῶν κειμένων μηδενί. ἐὰν δέ τις λύσας τινὰ τῶν νόμων τῶν κειμένων ἕτερον ἀντιθῇ μὴ ἐπιτήδειον τῷ δήμῳ τῷ Ἀθηναίων ἢ ἐναντίον τῶν κειμένων τω, τὰς γραφὰς εἶναι κατ' αὐτοῦ κατὰ τὸν νόμον ὃς κεῖται, ἐάν τις μὴ ἐπιτήδειον θῇ νόμον. Cf. *Ath. Const.* c. 59.

[2] Ditt. *Syll*[3]. I, 226, 1, 37 τὸν ταμίαν τοῦ δήμου τὸν ἀεὶ ταμιεύοντα διδόναι Πεισιθείδῃ δραχμὴν τῆς ἡμέρας ἐκ τῶν κατὰ ψηφίσματα ἀναλισκομένων τῶι δήμωι· ἐν δὲ τοῖς νομοθέταις τοὺς προέδρους οἳ ἂν προεδρεύωσιν καὶ τὸν ἐπιστάτην προσνομοθετῆσαι τὸ ἀργύριον τοῦτο μερίζειν τοὺς ἀποδέκτας τῶι ταμίαι τοῦ δήμου εἰς τὸν ἐνιαυτὸν ἕκαστον.

The law is not one of those passed as a general rule and valid as long as it is not abrogated; but it is clear that these financial measures had to pass the scrutiny of the judicial commission in the same way as actual laws. In this case the νομοθέται acted as a Court with yearly legislative powers.

The νομοθέται were a judicial commission consisting of six hundred members selected from among the sworn judges, and this, no doubt, was one reason why the elaboration of laws was entrusted to them rather than to the Assembly; since the latter body took no oath it was regarded as less responsible. The oath of the νομοθέται made the process of legislation more solemn, and provided an extra safeguard against hasty action.

Another important difference consisted in the fact that judges were mute, while members of the Assembly were free to discuss and to vary proposals. There was always a great risk of confused and contradictory drafting of decrees, while the adversaries pitted against each other before a Court were bound to formulate and to argue on definite issues, decision resting meanwhile with the δικασταί.

By the side of ordinary legislation there were occasions when general reforms or revisions were carried out by special processes resembling the Roman method of legislation by means of a *dictator rei publicae constituendae.* Solon was such a dictatorial legislator; so was Kleisthenes and, probably, Ephialtes. It was recognized on such occasions that it was impossible to carry out sweeping reforms through the entanglements of ordinary legislative procedure. Confirmation of the People was expressed by the approval of the whole complex of laws and by an oath to abide by them for ever, or for a certain stated period. The revisions of laws after the fall of the Four Hundred and after the pacification of 403 B.C. must have been carried out by similar methods.

Some light on these methods is shed indirectly by facts which took place outside Athens. Under the Makedonian kings wholesale legislative reorganization was not uncommon; Philip and Alexander insisted, for instance, on a return to democratic systems in the Greek cities on the islands and on the coasts of Asia Minor.　We have an inscription recording an order of Alexander the Great to the city of Chios.[1]　The decree enacts that democracy is to be restored; legislators are to be elected to put down in writing the laws of a new Code.　Antigonos decreed about 303 B. C. that the cities of Teos and Lebedos should be joined into one commonwealth by synoikismos, and that a commission of νομογράφοι should draw up laws for that commonwealth, any differences between the legislators being referred for settlement to King Antigonos.　In the interval between the passing of the decree and the completion of the task of legislation the two cities agreed to be ruled by the laws of the neighbouring city of Kos.[2]

Νομοφυ-
λακία.

A characteristic supplement to legislative functions at Athens was provided by the *guardianship* or preservation of the laws.　In modern systems we do not make a definite opposition between conservation of laws and the general functions of legislation.　In English law every judicial decision aims at preserving law as well as deciding a particular case.　In other systems this opposition is more clearly marked : e. g. in the United States discussion in the Supreme Court starts from the point of view of private litigants, although indirectly it may result in testing the constitutional validity of a law.

In Athens there was no consolidated constitution ; but as laws were presumed to be passed in a solemn and regular manner they could be appealed to against a new law on the ground of infringement.　The development of the guardianship of law (νομοφυλακία) is so characteristic that it must be noticed, if only briefly.　It passed through three stages :

---

[1] DITT. *Syll*[3]. I, 283, 11, 4 ff. πολίτευμα δὲ εἶναι ἐν Χίωι δῆμον αἱρεθῆναι δὲ νομογράφους, οἵτινες γράψουσι καὶ διορθώσουσι τοὺς νόμους, ὅπως μηδὲν ἐναντίον ἦι τῆι δημοκρατίαι μηδὲ τῆι τῶν φυγάδων καθόδωι. τὰ δὲ διορθωθέντα ἢ γραφέντα ἐπαναφέρεσθαι πρὸς 'Αλέξανδρον.

[2] *Ibid.*, 344, § 3 εἰς δὲ τὸ λοιπὸν καὶ διδόναι καὶ λαμβάνειν δίκας κατὰ νόμους οὓς ἂν ὑπολαμβάνοιτε ἴσους ἀμφοτέροις εἶναι. ἀποδεῖξαι δὲ ἑκατέρους νομογράφους τρεῖς . . . οἱ δὲ αἱρεθέντες ὀμοσάντων γράψειν νόμους οὓς ἂν νομίσωσιν βελτίστους εἶναι καὶ συνοίσειν τῆι πόλει . . . τῶν δὲ εἰσενεχθέντων ὅσα μὲν ἂν ἐξ ὁμολογουμένων ὁ δῆμος ἐπικυρώσηι, χρᾶσθαι τούτοις, ὅσα δὲ ἀντιλεγόμενα ἦι, ἀναπεμφθῆναι πρὸς ἡμᾶς, ὅπως ἢ αὐτοὶ ἐπικρίνωμεν ἢ πόλιν ἀποδείξωμεν τὴν ἐπικρινοῦσαν· . . . συνομολογησάντων δὲ ἀμφοτέρων ὥστε τοῖς Κώιων νόμοις χρῆσθαι, ἐπικεκρίκαμεν, τοὺς δὲ Κώιους παρεκαλέσαμεν πρὸς τοὺς νόμους ὅπως δῶσιν ὑμῖν ἐγγράψασθαι.

at first it was in the hands of the Areiopagos; on this we
have definite information in the *Athenian Constitution*.[1]
Speaking of the laws of Drakon Aristotle says that the
Council of the Areiopagos was the guardian of the laws.
In describing Solon's constitution Aristotle repeats, that
Solon set the Areiopagos to guard the laws as it had
done before.[2] This accounts, according to Aristotle, for the
importance of the Areiopagos in political affairs down to the
time of Ephialtes.

The Areiopagos was an essentially conservative institution, the stronghold of the πάτριος πολιτεία. Developed
democracy could not leave such important powers in its
hands: therefore Ephialtes took them away; but in order
not to destroy the function of "guardianship of law"
a substitute had to be introduced. In the second stage
in the history of νομοφυλακία, according to a fragment of
Philochoros,[3] νομοφύλακες were instituted with the right
to watch over proceedings in the Council and in the
Assembly, where seats were assigned to them beside the
Presidents. This statement is definite, yet no instance
is recorded of interference by these supervisors in the
course of Athenian legislation. So much material has
come down to us in the speeches of the orators and in the
notices of scholiasts and lexicographers that the omission
cannot be accidental. The fact was that the arrangement
was not in harmony with the general trend of Athenian
politics and was in practice superseded by the "accusation
for illegality" (γραφὴ παρανόμων). The third period in the
history of the νομοφυλακία is represented by its revival
towards the end of the fourth century; at the "restoration"
of Athenian democracy under Demetrios of Phaleron an
attempt was made to re-establish it on Ephialtian lines.

---

[1] *Ath. Const.* c. 4 ἡ δὲ βουλὴ ἡ ἐξ ᾽Αρείου πάγου φύλαξ ἦν τῶν νόμων
καὶ διετήρει τὰς ἀρχὰς ὅπως κατὰ τοὺς νόμους ἄρχωσιν. ἐξῆν δὲ τῷ
ἀδικουμένῳ πρὸς τὴν τῶν ᾽Αρεοπαγιτῶν βουλὴν εἰσαγγέλλειν ἀποφαίνοντι
παρ᾽ ὃν ἀδικεῖται νόμον.
[2] *Ibid.*, c. 8 τὴν δὲ τῶν ᾽Αρεοπαγιτῶν (βουλὴν) ἔταξεν ἐπὶ τὸ νομοφυλακεῖν,
ὥσπερ ὑπῆρχεν καὶ πρότερον ἐπίσκοπος οὖσα τῆς πολιτείας.   Cf.
WILAMOWITZ-MOELLENDORFF, *Aristoteles und Athen*, II, p. 187 f
[3] *Fragm. Hist. Gr.* (Muller), I, Fr. 141 b τὰς δὲ ἀρχὰς ἠνάγκαζον
τοῖς νόμοις χρῆσθαι, καὶ ἐν τῇ ἐκκλησίᾳ καὶ ἐν τῇ βουλῇ μετὰ τῶν προέδρων
ἐκάθηντο κωλύοντες τὰ ἀσύμφορα τῇ πόλει πράττειν.

Γραφὴ
παρανόμων.

The ordinary course was to allow any one to bring an accusation for infringement of legal rules,[1] neglecting forms of procedure or some regulation bearing on the legislative process (νομοθεσία). That there was constant litigation of this kind is shown by the speeches of the orators. Aischines in his speech against Ktesiphon has a notable passage on this point.[2] Aristophon had prided himself on having been seventy-five times accused by γραφὴ παρανόμων; Aischines says that it is a greater claim to fame to be able to say, as Kephalos did, that no one living had proposed so many decrees as he had, and that without ever having been challenged by γραφὴ παρανόμων. The most important speeches dealing with this process are those of Demosthenes against Aristokrates and Timokrates; that against Leptines is also noteworthy as showing that even after a year had elapsed a person could be attacked, though not legally penalized. In Demosthenes' speech on the *Crown* and in Aischines' speech against Ktesiphon, to which the former oration was the reply, we notice the worst side of the practice, its use as a political weapon for personal motives.[3]

Rule of
law.

In the speeches mentioned above, however, there is more than personal hostility: Demosthenes made a genuine attempt to underline the principles which ought to be considered. In the speech against Aristokrates the facts were that Aristokrates had proposed a special measure prompted by gratitude to the Thrakian general Charidemos: one of the clauses provided that if any one attempted to murder or actually murdered Charidemos he should be seized and put to death without trial. Demosthenes attacks Aristokrates on the ground that such a procedure would amount to a denial of judicial discussion, and that it would be emphatically a case of privilege for a single person, an illegal νόμος ἐπ' ἀνδρί. As we have seen before, there was only one way of legislating in a case of this kind: the proposal

---

[1] DEM. XXIV. 36 βουλόμενος φύλακας ὑμᾶς τῶν νόμων καταστῆσαι.
[2] III, §§ 193, 194.
[3] Cf. also HYPEREIDES, II (IV), 17. In this case the proposed measure was not in itself illegal, though open to criticism, and the use of the γρ. παρανόμων was an abuse of the purpose for which this procedure was intended.

had to be carried in a special assembly with 6,000
citizens present. This was, of course, an exceedingly high
quorum, as there were only 20,000 citizens on the ordinary
roll; many of these could not be present on account of
various duties both public and private, including military
service at home and abroad:[1] but the difficulty of securing
this large attendance was just the reason why it was
required. We know that in the case of ostracism 6,000
had to vote in the Assembly, and though in the case of
privilege the voters would not be ekklesiasts merely, but
heliasts, there is some evidence to show that the number
could be used for the legislative purpose, that is, the proposal could be put before them as δικασταί.[2] In any case it
is clear that the Athenians had a rule that the ordinary
legislative process could not be employed to proclaim either
privilege or proscription of an individual.

Another point, illustrated in the speech against Timokrates, is the prohibition of *ex post facto* legislation. In
this case Timokrates had contrived to carry a law which
defied legislative guarantees. Three Athenian ambassadors
were on their way to Halikarnassos when the ship on
which they were sailing captured an Egyptian vessel.
Egypt being at war with the Athenians, the vessel was
declared a prize. The money thus acquired was entrusted
to the ambassadors to be paid into the treasury; but they
kept it for a long time. They were accused and condemned
to repay the money, and not only the actual sum but double
the amount. Timokrates, coming to their assistance, brought
in a bill by which persons who were debtors of the State
and subject to imprisonment in default of payment should
be exempt from imprisonment if they could produce three
sureties, and should then be allowed to pay the debt by
instalments; up to the ninth Prytany of the year simple
payment of the money should satisfy the claim. It was
not difficult to show that this proposal was made for the
benefit of the three ambassadors, and, as being contrived
post factum, was illegal.

This shows that the Greeks recognized the principle

---

[1] FRAENKEL, *Die attischen Geschworenengerichte*, 15 f.
[2] See above, p. 84, App. to Ch. IV.

clearly stated in the constitution of the United States of
America that no law should be retroactive, that no person
ought to be affected by a law which was not in force when
his case was decided.

2. *Control of the Administration.*

Position
of officials.
The next point with which we have to deal is the treatment of executive officials. In the sixth book of the
Politics Aristotle dwells on the general attitude of the
Athenian Demos as regards officers, taking Athens as an
example of extreme democracy.[1] There are two main
directing lines : the first principle is to make it possible
for every citizen in turn to become an official or magistrate.[2]
Offices were therefore arranged in colleges of ten, and
iteration was prohibited as a rule except in the case of the
στρατηγία, where such a prohibition was deemed impossible
because commanders must have technical knowledge and
recognized talent. Thus Perikles held office for fifteen
years as στρατηγὸς αὐτοκράτωρ. All the other officials
were chosen for a period limited to one year, or for those
of lower grade—curators and delegates—to six or even
three months. Thus access to honorary offices (τιμαί) was
open to very many people.

The second principle is that election is by lot, except, as
before, in the case of the generals. This is a direct consequence of the number of claims to a share in power.
Aristotle's remarks in the *Ethics* on the distribution of
advantages [3] show that τιμαί are thought of as a benefit or
boon to which every one has a claim, and for which every
normal citizen is deemed fit. It is obvious that the use of
the lot is not the best way to select magistrates ; and the
drawing of lots was supplemented by a δοκιμασία, a test of
fitness ; every candidate must have passed this scrutiny, in
which he had to defend himself eventually against accusations and criticism. In the case of the generals it was

---

[1] See WILAMOWITZ-MOELLENDORFF, *Aristoteles und Athen*, I. 217 f.

[2] *Pol.* VIII (VI), 2, 1317 b ὑπόθεσις μὲν οὖν τῆς δημοκρατικῆς πολιτείας
ἐλευθερία· . . . ἐλευθερίας δε ἐν μὲν τὸ ἐν μέρει ἄρχεσθαι καὶ ἄρχειν.

[3] *Eth. Nik.* V, ii and iii, 1130 b 30, 1131 a 25. See above, pp. 52 f.

still required that they should be landowners and fathers of families.

There are three speeches of Lysias written in cases of δοκιμασία; in two of them he defended persons attacked, and in the third he accused an archon-elect, named Evander. In these speeches the main object was to scrutinize the conduct of candidates during the rule of the Thirty. Lysias tried to prove that his clients had not taken an active part in the crimes of the Thirty, and on the contrary that Evander did take part in an execution ordered by the Thirty. The scrutiny dealt with no definite offence, no single act or fact, but bore on the whole tenor of a man's conduct and involved a general review of his career. Even in the case of Evander no special crime is alleged, and Lysias only censures his general conduct. Such a scrutiny counteracted to some extent the influence of chance in the lot; it provided a possibility of revision. The candidate's personal capacity for the post he was to hold was not, however, considered; this was not necessary, since each individual's part was reduced to a minimum so that he could not personally do much harm or much good.

Another point to notice is the processes εὔθυναι and ἐπιχειροτονία. Every official when selected, though he had certain prerogatives, knew that he had to stand a strict examination not only by εὔθυναι at the end of his term of office, but even in the course of his tenure by ἐπιχειροτονία. The εὔθυναι had two aspects: receipts must be presented and expenditure justified before the auditors (λογισταί): but besides this there was an examination before the εὔθυνος, and in the case of high offices before the Council and the Judicial Courts.[1] All sorts of accusations could be brought up here. The ἐπιχειροτονία went further than this: at any moment during one of the regular Assemblies (κυρία ἐκκλησία, the first of each prytany), an official could be suspended and brought up for examination. The generals were liable to this as well as other officials (as we learn from the *Athenian Constitution*), the question being whether it seemed to the People that the magistrate in

(margin) Ἐπιχειρο- τονία.

---

[1] Cf. HERMANN-SWOBODA, *Griech. Antiqu.* III, 152 f.

question was performing his duties properly.[1] Much confusion might be caused in this way. We hear e. g. of the
θεσμοθέται being suspended on a certain occasion.[2]

The Five Hundred. Another point comes for consideration here: the wish of
the Demos not to leave delegates in full possession of the
powers given to them, but to intervene directly in administration. The Assembly being too numerous for that purpose the Council of Five Hundred was charged with the
supervision of the current administration ; it came therefore to occupy an anomalous position. In one sense it was
an ἀρχή : the members were chosen by lot, and had to submit
to scrutiny (δοκιμασία). Single members could be subjected
to εὔθυναι, while the conduct of the Council as a body could
be approved or censured by indirect means. At the end of
the year the usual practice was to propose that a crown
should be offered to the Council in acknowledgement of its
good services. Demosthenes in his speech against Androtion
accused the latter of bringing his proposal without the
necessary προβούλευμα. As the proposal concerned the
Council itself, it was somewhat difficult for that body to
make the ordinary draft. It may be inferred from this
speech, especially from §§ 33–38, that the gift of the crown
was regarded as covering the actions of the Council in all
directions. Certain members wished by means of Androtion's proposal to shield themselves and escape responsibility
for their actions. The Council, being a permanent delegacy
of the people, came to be the most important administrative
organ of the State; through the system of prytanies it
was always in session. It controlled the democratic
machinery of finance, according to which no money was
kept for more than a couple of days in the central office,
but all was distributed as soon as possible for definite
purposes (e. g. the θεωρικόν). It was the business of the
Council to see that there was no large amount of money
accumulating in the hands of the clerks of the treasury.
The main payments were made in the ninth prytany (20th
of Thargelion).

---

[1] Ar. *Ath. Const.* 61 ἐπιχειροτονία δ᾽ αὐτῶν (*sc.* τῶν στρατηγῶν) ἐστὶ
κατὰ τὴν πρυτανείαν ἑκάστην, εἰ δοκοῦσιν καλῶς ἄρχειν.

[2] Dem. LVIII, 27 f.

The question also arises : Is the Council to be considered *only* as an administrative organ, or as a kind of "Upper House" taking a share in the sovereign power of Athens ? When it was created by Solon the latter was, no doubt, intended. This aspect is manifested e. g. in the form of the decrees, ἔδοξε τῇ βουλῇ καὶ τῷ δήμῳ ; and in the fact that the Council prepared the προβουλεύματα. In its executive capacity the Demos could not do without delegation of some kind ; a definite framework for activity was required, and in this respect the Council acted as a kind of standing Committee of the Assembly. In the history of the Council, however, as in other matters, we see a process of gradual encroachment on the part of the democratic Assembly which represented the people most directly.

3. *Judicial Functions of the People.*

There is a necessary separation of functions between governmental and judicial action, and while the Greeks laid chief stress as regards the former on *deliberation*, the attribute of *decision* (κρίνειν) was naturally prominent in the latter. However, the separation of functions could not be carried out consistently, and in Athens, at any rate, an attempt was made to combine in the highest instance—that of the Heliaea—the function of the People in judgement with that of the People as a deliberative body. In some of the extant speeches the pleaders address the juries as citizens of Athens, not technically as δικασταί, and it is clearly realized that the main difference does not consist in the fact that the judicial body forms a special institution, but in the fact that citizens of mature age are acting under oath. Now the recognition of a unity of political and judicial functions led of itself to the very democratic constitution of the tribunals. It is hardly necessary to repeat that we have to deal in this case with bodies of 201, 401, sometimes even 1,001 and 1,501, in session. The drawbacks of such a constitution of the judicature are obvious. Aristotle treats of them specifically in two or three instances in his *Politics*. The most important passage is in the second

Demo-
cratic
tribunals.

book,[1] where, after making a statement as to the proposals of Hippodamos of Miletos for an improved arrangement of democratic tribunals, Aristotle turns to the actual practice of such tribunals.

Aristotle's line of argument in this case seems reasonable, and one cannot but agree with him that the introduction of variety of opinion would have led in such large democratic tribunals to inextricable confusion. The other objection which Aristotle meets in another passage [2] bears on the wisdom of allowing large crowds to pronounce sentences in judicial disputes. Here again Aristotle presents an apology on the ground that although each single member of such a crowd may not be very competent or wise, there is reason to suppose that many acting together are usually capable of finding out a common-sense solution of difficulties. In any case the system provides against corruption, as a large quantity of water is more free from any taint of corruption than a small quantity of the liquid. These characteristic explanations and apologies must be accepted as the ultimate result of doubts and controversies on the part of thinkers, and there is a good deal of sound common sense about them.

From our own experience of the speeches as preserved in the various collections of the works of Demosthenes, Lysias, Isaios, &c. we may come to the conclusion that on the one hand the Athenian jurors were very apt to be caught by sophistical arguments and impressionist suggestions, so that from the point of view of strict application of the law the system left very much to be desired. But on the other hand it is clear that, at any rate during the best period of democratic Athens, there was good reason to trust the jurors in their general estimates of the rights and wrongs of a case. The analysis of νόμοι may have been often faulty, but the exercise of equity (ἐπιείκεια) on the part of jurors was aimed at as the principal guarantee that the legal process would follow the line of public opinion, the standard of justice being much influenced, of course, by the demo-

---

[1] *Pol.* II, v, 3, 1268 a. See above, p. 49.
[2] *Ibid.* III, 15, 1286 a 30 ff. Cf. *Ath. Const.* c. 41, § 2.

ratic conception of the superior right of the community at large. After all it may be worth noting that even in Rome, where of course the professional point of view was much more prominent and led to remarkable results, the notion as to the part played by the *judex* was clearly governed by the assumption that a man representing the lay element of the community must be guided by a general appreciation of the merits of a case, and cannot be fettered by very strict rules as to evidence and as to the value of the arguments produced by pleaders.[1]

In any case, in order to work such a system with tolerable results, it had to be surrounded with certain guarantees and technical restrictions. The principal way out of the difficulty was sought in a kind of dualism between the preliminary steps leading to a discussion and possibly conciliation, and the ultimate stage of adjudication. In Rome this dualism found an expression in the clearly-cut formulary arrangement by which the procedure *in jure* appertaining to the magistrate and guided by jurisconsults was quite distinct from the procedure *in judicio* which culminated in the verdict of the *judex*. It would be misleading to look for an exact parallel to this dualism in Greek procedure. Nevertheless one must reckon seriously with the preliminary action of the magistrate of Athens or other democratic cities in directing the trial along certain specific lines. The ἀνάκρισις of the magistrate who had to preside in the δικαστήριον, or the arbitration of the διαιτητής, was evidently a very important part of the process, although we do not hear much about it. This preparatory action is generally relegated to the background by the display of forensic eloquence in the speeches; nevertheless one may sometimes perceive certain vestiges of it in the trials. In the διαδικασία as to the succession of Hagnias, for instance, it is evident from the argument of the parties that the archon who instructed the case, and who presided at the trial, had settled the question as to the persons to be admitted and the formula at issue in a manner which established a definite line of prejudicial settlement

Two stages in trial.

---

[1] AULUS GELLIUS, *Noctes Atticae*, XIV, 2.

for the various parties.   The mother of one set of claimants
(Glaukon and Glaukos) was admitted to claim, and an urn
was put up for the votes likely to be cast in favour [1] of her
and of her sons.   Such an arrangement was much more
than a purely technical decision as to the number of
claimants.   It was the result of the recognition by the
archon of certain views as to the relative rights to suc
cession of various members of a family, and the claim of a
mother as a member of a family seems in this case to be in
advance of the rules of strict law.   The importance of the
juridical functions of the magistrate conducting an ἀνά
κρισις, and eventually deciding on the avenue which an
action was to follow (εἰσαγωγή), is indirectly indicated by
the fact that the principal magistrates who had to act in
law were regularly helped by legal advisers (συνήγοροι).
At the same time one cannot suppose that the decision of
an archon or any other investigating and presiding magi
strate was absolute and could not be reversed.   As a matter
of fact in this speech against Zenothemis, for example, the
παραγραφή or exception of Demon is directed really against
the procedural course adopted by the investigating magi
strates (the θεσμοθέται).   The affair was being tried on
lines of commercial jurisdiction, and Demon contested this
by raising the παραγραφή.   This means that although
the case had been treated as a δίκη ἔμμηνος, the party
who was interested in having a trial on general lines
of contract could plead in that direction even when the
process had been opened in the δικαστήριον.   In other
words the question could not be considered as finally
decided by the presiding magistrate.[2]

Another line of restrictions arose from the practice of the
διαιτηταί.   It is quite evident that this institution of arbi
trators played an exceedingly important part in the judicial
life of Athens.   Most of the civil cases went through this
channel, and a great many of them did not reach the stage
of the δικαστήριον at all.   Our information as to the
διαιτηταί shows to begin with that the membership of

---

[1] Isaios, XI. Cf. Wyse, p 673 ; [Demosthenes], XLIII, §§ 8-10.
[2] On the παραγραφή see Lipsius, 848 f.

hat college was a very numerous one, and that the position
f a διαιτητής was highly considered and connected with
very grave responsibility. We hear of appeals to the general
body of arbitrators by which διαιτηταί who were supposed
o have acted wrongly were put to trial and condemned to
severe penalties.[1]

This is one side of the matter, but what is even more
mportant is that the practice led to definite limitation in
he procedure of the Heliastic tribunal itself. Aristotle states
n the *Athenian Constitution* [2] that the procedure in the
Heliaea was restricted to the use of documents which had
been produced before the διαιτητής: " It is not allowed to
make use either of laws or of judicial demands or of evidence
other than such as has been produced before the arbitrator
and has been included by him in the sealed casket." This
hardly requires a commentary: the notice shows conclusively that the parties had to take great care in the
discussion before the arbitrator not to omit any part of the
evidence or anything which might turn out to be of material
importance for their case, as this would have prejudiced
their position before the Heliastic Court.

There is also another point of view on which depended a Summary
proce-
dure.
supplementary kind of justice. In Athenian law cases of
flagrant crime were treated by summary methods, and self-
help and the interference of police magistrates were allowed
to a considerable extent.[3] A thief, for example, caught in
the act could be taken, bound, and led off to prison by the
injured party (ἀπαγωγή). Or else the assistance of the
police in the shape of the interference of the Eleven
(οἱ Ἕνδεκα) could be required. These cases very often
resulted in summary sentences, and evidently the convicts
were not always able or willing to appeal by ἔφεσις to
the δικαστήριον, in spite of the fact that theoretically
such a way was open to them, at any rate against condemnations of a serious kind.

[1] DEM. XXI, 86 f. Cf. *Ath. Const.* 53, 6.
[2] *Ath. Const.* c. 53 οὐκ ἔξεστι δ᾽ οὔτε νόμοις οὔτε προκλήσεσι οὔτε
μαρτυρίαις ἀλλ᾽ ἢ ταῖς παρὰ τοῦ διαιτητοῦ χρῆσθαι ταῖς εἰς τοὺς ἐχίνους
μβεβλημέναις.
[3] See on the subject LIPSIUS, *Attisches Recht und Rechtsverfahren*,
309 ff.

Another set of measures of summary jurisdiction arose from cases in which the safety of the People was involved directly or indirectly. The Greeks were very sensitive in this respect, and allowed great latitude to denunciation. There were various forms of procedure of this kind; the most common were φάσις and μήνυσις, the first arising from a denunciation made by a citizen, the second from one made by a denizen or a slave. In both cases the administrative authorities took the matter up and acted, as it were, on the lines of prerogative for the sake of the " defence of the realm." A third variety was connected with attempts of men who for some reason had been deprived of civil rights to exercise any of these rights—breaches of ἀτιμία. These led to an ἔνδειξις, a special form of delation coupled with administrative action against a person supposed to be guilty of the infringement. Without attaching too much importance to these forms of procedure one has to take stock of them because we have to account for many cases in our records which spring from the exercise of these special methods. The peculiarity of all actions proceeding from denunciation was that the delator had a personal interest in bringing the action, as he could claim a part of the fine in case of pecuniary condemnation or confiscation.

Before leaving this subject of supplementary measures of a judicial character we must notice the attempt to create local judges for cases in which it would have been a hardship to call up the litigants to Athens. A special tribunal was instituted for such cases by Peisistratos, the δικαστα κατὰ δήμους; in the legislation of the tyrant the institution had a political meaning: he wanted to decentralize as much as possible the life of Attika, so as to secure more or less the quiet possession of central power for himself and for his successors; there is evidence as to a policy of the tyrants in preventing people from coming too often to Athens, and of course the creation of justices for local cases tallied well with such a policy.[1] But the idea had a meaning for ordinary purposes in the administration of law

---

[1] *Ath. Const.* c. 16.

especially as regards the settlement of less important disputes; therefore the δικασταὶ κατὰ δήμους reappeared as
the Thirty in the democratic period, and eventually the
number of these magistrates was increased to forty. They
acted partly on the spot in minor cases (up to ten drachmae),
and their decisions on such occasions were taken by each
judge personally.   Besides this they presided over the
decisions of tribunals in Athens, and this part of their
jurisdiction is connected with the settlement of disputes
which involved more considerable interests and were therefore taken over to the city.

Such are the principal features of the purely judicial State
organization from a general point of view. By the side of trials.
these we find an extensive use of State trials: the practice Προβολή.
is a characteristic side of the life of the city, in which
political conflicts could not be disentangled from the purely
technical treatment of lawsuits. The principal avenues in
this respect were provided by two forms of procedure, the
προβολή and the εἰσαγγελία. Harpokration's *Lexicon* supplies a definition of the προβολή in connexion with the
so-called καταχειροτονία.[1] The meaning of the passage is
that the Demos could in the course of a political assembly
decide that certain citizens, or magistrates, or pleaders who
had misused their right of accusation (συκοφάνται) should
be brought to trial. The first step in this case, however,
consisted in obtaining a declaration of the people that such
and such a person was in the opinion of the Assembly guilty
of a crime. After such a declaration the case went, however, its usual course in one or the other tribunal of the
people. The best illustration of the procedure in such
a case is given in the speech of Demosthenes against
Meidias. The speech starts from circumstances which are
not mentioned in Harpokration's notice. Meidias was accused
by Demosthenes of having insulted him when he was acting
for the people as Choragos, by tearing his vestments and
beating him. It is thus a case of an insult to a person

---

[1] HARPOKRATION's *Lexicon* (ed. Dindorf, 1853) s.v. καταχειροτονία :
ἔθος ἦν Ἀθήνησι κατὰ τῶν ἀρχόντων καὶ κατὰ τῶν συκοφαντῶν προβολὰς ἐν
τῷ δήμῳ τίθεσθαι· εἰ δέ τις καταχειροτονηθείη, οὗτος εἰσήγετο εἰς τὸ
δικαστήριον.

representing the People on a great ceremonial occasion.
The process which could have started in an ordinary course
by a δίκη βιαίων or a γραφὴ ὕβρεως is brought into a political channel, as Demosthenes explains, because he wanted
to emphasize the fact that the People had been attacked in
its dignity in the person of its representative.[1] The accusation was intended to provoke a prejudicial declaration by
the People, while the real trial with examination of the
evidence was to take place before a Court. But it is evident that the pronouncement of the Assembly was to be
reckoned with as a very serious support for the accuser in
the subsequent trial. The interest of the oration is increased by the fact that Demosthenes mentions several
similar accusations from recent Athenian history. In one
of the cases quoted by him we hear of a remarkable com-
plication of the usual procedure in the δικαστήριον. The
person who had brought the προβολή, a foreigner, was
willing to drop the case altogether, but the People proceeded with the investigation, and we hear that a special
proposal as to punishment (προστίμησις) was made at the
trial of the case in the δικαστήριον.[2] Unfortunately we
are not informed about the manner in which such a special
proposal as to penalty was carried through. It may be
guessed that this was done on behalf of the State by the
βουλή, or possibly by some συνήγορος representing the
People, but all such suppositions are based on general
inferences.

Εἰσαγγε-
λία.

A much more serious aspect was assumed by political
trials conducted as εἰσαγγελίαι. This was a denunciation made directly to the People in their Assembly, and
calling for an exertion of the People's authority and not
merely for an expression of opinion, as in the προβολή.
The procedure in this respect underwent a considerable
change in the fourth century. We have to reconstitute its
history chiefly on the strength of two cases: one is the
famous case of the εἰσαγγελία brought against the commanders at Arginusae, of which an account has been
preserved in Xenophon's *Hellenika*.[3] The second case is

---

[1] DEM. XXI, 33.   [2] *Ibid.* 176. Cf. above, p. 50 f.
[3] XEN. *Hellenika*, I, vii.

presented by Hypereides' speech in favour of Euxenippos, which gives us the law and illustrates the practice of the εἰσαγγελία about the middle of the fourth century B. C.[1] The Arginusae trial was obviously conducted by very irregular methods, but the legal process can be ascertained from the contention of men like Euryptolemos and Sokrates, who were opposing the rush of the extremists led by Kallixenos. It was material that the trial should be conducted through two stages resulting in two decisions; one was to establish the procedure to be followed and the law which had to be applied; in the second stage and by a second vote the actual facts were to be considered and the sentence had to be delivered. The law which it was proposed to apply was the decree of Kannonos as to high treason, with the eventual application of the death penalty in case of conviction.[2] As a matter of fact the decision was rushed through one session of the Assembly in disregard of the distinction between the scheme of procedure, which had to be settled by the Assembly in the first stage, and the material consideration of facts after adequate defence. It is important to establish that legally even in these political trials the settlement as to procedural form ought to have been clearly distinguished from the examination of the facts. In other words, although the political aspect of the trial gave the discussion a summary character and rendered it juridically incomplete, some guarantees were provided in law against purely arbitrary proceedings.

When we come to the time of Hypereides, we find that the experience gathered from the case of Arginusae and other precedents, like the trial of Miltiades or of Kimon, had led to a much more careful formulation of the law. The heads of possible accusation are stated in as many words in the quotation from the νόμος referred to by Hypereides. " For what offences," he says, " do you think impeachments are to be made? This you have already

---

[1] See below, p. 152.

[2] XEN. *Hell. loc. cit.*, § 20. (Εὐρυπτόλεμος ἔλεξεν) ὥστε δὲ ... πάντες ὅτι τὸ Καννωνοῦ ψήφισμά ἐστιν ἰσχυρότατον, ὃ κελεύει, ἐάν τις τὸν τῶν Ἀθηναίων δῆμον ἀδικῇ, δεδεμένον ἀποδικεῖν ἐν τῷ δήμῳ, καὶ ἐὰν καταγνωσθῇ ἀδικεῖν, ἀποθανεῖν εἰς τὸ βάραθρον ἐμβληθέντα, τὰ δὲ χρήματα αὐτοῦ δημευθῆναι καὶ τῆς θεοῦ τὸ ἐπιδέκατον εἶναι.

written down in detail in the law, so that no one should be
ignorant on the subject. 'If one,' says the law, 'destroys
the people of Athens . . . or conspires for the destruction of
the people or forms a (political) club or if one betrays a
town or some ships or a fleet or an army, or as an orator
says what is not best for the Athenian people in consideration of a bribe.'"[1] It is somewhat strange that by the side
of accusations of high treason appear processes against
pleaders misusing their power of private accusation (συκοφάνται), but this notice shows how important it was to
prevent the further growth of that particular abuse. It is
another question, of course, how far the method was an
appropriate one and what practical results it could achieve.
Hypereides does in fact complain that the terrible weapon
of εἰσαγγελία was being used for futile accusations about
all sorts of small matters, such as charging a high price for
the hire of musicians, enrolment in the wrong deme, or the
recital of dreams, as in the case of his own client, Euxenippos.[2] This wretched man had been dragged into an εἰσαγγελία process because he had reported to the people a
prophetic dream which he had dreamt in a sanctuary where
he had been sent by the people to ascertain the advice of
the gods. His report as to the dream had led to measures
which ended in disaster, and the dreamer was taken to task
by εἰσαγγελία. The whole procedure throws a strong light
on the lack of clear distinction between judicial and political
functions. It has to be added, however, that at any rate in
the fourth century the People did not give the decisions
directly in cases of εἰσαγγελία, but empowered the ordinary
Heliastic Courts to pronounce sentence as to facts—again
an application of the dualism between procedure in jure
and in judicio. Judicial authority was, however, directly
derived in this case from the intervention of the Sovereign
Demos.

[1] HYPEREIDES, IV (III), § 7 f. ἐάν τις ... τὸν δῆμον τὸν Ἀθηναίων καταλύῃ
... ἢ συνίῃ ποι ἐπὶ καταλύσει τοῦ δήμου ἢ ἑταιρικὸν συναγάγῃ, ἢ ἐάν τις πόλιν
τινὰ προδῷ ἢ ναῦς ἢ πεζὴν ἢ ναυτικὴν στρατίαν, ἢ ῥήτωρ ὢν μὴ λέγῃ τὰ
ἄριστα τῷ δήμῳ τῷ Ἀθηναίων χρήματα λαμβάνων.
[2] Ibid., § 3.

CHAPTER VIII

RELATIONS BETWEEN CITIES

1. *International Law and the Right of Reprisals.*

THE exclusiveness of Greek city-institutions has given rise to a fundamental misconception in regard to the treatment of international relations. It is a common error to suppose that the Greek world was deficient in this respect, that there could not be any talk of international law in societies sharply divided into a number of small republics.[1] As a matter of fact it was not so, and a closer study shows that on the contrary the world of Greek cities was particularly adapted to the development of a certain kind of international, or—to speak more correctly—intermunicipal relations. The point is that not one of these cities was really self-supporting in the sense attached to the term by Aristotle. Under stress of circumstances they could exist for some time in isolation, as it were in a state of siege or blockade. But under normal conditions each of these small political units was dependent in a high degree on supplies of goods and ideas from abroad ; in the existence of every one of them the intercourse with neighbours, the exchange of native products for foreign imports, was of first-rate importance. The case of Athens may serve as an illustration. Attika was deficient in the very first element of economic life—the poor soil could not provide the corn necessary to feed its population. Hence a series of protectionist measures and prohibitions of export,[2] etc. The opening of trade routes connecting Athens with granaries in the Bosporos and in Sicily played a great part in Athenian history ;[3] and at the time of its flourishing expansion Athens became a centre of international intercourse without ceasing to be the home of some 21,000 privileged citizens.

[1] E. g. LAURENT, *Histoire du droit des gens.*
[2] LYSIAS, XXII : DEMOSTHENES, XXXII.
[3] BELOCH, *Griechische Geschichte*, I, 395 ff.

The activity of intermunicipal intercourse in religious
and literary life, in games and competitions of all kinds,
was one of the most essential and remarkable features of
Greek history, and it would be impossible to understand
the influence of the Homeric poems, of Ionian philosophy,
of the art of Pheidias and Praxiteles,[1] without the background of this common intermunicipal organization.   It is
characteristic that the practice of the great national games
was not entirely interrupted even by feuds between the
various cities[2], and that consultations with the oracle of
Delphi were carried on at the same time by the Lakedai-
monians and by their enemies in Athens and in Thebes.

Commercial relations and the juridical effects of travel-
ling and settlement in foreign parts were not less necessary
and prominent consequences of the situation.   For our
purpose, the inter-municipal action of the ordinary institutions of Greek States is even more important than exceptional manifestations of solidarity, and the occasions for
such action in the classical period of Greek history were
numberless and varied.

Distress
and
reprisals.

The practices in this respect fall naturally into two
groups.   There were cities which, though not at war with
each other, had not established definite agreements as to
the treatment of disputes between their respective citizens,
and there were other cities which had come to some
understanding in this respect.   In the first case, apart
from the intervention of patrons, by means of which
a member of one State enforced claims against a member of
another, recourse had to be taken to procedure by self-help,
and, indeed, we commonly find men led away into captivity,
(ἄγειν) and property taken away by distress (φέρειν)
because offended persons were seeking to obtain compensation for wrongs or to assert some right.   This is termed
συλᾶν in the case of distress as well as in the case of
reprisals.   Needless to dwell on the arbitrary character of
such methods, but it must be borne in mind that such raids
were not by any means simple outbursts of lawless violence.

---

[1] E. MEYER, *Geschichte des Altertums*, III, 433 ff.
[2] Cf. HERMANN-THUMSER, *Lehrbuch der griech. Antiqu.* I, pp. 78 ff.
SZANTO, s. v. ἐκεχειρία in *Real-Enc.* V, 2162.

As frequently happens in ancient law, distress was used as a means of obtaining justice by self-help. Another feature of the procedure was that distress or reprisals are not necessarily directed against one's opponent, but might be levelled against relatives of his, or even against his countrymen at large. Such cases were considered as a justified taking of hostages, and designated by the special term ἀνδροληψία.[1]

This form of self-help, although exceedingly common, presented obvious inconveniences, and one of the principal objects of international agreement between Greek cities was to replace it by some form of regular jurisdiction. In order to put an end to the state of natural savagery in the relations of the citizens to those of neighbouring States, one city would "grant justice" (δωσιδικία) to another. A very good illustration of such a public act is to be found in the ancient treaty (fifth century B.C.) between two Lokrian cities—Chaleion and Oiantheia—preserved on a bronze tablet in the British Museum.[2] Self-help was not abolished by it, but reduced to juridical methods.

"It is forbidden to any man of Oiantheia to carry off a foreigner on the territory of Chaleion, and to any man of Chaleion to carry off a foreigner on the territory of Oiantheia, or to seize property by way of distress.

"Whosoever distrains property belonging to a foreigner shall be allowed without exposing himself to seizure to take away the goods by sea, except from the harbour below the city. If the seizure be made without right, the fine shall

---

[1] *Real-Enc.* s.v. ἀνδροληψία.

[2] MICHEL, 3 (HICKS, 31). A. Τὸν ξένον μὲ ἅγε[ι]ν ἐ τᾶς Χαλείδος τὸν Οἰανθέα μεδὲ τὸν Χαλειέα ἐ τᾶς Οἰανθίδος, μεδὲ χρέματα αἴ τι συλοῖ τὸν δὲ συλόντα ἀνάτος συλὲν τὰ ξενικὰ ἐ θαλάσας ἅγεν ἄσυλον πλὰν ἐ λιμένος τὸ κατὰ πόλιν. Αἴ κ᾽ ἀδίκος συλοῖ τέτορες δραχμαί αἰ δὲ πλέον δέκ᾽ ἁμαρᾶν ἔχοι τὸ σῦλον ἡεμιόλιον ὀφλέτο, Fότι συλάσαι. Αἱ μεταΓοικέοι πλέον μενὸς ἐ ὁ Χαλειεὺς ἐν Οἰανθέαι ἒ Οἰανθεὺς ἐν Χαλείοι, ταῖ ἐπιδαμίαι δίκαι χρέστο. B. Αἴ κ᾽ ἀνδιχάζοντι τοι ξενοδίκαι ἐπομότας ἑελέστο ὁ ξένος ὁπάγον * τὰν δίκαν ἐχθὸς † προξένο καὶ Fιδίο ξένο ἀριστίνδαν ἐπὶ μὲν ταῖς μναιαίαις καὶ πλέον πεντεκαίδεκ᾽ ἄνδρας ἐπὶ ταῖς μειόνοις ἐννέ᾽ ἄνδρας. Αἴ κ᾽ ὁ Fαστὸς ποῖ τὸν Fαστὸν δικάζεται κατὰς συνβολὰς δαμιοργὸς ἑελέσται τὸς ἡορκομότας ἀριστίνδαν τὰν πεντορκίαν ὁμόσαντας τὸς ἡορκομότας τὸν αὐτὸν ἡόρκον ὀμνύεν πλεθὺν δὲ νικὲν. DARESTE, *Revue des études grecques*, II, 318–21. Cf. OTT, *Zur Kenntniss der griechischen Eides*, Leipzig, 1896, p. 123.

* = ὁ ἐπάγων. † = ἐκτός.

be four drachmae. If the person distraining keeps the
thing seized for more than ten days, he shall pay the value
of it once and a half. If a man of Chaleion is a resident
established more than a month at Oiantheia, and *vice versa*,
he shall have recourse to the justice of the city. . . . If the
affair is carried before the judges who deal with foreigners,
the foreign claimant shall choose sworn persons from
among the notables, but *not* his proxenos nor any fellow-
citizen. For processes involving one mina or more he shall
have fifteen sworn persons, for those involving a smaller
amount he shall have nine. If a citizen pleads against
another citizen in virtue of the treaty, the demiurgi (magistrates) shall choose sworn assessors from among the
notables, after having taken the quintuple oath. The
sworn assessors shall in their turn take the same oath, and
the verdict shall follow the majority."

Even in cases of treaty relations between two cities, self-
help may play a part in the defence against illegal distress
or violence. The way was open in such case to the intervention of a *vindex*, to use the Roman term and notion.
Striking illustrations of this counter-action by any member
of the contracting States may be found in the manumission
inscriptions of Delphi,[1] and in the inscriptions commemo-
rating the consecration of Teos to Dionysos, accompanied by
guarantees of ἀσυλία on the part of neighbouring cities.[2]
The formulae are:—αὐτοσαυτὸν συλέων καὶ οἱ παρατυγχά-
νοντες ἀζάμιοι ὄντες καὶ ἀνυπόδικοι πάσας δίκας καὶ ζαμίας.
ὁ βουλόμενος, ὁ θέλων, ὁ παρατυγχάνων κύριοι ἔστωσαν ἀφε-
λόμενοι καὶ ἀποδιδόντες τοῖς ἀδικημένοις.

2. *The Granting of Justice* (δωσιδικία).

The
"granting
of jus-
tice."

In contrast with these methods of self-help stood the
system by which the citizens of a foreign city obtained
a standing before the Courts of a State according to certain
rules: this is described as the "granting of justice,"
δωσιδικία or δικαιοδοσία, and the agreements regulating

---

[1] *Griech. dial.-Inschriften*, 1721, 1749, 1857, 1936.
[2] MICHEL, 51 ff. See HITZIG, *Altgriechische Staatsverträge über
Rechtshilfe*, 39, 40.

the procedure in such cases were called συμβολαί or σύμβολα and the procedure itself δίκη ἀπὸ συμβόλων.[1]

When justice is "granted" to a foreigner the simplest way is to apply the laws of one or the other State according to certain rules appropriate to the various modalities of the controversy. Thus a so-called "conflict of laws" takes place. The account of the struggle between Sparta and Argos in the fifth book of Thukydides (c. 79) presents a good example of the application of this method in classical Greece. The sixth clause of the treaty of 418 B. C. provided that "justice shall be administered to individual citizens of each State according to their ancestral customs." This can only mean that the tribunal before which the case was brought was to apply either the law of Argos or the law of Sparta, and, as the choice of the particular law to be applied was made dependent on descent, the only outstanding question is whether it was the status of the plaintiff or of the defendant that was considered decisive. The common practice in Greece was that, *ceteris paribus*, when personality was taken as the standard of selection, litigation proceeded in accordance with the status of the defendant. The personality principle was sometimes modified by taking account of the *forum domicilii* of the defendant.[2]

In the treaty between Athens and Phaselis (395–385 B. C.)[3] two different principles are mentioned side by side. The principle of the *forum contractus* is introduced for conventions made in Athens, but on other occasions the direction of the case depends on the defendant's domicile. Conventions made outside Athens were not to be interpreted in accordance with Athenian law, and this can hardly mean anything else but the concession to the Phaselites of the application of their laws in the case of contracts made with their city.

An important consequence of the frequency and multiplicity of intermunicipal relations was the tendency of the

Generalization of laws.

---

[1] AR. *Pol.* III, 9, p. 1289 a σύμβολα περὶ τοῦ μὴ ἀδικεῖν. See HITZIG, *op. cit.* 31.

[2] WILAMOWITZ-MOELLENDORFF, *Hermes*, XX, 240 GILBERT, *Staatsalterth.*, I, p. 487. LIPSIUS, p. 966.

[3] MICHEL, 6. Cf. COLEMAN PHILLIPSON, 120.

various city customs and laws towards generalization and unification. Rules of common law grew up on an inter-municipal basis, and towards the end of the fourth century one may speak of a private international law of Greece, which, though not codified, was governed in most important respects by similar if not identical principles. This is stated in as many words in Demosthenes' oration against Lakritos concerning commercial laws.[1]

In the speech against Zenothemis a similarity of trade customs is implied by the fact that in a trial conducted at Athens one of the parties proposes to obtain evidence as to a transaction concluded at Syrakuse, while a Massaliote trader pleads on the strength of a document executed at sea with a skipper, and the magistrates of Kephallenia order a Massaliote ship to sail to Athens in view of its original destination to that port. Nor is that community of legal principles restricted to commercial affairs, as may be gathered from Isokrates' Aiginetic speech, dealing with the validity of a will.[2]

The processes which led to the building up of a Common Law of Greece can be clearly discerned. To begin with, there was colonization, in which all the Greek cities of any importance took part. It resulted in the transfer of rules and usages across the seas to different places. Thurioi, Kerkyra, Olbia, the Chalkidike, &c., were as many centres for the spread of the customs of Athens, of Korinth, of Miletos, of Chalkis, &c.[3] The compulsory tie of political allegiance was sometimes altogether discarded, but, as in the case of the United States as regards England, the legal traditions of the metropolis persisted in the new surroundings, although with some variations in detail.

Leagues and fede-rations.   A second powerful influence brought to bear on the unification of intermunicipal law was the action of leagues and confederacies. The most potent influence in this respect was, of course, exercised by the first Athenian-

---

[1] XXXV, § 45. See above, p. 4.
[2] See above, p. 5. Cf. E. WEISS, *Z. SS. Rom. Abth.* XXXIII, pp. 215 f.
[3] See e.g. the treaty between the Epiknemidian Lokri and the Lokrian colonists in Naupaktos (fifth century B.C.), ROEHL, *I G. A.* 321, MICHEL, 285. *Griech. dial.-Inschr.* 1478.

Delian league.[1] Its power made itself felt through the
greater part of the fifth century, and the gradual assumption by Athens of jurisdiction in important cases led
necessarily to the introduction of Athenian methods and
principles in the administration of law.[2] This " reception "
of Attic law by the allies of Athens was, however, the effect
of governmental pressure rather than that of intermunicipal agreements, and, although its results were permanent
and important, their discussion does not lie within the
scope of our inquiry. The methods adopted by the second
Athenian league in the fourth century are more interesting from our point of view.[3] This alliance was framed
with the distinct object of avoiding the subjugation of the
allies by Athens, and, in the treaties with various members of the league, the leading city had to renounce expressly the right to keep garrisons and to acquire land
within the territory of the allied commonwealths.[4] As
regards jurisdiction, it was to follow the ordinary lines of
the conflict of laws, while appeals had to be decided not
by the Heliaea but by the Council of the League.[5]

The report of a case has been preserved in which the
decision fell against an Athenian who had infringed the
rule forbidding the acquisition of landed property in an
allied State (*C. I. A.* II. 17). As a matter of fact, the leading city did encroach in many ways on the autonomy of
the fellow-republics, and turned its hegemony to advantage
in order to increase its political power. But this is matter
of political history rather than of law.

The oligarchical confederation of Boiotia in the fifth
century, whose organization has been made known to us in
detail through the discovery of the Oxyrhynchus fragment
of Theopompos' *Hellenika*,[6] was constructed on a principle
of genuine representation of the eleven sections ($\mu\acute{\epsilon}\rho\eta$) of

---

[1] MORRIS, *American Journ. Phil.*, V (1884), 298 ff.
[2] H. WEBER, *Attisches Prozessrecht in den attischen Seebundstaaten.*
On the συμμαχία turned into an ἀρχή see Hermokrates' speech in
Syrakuse. THUK. VI, 76.
[3] See on the subject BUSOLT, *Der zweite attische Bund.*
[4] *C. I. A.*, II, 17, 49, 49ᵇ.
[5] Cf. *C. I. A.*, IV, 2, n. 54ᵇ (DITT. *Syll³.* I, 173), ll. 45 f. IV, 2, n. 88ᵈ,
1, 13 f. *C. I. A.*, II, n. 546, l. 21.
[6] *Hellenica Oxyrhynchia*, ed. Grenfell and Hunt, ch. 4.

the land, and the hegemony of Thebes was based mainly
on the greater number of its representatives in the regional
and in the central councils. Disputes between the members of the confederacy were brought before a Federal
Court composed on the usual proportional basis; it is not
known to what extent this Court acted as a tribunal of
appeal, or of first instance, but it may be supposed that
the ordinary rules as to domicile and *lex contractus* applied,
subject to occasional revision of judgements by the central
Court.

Arbitra-
tion.

Apart from articles of Confederation, international
intercourse was conducted under customary rules and
under treaties. A number of the latter have come down
to us in their documentary form, and we can judge from
them to what extent the device of *arbitration* was
resorted to in this world of independent States. It was
the natural outcome of conflicts between cities anxious to
settle disputes by legal process.[1] The Kerkyraians complained in Athens in the course of the negotiations which
preceded the Peloponnesian war that the Spartans did not
want to try conclusions on equal terms according to convention, but preferred force to justice.[2] The ordinary
expedient was to agree upon an umpire—either a foreign
statesman like Periander or Themistokles, or, more often,
a city in whose impartiality both parties had confidence.[3]
The πόλις ἔκκλητος thus selected conducted the proceedings
with all formalities necessary to secure careful examina-
tions of claims and evidence. A classical example of such
an arbitration is presented by the inscription commemora-
ting the proceedings in a trial before a court of Knidos
between the cities of Kos and Kalymna.[4] This case falls
into the second century B.C., but there are many notices
of similar proceedings on earlier occasions, and there

---

[1] M. N. Tod, *International Arbitration*, Oxford, 1913.
[2] Thuk. I, 34.
[3] Dem. XVIII, 134.
[4] *I.J.G.*, I, 158 ff.   Cf. Tod, *op. cit.*, p. 49: "The inscription
consists of four parts. A. The oath taken by members of the Knidian
tribunal. B. Directions regarding the production of evidence and
the conduct of the trial. C. A statement of the case for the claimants
and of the amount of their claim. D. A record of the verdict and
a list of the advocates on each side."

can be no doubt that similar methods of procedure were commonly recognized and developed in the most minute particulars.[1]

An important variety of intermunicipal justice arose Δίκαι ἀπὸ when law had to be administered not by arbitral, but συμβόλων. by municipal Courts. Such cases were of daily occurrence in connexion with commercial transactions. If a ship belonging to a Milesian citizen came to Athens and discharged a cargo owned by merchants of Smyrna, all sorts of disputes might arise out of transactions and delicts of the shippers, the crew, the passengers, the consignees. Apart from ordinary rules of conflict of laws, Athenian Courts had to take cognizance of disputes under intermunicipal agreements—δίκαι ἀπὸ συμβόλων—of customs of trade and navigation, of general principles of law and equity in the punishment of delicts and the award of compensation.[2] Unless the dispute grew into an international quarrel, it was regularly considered and decided by Athenian Courts—by the ναυτοδίκαι or, later on, by a section of the jury, under the chairmanship of θεσμοθέται.[3] The procedure in these cases when they did not assume the character of public law trials (γραφαί) was of a simplified kind, as befits commercial jurisdiction. In Athens it was provided in the fourth century that the case should be tried within a month after the action had been brought.

The provision of treaties and agreements between inde- Sanctions. pendent States raises the fundamental question of sanctions for the fulfilment of the obligations laid down in them. Sometimes the payment of fines in case of infringement is mentioned in the text, as e. g. in the case of the treaty between

---

[1] Cf. LÉCRIVAIN, s.v. *ephesis* in DAR. et S. TOD, *op. cit.*, *assim.*

[2] THUK., I, 77. Cf. LIPSIUS, *Attisches Recht und Rechtsverfahren*, p. 972.

[3] DAR. et S., s.v. θεσμοθέται. LIPSIUS, *op. cit.* 86. It is not unlikely that the transfer of the jurisdiction from the ναυτοδίκαι to the θεσμοθέται was connected with the regulation of appeals to the Heliaea. The ναυτοδίκαι probably judged without juries in order to expedite commercial cases; when this jurisdiction was passed on to the θεσμοθέται it was found necessary to set a definite term for the discussion of the cases. The procedure in ἐμπορικαὶ δίκαι may be illustrated by DEM., XXXIII and XLV.

Elis and Heraia [1] (588–572 B.C.) in which we find stipulated
the payment of one talent of silver to the Olympian Zeus.
Wagers are made in litigation with corresponding deposits to
satisfy the winning party; sometimes, again, hostages are
given to ensure the carrying out of the provisions; this latter
expedient was, of course, chiefly used in cases of public obligations. But the principal guarantee of the fulfilment of treaties
and conventions was the *oath* of the parties. Now this may
mean very little or a great deal. We know by experience that
interests and passions may turn the most solemn assevera-
tion into a scrap of paper, and the history of ancient Greece
provides many examples of treachery of that kind. But
it would be a gross error to suppose that the religious
sanction implied by the oaths and imprecations had no
real meaning or weight. Its breach entailed not only
loss of credit—a most important source of influence in
the world—but it clashed with beliefs and moral feelings
which were strongly established and powerful in the
classical world. It is not for nothing that treaties, when
concluded and ratified, had to be confirmed by the oath
of the whole population of a State, or at least of large
and influential sections of its population.[2]

The formulae of these oaths are characteristic: they are
personal and not representative, because the ancient city
was a concrete reality, and not a corporation in the modern
sense, with the attributes of a *persona ficta*. In the earlier
stages of Greek history the fear of the ἄγος incurred by
the violation of an oath was certainly a strong deterrent,
though, of course, like all deterrents, it did not prevent
occasional breaches of faith under temptation. Even in
later times the religious sanction had not lost its meaning,
because religion afforded the natural channel for those
supermunicipal and supernational feelings which form, as
it were, the second root of international law.

Princi-
ples of
humanity.
The claims of civilization and of humanity were not vain
words for the Greeks; in spite of the narrowness of their
civic organizations, they had a vivid sense of personal

---

[1] *C. I. G.*, 11. MICHEL, I, 1 αἰ δὲ μὰ συνέαν τάλαντόν κ' ἀργύρω
ἀποτίνοιαν τôι Δὶ 'Ολυνπίοι.

[2] See above, pp. 107 f.

dignity and of moral restraint, as well as a sense of beauty
and a thirst for truth.   No one who has read the story of
the interview between Priamos and Achilles in the *Iliad*
can fail to recognize that, amidst all the horrors of ruthless
fights, Greek youths were brought up to harbour humane
feelings towards the unfortunate and the vanquished.   The
way in which Thukydides relates the atrocities committed
by his countrymen as well as by their enemies—the slaughter
of Mytilene, the slaughter of Melos, the slaughter of sailors
on neutral ships, is in itself a piece of evidence and a lesson.
And the popular roots of these feelings were intertwined
with religious conceptions.   It is to the Ζεὺς ξένιος that
a wanderer in a foreign land appealed for protection.   It is
at the sacred hearth that a refugee sought an asylum from
vengeance and pursuit,[1] and when the refugee took on his
lap the child of the householder, he made the latter think
of what fortune might have in store for his offspring.
A curious set of commandments bearing on humane conduct has come down to us in connexion with the traditional
lore of a noble family in Athens, the Buzygae.[2]   A similar
though much shorter set of commandments was adopted by
the Amphiktyonic League of Delphi and Thermopylae.[3]
This League might be regarded rightly as an embryonic The Am-
League of Nations; its constitution goes back to a very phikty-
onic
early period in the colonization of Greece by Hellenes— tribunal.
its membership [4] was restricted and its methods rudimentary,
but it was an attempt to embody the notion of international
justice in an organized institution.   The religious authority
of Delphi gave it powerful support, and it was not devoid
of compulsory sanctions.   In this respect its endeavours
stranded, as usual, on the divergence of interests and the
inequality of forces of its component members.   Twice the
League, in order to enforce its decrees, carried on prolonged

---

[1] E. g. Themistokles at Admetos' hearth.   See above, p. 101.
[2] TOEPFFER, *Attische Genealogie*, p. 139.
[3] Cf. as to free trade between allies, PLUT. *Perikles*, 29 προσεγένοντο
Μεγαρεῖς, αἰτιώμενοι πάσης μὲν ἀγορᾶς ἁπάντων δὲ λιμένων ὧν ᾿Αθηναῖοι
κρατοῦσιν εἴργεσθαι καὶ ἀπελαύνεσθαι παρὰ τὰ κοινὰ δίκαια καὶ τοὺς γεγενη-
μένους ὅρκους τοῖς ῞Ελλησιν.
[4] See on the subject BUERGEL, *Die pyläeisch-delphische Amphik-*
tyonie.   Cf. HERMANN-THUMSER, I, 90 ff.

wars with the help of coalitions of cities. In both cases these wars were made to serve the interests of the great powers—Sparta and Makedon. This is, however, a difficulty common to all states of society dominated by territorial sovereignty, a difficulty which could only be removed by the building up of a World State—a contingency very distant even in our own time.

As for the Greeks, their intermunicipal humanity was undoubtedly restricted during the early and the classical period to the circle of Hellenic civilization. The barbarians were regarded as inferior by nature; notice, for instance, Aristotle's account of the barbaric roots of slavery.[1] But this pride of race begins to undergo a remarkable transformation towards the end of the classical age. Instead of the racial it is the cultural aspect that is thrust into the foreground, and hereby a transition is provided to a different world in which Hellenism appears not as a national peculiarity, but as a badge of civilization. One of the forerunners of the Hellenistic age, Isokrates, has expressed this in as many words:[2] "Our city has so far surpassed the rest of mankind in power of thought and speech that her disciples have become the teachers of the rest; she has made the name of Hellene seem to belong no longer to the race, but to the mind, so that the name is given to those who share in our culture more than to those who share the common blood."

---

[1] *Pol.* I, 3–6.   [2] ISOKR. IV, 50.

CHAPTER IX

CRIME AND TORT

1. *Penal actions* (γραφαί).

THE treatment of criminal law in Blackstone's *Commen-* Classifica-
taries starts from a distinction between public and private tion of wrongs.
wrongs—the former affecting the community at large, while
the latter are taken to injure primarily private persons.
Blackstone's definition has been criticized on the ground
that any infringement of legal right is directed against the
commonwealth which has acknowledged and guaranteed
these rights.[1] But although the opposition between private
and public wrongs may not be an absolute one, it is fully
justified from the "subjective" point of view in so far as
breaches of law may be opposed either by the individuals
immediately concerned or by the community at large, if the
latter deems itself directly menaced in its interests or in
the fundamental principles of its political and legal order.
These two aspects of legal redress are sharply distinguished
in Greek jurisprudence.   Individuals seek to enforce their
rights contested or infringed by other persons by means of
"appeals to justice"—δίκαι. If the interests of the city are
directly affected by the act or omission of a person subjected
to its jurisdiction, a penal action is instituted by an accusation in writing—γραφή.[2] In both cases the trial starts, as
a rule, in the shape of an action brought by a citizen, or in
certain cases by a denizen or a foreigner, as there did not
exist in Athens or in other Greek cities any office corresponding to the public prosecutor of English law or the
procureur of Continental systems; but the contrast between
private prosecution (ἰδίᾳ) and the redress of public wrongs
(δημοσίᾳ) is clearly perceived and followed up to its consequences as regards compensation and punishment. The

[1] KENNY, *Outlines of Criminal Law*, pp. 5 f.
[2] Cf. G. M. CALHOUN, On *Oral and Written Pleadings in Athenian
Courts* in *Transactions of American Philological Association*, vol. L
(1919), pp. 177 ff.

contrast may be illustrated, for example, from Demosthenes' speech against Meidias. The orator brought a προβολή, that is, a political accusation, against his enemy, who had treated him in a humiliating manner on a solemn occasion, and he asserted that he had renounced the more profitable course of bringing a private action for compensation, in order to punish Meidias signally for the public wrongs inflicted on the city in the person of her Choragos.[1]

Choice of actions.

Readers of the Greek orators are familiar with these two kinds of suits : δίκαι, private actions, dealing with the settlement or adjudication of rights as between members of the community, and γραφαί, actions in writing, arising when the object of the suit was punishment. The Greeks used them in a way very different from the legal practice of the present day ; they had a much wider scope in choosing between criminal and civil action. Special emphasis was laid on the *freedom* of the party in choosing the form of procedure. An orator is often at pains to explain to his hearers that various alternatives were open to him, giving also the reasons for his choice. Sometimes he even goes so far as to confess that he was not strong enough to carry through the more drastic alternative, and therefore confined himself to the easier course. To take a familiar example from the private orations of Demosthenes [2]: Ariston brought an action of assault (αἰκία) against Konon. He describes how this man and his friends set upon him, beat him, and robbed him of his clothes ; he explains that these crimes rendered Konon liable to actions for robbery and contumelious aggression (ὕβρις), but in the circumstances the plaintiff and his friends did not think it wise to institute *criminal* proceedings, and he decided to seek only

---

[1] DEM. XXI, § 28 εἰ δ' ἐγὼ τὴν ἐπὶ τῶν ἰδίων δικῶν πλεονεξίαν ἀφείς, τῇ πόλει παραχωρῶ τῆς τιμωρίας, καὶ τοῦτον εἱλόμην τὸν ἀγῶν' ἀφ' οὗ μηδὲν ἔστι λῆμμα λαβεῖν ἐμοί, χάριν, οὐ βλάβην δήπου τοῦτ' ἂν εἰκότως ἐνέγκοι μοι . . . Cf. §§ 25 and 32.

[2] Id. LIV, § 1 . . . ἔλαχον αὐτῷ τὴν δίκην τῆς αἰκείας ταυτηνί. πάντων δὲ τῶν φίλων καὶ τῶν οἰκείων οἷς συνεβουλευόμην, ἔνοχον μὲν φασκόντων αὐτὸν ἐκ τῶν πεπραγμένων εἶναι καὶ τῇ τῶν λωποδυτῶν ἀπαγωγῇ καὶ ταῖς τῆς ὕβρεως γραφαῖς, συμβουλευόντων δέ μοι καὶ παραινούντων μὴ μείζω πράγματ' ἢ δυνήσομαι φέρειν ἐπάγεσθαι, μηδ' ὑπὲρ τὴν ἡλικίαν ὧν ἐπεπόνθειν ἐγκαλοῦντα φαίνεσθαι, οὕτως ἐποίησα καὶ διὰ ἐκείνους ἰδίαν ἔλαχον δίκην, ἥδιστ' ἂν . . . θανάτου κρίνας τοῦτον.

damages. In another speech[1] there is a general statement
about choice of action. "Take theft: if you have lost
something, many methods are open to you.—Are you able-
bodied and confident in yourself? Take the thief to
prison; but you risk the penalty of a thousand drachmae.
Are you not so strong? Take the archons with you; they
will do it. Are you afraid of this too? Indict him. Do
you distrust yourself, and are you too poor to pay the
thousand drachmae? Sue him for larceny before the
Arbitrator, and you will run no risk."

The sharpness of the contrast is, however, modified by
the fact that a very important group of offences, treated
by all modern systems under the general rubric of crimes—
murder, manslaughter, poisoning, arson—are initiated by
δίκαι and brought to trial, not by any qualified citizen who
wished to do so, but by the offended party or by relatives
of the latter. These actions are, therefore, private as
regards procedure, but they come before special courts of
great traditional authority—the Areiopagos and the Ephetae in Athens—and result in the infliction of heavy penalties. The reason is not far to seek—the trials in question
were still conducted in accordance with ancient customs of
tribal oligarchy (τὰ πάτρια) and projected, as it were, like
a primeval rock in the midst of the more recent layers of
enacted law. It would be an anachronism to apply to them
the concepts of private and public wrongs, in the same way
as to other modernized forms of action; they must be
treated as a group by themselves.

The first thing that strikes one in the study of Greek
criminal law is the extraordinary development of repressive
actions against officials.

Accusations against officials.

After the reforms of Ephialtes and Perikles the Areiopagos lost its high position as a court of redress in administrative cases.[2] These loom large in the jurisdiction of the

---

[1] DEM. XXII, § 26 πολλὰς ὁδοὺς . . . διὰ τῶν νόμων ἐπὶ τοὺς ἠδικηκότας,
οἷον τῆς κλοπῆς. ἔρρωσαι καὶ σαυτῷ πιστεύεις· ἄπαγ᾽, ἐν χιλίαις δ᾽ ὁ κίνδυνος. ἀσθενέστερος εἶ· τοῖς ἄρχουσιν ἐφηγοῦ· τοῦτο ποιήσουσιν ἐκεῖνοι.
οὐδέτερον βούλει τούτων· γράφου. καταμέμφῃ σεαυτὸν καὶ πένης ὢν οὐχ ἂν
ἔχοις χιλίας ἐκτεῖσαι· δικάζου κλοπῆς πρὸς διαιτητὴν καὶ οὐ κινδυνεύσεις . . .
τῆς ἀσεβείας κατὰ ταῦτ᾽ ἐστ᾽ ἀπάγειν, γράφεσθαι, δικάζεσθαι πρὸς Εὐμολπίδας,
φαίνειν πρὸς τὸν βασιλέα.

[2] ARIST., *Ath. Const.*, 8.

democratic institutions—the Heliaea, the Council of Five Hundred, and, on certain occasions, the Assembly. Magistrates, commissioners, and their subordinates were examined in a searching manner on their appointment (δοκιμασία) and were sometimes suspended from their functions (at the ἐπι-χειροτονία) in order to answer some charge against their conduct in office.[1] They were subjected to a stringent audit before the λογισταί on laying down their office, and also threatened by specific accusations before the εὔθυνος of their Phyle (tribe).[2]

Besides, there was, of course, always the possibility of an attack prompted by political motives and directed indiscriminately against the entire activity of a statesman : the process against Perikles with its undefined charge of embezzlement and corruption, or injustice (κλοπῆς καὶ δώρων, ἢ ἀδικίου) is a well-known example of such vague accusations.[3] But Athenian procedure took cognizance also of a great variety of specific delicts, for which members of the administration could be sued. Failure to conform to laws or rules in the exercise of the duties of a πρόεδρος or an ἐπιστάτης gave rise to a γραφὴ προεδρική or to a γραφὴ ἐπιστατική; failure to present accounts within the prescribed times to a γραφὴ ἀλογίου; misconduct of ambassadors to a γραφὴ παραπρεσβείας; failure to inscribe the name of a public debtor on the list of persons liable—to a γραφὴ ἀγραφίου; failure to render an account of the exploitation of mines—to a γραφὴ ἀναπογράφου μετάλλου; the acceptance of bribes—to a γραφὴ δώρων corresponding with a γραφὴ δεκασμοῦ in the case of corruption of judges. The γραφὴ ἀδικίου was directed against the misuse of judicial or administrative authority, while the γραφὴ κλοπῆς δημοσίων χρημάτων was used to prosecute officials guilty of embezzlement. It is hardly accidental that we are informed with such details of the varied forms of procedure against magistrates and employees. Many of our notices are derived from the lexicographers, who had

---

[1] HERMANN-SWOBODA, *Griech. Staatsalt.*, III, 121.

[2] WILAMOWITZ-MOELLENDORFF, *Aristoteles und Athen*, II. 217 ff.

[3] It is hardly necessary to say that on all questions of procedure our chief authority is LIPSIUS (*Attisches Recht und Rechtsverfahren*).

at their disposal a much greater store of materials than we
possess now, as they could refer to many pleadings which
have been lost since.   The reason for this wealth of information is not far to seek—the holders of office in democratic cities like Athens were not only persons invested
with temporary authority, but in a sense the targets of
popular distrust and envy, and the professional accusers
(the συκοφάνται) aimed their darts chiefly at them.

In connexion with these actions stand a number of
political offences attributable both to officials and to plain
citizens.   There were of course actions (γραφὴ ἀστρατείας,
λιποστρατίου, λιποταξίου, λιποναυτίου), against deserters
and men who had shirked military duties, and (γραφὴ
δειλίας, γραφὴ περὶ τοῦ ἀποβεβληκέναι τὴν ἀσπίδα) against
cowards.   High treason gave rise to two distinct forms of
prosecution : the crime was termed either κατάλυσις τοῦ
δήμου or προδοσία, and, in view of the grave danger to the
State and the necessity of stringent measures the procedure
indicated for regular prosecution was the εἰσαγγελία, in
which the accusation proceeded not from private persons,
even if the accused had been denounced by them, but from
the Council, while the decision was to be pronounced by the
people in the Assembly.   The contents of the charges are
definitely stated in the law by which the εἰσαγγελία procedure was regulated in the fourth century.   In his speech
on behalf of Euxenippos [1] Hypereides compares his own
(correct) mode of procedure in such cases with the incorrect
methods of Euxenippos' accuser, Polyeuktos: "When I
accused Philokrates," he says, "I brought him into Court
and wrote a proper charge as the law directs ; I stated that
' he being an adviser of the people (ῥήτορα) said what was
not in the best interest of the people of Athens, having
received money and presents from those who were working
against the people.'   And," he continues, "I repeated this
many times in the charge."

But although the law is reported in the most definite
form in this speech of Hypereides, the prosecutions against
persons suspected or accused of high treason and of attempts
to subvert democracy go back to the age of Solon, and

Political crimes.

[1] HYPER., IV, 29 f.   Cf. 39.   Cf. above, Chap. VII, p. 151.

were formulated more and more sharply. Andokides tells
us of a decree in this sense carried by Demophantes after
the fall of the Four Hundred,¹ and Xenophon in relating
the proceedings against the commanders at Arginusae
refers to a decree of Kannonos on the subject, disregarded
by the enraged people²; and Lysias mentions similar dispositions after the fall of the Thirty.³ The γραφὴ ξενίας was
used against foreigners or unfree persons who had surrepti-
tiously obtained admission into the ranks of citizens.⁴

An action has to be mentioned here which has been
already considered in another chapter,⁵ namely the γραφὴ
παρανόμων, the accusation of illegality. One point has,
however, to be noticed now in addition to what has been
stated before. In the extant speeches of the Attic orators
in cases of alleged illegality, e. g. in Demosthenes' speeches
against Timokrates, Aristokrates, Aristogeiton, the pleaders
are never satisfied with urging the formal reasons for in-
validating the law : they always dwell a great deal on the
substantial inconvenience or injustice of the law they are
attacking as well as on the supposed bad motives and bad
character of the prompter of the impugned enactment.
This is of course a feature common to Greek pleadings in
general, a feature conditioned by the fact that the judges
in the case were not trained lawyers but men of the world
more amenable to impressions and suggestions than to
juridical deductions. There is, however, yet another consideration which acted in the same sense—a consideration
embodied in various forms of action. A legislator, a statesman, an orator, who had persuaded the people, was not
absolved from responsibility when the people had adopted
the measures advocated by him. On the contrary, he
remained responsible for the results, and if they were disas-

¹ ANDOK., I, § 95 ὁ δὲ νόμος τί κελεύει, ὃς ἐν τῇ στήλῃ ἔμπροσθέν
ἐστι τοῦ βουλευτηρίου ; "ὃς ἂν ἄρξῃ ἐν τῇ πόλει τῆς δημοκρατίας κατα-
λυθείσης, νηποινεὶ τεθνάναι" κτλ. § 96 ἐάν τις δημοκρατίαν καταλύῃ τὴν
Ἀθήνησιν ἢ ἀρχήν τινα ἄρχῃ καταλελυμένης τῆς δημοκρατίας.
² See above, Chap. VII, p. 151.
³ LYSIAS, XXXI, §§ 8, 26.
⁴ LIPSIUS, 412.
⁵ See chapter VII. It applied of course not only to legislation, but
to illegal proposals of all kinds ; e. g. DEMOSTHENES, XXII.

trous or discreditable he became the scapegoat on whom
the Demos took revenge for its own folly. Turning to the
procedure against misconceived legislation, we notice that
closely allied to the γραφὴ παρανόμων stand attacks against
unprofitable laws and against their promoters—γραφὴ τοῦ
μὴ ἐπιτηδείου νόμου. Lipsius cites in illustration the well-
known speech of Demosthenes against Leptines. The
argument of the orator is almost entirely directed against
the material injustice and lack of generosity of Leptines'
law; its clauses are contrasted with those of a bill advocated by Demosthenes' client and his companion. Twice
the measure carried through by Leptines is expressly
characterized as unprofitable (μὴ ἐπιτήδειος).¹ Lipsius'
conclusion that there was a specific action which took its
name from the unprofitable character of the law seems,
however, too bold,² and technically this side of the attack
might well be combined with the usual γραφὴ παρανόμων.
Anyhow, the close connexion between formal and material
grounds shows the force of the view that a legislator is
answerable for the consequences of his measures even to
the extent of criminal responsibility. In the case of
Leptines this liability did not arise, as we know, because
a year had elapsed since the impugned enactment had
been approved and confirmed by the people.

There was yet another form of action based on an accusation of "deceit of the people" (γραφὴ ἀπάτης τοῦ δήμου).
A charge of this kind would naturally lead to prejudicial
proceedings (προβολή), and possibly to an impeachment by
εἰσαγγελία. Miltiades was tried in this manner after the
failure of the expedition to Paros.³ As a supplementary
guarantee against misdirection by insidious proposals
Athens demanded from orators in the Assembly a clean
record as regards fundamental requirements of morality.
Aischines enumerates four such requirements in his speech

---

¹ DEM. XX, § 88 ἀναγνώσεται τὸν νόμον ὑμῖν, ὃν παρεισφέρομεν
γράψαντες ἀντὶ τοῦδε, ὃν οὐκ ἐπιτήδειον εἶναί φαμεν.
² LIPSIUS, Att. Recht, 383–6.
³ HERODOTOS, VI, 136 Ξάνθιππος . . . θανάτου ὑπαγαγὼν ὑπὸ τὸν
δῆμον Μιλτιάδεα ἐδίωκε τῆς Ἀθηναίων ἀπάτης εἵνεκεν. Cf. DEM. XLIX,
§ 67 νόμων ὄντων, ἐάν τις τὸν δῆμον ὑποσχόμενος ἐξαπατήσῃ, εἰσαγγελίαν
εἶναι περὶ αὐτοῦ.

against Timarchos[1]: an orator addressing the people must
not be guilty of any of the following four misdeeds: beating his father or his mother or refusing to support them
in need; failure to perform military service, or cowardice
in the field (throwing away of the shield); prostitution
(ἑταίρησις); squandering of inherited property, On these
grounds a citizen might be prevented by εἰσαγγελία from
delivering a speech to the Assembly. If he had already
done so, the way was open for a prosecution. Demosthenes brought a charge of this kind against Androtion,
whom he accused amongst other things of having addressed
the people in spite of the fact that he had practised
ἑταίρησις.[2]

The people of Athens had to guard not only against
deception and misdirection by demagogues. Their system
of accusation by private citizens lent itself to flagrant
abuses. It was often openly recognized by accusers that
they were prompted by personal hatred or revenge in
trying to subject the defendants to public condemnation.[3]
No wonder we are told that public accusation came to be
practised as a craft and an art: Aristophanes' Kleon is the
caricature of the demagogue who relies on his skill not
only in flattering Demos, but in exciting his wrath; and
a number of political leaders are described as professional
sykophants, e. g. Androtion,[4] Theokrines.[5] As an antidote
against this evil Athenian law allowed a criminal action
for malicious prosecution, γραφὴ συκοφαντίας.[6] A syko-
phant was not merely one who spread false and defamatory information about a person, but one who made use of
public accusation for a malicious and unjustified purpose.
Unfortunately, although we constantly come across charges
of this kind in various speeches, no oration held in a specific trial for συκοφαντία has been preserved.

To the already mentioned public wrongs are to be added
offences against the gods of the city. As the life of the

---

[1] AISCH. I, § 28. See below, p. 190. Cf. § 54.
[2] DEM. XXII, §§ 25-34. § 30 ἐκ τούτου τοῦ νόμου, μήτε λέγειν μήτε
γράφειν ἐξεῖναι τοῖς ἡταιρηκόσιν.
[3] E. g. DEM. XX, 1-3. LYSIAS, XII, § 2.
[4] DEM. XX, 65-7.   [5] Ibid., LVIII, 2, 12, &c.
[6] LIPSIUS, op. cit., p. 448.

State was intimately connected with their worship,[1] any infringement of their rights and interests constituted a heavy public delict. Two actions could be brought to safeguard these rights—the γραφὴ ἀσεβείας and the γραφὴ ἱεροσυλίας. The first was directed against those who subverted the creed and worship of the national deities, and the trial of Sokrates is the best-known example of it [2]; the other was aimed at offenders who had violated the right of property of the gods. Such sacrilege was treated quite differently from ordinary theft or burglary.

The only department of common law, apart from the political one, which is safeguarded with minute precautions by many and various forms of action is family law. All relations connected directly or indirectly with family organization were protected by γραφαί. Foremost stand proceedings against κάκωσις, a term which may be rendered by "ill-treatment". The First Archon, on whom lay the supervision and protection of citizen families and of their property, received accusations against those who had illtreated their parents (κάκωσις γονέων), or orphans (κ. ὀρφανῶν), or daughters inheriting landed property in the absence of sons (κ. ἐπικλήρων), or wards (κ. οἴκου ὀρφανικοῦ).[3] In all these cases the damage to property was estimated as well as the ill-treatment of persons, and the actions for κάκωσις are matched by another group of accusations which aim at preventing the squandering of patrimony by extravagance and inefficient management. There was a γραφὴ τοῦ καταδεδωκέναι τὰ πάτρια, dispersing ancestral property,[4] and also a γραφὴ παρανοίας, aiming not merely at putting insane persons under curatorship—a proceeding which does not involve criminal responsibility—but at inhibiting the squandering of property to the detriment of eventual heirs.[5] Lastly, the γραφὴ ἀργίας mentioned in historical narratives can hardly have been directed against sloth and laziness as a vice: its probable justification lay in the neglect of family interests and the resulting material damage to the family.[6] The great development of actions protect-

Offences against the family.

---

[1] See above, Chapter V. Cf. (LYSIAS), VI, § 10.
[2] Cf. THONISSEN, *Droit pénal*, 180.
[3] AR., *Ath. Const.*, 56. 6.   [4] LIPSIUS, p. 340.
[5] *Id.*, p. 353.   [6] *Id.*, p. 340.

ing family relations and property may be considered in itself as an expression of the importance of family organization in the political structure of the city. As we have already noted, the latter was considered in a sense as a federation of kindreds, and its social order was based even in democracies on the privileges of citizens of pure descent.[1]

Ordinary crimes. In comparison with the manifold remedies provided against political offences, the domain of criminal law relating to ordinary crimes appears very restricted and undeveloped; a crime of that kind may either be an attack on the person of the plaintiff or a violation of his property rights. We find accordingly in Athenian law two main actions corresponding to these aspects—the γραφὴ ὕβρεως for offences against the person and the γραφὴ κλοπῆς for certain kinds of theft. Outside those two main actions there are only two crimes giving rise to a public action, namely procuration (προαγωγεία) and adultery (μοιχεία) ; the treatment of the former offence is not particularly characteristic of Athenian jurisprudence, but the manner in which the main actions mentioned above were conducted is worthy of attention.

Physical and moral injury to a person may be inflicted in several ways—by blows, by defamation, by contumelious treatment in general. In Athenian law the first two varieties give rise to private suits for compensation (δίκαι)—the δίκη αἰκίας and the δίκη κακηγορίας. On the contrary, contumelious treatment and intentional insults are considered to be public wrongs, and the accuser is entitled to a γραφὴ ὕβρεως. The consequences for the defendant, if convicted, are entirely different—in one case a fine estimated by the parties and decreed by the jury, in the other *infamia* (ἀτιμία), heavy fines or confiscation, sometimes even the death penalty. The classical illustration of ὕβρις is the behaviour of Meidias to Demosthenes, although the extant speech of the latter was delivered not before a tribunal, but before the Assembly in support of a prejudicial impeachment (προβολή).[2] The fact that Meidias had insulted a choragos made the offence an aggravated one, but any free citizen exposed to contumelious treatment of that

---

[1] Cf. above, Chap. V.   [2] DEM. XXI. See above, p. 61 f.

sort was entitled to have recourse to the penal action (γραφὴ ὕβρεως). The motive of the Athenian legislator in instituting a criminal prosecution for ὕβρις was evidently their intention to suppress the perverse habit of insulting behaviour as a vice tending to corrupt public morality. Therefore even ὕβρις against slaves was considered to be a public offence and threatened with punishment. In practice, however, there could hardly be much chance for a slave to carry through such an accusation, unless a citizen took up the case. It is in connexion with the injury to the strongest feelings of a family man that adultery was considered to be a public wrong and a subject for public prosecution. The γραφὴ μοιχείας was a substitute for private vengeance in these cases. Lysias' speech on the death of Eratosthenes illustrates the legality of personal revenge not only of an offended husband, but even of one who lived with a concubine.[1] If the adulterer was not killed on the spot, however, he could be captured, held in captivity by the offended party, and eventually brought to judgement by means of a penal action—γραφὴ μοιχείας. If there was no ground for such self-help the arrested defendant could, on his part, bring a counter-accusation for "false imprisonment as an adulterer" (ὡς μοιχὸς εἱρχθῆναι ἀδίκως). These penal actions were evidently intended to restrict as far as possible the range of allowable private self-help and revenge. In granting them, Athenian law established the point of view that a grave injury to the feelings, the honour, and the reputation of a citizen entitled him to seek, instead of ordinary compensation, a grievous punishment for the culprit.

Whether there was a corresponding penal action in regard to the rape of a virgin we do not know; to judge from the analogy of the Code of Gortyn[2] there may have been one. The matter may have been also taken up, however, from the point of view of damages, and therefore connected with a δίκη and not a γραφή.

[1] LYSIAS, I, §§ 30, 31 Ἀκούετε . . . ὅτι αὐτῷ τῷ δικαστηρίῳ τῷ ἐξ Ἀρείου πάγου . . . διαρρήδην εἴρηται τούτου μὴ καταγιγνώσκειν φόνον, ὃς ἂν ἐπὶ δάμαρτι τῇ ἑαυτοῦ μοιχὸν λαβὼν ταύτην τὴν τιμωρίαν ποιήσηται. καὶ οὕτω σφόδρα ὁ νομοθέτης ἐπὶ ταῖς γαμεταῖς γυναιξὶ δίκαια ταῦτα ἡγήσατο εἶναι, ὥστε καὶ ἐπὶ ταῖς παλλακαῖς . . . τὴν αὐτὴν δίκην ἐπέθηκε. Cf. DEM. XXIII, § 53.

[2] I. J. G. I, xxvii, 8–17.

A person bringing a γραφή of the kind described above exposed himself to the risk of a fine in case of defeat. The law allowed him therefore to choose his mode of procedure and to avoid the pitfalls of the criminal action by restricting his claim to one of civil compensation. This choice in regard to blows and abuse is discussed in the speeches of Isokrates against Lochites and Demosthenes against Konon.[1] The plaintiffs in both cases had certainly been treated in a most contumelious manner—one being thrashed by his enemy and the other (literally) " aspersed " from a slop-basin. Both inveigh passionately against the offenders, but both consider discretion the better part of valour and abstain from the risky venture of the trial for ὕβρις. It is interesting to find that the point of honour made all the difference between the civil and the criminal accusation in such cases, but it is also noteworthy that the People took up the high ground of a prosecution for crime not because it considered itself directly offended in the person of its citizens, but because the latter insisted on trying conclusions on these lines with their opponents. Similar peculiarities are to be observed in the treatment of offences against property. The action κλοπῆς is not necessarily a criminal action. A thief who had penetrated into a house might be exposed to various treatment according to circumstances. If he was caught in flagrante delicto he might be imprisoned and, at night, even killed. If he was pursued immediately after the theft and tracked to a neighbouring house, that house could be searched (φωρά) provided that certain conditions were observed by the search party. If the accusation rested on inference and was undertaken when some time had elapsed, an action κλοπῆς had to be brought, and it was conducted as a criminal action initiated by a charge in writing (γραφὴ κλοπῆς) only if the theft had been committed in the market-place, in the bath-house, or in some other public place. It is explained that a theft aggravated in this manner was deemed to affect directly the security of the city, which was particularly interested in the safety of the public buildings and places of public intercourse. Otherwise trial proceeded as a civil action[2] (δίκη κλοπῆς)

---

[1] ISOKR., XX ; DEM. LIV.   [2] LIPSIUS, p. 438.

with a prospective penalty amounting to double the value of the stolen goods.[1] Housebreaking does not seem to have given rise to a special action.[2]

2. *Archaic forms of Criminal Procedure.*

A striking peculiarity of criminal jurisprudence in Athens Murder was that the most grievous offences against the life of citizens and man-slaughter. were not considered to be directly within the range of public coercion. When an individual was killed the city left the prosecution to the relatives, and if there were no relatives or if they preferred entering into a bargain with the slayer, the latter was let off without further punishment.[3] There were δίκαι φονικαί, but not γραφαὶ φονικαί in case of homicide, and this means that the affair was considered primarily as a private feud to be settled between the two parties by revenge or composition. This point of view had, however, to be reconciled with the existence of a well-ordered community: hence the peculiar procedure described in an inscription of 409 B.C. bearing a copy of the law of Drakon as to manslaughter,[4] and in the speech of Demosthenes against Aristokrates,[5] and mentioned with some additional details in Aristotle's *Athenian Constitution*[6] and in Plutarch's biography of Solon.[7] We need not rehearse the well-known enactment on unpremeditated homicide (φόνος ἀκούσιος) which gives leave to the members of the household (father, sons, and brothers) to declare a feud against the slayer, and to relatives of a second circle down to cousins and their sons to join in the pursuit, nor the clause which entitles them to effect, by unanimous consent, a compromise with the slayer allowing him to return from exile. Certain other points, however, require some attention. I have already noticed in a former chapter[8] the fact that in the absence of relatives of the inner circles

---

[1] ARISTOTLE, *Problemata*, xxix, 14 ἐὰν μέν τις ἐκ βαλανείου κλέψῃ ἢ ἐκ παλαίστρας ἢ ἐξ ἀγορᾶς ἢ τῶν τοιούτων τινός, θανάτῳ ζημιοῦται, ἐὰν δέ τις ἐξ οἰκίας, διπλοῦν τῆς ἀξίας τοῦ κλέμματος ἀποτίνει.

[2] LIPSIUS, p. 442.

[3] GLOTZ, *La Solidarité de la famille*, pp. 309 ff.   LIPSIUS, p. 610.

[4] *I. J. G.* II, xxi, pp. 1 ff.   [5] DEM. XXIII.

[6] *Ath. Const.* 54.   [7] c. 19.

[8] Chapter V, p. 90.

ten members of the phratry chosen in accordance with
precedence in birth rank (ἀριστίνδην) by the assessors
(ἐφέται) are bound to take up the prosecution and entitled
to settle with the slayer.   The γένος—the intermediate
unit between the family and the phratry—is passed
over, evidently because a number of citizens were only
ὀργεῶνες of some kind and not members of old γένη ; and
as the law had to formulate a general rule applicable to
all, such men had to be content with a representation
of their interest by their noble comrades in the same
phratry.   Aischines, for example, would have been represented in such a case by some of the Eteobutadae,[1] plebeians
of the phratry of the Demotionidae by some scions of the
house of Dekeleia,[2] etc.   The point is of great interest
in so far as it shows that the ancient scheme of avengers
was originally constructed on agnatic lines, while in its
modified form it proceeded from the household to the
nearest heirs (the ἀγχιστεῖς) on both sides—through males
and through females—to return to the agnatic organization of the phratry with its leading patriarchal kindreds
(ἀριστίνδην).

Another point to be noticed is the distribution of cases
of homicide among the three principal tribunals.   Trials
for murder were assigned to the Areiopagos, composed
of acting and former Archons; unpremeditated homicide
(manslaughter) was of the province of the Ephetae, the
fifty-one representatives of the federation of kindreds in
the Palladion, and justifiable homicide was tried by the
Ephetae in the Delphinion.   The question arises by what
means the competence of one or the other of these Courts
was to be determined.   Lipsius solved the difficulty by
suggesting that evidently the choice of the tribunal was
determined by the nature of the plaintiff's action or of
the defendant's opposition.[3]   This means, I suppose, that
if the avengers did not feel confident of obtaining a
verdict of wilful murder, they would not approach the

---

[1] AISCHINES, II, § 147.
[2] MICHEL, 961. Cf. above, Chap. V, p. 89.
[3] LIPSIUS, p. 26. PHILIPPI, *Der Areopag und die Epheten*, seems
to me to be in the right when he draws the inference that the assign-
ment to a court was made by the kings.

Areiopagos but would bring their action before the king in the Palladion. This may sound plausible, but how would this account for the Delphinion? There could be no motive for the plaintiff to seek justice before a tribunal trying the question of legal homicide; this kind of trial would surely arise in most cases in consequence of a *defence* of the accused. If so, the attribution of the case must have been determined, not by the parties—especially not by the plaintiffs—but by a preliminary investigation carried out by some court or by the presiding magistrates (the king or kings).[1] When Antiphon informs us that even in a case of murder the accused could take to flight before the first decision had fallen, he may have had in view the result of such an ἀνάκρισις.[2] The uncertainty of the situation before the pronouncement of the judges as to the tribunal competent to try the case may also explain the passage of the pseudo-Demosthenic speech against Theokrines, in which the latter is said to have arranged a compromise with the slayers of his brother.[3] The imputation cannot concern manslaughter, because compromise for φόνος ἀκούσιος was legal and constantly practised.[4] It would also be out of place in a clear case of φόνος ἑκούσιος, in which perpetual exile was the only means of avoiding capital punishment. It is significant that the expressions of the speaker in the oration against Theokrines point to homicide in general and leave it undecided whether the case should have been tried by the Areiopagos or gone before one of the other tribunals.[5]

---

[1] I incline to refer to this function the words of Drakon's law, 1, 35: *I. J. G.*, p. 2 δικάζειν τοὺς βασιλέας αἰτιῶν φόνου, . . . τοὺς δὲ ἐφέτας διαγνῶναι. The duty of the king was to determine the point of law and the mode of trial; the Ephetae gave the verdict as to fact.

[2] ANT. V, § 13 καίτοι ἐμοὶ εἰ μηδὲν διέφερε στέρεσθαι τῆσδε τῆς πόλεως, ἴσον ἦν μοι καὶ προσκληθέντι μὴ ἐλθεῖν, ἀλλ' ἐρήμην ὀφλεῖν εἶναι τὴν δίκην, τοῦτο δ' ἀπολογησαμένῳ τὴν προτέραν ἐξεῖναι ἐλθεῖν· ἅπασι γὰρ τοῦτο κοινόν ἐστι.

[3] DEM. LVIII, § 28 τελευτήσαντος αὐτῷ τοῦ ἀδελφοῦ βιαίῳ θανάτῳ, . . . ζητήσας τοὺς δράσαντας καὶ πυθόμενος οἵτινες ἦσαν, ἀργύριον λαβὼν ἀπηλλάγη.

[4] DEM. XXXVII, § 58 ἀλλ' ὅμως ἁπάντων τούτων ὅρος καὶ λύσις τοῖς παθοῦσι τέτακται τὸ πεισθέντας ἀφεῖναι. Cf. XXVIII, 22.

[5] GLOTZ comes to the same result by another way (*Solidarité*, p. 381); I am, however, unable to follow his argument as to the distinction between compromises before and after sentence.

The next point to be established concerns the part played by the city in determining the condition of citizens convicted of homicide. When the Areiopagos pronounced a capital sentence on a murderer it was carried out by the public executioner in the presence of the relatives of the deceased. Thus the avengers were prevented from taking the law into their own hands when the murderer had not been killed ἐπ' αὐτοφώρῳ, on the spot. They had to be content with the moral satisfaction of having destroyed their enemy at the hands of public justice. The murderer could save himself by flight, and the law protected him from the "vendetta" of the offended family if he kept away from the soil of Attika (ἀειφυγία).[1] But if he returned, he exposed himself to the vengeance of the hostile kindred—he was considered as an outlaw, and could be killed by any one with impunity.[2] There is no reason to suppose that the fate of a person guilty of manslaughter and sentenced to conditional exile was different if he returned without having arranged a compromise with the relatives of the victim. His case would be covered by the clause on the ἀνδροφόνοι in the same way as that of the murderer. The city forbade, however, wanton cruelty to such outlaws: they might be killed, but it was not lawful to cripple or otherwise to ill-treat them. The clause may be part of a later addition to the original text of Drakon's law indicated by the words "ὡς ἐν τῷ ἄξονι εἴρηται" in the speech against Aristokrates.[3] The point about the protection accorded to fugitives who keep outside the frontiers seems to belong to the later amendment which may have been added when Drakon's law was re-copied and re-enacted in 409 B.C.[4]

The jurisdiction of the Areiopagos.

The Areiopagos was certainly the central tribunal for the decision of criminal cases according to traditional custom (τὰ πάτρια); the courts in which the king sat with the Ephetae as

---

[1] *I.J.G.* II, XXI, § 7, p. 4 (7) τοὺς δὲ ἀνδροφόνους ἐξεῖναι ἀποκτείνειν καὶ ἀπάγειν ἐν τῇ ἡμεδαπῇ, λυμαίνεσθαι δὲ μή, μηδὲ ἀποινᾶν, ἢ διπλοῦν ὀφείλειν ὅσον ἂν καταβλάψῃ. Cf. DEM. XXIII, 28 ff. See below, p. 186.

[2] *Law of Drakon*, § 7. See above, note 1.

[3] DEM. XXIII, § 31.

[4] GLOTZ, *op. cit.*, pp. 319 ff, builds up a hypothetical and complicated theory on the analysis of the clause as given in Demosthenes' oration. Cf. LIPSIUS, p. 943.

his assessors were engrafted, as it were, on the more ancient institution of the Council on the hill of Ares. Indirect consequences of this later formation may be traced in certain facts of Athenian institutional history. In a sense the tribunal of the 300 representatives of the Eupatrid clans (ἀριστίνδην αἱρεθέντες) may be said to have been an enlarged and extraordinary commission of Ephetae appointed to try the accomplices of Kylon or their slayers.[1] The fifty-one (or fifty if the king was numbered as the fifty-first) assessors of the Palladion and of the Delphinion held their ground for a considerable time, but were replaced by heliasts either in connexion with the reform of Ephialtes or at the revision of the laws after 403 B.C. In any case the heliasts are found acting in the first half of the fourth century, so that the re-enactment of Drakon's law in 409 B.C. cannot have had a durable effect as to the composition of the Courts formerly held by Ephetae. On the other hand the Areiopagos remained master of the stronghold of criminal jurisdiction even though it was stripped of political power.[2]

Aristotle enumerates in the *Athenian Constitution* the criminal actions within the jurisdiction of the king archon,[3] and his account is corroborated by Demosthenes' speech against Aristokrates. Apart from homicide, the king archon was the presiding judge in trials for attempting to establish tyranny, wounding with intention to kill, poisoning, and arson, and the central Court for all these trials was the Areiopagos.[4] The duty of prosecuting persons conspiring to obtain tyranny was entrusted to the Areiopagos by the decree of Patrokleides[5] in 405 B.C. The psephism was evidently voted by the people in a state of great excitement

---

[1] AR., *Ath. Const.* c. 1. Cf. PLUTARCH, *Solon*, 19 ὁ δὲ τρισκαιδέκατος ἄξων τοῦ Σόλωνος . . . ἔχει . . . γεγραμμένον· ᾿Ατίμων ὅσοι ἄτιμοι ἦσαν πρὶν ἢ Σόλωνα ἄρξαι, ἐπιτίμους εἶναι πλὴν ὅσοι ἐξ ᾿Αρείου πάγου ἢ ὅσοι ἐκ τῶν ἐφετῶν ἢ ἐκ πρυτανείου καταδικασθέντες ὑπὸ τῶν βασιλέων ἐπὶ φόνῳ ἢ σφαγαῖσιν ἢ ἐπὶ τυραννίδι ἔφευγον ὅτε ὁ θεσμὸς ἐφάνη ὅδε.
[2] Cf. DEM. XXIII, §§ 65 f.
[3] c. 57. 3.
[4] DEM. XXIII, 22 δικάζειν δὲ τὴν βουλὴν τὴν ἐν ᾿Αρείῳ πάγῳ φόνου καὶ τραύματος ἐκ προνοίας καὶ πυρκαϊᾶς καὶ φαρμάκων, ἐάν τις ἀποκτείνῃ δούς. Cf. ANTIPHON, VI.
[5] ANDOKIDES, I, § 78.

and apprehension, in view of the desperate situation in Athens with the prospect of defeat and capitulation. We do not hear of its application in any particular case.

On the other hand all the other crimes in which jurisdiction is attributed to the Areiopagos are illustrated by forensic speeches. The wounding with intention to kill (δίκη τραυμάτων ἐκ προνοίας) is represented by a tetralogy of Antiphon,[1] and by Lysias' speech on the death from a wound of an Athenian whose name has not come down to us.[2] Poisoning is the subject of two important speeches of Antiphon, in which the principal argument for the defence consists in trying to prove that a fatal beverage was administered not as a poison but as an aphrodisiac charm or a medicinal drink.[3] As for accusations of arson (πυρκαϊά), they seem to have been placed within the competence of the Areiopagos because the setting fire to a neighbour's house was regarded as an act of private feud. It may be supposed that if no casualties were caused by the fire, the matter would be considered merely from the point of view of material damage and give rise to a simple δίκη βλάβης.[4]

3. The Elements of Crime.

Mens rea.   The differentiation of tribunals for the trial of homicide shows the importance attached by the Athenians to the psychological element in criminal proceedings. The fundamental distinction between φόνος ἑκούσιος and φόνος ἀκούσιος turns on the presence or absence of the intention to slay (πρόνοια). In what circumstances was it allowable to put up a defence of this kind (μὴ ἐκ προνοίας)? Unquestionably death caused by an accident entitled a person to do so. Accident and self-defence were defined in a peculiar way in a law quoted in Demosthenes' speech against Aristokrates.[5] Death arising from a blow which was meant to be inflicted on an enemy in battle, or from rough handling in a wrestling match, was deemed "bootless," and the orator goes on to explain that if a wrestler succumbs in a contest this must

[1] ANTIPHON, IV.   [2] LYSIAS, IV.
[3] ANTIPHON, I, § 9; cf. VI, § 19.   [4] LIPSIUS, p. 984.
[5] DEM. XXIII, § 53. Cf. LIPSIUS, p. 610.

be regarded as an act of the gods. The rule as to slaying
on the road (ἐν ὁδῷ) is not clearly expressed and does not fit
well into the context. But there was evidently a tendency
of defendants in cases of this kind to avail themselves of
any proof of contributory negligence on the part of the
victim to claim complete absolution. The imaginary defendant in Antiphon's second tetralogy [1] tries to make out
that a boy killed by his spear was himself responsible for
his death, because he ran over the course when it was forbidden to do so. The accuser sets up against this plea the
curious assertion that an unfortunate accident of this sort
shows that the gods were discontented with the slayer, and
punished him for his want of piety by making him the
agent of a homicide, however involuntary. This seems
a far-fetched deduction, but as it was meant to serve as an
example of an argument before the Ephetae at the Palladion
it cannot be regarded as a mere attempt to mislead a popular court by sophistical suggestions. The delimitation
between negligence and accident mentioned by Aristotle
in the *Rhetoric* [2] evidently formed the subject of judicial
controversies among the venerable assessors of the Palladion.

On the other side there lay the indefinite borderland
between murder and manslaughter. According to Plato's
Laws, death following on blows inflicted in a fit of anger
was not treated in the same way as deliberately prepared
murder; [3] but this distinction, corresponding to our modern
rules on the subject, can hardly have been clearly recognized by Athenian jurisprudence. There is, however,
evidence that the defence was set up in some cases that
as no weapons had been used, or prepared for use, there
could not have been an intention to kill. This was urged
by Lysias' client in the oration about a deliberately inflicted
wound that caused death (περὶ τραύματος ἐκ προνοίας).[4]
He contended that as the wound in question had been inflicted by a blow with a shell picked up on the road, there
had certainly been no premeditated attempt to kill. An-

---

[1] ANT. III, § 8.
[2] I, xiii. 16 ἔστι δ' ἀτυχήματα μὲν ὅσα παράλογα καὶ μὴ ἀπὸ μοχθηρίας,
ἁμαρτήματα δὲ ὅσα μὴ παράλογα καὶ μὴ ἀπὸ πονηρίας.
[3] PLATO, *Laws*, IX, 9.   [4] LYSIAS, IV, § 6.

other point of view from which the inquiry as to πρόνοια
might be productive of doubt and discussion arose in connexion with the possibility of mistake in the use of
dangerous ingredients. Antiphon's oration against the
stepmother [1] was delivered in a case in which two men had
perished from the effect of a drug which was served to them
in some wine. For the defence it was pleaded that the
drink had been drugged by the concubine of one of them
in order to excite his amorous inclination. The plaintiff
did not dispute that a mistake of that kind had been made
by the concubine who served the cups, but he maintained
that she had been deliberately misled by his stepmother, who
wanted to get rid of her own husband. The decision rested
with the Areiopagos, but the fact that such arguments were
used by a prominent pleader shows that defences of that
kind were common, and had to be considered on their merits.
In another speech of Antiphon the whole force of the defence
consists in the proof that a choragos who caused the death
of a singer by treating him to a certain drink could not on
any account be made responsible for poisoning, but only for
a most unfortunate mistake.[2] The importance attached to
criminal intention explains why no material difference was
recognized between the actual perpetrator of a homicide
and its instigator. In the case of the stepmother just mentioned Antiphon puts side by side the action of the person
who administered the drink without realizing what it might
produce, and that of the woman who remained behind the
scenes but was the real agent of the misdeed.[3] The speech
just referred to indicates at the same time that no attempt
was made to draw distinctions in law between principals
and accomplices or accessories, although pleaders would be
sure to avail themselves of any circumstance likely to produce mitigation of the verdict. Another consequence of
the principle of moral responsibility for crime was that
conspiracy or plotting some one's destruction, if there was
any attempt to carry the plot into execution, was tanta-

---

[1] ANT. I.   [2] ANT. VI.

[3] ANT. I, 20 ἀνθ' ὧν ἡ μὲν διακονήσασα καὶ χειρουργήσασα ἔχει τὰ
ἐπίχειρα ὧν ἄξια ἦν, οὐδὲν αἰτία οὖσα—τῷ γὰρ δημοκοίνῳ τροχισθεῖσα παρε-
δόθη—ἡ δ' αἰτία τε ἤδη καὶ ἐνθυμηθεῖσα ἕξει, ἐὰν ὑμεῖς τε καὶ οἱ θεοὶ θέλωσιν.

mount to actual homicide. The king was in charge of the trial βουλεύσεως as well as of those of murder and manslaughter.[1] The root idea was the reaction of society against violence produced by hatred or self-will.

Yet, even apart from criminal intention, the shedding of blood had to be expiated as being a pollution of the city's soil.[2] All the forms of trial for homicide, with the possible exception of the one ἐν Φρεαττοῖ, were connected with shrines and sacred rites. On the hill of Ares the solemn oaths and sacrifices forcibly recalled to the mind the presence of deities watching over truth and justice. At the shrines of Pallas and of Apollo the wisdom of the judges was directed towards distinguishing between manslaughter and lawful homicide in self-defence, or in revenge. The trial resolved itself, if the latter defence was accepted, into expiatory rites at the shrine of Apollo. Even when death had been caused by an animal or an inanimate object, a stone or a beam, the kings of the city and of the tribes went through the ceremony of a judgement ending in expiatory sacrifices.[3] In all cases the ἄγος, the curse called forth by violent death, had to be removed from Attika, and some of the principal acts of the pacification of civil strife in the seventh century were the expiatory functions performed by Epimenides of Krete. A poetic expression of popular beliefs on such matters has been preserved in the *Oresteia* of Aischylos: the Erinyes pursue the murderer up to the last, and he is absolved by a judgement of the Areiopagos under the direct intervention of Pallas and Apollo. It is not without meaning that the high tribunal stands in its original unity and that the two titular deities of the Ephetae Courts appear as protectors of the accused man. A tragedy is, of course, not a historical statement, but Aischylos would hardly have omitted to mention the subsidiary Courts if they had not been regarded as the offshoots of the Areiopagos.

Religious transgression.

The trial.

---

[1] AR., *Ath. Const.* c. 57.
[2] Cf. GLOTZ, *op. cit.*, 62 ff. We may expect an attempt to reopen the question on the part of G. M. CALHOUN; see *Proceedings of the Classical Association*, Vol. XVIII (1921), pp. 87 ff.
[3] DEM. XXIII.

Private
violence
and public
danger.

It is not necessary to dwell long on the exercise of self-help in the struggle against criminals.   The latitude left to vengeance by kinsmen has been sufficiently and frequently described.[1]   One point of detail may be noticed now, as it shows to what extent the pursuit of men guilty of inflicting mortal wounds was regarded as an act of private revenge.   We learn from Demosthenes' speech against Pantainetos that if a person who had been mortally wounded pardoned his assailant before his death, this pardon barred further prosecution by the relatives.[2]   The proof that a plaintiff in a case of wounding, or the man slain in a case of homicide, had himself begun the fight was considered a sufficient ground to establish a plea of self-defence ($\mathring{\eta}\rho\xi\epsilon$ $\chi\epsilon\iota\rho\hat{\omega}\nu$ $\mathring{a}\delta\acute{\iota}\kappa\omega\nu$).[3]   The same defence held good in the case of a culprit being taken *in flagrante delicto* ($\mathring{\epsilon}\pi'$ $a\mathring{v}\tau o\phi\acute{\omega}\rho\omega$).   In the latter case it was common practice, however, not to risk an accusation of homicide, and to content oneself with the forcible arrest of a burglar or thief and his delivery to the public authorities for imprisonment ($\mathring{a}\pi a\gamma\omega\gamma\acute{\eta}$).[4]   The private arrest ($\mathring{a}\pi a\gamma\omega\gamma\acute{\eta}$) starts in this way from the seizure *in flagrante* ($\mathring{\epsilon}\pi'$ $a\mathring{v}\tau o\phi\acute{\omega}\rho\omega$), but the notion was extended in several directions. From Lysias' speech against Agoratos we learn that the Eleven, to whom the arrested persons had to be handed over, required from the accusers that they should state expressly that the arrest had been made $\mathring{\epsilon}\pi'$ $a\mathring{v}\tau o\phi\acute{\omega}\rho\omega$, and yet Dionysodoros, whose death Lysias' client is trying to avenge, was neither killed nor wounded by Agoratos, but only supposed to have fallen a victim in consequence of Agoratos' denunciation.[5]   It was admitted to be sufficient that the accused should be regarded by public opinion as miscreants ($\kappa a\kappa o\hat{v}\rho\gamma o\iota$) in order to enable accusers to arrest and to conduct them before the Eleven.[6]   A third case where arrest was allowed by the side of self-help was that

---

[1] See especially GLOTZ, *op. cit.*, 76 ff.
[2] DEM. XXXVII, § 59.
[3] ANTIPHON, IV β, § 1.
[4] Cf. LIPSIUS, *op. cit.*, p. 38.
[5] LYSIAS, XIII, §§ 85–87.
[6] ANTIPHON, V, § 9 κακοῦργος ἐνδεδειγμένος φόνου δίκην φεύγω, . . . καὶ ὡς μὲν οὐ κακοῦργός εἰμι οὐδ' ἔνοχος τῷ τῶν κακούργων νόμῳ... οὗτοι... μάρτυρες γεγένηνται.

of outlaws and persons deprived of civic rights (ἄτιμοι)
when they showed themselves in the market or in temples
or exercised public office. The first prohibition concerned
those who had perpetrated a homicide and had been sentenced, or at any rate had not obtained reconciliation with
the kinsmen of the deceased. The second came into operation in the case of state debtors who had not acquitted
themselves of their debt, and yet had taken part in public
life : we hear of capital sentence against such individuals.[1]

In such cases the exercise of private force against the
accused was justified partly by the strong feeling of personal hatred—as regards persons guilty of homicide,—
partly, and even more, by considerations of public safety.
The debtor who was remiss with his payment, the outlaw,
the professional miscreant, were sources of danger to the
State, and when their transgression was a matter of public
notoriety they could be arrested and imprisoned either by
other citizens or by the authorities—usually the Eleven—
on a written accusation presented by a citizen (ἔνδειξις).
This procedure rendered ineffective the usual guarantees of
civic rights : the accused had to submit to the hardships
and indignities of imprisonment; he was deprived of the
liberty necessary to prepare an effective defence ; his plight
created an unfavourable impression and made it difficult to
collect witnesses for the defence. Generally the person
arrested in such a manner had leave to obtain bail if he
was able to present three sureties, but in the case of the
murder of Herodes treated in Antiphon's fifth speech such
bail was refused and the accused man incarcerated on the
strength of the deposition of a slave under torture.[2] No
wonder procedure by ἔνδειξις played a great part in State
trials for treason and infringement of the constitution.[3]
On the whole these summary forms of accusation and
arrest throw vivid light on the police of public safety in
Athens : the usual safeguards against arbitrary treatment
of citizens gave way when the principle of public safety
was invoked against them.

[1] DEM. XXI. ANDOK. I. LYS. VI.
[2] ANT. V.
[3] AR., *Ath. Const.* 29, 4.

4. *Punishment.*

In our age of extreme sensitiveness as to social responsibility for the evils of punishment it seems strange that the
highly civilized Greeks were exceedingly callous as to the
fate of individuals who had excited the wrath of the city.
Even the best and most idealistic Greek thinkers were
never troubled with misgivings on this point: they considered the infliction of evil, including the death penalty,
as the most effective means of attaining civic virtue and
of preventing vice and crime. Demokritos, for example,
speaks of the necessity of destroying criminals as we destroy
wild animals.[1] Plato in the *Laws* classified offences carefully, and decreed the death penalty for a number of them.[2]
Protagoras, according to the statement in the dialogue
bearing his name, argued that the chief means of political
education was the enactment of laws likely to deter men
from wrongdoing.[3]

The practice fully corresponded to the theory in this
case; the death penalty was constantly decreed in laws
and adjudged by the courts. An instance like that of
Pyrrhos the Eteobutad, whom some of the judges wanted
to condemn to death because he had sat as a juror in a
tribunal while not absolved from a debt to the Commonwealth, and this not on account of arrogance, but of
poverty—such an instance of harshness seems appalling to
us,[4] and yet it is by no means exceptional in the annals of
Athenian judicature. The most terrible penalties are
threatened against attempts to seize tyrannic power; the
usurper and his offspring are doomed to extermination.[5]

Infamia.

I have already had occasion to mention the loss of civic
rights by fugitive murderers (ἀνδροφόνοι).[6] It extended
also to those convicted of manslaughter who had not been
admitted to pay composition (ποινή) by the relatives of the
victim. Such a condition was, however, exceptional.

---

[1] DIELS, II. *Fragm.* 257, 258, 259, 260.
[2] *Laws,* IX, *passim.*
[3] PLATO, *Protagoras* 324 a b. Cf. above, p. 35.
[4] DEM. XXI, 182.
[5] E. g. *Law of Ilion, I. J. G.,* II, xxii, pp. 26 ff. and *Judgement of
Eresos, ibid.* xxvii, pp. 161 ff.
[6] Above, p. 180. Cf. GLOTZ, *Solidarité,* 485 ff.

Usually the loss of rights was connected with a declaration
of ἀτιμία which did not involve the withdrawal of all protection, but only the loss of honour, of consequent political
privileges, and in some cases confiscation of property.[1]   A
detailed but yet incomplete enumeration of different kinds
of ἀτιμία is given by Andokides in his speech on the
Mysteries.[2]   He cites three groups of persons branded as
infamous (ἄτιμοι): public debtors who had not acquitted
themselves of the payments to which they were liable;
persons who had incurred an ignominious sentence, e. g.
citizens guilty of male prostitution (ἐταίρησις), convicted
of theft, &c.; persons who had been deprived of specific
rights—e. g. who were forbidden to bring a public action
because they had made use of this right in a frivolous
way and had failed to prosecute in actions brought by
them.   Convicts of the first category, according to Andokides, were punished in their property as well as in their
persons, their land and goods being confiscated if they
failed to pay.   The second category suffered only in their
persons (σώματα).   Their principal disability was that they
were debarred from participating in political life, standing
as candidates for office, sitting on juries, &c.   The third
category was treated even more leniently in so far as the
deprivation of active right concerned only certain specific
functions like giving evidence on oath or bringing an action
for illegality (παρανόμων).

So far Andokides' enumeration corresponds to the facts.
But ἀτιμία was pronounced on several other very important
occasions.   It could be decreed, for instance, against any one
attempting to abrogate or to modify a law.   Witness the
psephisma concerning the foundation of the colony of Brea
in Thrace in the age of Perikles[3] and a similar prohibition
in the statute of the Second Athenian League.[4]   It was
a necessary corollary of all condemnation in trials for
high treason.[5]   It threatened persons guilty of misconduct

---

[1] This distinction is often disregarded.   See e. g. THALHEIM in
R.-Enc. II, 2101 s.v. ἀτιμία.
[2] ANDOK. I, 73 ff.
[3] C. I. A. I, 31.   DITT. Syll³. I, 67, l. 25.
[4] C. I. A. II, 17.   DITT. Syll³. I, 147, l. 53.
[5] PLUTARCH, Solon, c. 19.

against their parents. All professional vagrants and miscreants (κακοῦργοι) were *ipso facto* deprived of the ordinary guarantees of civic freedom.[1] Besides, we hear of many cases in which personal dishonour involves public ἀτιμία, as for instance in the case mentioned in a pseudo-Demosthenic speech, when a man was declared to be ἄτιμος because he had continued to live with his wife who had committed adultery.[2] One striking feature of ἀτιμία is described at great length in Aischines' speech against Timarchos. The orator dwells on the care with which the law prescribes to keep undesirable people from taking part in government or legislation.[3] He mentions four types of "evil livers" debarred from political life: those who maltreat their parents or refuse them housing; those who shirk military service or play the coward; those guilty of bodily vices; those who squander their patrimony. These are excluded from the public platform, and if they still presume to use—or worse, to abuse—the privilege of speech they are to be subjected to δοκιμασία, and the verdict upon them rests with the Courts. On the whole, the prominence of ἀτιμία as a punishment of crime and vice seems as characteristic of the highly-strung sense of civic honour entertained by the Athenians as the importance attached to contumelious treatment in trials for ὕβρις.

Fines and imprisonment.

The penalty of imprisonment, so common in modern times, hardly existed in Greece, although temporary captivity was recognized as a means of preventing flight; it was the usual outcome of an ἀπαγωγή. As a substitute for this kind of compulsory seclusion the Athenians sold

[1] ANTIPHON, V.
[2] DEM. LIX, 87.
[3] AISCHINES, I, 28–32 τίνας δ' οὐκ ᾤετο δεῖν λέγειν ; τοὺς αἰσχρῶς βεβιωκότας· . . . καὶ ποῦ τοῦτο δηλοῖ ; "δοκιμασία," φησὶ, "ῥητόρων· ἐάν τις λέγῃ ἐν τῷ δήμῳ τὸν πατέρα τύπτων ἢ τὴν μητέρα, ἢ μὴ τρέφων, ἢ μὴ παρέχων οἴκησιν." . . . καὶ τίσι δεύτερον ἀπεῖπε μὴ λέγειν; "ἢ τὰς στρατείας μὴ ἐστρατευμένος, ὅσαι ἂν αὐτᾷ προσταχθῶσιν, ἢ τὴν ἀσπίδα ἀποβεβληκώς." . . . τρίτον τίσι διαλέγεται; "ἢ πεπορνευμένος ἢ ἡταιρηκώς." . . . τέταρτον . . . "ἢ τὰ πατρῷα κατεδηδοκώς, ἢ ὧν ἂν κληρονόμος γένηται." . . . τούτους οὖν ἐξείργει ἀπὸ τοῦ βήματος, τούτους ἀπαγορεύει μὴ δημηγορεῖν. ἐὰν δέ τις παρὰ ταῦτα μὴ μόνον λέγῃ ἀλλὰ καὶ συκοφαντῇ καὶ ἀσελγαίνῃ, καὶ μηκέτι τὸν τοιοῦτον ἄνθρωπον δύνηται φέρειν ἡ πόλις, "δοκιμασίαν μὲν," φησιν, "ἐπαγγειλάτω 'Αθηναίων ὁ βουλόμενος, οἷς ἔξεστιν," ὑμᾶς δ' ἤδη κελεύει περὶ τούτων ἐν τῷ δικαστηρίῳ διαγιγνώσκειν.

certain culprits into slavery; this manner of getting rid of
undesirable elements is mentioned, for instance, in connexion with attempts by foreigners to get admission into
the ranks of citizens.[1]   Free men were not subjected to
corporal punishment, which could always be inflicted on
slaves.   Indeed it was considered a principle of common
law that the main difference between free men and slaves
consisted in the fact that the former had to suffer in their
property while the latter were coerced in their bodies.[2]

Fines and confiscations were indeed the ordinary penalties meted out to citizens and to foreigners of free status.
It is unnecessary to recite the numberless references to
fines in the laws, the decrees, and the speeches of pleaders.
They were so varied and so oppressive that critics of democracy came to accuse popular governments, like that of
Athens, of multiplying unjust condemnations in order to fill
the public purse.[3]   As there was really no option but to
condemn either to death (or to its substitute, banishment)
or to a fine, it is difficult to see in what way the
material losses to the convicted persons could be consider-
ably mitigated.   The distinction between fixed fines in
trials without assessment (ἀγῶνες ἀτίμητοι) and varying
fines in trial with free assessment (ἀγῶνες τιμητοί) depended
entirely on accidental circumstances and had nothing to do
with differences in principle.   Confiscation was naturally
reserved for particularly serious offences.

5. Actions in Tort (δίκαι κατά τινος).

Claims for legal redress of private wrongs were brought Classifica-
by means of actions of two different kinds: a plaintiff tion of
insisting on a right disputed or infringed by the defendant actions.
sued the latter by a δίκη πρός τινα which involved no
penalty, although it might lead to certain payments in
compensation of damages.   On the other hand there was
a group of actions—δίκαι κατά τινος—which started with
an accusation against the defendant for a wrong supposed

[1] DEM. LIX; ISAIOS, VI.
[2] DEM. XXII, 55.
[3] [XENOPHON], Resp. Ath.

to be inflicted on the plaintiff.   While the first set of trials
turned mainly on questions of property and of contract, the
second set was concerned with matters in which public
force had to intervene for the restoration of disturbed legal
order, although the questions at issue were considered
mainly from the point of view of the infringement of
private rights and of the consequent necessity of com-
pensating for incurred material and moral damages.   Besides these two classes of actions there was a third, covering
what may be called prejudicial declarations of right—
διαδικασίαι. These latter are closely allied to the δίκαι πρός
τινα and their consideration may be postponed till the next
chapters.   The δίκαι κατά τινος, on the other hand, which
correspond to English actions in tort, have to be considered
in close connexion with criminal jurisdiction, as they apply
frequently to the same or to similar subjects.

The simplest kind of prosecution for the illegal use
of force arose in connexion with assault and battery.   A
person who had received blows could bring an action
αἰκίας, in which the plaintiff was expected to prove that
he had not been guilty of beginning the brawl himself.
Isokrates' speech against Lochites and Demosthenes' speech
against Konon deal with trials of this kind.   Both pleaders
lay stress on the fact that they might have prosecuted
their adversaries by penal actions ὕβρεως, but as Athenian
plaintiffs had a free choice of remedies and were by no
means bound to give to the prosecution the character of
a penal accusation, they both preferred the less hazardous
course of an action in tort, with the prospect of substantial
compensation in damages.[1]   They magnified the losses
incurred in order to be able to claim a high compensation
(τίμημα) when the time came to estimate the material and
moral damages suffered by them.

The action βιαίων covered various forms of wrong caused
by violence.   It was used in pursuance of a law of Solon[2]
in cases of rape.   The plaintiff must have been usually the
father or κύριος of the maiden or boy who had been
assaulted.   It may be noticed that originally the compen-

---

[1] ISOKR. XX, §§ 5 ff. DEM., LIV, §§ 13 ff.
[2] PLUTARCH, Solon, c. 23.

sation was a fixed sum of 100 drachmae. Later on, however, as can be inferred from a speech of Lysias,[1] the culprit had to pay the " double price of the person " as compensation, one half of the fine accruing to him and half to the city. This notice is interesting in two ways : it shows that the Commonwealth did not disinterest itself in cases of tort, but claimed part of the fine as a fee for its services ; the amount of the compensation is estimated at double the value of something or of some one. The most likely explanation seems to be that the citizens and other inhabitants of Attika were appreciated according to certain standards of value, somewhat in the manner of the mediaeval wergelds. The law of Gortyn gives a definite tariff of this kind in connexion with rape.[2]

In another direction the action βιαίων was used by those who had to complain of violent deprivation of their goods. The corresponding action as to immovable property was the δίκη ἐξούλης of which we shall have to speak at length in the next chapter.[3] Here again the fine to be paid by the convicted defendant was estimated at double the value of the chattels " disseised." The unjustified claim of liberty for a slave was also treated as disseisin of a chattel ; the action directed against the citizen making the claim bore the specific designation of δίκη ἐξαιρέσεως or ἀφαιρέσεως εἰς λευθερίαν.[4] As the slave had no standing in justice against his master, and any one who claimed to be the master of a slave could seize the latter by way of distress, the only remedy against fraudulent assertions of this kind lay in vindication. The δίκη ἀφαιρέσεως was introduced to prevent abuses on the part of those who assumed the responsibility of vindication.

The δίκη κακηγορίας may be mentioned here, as it was intended to protect persons against humiliating abuse. A law had been framed against this kind of wrong by

---

[1] LYS. I, § 32.
[2] I.J.G. xvii, §§ 8, 9, p. 358. GLOTZ, Solidarité, pp. 393 f. takes the application to apply to the price of a slave as the lowest unit of compensation. But the double fine occurs in all kinds of the δίκη βιαίων and not only in those in which slaves may be concerned.
[3] DEM. XXI, § 44. Cf. below, p. 225.
[4] DEM. LIX, § 40. ISOKR. XVII, § 14. Cf. LIPSIUS, p. 64 f.

Solon,[1] but it is characteristic that what may be called ordinary abuse was not punishable. Plutarch offers the very plausible explanation that it would have been out of the question to proceed effectively against every kind of angry utterance or retort; legislators must not attempt too much, and had better restrict their action to what is really important. Thus Solon forbade the levelling of abuse at the dead, or, as to the living, the indulging in it in certain specially protected localities—temples, tribunals, political assemblies. Certain particularly obnoxious terms of abuse like ἀνδροφόνος or πατραλοίας were also actionable. Magistrates were protected, by the severe threat of ἀτιμία against any abuse. There is also a curious notice that it was illegal to reproach a tradesman with the exercise of his trade. Fines in these cases ranged from the trifling sum of five drachmae to heavier penalties.

Damage to material interests. An action of great importance and very general application was the δίκη βλάβης, corresponding more or less to the action *ex lege Aquilia de damno injuria dato* of Roman law. It lay on two principal occasions: if some one had deliberately inflicted damage on the plaintiff, and if the plaintiff had been hurt or suffered damage by the act of a slave or animal belonging to the defendant. The first eventuality presented the simplest basis for a prosecution. It occurred, for instance, in a trial mentioned in Demosthenes' speech against Kallippos,[3] in which it is was contended by the plaintiff that the banker Pasion had paid out a certain sum sent to a wrong addressee contrary to the direction of a correspondent of his and to the detriment of Kallippos; or again in the case referred to in the speech against Pantainetos,[4] who complained of the arbitrary distress practised by Nausimachos on Pantainetos' agent, with the result that Pantainetos was unable to acquit himself. was natural in such trials that an intention to harm should

---

[1] PLUTARCH, *Solon*, 21 Ἐπαινεῖται δὲ τοῦ Σόλωνος καὶ ὁ κωλύων νόμ τὸν τεθνηκότα κακῶς ἀγορεύειν. ... ζῶντα δὲ κακῶς λέγειν ἐκώλυσε πρὸς ἱερ καὶ δικαστηρίοις καὶ ἀρχείοις καὶ θεωρίας οὔσης ἀγώνων· ... τὸ γὰρ μηδαμ κρατεῖν ὀργῆς ἀπαίδευτον καὶ ἀκόλαστον· τὸ δὲ πανταχοῦ χαλεπὸν, ἐνίοις ἀδύνατον· δεῖ δὲ πρὸς τὸ δυνατὸν γράφεσθαι τὸν νόμον.

[2] LYSIAS, XI, 3, 4. Cf. LIPSIUS, pp. 649 ff.

[3] DEM. III, § 14.

[4] DEM. XXXVII, § 4, 22.

ve to be proved in order to justify penal proceedings,
d the principal point of dispute was therefore whether
e damage had arisen accidentally or in consequence
spiteful intention. In the trial between Kallikles and
e son of Teisias, Demosthenes for the defendant tried
prove that the damage done to the plaintiff's plot by
undation was not the result of any building operations
rried out recently and intentionally on the estate of
s client, but the consequence of accidental torrential rain
ndered more noxious by certain acts of the plaintiff
mself.[1] If compensation had to be paid at all, it ought
be paid, according to this defence, only in reparation of
e material damage sustained, and not in double, as would
the case in a penal action.

In view of the stress laid on harmful intention, it seems
ubtful whether a case like that against Boiotos, in which
e plaintiff Mantitheos objected to the use of his name
y the defendant, could be treated as a δίκη βλάβης.[2]
spite of the usual attempts to cast suspicion on the
otives of defendants and to depict the consequences of
e latter's success in the trial in the darkest colours,
seems to me that the juridical situation did not warrant
y claim for compensation either penal *in duplum* or
vil *in simplum*, although it gave ground for a con-
oversy as to the use of the name—a διαδικασία—directed
wards a result which would be obtained in English law
y an injunction.[3]

The second group of δίκαι βλάβης was the subject of
e of Solon's laws[4] which treated of damage occasioned
y four-footed animals. Dogs are especially mentioned in
is connexion, but there can be no doubt that cattle and
her domestic animals were covered by this rule. The
sponsibility of the master extended also to the acts of
aves.[5] All these eventualities are discussed with many
ncrete details by Plato in the *Laws*, and we may safely

[1] [DEM.] LV.
[2] DEM. XXXIX.
[3] Thalheim in the article on δίκη βλάβης in *R.-Enc.* III, 554 ex-
esses a different view.
[4] PLUTARCH, *Solon*, 24.
[5] An oration on the subject was ascribed to Lysias.

suppose that he drew his precepts in this case from th practice of his native city.[1]

I have already had occasion to notice the strange fa that theft was considered to be a matter for private an not for public prosecution. In ordinary cases the suffer brought a δίκη κλοπῆς, while the γραφὴ κλοπῆς was reserve for certain qualified transgressions, like stealing in a bath house or in a court of justice.[2] This does not preclud the infliction of a fine on the thief: he had, as on som other occasions, to pay compensation in double, and ha of the fine went as a penal payment to the city.

It seems even more strange from our modern point c view that false evidence in a trial at law gave rise no to a public but to a private prosecution. Such lenienc was evidently suggested by similar considerations of polic as the impunity of ordinary abuse: false testimony was c too common occurrence to call for criminal prosecution i every instance.[3] An attempt was made, however, to penaliz false evidence treated as a profession. If some one was co victed three times in actions ψευδομαρτυριῶν he lost th right to tender evidence in a court of law. Otherwis that action was treated purely as an action in tort. A co responding action lay against a person who had contrive the production of such false testimony. He was actionabl by a δίκη κακοτεχνιῶν.[4] Another penal action akin to th δίκη ψευδομαρτυριῶν was the prosecution for referrin to witnesses who had not really been called in to testif to an action in law—δίκη ψευδοκλητείας.[5] In this cas again Athenian law entrusted the prosecution to the priva person whose interests were directly affected by the fals assertion.

[1] *Laws*, XI, 936.
[2] See above, p. 176.
[3] Cf. LIPSIUS, p. 778.
[4] DEM. XLIX, § 56.   Cf. LIPSIUS, p. 783.
[5] LIPSIUS, p. 446.

CHAPTER X

PROPERTY AND POSSESSION

1. *General Terms and Distinctions.*

THE essence of the law of property is the attribution to ertain persons of exclusive rights of disposal over certain hings. Modified and conditional rights are derived from his main position, and they will have to be examined in .me, but the first thing to be ascertained in any given ystem of law is to what extent and on what basis things re attributed to persons as belonging to them or *owned* y them. It is evident at first glance that there are two spects of the matter. Things may belong to me because have made them or got hold of them; they may also be->ng to me because they have been granted or guaranteed) me by some community of which I am a member. In ther words, ownership has been produced by private force a the shape of labour or occupation; it has roots also in ublic force in the shape of laws protecting certain interests s against other interests. For the sake of analysis it is seful to examine these various elements separately and one y one, but in reality social life always presents a combina-.on of both tendencies. Such combinations vary greatly ccording to systems, and their characteristic turn depends) a great extent on the social type which serves as a basis or the particular legal system under investigation. The :udy of Greek jurisprudence is highly interesting from this oint of view. Although it cannot be reduced to a series f simple deductions from the principle of city democracy, , gives this principle a prominence which greatly restricts nd modifies all other influences bearing on the case.

The most striking feature of this formation is its contrast ith the Roman treatment of the subject. Rome and Athens osely resembled each other in the initial stage of their

The elements of pro- perty.

development as city federations of kindreds, but later or
with the growth of their imperial policy, they came i
many respects to follow divergent roads. As to the probler
under discussion, Rome developed the conception of absolut
property for the citizen—the *dominium ex jure Quiritiun*
—while Athens worked out a conception of *relative* pro
perty rights (κυρίως κτῆσθαι or ἔχειν καὶ κρατεῖν).[1]   It i
significant enough that there is no Greek term correspond
ing to the *dominium* of the Romans. It has been con
jectured that this is to be explained by the insufficien
development in Greece of the rules as to occupation an
usucapion.   Under these circumstances, it is said, a Greel
attempting to assert absolute ownership ' against the whol
world' would have had to run the gauntlet of an endles
string of references to one *auctor* after another, truly
probatio diabolica.[2]   I must own that I fail to understan
this line of reasoning: the Greek world traced property i
a multitude of cases to definite acts of State—to th
distribution of lots or to the public inscription of the tenur
in the presence of witnessing officials,[3] and nothing coul
have been easier than to assert absolute *dominium* at leas
in such cases—provided that absolute *dominium* had bee
recognized.   In reality the point established was only
recognition of better right (καρτερὸν εἶναι), and not o
absolute right.   And there was yet another point, not les
important than the first—in all cases of allotment, officia
registration, adjudication, etc. the title of the proprietor wa
emphatically derived not from the assertion of private wi
(*hunc fundum meum esse aio ex jure Quiritium*), but fror
a concession by the city.   The public element was clearl
predominant, and this fact goes far to explain why occupa
tion and usucapion did not come to play the part that the
played in Rome.

Another term conspicuously vague in Greek law is th
term οὐσία:[4] it means fortune, patrimony, the complex o

---

[1] DITT. *Syll*[3]. I, 167.   MITTEIS in *Z. SS. Rom. Abth.* XXIII.

[2] BEAUCHET, *Droit privé*, III, 53.

[3] See, for example, the inscription of Halikarnassos, *I. J. G.* I, p.
καρτερὸς δ' εἶναι γῆς καὶ οἰκιῶν, οἵτινες, τότ' εἶχον ὅτε 'Απολλωνίδης κ
Παναμύης ἐμνημόνευον, εἰ μὴ ὕστερον ἀπεπέρασαν.

[4] Οὐσία, BEAUCHET, *op. cit.*, III, 367.

objects owned and held, but not the right of property. Δίκη οὐσίας means an action concerning the patrimony of a person or the interests of a person in certain objects, but it does not mean a *rei vindicatio* in opposition to a personal action. By calling attention to these peculiarities of legal terminology I do not wish to create the impression that the rules as to property in Greece were entirely built on a foundation of public law and disregarded the influence of individual will and interests. It is not necessary to rush to such absurd exaggerations in order to appreciate at their due value the importance of the public elements in the Greek legal system. It is well, however, to take stock from the very beginning of certain characteristic peculiarities in the use of juridical terms and in the general treatment of property in Greece.

Before examining in detail the juridical theory of pro- *Kinds of* perty, let us ascertain what different species the Greeks *property.* distinguished within the generic conception of things belonging to persons. We are accustomed in modern systems to oppose real to personal property; or property in land, including houses, to chattels; or again, ancestral to self-acquired property. The first of these distinctions is connected with the mediaeval history of tenure and has no parallel in Greek law. The other two classifications are represented in somewhat modified forms in Greek law.

The contrast between land and chattels and its bearing on legal rules is often noticed in the sources of the classical period. We read, for instance, in Isaios' speech on the inheritance of Kiron [1] that the latter possessed property of various kinds: land (ἀγρόν) worth a talent, two houses (οἰκίας) in the town, one leased, bringing in two thousand drachmae, the other, in which he lived, worth thirteen minae. Also slaves let out on hire (ἀνδράποδα μισθοφοροῦντα) and two maidservants and a girl; furniture (ἔπιπλα) used in the house, worth, with the slaves, thirteen minae; and property clearly ascertainable (φανερά) worth more than ninety minae; besides this considerable loans, from which he received interest. Aischines in his oration against Timarchos lays

---

[1] ISAIOS, VIII, § 35.

particular stress on the dissipation of various kinds of fortune by his opponent.[1] In these cases and in similar ones,[2] while the various elements of a person's fortune are enumerated, the principal place is naturally assigned to land and houses.   The expression ἔπιπλα, used originally for furniture, came to be gradually extended to all sorts of goods kept in a house or on an estate,[3] although cattle, slaves, and money were generally mentioned as separate categories of goods.   Like the *familia pecuniaque* of Roman law,[4] they were considered in Greek law from another point of view than land and houses.

Slaves as well as cattle and agricultural implements were often economically bound up with the cultivation of an estate, and the *instrumentum fundi* came to be considered in Roman law as a part of the *fundus* which could not be detached from it at random.   There are definite indications of a similar view in Greek law, although it was not neatly reduced to a formula as in the French *Code Civil* under the heading of *immeubles par destination*.   Plots are mentioned with some slaves connected with them, as for instance in Demosthenes' first speech against Aphobos.[5]   In the oration against Onetor Demosthenes tried to refute his adversary's contention that he held a certain estate in mortgage for his sister by showing that he had let his brother-in-law, Aphobos, denude the estate by removing the slaves and other elements of the *instrumentum* necessary to its cultivation.[6]   " He went off with all that he could carry away, the crops and the agricultural implements, all except the jars ; but what he could not carry off he of necessity left behind, so that it is possible now for this man to claim the land itself."   If it had been a dower estate he would have been careful to treat it like a provident *paterfamilias*.

An indirect, but most important indication as to the exceptional importance of land tenure is to be found in the prohibition of the acquisition of land (ἔγκτησις) by

---

[1] AISCH. I, 97 f.   [2] Cf. ISAIOS, VI, 30.
[3] AR. *Rhet.* I, 5, 7 ; *Pol.* II, 4, 10.
[4] MITTEIS, *Rom. Privatr.* I, p. 80.
[5] DEM. XXVII, 35.   Cf. XXXVII.
[6] *Id.*, XXX, § 28.

foreigners. While the ports and markets of Athens were
full of business men from all parts of the world, who
bought and sold goods and entered into all sorts of contractual relations with citizens and among themselves,
while denizens (μέτοικοι) formed one of the principal elements of the population of Attika, all these persons, fully
safeguarded as regards money, goods, and conventions by
Athenian law, were deprived of the right of owning land,
except in certain specified cases. I have already had
occasion to refer several times to the endeavours of autonomous allies of Athens to exclude the citizens of the capital
city of the League from their respective territories.[1] The
reason is obvious: each independent city was afraid of
letting in foreign colonists and capitalists who might
acquire undue political influence as landowners, and prohibitions against such invasions are generally coupled
with promises that no foreign garrisons should enter the
territory of free allied cities. It will be necessary later on
to return to the prominent part played by land tenure in
Greek law.

The distinction between ancestral (πατρῷα) and self-
acquired (ἐπίκτητα) is not often made the text of definite
declarations in Athens, but it played a conspicuous part in
the law of Gortyn, especially in cases of dowry and divorce,[2]
and it made itself felt in Athenian procedure by the wide
scope of the action directed against spendthrifts. It was
designated emphatically δίκη κατά τινος περὶ τοῦ τὰ πατρῷα
δεδωκέναι, and there was sufficient material for such an
accusation in the case of Timarchos, if the assertions of
Aischines are to be believed even in part. The speaker
declares that property of great value was left by the father
of Timarchos—enough to warrant the undertaking of a λει-
τουργία—estates, skilled slaves, furniture, money on loan,
and cites proof that Timarchos received this property and
dissipated it.[3] These facts point to another social aspect of

---

[1] See above, p. 159.
[2] Code of Gortyn, I. J. G., §§ 14, 17, 36.
[3] AISCH. I, §§ 96 ff. § 97 τούτῳ γὰρ κατέλιπεν ὁ πατὴρ οὐσίαν, ἀφ' ἧς
ἕτερος μὲν κἂν ἐλητούργει, οὗτος δὲ οὐδ' αὑτῷ διαφυλάξαι ἐδυνήθη· οἰκίαν
μὲν ὄπισθεν τῆς πόλεως, ἐσχατιὰν δὲ Σφηττοῖ, Ἀλωπεκῆσι δ' ἕτερον χωρίον,
χωρὶς δὲ οἰκέτας δημιουργοὺς τῆς σκυτοτομικῆς τέχνης ἐννέα ἢ δέκα, ὧν ἕκαστος

property—to the economic and juridical connexion with family organization. Here again the ancestral character of the property could hardly be established except on the basis of land tenure.

One more distinction has to be noticed in connexion with management of property by the Greeks, namely the distinction between openly acknowledged (φανερά) and concealed property (ἀφανὴς οὐσία). Orators often use these terms,[1] but it is evident that they do not deal in such cases with juridical attributes, but rather with facilities for keeping one's wealth concealed in order to avoid the imposition of public services and taxation. It was easier to do so by placing one's capital in the hands of bankers or lending it out. Money was altogether less ostensible as an element of one's fortune than land, or houses, or workshops. These terms need not detain us any longer, as they reflect tendencies of economic management rather than legal peculiarities.[2]

2. The Public Element in Property.

Assignation.

In theory every private estate in Greece was considered as an allotment (κλῆρος, κλᾶρος) assigned by the State. Nor was this theory a mere juridical fiction or antiquarian speculation. In the frequent cases of the swarming of colonies from some city (ἀποικία), the emigrants led by an οἰκιστής established themselves in their new home as κληροῦχοι. In the precious inscription bearing on the colonization of Brea in Thrace (about 444 B.C.) we read that the first act of the new settlers was to divide the land among themselves. Ten γεονόμοι—one from each Athenian tribe—marked off and distributed the lots; the temple and temple grounds which had belonged to the former inhabitants were to be taken over by the new settlers, but no religious estates

τούτῳ δύ᾽ ὀβολοὺς ἀποφορὰν ἔφερε τῆς ἡμέρας, ὁ δ᾽ ἡγεμὼν τοῦ ἐργαστηρίου τριώβολον· ἔτι δὲ πρὸς τούτοις γυναῖκα ἀμοργὸν ἐπισταμένην ἐργάζεσθαι καὶ ἔργα λεπτὰ εἰς τὴν ἀγορὰν ἐκφέρουσαν, καὶ ἄνδρα ποικιλτήν, καὶ ὀφείλοντάς τινας αὐτῷ ἀργύριον, καὶ ἔπιπλα κτλ.

[1] E. g. ISAIOS, VII, § 35; DEM. XLVIII, § 12.
[2] Cf. BEAUCHET, Droit privé, III, 13.

were to be formed.[1] After the conquest of Chalkis 4,000
lots were formed;[2] after the conquest of Lemnos 3,000, of
which 300 were to be dedicated to the gods.[3] Plutarch has
preserved in the biography of Perikles a list of colonies
sent out from Athens in his age,[4] and there can be no doubt
that each citizen householder was assigned a plot of land by
lot. By instituting his hearth in the plot he dedicated it
to the permanent use of his family. The ἰστία of the
Lokrian colonists in Naupaktos was to remain undisturbed
even if the new colonist changed his mind and went back
to the mother city: he was obliged by law to leave a successor in the person of a grown-up son or of a brother. If
he died without leaving near relatives, his hearth was kept
for relatives living among the Epiknemidian Lokri of the
metropolis.[5]

Nor was the assignation of landed property by the city
a feature restricted to colonial institutions. The law of
succession was not designated as κληρονομία, the heir as
κληρονόμος, without valid grounds. The complex of estates
in Attika was regarded in law as a set of κλῆροι distributed
as far as possible permanently among a set of citizen
households (οἶκοι), and the Archon Eponymos had to watch
over this distribution and to guard against the disappearance of any of these ancient households.[6] This
principle went back to a period when kindreds and families
were still ruled by tribal rather than by civic law, when
the κλῆρος, like the ἀρχαῖαι μοῖραι of Sparta, was inalienable, and this aspect of their history will have to be considered at greater length later on. But the notion of the
public character of the κλῆρος was expressed in many
features of later law. The frequent use of confiscation as
a means of repression in political struggles as well as in
criminal justice gave occasion for constant reassertion of
the eminent domain of the State. Take, for instance, the
law of Iasos passed about 367 B.C. against the enemies of

[1] DITT. *Syll*[3]. I, 67.
[2] HEROD. V, 77.
[3] ED. MEYER, *Forschungen*, I, 13 ff.
[4] PLUTARCH, *Per.*, c. 11.
[5] *I. J. G.* I, xi, 180 ff.
[6] AR. *Ath. Const.* I, 56, § 7.

Molossos, the satrap ruler of Asia Minor under Artaxerxes
Memnon.   Their estates were to be confiscated and sold by
a numerous commission for the benefit of the city. A great
part of the territory affected was distributed in lots ($\kappa\lambda\hat{\eta}\rho o\iota$),
the size of which seems to have varied in the course of suc-
cessive adjudications. The validity of the bargain depended
on its confirmation by *mnemones*—a kind of public notaries.[1]
In another inscription—that of Mylasa,[2] connected with the
same struggle between the cities of Asia Minor and the
Persian authorities, the transfer of the plots is declared to
produce complete ownership ($\dot{\epsilon}\kappa\tau\hat{\eta}\sigma\theta\alpha\iota\ \kappa\nu\rho\dot{\iota}\omega\varsigma$). The officials
charged with the duty of supervising dealings in land and
of giving decisive testimony as to the attribution of plots
(the *mnemones*) play a conspicuous part in the law of
Halikarnassos on the restitution of estates to amnestied
exiles.[3]   The practice of public registration of documents
concerning land tenure assumed important dimensions,[4] and
made it possible to avoid many controversies. But although
it helped to prove private rights, it detracted in no way
from the prerogatives of the city, and made it much easier
for officials to proceed when necessary to the application of
sanctions against convicts or insolvent debtors.

Confisca-
tion and
expropria-
tion.

A most drastic intrusion of the State in the domain of
private transactions is reported in an inscription of Ephesos.
It commemorates measures of public safety decreed by the
city authorities during the war against Mithridates (87 B.C.).
The date is a late one, but the legislation mentioned in the
inscription is entirely in keeping with the practice of Greek
cities during the classical period—in fact it can be referred
to as the closest parallel to Solon's celebrated $\sigma\epsilon\iota\sigma\dot{\alpha}\chi\theta\epsilon\iota\alpha$,
although it was called forth not by internal struggles, but
by external danger.[5] In a first law, passed in 87 B.C., all
public debts contracted before the current year except those
resulting from the farming of taxes or from mortgages
made to colleges of priests were cancelled and the insolvent
debtors liberated from the $\dot{\alpha}\tau\iota\mu\dot{\iota}\alpha$ into which they had

---

[1] DITT. *Syll*[3]. I, 169.   [2] *Ibid.*, 167.
[3] *Ibid.*, 45 (4th cent.), l. 20.
[4] *The register of Tenos, I. J. G.* I, vii, pp. 64 ff.
[5] *Ibid.*, 1, iv, p. 23, l. 27 ff.

fallen. Private debts also were to be remitted without
prejudice to the state of property rights in the year when
the law was passed. A second law was passed in 85 B.C.
authorizing a division of mortgaged estates between mort-
gagors and mortgagees by judicial arbitration [1] in accordance
not with strict laws, but with equity.

No sweeping measure of this kind is known in the history
of Athens after the reform legislation of Solon. In fact
the heliasts are reported to have been pledged to swear an
oath at their assumption of office not to advise or allow the
repudiation of debts or the redivision of the land.[2] But
the historians and orators of the fourth century tell us
repeatedly that the people in its impoverished condition
had recourse to confiscations and expropriations which
were not justified in law, but helped to fill the treasury at
the expense of wealthy citizens.[3] A characteristic consequence of the protection afforded to interests derived from
public sources is to be seen in the rule that the title of
a person who had acquired property from the city could
not be disputed under any circumstances.[4] Those who
thought that they had been unjustly deprived of land or
houses by the city could contest the application of a decree
of confiscation or expropriation, and a διαδικασία might
arise in consequence of such a protest, but even if it were
proved that the city authorities had been in the wrong the
property transferred by them to private owners (δημόπρατα)
remained in the hands of those who had acquired it from
the State, while the latter had to compensate those who
had incurred the loss through an error of the magistrates.[5]

It ought to be noticed in this connexion that there was
no distinction in principle between State domains and
property of temples. The latter was considered a special
class of public property. In ordinary circumstances the
gods, for instance Athene in Athens, received their proportionate share, but the rules and administrative practices
obtaining in the temples were subject to supervision and

---

[1] *I. J. G.* I, v, pp. 30 ff.
[2] HERMANN-THUMSER, II, 377.
[3] XENOPHON, *Resp. Ath.*   [4] DEM. XXXVII, § 19.
[5] BEAUCHET, *Droit privé*, III, 31.

revision by the people.[1] Goods and land, though kept together from reasons of provident economy, were in no way *extra commercium,* and could be sold or mortgaged if necessity required.[2] Above all, the city could fall back on the wealth of the temples in extreme emergencies, and Athens, for instance, had recourse to them in the critical period of the Peloponnesian war. Expropriation for the sake of public utility was admissible in the case of temple goods, and there are recorded cases of it.[3]

Archaic features in City law.

I have abstained hitherto from discussing the lingering influence of tribal institutions on the law of the classical period. But it would be impossible to omit a reference to the law of succession ; it proves that certain fundamental rules obtaining in the fifth and in the fourth centuries were derived from the archaic customs of an epoch when the Greeks lived in kindreds loosely knit together around tribal centres. Guiraud has said with some reason that land tenure was created not by the city, but by the family groups of older ages.[4] He ought to have added that these family groups were themselves political associations, and therefore units of public law, and not merely the private combines of relatives which we usually have in view when we speak of families and kindreds. It is even more important to make up our mind from the outset as to the part played in family economy and law by the religious element. Fustel de Coulanges' famous campaign against primitive collectivism hinged on the view that early land law was governed by principles derived from the cult of ancestors. Private ownership, according to this theory, arose specifically from the appropriation of plots of land for family burial grounds, and the main purpose of succession was the continuance of rites and sacrifices in honour of deceased ancestors, the shrine for these rites being connected with the household hearth. Both Guiraud and Beauchet have accepted this theory and developed it further by distinguishing between the family root and the religious root of pro-

---

[1] E.g. DITT. *Syll*³. I, 94. See above, p. 112.

[2] BEAUCHET, *op. cit.* III, 39.

[3] Delos accounts are referred to by HOMOLLE, s.v. *Donarium* in DAR. et S. III, 331.

[4] GUIRAUD, *La Propriété foncière à Athènes,* pp. 1 ff.

perty and succession.[1] I submit that when the religious
source is separated from the family interests of which it is
the symbol, it loses its material meaning and remains, as it
were, in the air, as a mystic doctrine which might have
satisfied priests and superstitious clients looking out for
supernatural guidance, but could hardly have formed the
core of almost universal folklore. If, on the other hand,
we were to hold to Fustel de Coulanges' notion of a cult
creating positive laws and private economics, we might be
accused—and, I think, with much reason—of setting things
upside down, treating causes as effects, and *vice versa*. It
requires a more vivid imagination than is generally possessed by scholars nowadays to accept the view that men
appropiated fields not for the sake of the harvest, but
because they had buried their parents in some part of the
compound. A pasture and a tilled field have their own
raison d'être for men in all ages, and the only question to
be decided is, how far the use of a piece of land by one set
of persons is compatible with its use by other sets of persons.
In the solution of this problem considerations of defence, of
co-operation, of capital outlay, certainly play a great part, and
the religious sanctification of the relations arising on the land,
although by no means a negligible factor, serves chiefly to
embody and to vivify group conceptions which would
otherwise remain abstract and utilitarian. As in the case
of the State, the corporate life of the household, the kindred,
and the tribe tends to present itself in concrete forms of
hero-worship, of ancestral cults, of the tradition of the
hearth. In this way there is no reason either to oppose
the religious source of land law to the familial, or to subordinate the latter to the former.

We have an exceptionally favourable opportunity for
reconstituting the leading principles of the Greek law of
property at the early stage of city life, when they had
ceased to follow tribal habits of settlement, but had not
yet thrown off legal rules derived from the powerful influence of organized kindreds. This opportunity is given
by the Code of Gortyn, which affords insight into the

---

[1] GUIRAUD, pp. 29 ff. ; BEAUCHET, III, 68 f.

customary law of the outgoing sixth century. To be sure the Code treats of Kretan Dorians, but the institutions which it describes and implies are to be met with in a similar, though not so complete a form, among Ionians and Aiolians. Indeed, their study is indispensable if we want to understand the somewhat fragmentary accounts of the state of Attika before Solon.

Now, while the Code of Gortyn describes a perfectly developed system of property in movable goods, with carefully drafted rules as to the rights of husband and wife, father, mother, and children, in the clauses dealing with divorce, dower, succession, partition, we find the land holding (κλᾶρος) excepted from the operation of these rules. Sheep, cattle, dress, ornamental objects, and other movable goods are to be partitioned among the heirs, the sons taking the town houses and cattle and two-thirds of other goods, and the daughters one-third of the latter.[1] We learn from clauses dealing with eventual difficulties in partitioning articles of a perishable nature, or of a nature that does not admit of division by number, that failing agreement the judges had power to decide to whose share they should be consigned.[2] What is more, in some cases the successional mass of goods might be sold with a view of dividing the sum obtained as price.[3] The town houses were evidently included in the processes of partition and sale, but the rural holding cultivated by serfs (Ϝοικῆες) is distinctly excluded,[4] and remains unaffected by the change of ownership. Such difference between town property on one hand and rural holdings on the other was, of course, connected with the subjection of a population of rural serfs to Doric masters. The Ϝοικῆες—or κλαρῶται, as Hesychios calls them—were attached to the holdings for their cultivation and the payment of fixed dues to the masters. The whole system of rural exploitation was regulated by public

---

[1] *I. J. G.* I, xvii, p. 366, § 26 Ἡ δέ κ' ἀποθάνηι τις 'τέγανς μὲν τὰνς ἐν πόλι κ' ἅ τί κ' ἐν ταῖς 'τέγαις ἐνῆι, αἷς κα μὴ Ϝοικεὺς ἐν Ϝοικῆι ἐπὶ κώραι Ϝοικίων, καὶ τὰ πρόβατα καὶ καρταίποδα, ἅ κα μὴ Ϝοικέος ἦι, ἐπὶ τοῖς υἱάσι ἦμεν, τὰ δ' ἄλλα κρήματα πάντα δατήθθαι καλῶς, καὶ λανκάνεν τὸς μὲν υἴυνς, ὀπόττοι κ' ἴωντι, δύο μοίρανς Ϝέκαστον, τὰδ δὲ θυγατέρανς, ὀπότται κ' ἴωντι, μίαν μοίραν Ϝεκάσταν.

[2] § 33.   [3] § 34.

[4] § 26, see above.

aw and not dependent on the vicissitudes of private
rosperity or misfortune. Some features of this dualistic
wnership are worth special notice. The Code of Gortyn
eckons with the possible absence of heirs succeeding on
he strength of relationship, however remote, and calls in
his case the Ϝοικῆες to succession—a most remarkable
ecognition of the tenant right of the latter.[1] On the other
and the class of goods treated in the same way as town
ouses extends to cattle and sheep as well, and therefore
ome margin must be left for the use of pasture-land besides
hat distributed among the holdings. In the minute regu-
ations about the marriage of heiresses (πατρωιῶκοι) the
ttribution of chattels and of proceeds (καρπῶ) is determined
n connexion with all sorts of eventualities, and the general
im of the law is certainly to prevent as far as possible the
ispersion of family property. But the *klaros* is never
nentioned, and it is evident that the heiress and the agnate
hom she is expected to marry are only concerned with
he income or proceeds, but not with the property of the
olding.[2]

A curious corroboration of the tribal character of early
Doric land tenure may be found in an Argive inscription of the
eventh century B.C. discovered on the site of the Heraion,
he common sanctuary of the cities of Argos, Tiryns, and
[M]ykenai.[3] It treats of the consequences of a crime com-
nitted by a person and visited by the penalties of banish-
nent and confiscation. The latter concerned the goods
(τάματα) of the culprit, not his plot, and even these goods
ere not sold indiscriminately to any one who offered a good
rice for them, but either to the magistrates of the city or to
he members of the kindred to which the fugitive belonged.

---

[1] *I. J. G.* I, xvii, p. 368, § 31 αἰ δὲ μὴ εἶεν ἐπιβάλλοντες, τᾶς Ϝοικίας
τινές κ' ἴωντι ὁ κλᾶρος, τούτους ἔκεν τὰ κρήματα.

[2] *Ibid.*, pp. 376 ff., § 46 ἐπὶ τᾶι πατρωιώκωι ἦμεν τὰ κρήματα πάντα καὶ
υ καρπὸν πρείν κ' ὀπυίηι. (Cf. § 45.)

[3] *American Journal of Archaeology*, Second Series (1901), edition
nd commentary of J. Dennison Rogers. Cf. First Series (1894),
rticle by Prof. Wheeler. The term πάματα can hardly be inter-
reted otherwise than as "goods"; in early law it seems to have
orresponded to the *familia pecuniaque* of Roman custom. The
rτιοπάμων was the head of the Doric household entitled to legal
narriage and to the administration of family goods and interests.

Only if none of these wished to acquire them, might the
be disposed of by auction conducted by the tribe of th
Hyllaeans.

The law took a different shape in Athens, where ther
was no social substratum similar to the ϝοικῆες of Krete α
the *penestae* of Thessaly.   The condition of affairs obtainin
before the reform of Solon might conceivably have develope
into something analogous, if the Attic θῆτες had been r
duced into a state of subjection regulated by the cit
Solon's reform, however, prevented this and led to th
individualization and the mobilization of landed propert
Before considering its results let us attend for a mome
to the epoch immediately preceding the reform.   It is n
necessary to dwell on the well-known economic features
the situation clearly outlined in the sources and commente
upon innumerable times by modern historians.[1]   It
obvious that the main cause of the wretched state of th
peasants was want of capital and their consequent depen
ence on those who for some reason did possess money
stock and could lend them at high interest.   What is pa
ticularly noticeable from our point of view is the inabilit
of the peasantry to repay debts by alienating part or th
whole of their land.   The κλῆρος of the Athenian peasa
was as inalienable as the κλᾶρος of the Doric tenan
(ϝοικῆες).   It could not be given, sold, or bequeathed o
of the family course of tenure.   This being so, nothir
remained but to pledge income and labour, and the
pledges took the shape of ever-accumulating heaps
recognizances in stone.   Five-sixths of the income h
commonly to be surrendered in this way, while person
indebtedness might end in the sale of the debtor out of th
country or in his reduction to the status of a hand laboure
a *thes*.[2]

The cure adopted by Solon was not only a drastic redu
tion of the burden of debts by subtracting interests pa
from the capital owed, and the remission of a certain quo
of the loan, but also the introduction of limited free tra
in land.   It is this latter feature which concerns us imm

---

[1] See, e.g. MEYER, *Gesch. des Altertums*, II, § 401 ff.
[2] PLUTARCH, *Solon*, c. 16 ; AR. *Ath. Const.*, c. 12.

diately. Unfortunately we are not told to what extent the
heavily indebted peasants threw their farms into the
market in order to achieve their liberation, but it is
evident from the economic state of Attika in the sixth and
fifth centuries that the social struggle went on for a good
while even after the opening of the market in land, and
that it is only thanks to the unexpected outlets created by
the Persian wars and the policy of State colonization that
Athens succeeded in attaining for a time a certain equilibrium between her agrarian and her commercial relations.
Anyhow, the legal basis for this ulterior development had
been created by the reform of Solon, and it remains for us
to notice that in spite of its radicalism it did not do away
with some traces of the previous archaic order.   The most
characteristic of these traces are to be found in the law of
succession and in arrangements of family property dependent
on it.   Solon's legislation recognized the ἐπίκληρος, the
heiress who serves as a link for the transfer of the family
holding to the nearest agnate.   Her position is often discussed in the speeches of the pleaders,[1] but the details
supplied by them can add nothing to the minute regulations of the Gortyn Code in familiarizing the modern
student with this particular device for preventing the
dispersion of the κλῆρος.   Intestate succession takes its
course, exactly as in Krete, on the lines of successive
parentelae—the descendants of the deceased coming first,
the males having precedence over the females ; then come
the descendants of the father of the deceased, that is, his
brothers and nephews (eventually sisters and nieces) : in
the third rank the descendants of the grandfather, that is,
uncles, cousins, and sons of cousins, with the corresponding
female relatives behind them.   This closes the ἀγχιστεία
or narrow circle of relatives, and leaves the way open
to succession according to relative proximity of degree.[2]
Partition and sale may supervene and break up the actual
estates into new plots, and evidently no kind of regularity
could be traced in the distribution of the soil, say in the
time of Perikles.   But the public supervision of the κλῆρος

---

[1] E.g. Isaios, III, 31, 2 ; 65, 7 ; VIII, 31, 4, 5.
[2] Dem. XLIII, § 51.

was never abrogated, and the Archon Eponymos continued
to perform onerous duties in connexion with the marriage
of heiresses, the appointment of guardians, the introduction
of new blood by adoption in cases when a household was
threatened with extinction. In this way, although a specific
law of Solon limiting sale and acquisition of land has only
left a vestige of its existence in an obscure sentence
of Aristotle's *Politics*,[1] the general tendency of Athenian
democracy to preserve the family holdings as economic and
religious units is sufficiently indicated. The recognition of
the household estate as the normal basis of social life and
of juridical relations finds expression also in some of the
laws concerning testaments. In the early or tribal period
the institution of a stranger to take the place of a natural
heir was effected by adoption, and this method remained in
common practice even after the introduction of direct
testament. It was quite usual for a dying man to adopt
some one on the condition that he should marry his daughter
or even his widow.[2] Solon gave leave to bequeath property by will, but on the condition that there were no
children and that the testator were in his sound mind
and not under undue influence.[3] Thus a certain family
solidarity asserted itself even in cases of disposal of property
by will.

Altogether it may be said that although democratic
cities gave a wide scope to individual will and private
interests, they never lost sight of the public element of
ownership and allowed it sometimes to manifest itself in
a manner quite foreign to our own notions and habits.

3. *Private Appropriation.*

Occupa-
tion.

The assertion of private power over things assumed
a different character in Greek and in Roman law. While
the Roman agriculturist stubbornly asserted his right to
a field which he had occupied for cultivation, in Greece
private enterprise was mainly exercised by the trader

---

[1] AR. *Pol.* II, 4, 12. Glotz (*op. cit.*) tries to explain away this
reference, but as it seems to me without convincing reasons.
[2] DEM. XXVII.
[3] DEM. XLVI, § 14; XLIV, § 68; ISAEOS, II, § 13; VI, § 9.

while peasants rarely detached themselves from their
fellows in the kindred or the colonizing group. As a result,
occupation of land as an act of private force is hardly mentioned in Greek legal sources, while appropriation of chattels
is noticed and recognized as a juridical source of property.
Aristotle calls it the natural source of property in regard
to the proceeds of hunting and fishing.[1] The domestication
of bees also gave rights to the person who had tended
the insects on his ground and arranged skeps for them.
As for goods acquired by means of trade, it was sufficient
to establish title by referring to the original seller or producing a receipt of his as regards the sale.[2] This was,
however, only a means of proof, and not absolutely necessary to establish title. In fact, although the famous rule of
the Code Napoléon—" en fait de meubles la possession vaut
titre " (Art. 2279)—was not proclaimed in as many words,
a very short period—one year—was sufficient to protect the
possessor against litigation, and as a matter of fact we do
not read in any of the speeches that have come down to us
of any disputes arising from uncertainty as to title in the
case of chattels.

This is different in regard to land, but the position there Usucapion
is peculiar when compared with Roman law. It is well and pre-
known what an important part was played by acquisitive scription.
prescription or usucapion in the latter system.[3] It served
to justify title arising out of mere occupation, and was often
used by the praetors to avoid the cumbersome technicalities
of acquisition *jure Quiritium*. Now, acquisitive usucapion
is never mentioned as a legal source in Greek law. True,
in a speech of Isokrates dealing with the claims of Sparta
to the possession of Messenian territory the orator urges as
a recognized maxim the view that possession lasting many
years establishes ownership,[4] and it will not do to challenge
this text on the ground that it deals with a purely international dispute.[5] Isokrates has taken care to point out

---

[1] Ar. *Pol.* I, 3.
[2] Notice e.g. the proposal of Protos in Demosthenes' speech
against Zenothemis.
[3] Buckland, *Text-book of Roman Law*, 244, 386 ff.
[4] VI, § 32 πρὸς δὲ τούτοις καὶ τῷ πλήθει τοῦ χρόνου.
[5] Beauchet, *Droit privé*, argues in this sense.

that the principle in question obtains both in public and in private law. But, on the other hand, as the reference is couched in general terms and bereft of any specific determination as to a number of years—say thirty, or twenty, or ten—it appears rather as an appeal to equity than as a definite rule of usucapion. It is also characteristic that the question of good faith does not arise in any of the trials known to us, while it could hardly have been passed over in any system attaching importance to acquisitive usucapion.

On the other hand there is a certain number of instances in which a defence is opposed to claimants on the ground of what may be termed limitation of actions, that is, prohibition to initiate a trial when a considerable time has elapsed since the occurrence of the fact complained of. A προθεσμία of this kind limited to five years is mentioned in connexion with actions of debt and of accounts of guardians.[1] As to pleas of land the evidence is confused and does not admit of a clear solution. There are some passages which seem to suggest the conclusion that the προθεσμία of five years was applied also in trials as to landed property, the most important reference being that of Isaios in the speech on the succession of Pyrrhos, in which it is said expressly that the law puts a term of five years to claims of adjudication as to inheritance.[2] But the reference is complicated by the adjunct that this term is running not from the death of the original owner but from that of his first successor. That these enigmatic words are not the result of some copyist's blunder may be gathered from the fact that in well-known instances the trials to which extant speeches belong took place some twenty or twenty-two years after the death of the first *de cujus*. This was the case with Isaios' clients in the trials as to the succession of Pyrrhos and of Dikaiogenes.[3] As for Demosthenes, he meets the reproach that an action has been brought late[4] by the observation that his opponent should

---

[1] DEM. XXXIV; XXXVIII, § 17.

[2] ISAIOS, III, § 58 ὁ δὲ νόμος πέντε ἐτῶν κελεύει δικάσασθαι τοῦ κλήρου, ἐπειδὰν τελευτήσῃ ὁ κληρονόμος.

[3] *Id.* III and V.   [4] DEM. XLIII, § 16.

not complain of having been left unmolested for a long while, but rather attend to proving his right. A rhetorical counter-thrust of this kind does not help much to clear up doubts; the only inference that one is able to draw from it seems to be that there was no legal prohibition against taking action after long delay, although one would expose oneself thereby to unpleasant retorts on the part of the man in possession. The speech of Isaios on the succession of Aristarchos presents a similar situation. It is not denied that the plaintiff's father abstained from bringing an action when the inheritance was taken over by the brothers of the deceased because he did not want to be separated from his wife, the only remaining daughter of Aristarchos, who might otherwise have been claimed as an *epikleros* by one of these brothers.[1] Afterwards there were other delays occasioned by service in the Korinthian war, and by other untoward circumstances. Yet in spite of considerable procrastination Isaios' clients did eventually bring an action.

When we put all these fragmentary notices together, it seems that we have to formulate two main conclusions : (1) any exception based on prescription could only be pleaded against the successor of the original heir ; this may be a consequence of the fact that in the first instance the adjudication was made by an ἐπιδικασία which could not be met by a παραγραφή if the claimant made out a *prima facie* case before the archon. The appearance of new claimants, relying on new evidence, could thus lead to a number of trials concerning the same inheritance. (2) When the right of a first heir had not been contested, or he had succeeded in defeating his opponents, his successor derived additional security from the fact that his *de cujus* had maintained himself, and in strict law an exception by προθεσμία was allowed to him after five years' possession.[2]

---

[1] ISAIOS, X, § 19 ὁ γὰρ πατὴρ οὑμὸς ἐπὶ προικὶ ἐγγυησάμενος τὴν ἐμὴν μητέρα συνῴκει, τὸν δὲ κλῆρον τούτων καρπουμένων οὐκ εἶχεν ὅπως εἰσπράξαιτο. ὅτε γὰρ περὶ αὐτοῦ λόγους ἐποιήσατο τῆς μητρὸς κελευούσης, οὗτοι ταῦτα αὐτῷ ἠπείλησαν, αὐτοὶ ἐπιδικασάμενοι αὐτὴν ἕξειν, εἰ μὴ βούλοιτο αὐτὸς ἐπὶ προικὶ ἔχειν. ὁ δὲ πατήρ, ὥστε τῆς μητρὸς μὴ στερηθῆναι, καὶ δὶς τοσαῦτα χρήματα εἴασεν ἂν αὐτοὺς καρποῦσθαι.

[2] *Id.* III, § 58.

However, it seems that this rule was not always followed
by the heliastic Courts, and there were occasions when
vindication of property remained open to claimants even
after the five years of the προθεσμία had elapsed.[1]   Such
deviations from strict law were by no means uncommon in
the practice of the Athenian Courts.   In any case, even if
we admit the operation of a certain procedural exception on
the ground of a statute of limitations, the fact remains that
acquisitive prescription or usucapion was unknown to the
law of the classical period and this is a most important
feature in the jurisprudence of the Greek city.   Procedural
limitations correspond to one set of social requirements and
usucapion to an entirely different one.   In the first case
the object is to put an end to vexatious demands and to
fraudulent devices of pettifoggers.   This is why the limitations are so prominent in claims as to debts in which the
defendants cannot fall back on any assertion of title.
Usucapion, on the other hand, proceeds from the recognition
of an acquisitive value in protracted possession.   It arises
naturally in situations in which a number of persons hold
the soil without any other title but occupation and use, but
eventually claim protection for their tenure on the strength
of long user.   While this juridical process is definitely
recognized by Roman law with its various forms of occupation, it is not apparent in Greek law, at any rate in the
period of the classical city; and the reason for this stunted
development has to be sought, it seems, in the tendency of
Greek law to derive title to land either directly from
allotment (κληρονομία) or from transfer by conveyance.
Under this last head the practices of registration and
warranty [2] deserve special notice, although they are too
technical to form the subject of discussion in a work
dealing with principles of jurisprudence.

Cultiva-
tion as a
source of
land
tenure.

There is, however, one group of rules in Greek law, in
which the influence of men's labour—of the exertions and
enterprise displayed by them for purposes of culture—is

---

[1] This is particularly suggested by the case of Dikaiogenes (ISAIOS,
V, 7, 37).   See on the subject E. CAILLEMER, Études sur les antiquités
juridiques d'Athènes, no. 7 (1869).

[2] On βεβαίωσις see e.g. DEM. XXXVII, § 12.

recognized as generating real rights, although these rights
do not reach the standard of full property. I mean the
growth of protected tenant right on territories reclaimed
from the waste. While land bearing fruit (καρποῦσα γῆ)
appears in the market as a commodity subjected to the
common law of leases, barren soil (γῆ ψιλή) requires an
entirely different treatment. In the later law of the
Empire the exploitation of such plots was termed ἐμφύτευσις;
in the classical period of the Greek city this generic term
was unknown, but the relations that corresponded to it
existed and gave rise to important juridical consequences.

Although the most characteristic particulars are presented
by the treatment of deserted or barren plots, the evidence
to be examined is mainly derived from leases made by
temples and priestly colleges which included soil of different
quality. One of the best examples is that of the fourth-
century leases of Heraklea in southern Italy.[1] Certain
lands belonging to Dionysos were measured and divided
into lots (μερίδες) by surveyors in execution of a decree
made by the people of Heraklea in a regular assembly (ἐν
κατακλήτῳ ἁλίᾳ). The proportion of cultivated land to
wild grounds may be illustrated by reference to the first
lot, which contained 201 schoinoi of arable land (ἐρρηγεία)
and 646½ schoinoi of untilled (ἀρρήκτω) covered with wood.[2]
Some 700 schoinoi had been appropriated by outsiders and
recovered by summary actions before the tribunals (ἐγδι-
καξαμένοι δίκας τριακοσταίας). Both the recovered territory and the other grounds belonging to Dionysos are leased
for life (ἐμισθώθη ἁ γᾶ κατὰ βίω) for a yearly rent of some
measures of corn.[3] Although the term of the lease is
nominally during lifetime, the conditions of the subjoined
contract as to the lands of Dionysos show that a lease in
perpetuity was intended. In the first clause it is specified
that the tenants are to hold their plots for ever, provided
they supply the securities required and pay their yearly
rent.[4] The third clause of the contract lays down that if

[1] *I. J. G.* I, xii, pp. 195 ff.
[2] *Ibid.*, p. 196, § 3, cf. § 7. The total of cultivated land amounted
to 1,095 schoinoi, of uncultivated to 2,225 schoinoi.
[3] *Ibid.*, § 9.   [4] *Ibid.*, p. 200, § 1.

the tenants sublet the plots to third persons, bequeath them
by will, or sell the right to collect the fruits, the assigns,
legatees, or purchasers are bound to provide securities in
the same manner as the original tenants.[1] Besides the
payment of the moderate rent in kind, the lessor is required
to plant a certain number of vinestocks and of olive trees
in proportion to the size of the plot. If he declares that
the soil is not appropriate for the culture of olives, experts
are to report to the popular assembly after having made
a comparison of the soil with that of neighbouring plots.
Every fifteen years the *polianomoi*, together with ten
citizens chosen from among the people, have to examine
the progress of the plantations, and those tenants who have
not carried out their obligations incur a corresponding fine.

The beginning of a similar record has been preserved in
regard to the lands of Athene Polias,[2] which had been
partly invaded by private settlers, and had to be reclaimed.
The greater portion of the lots are described as γῆ ψιλή,
while the rest consisted of valuable plantations.

The particular points mentioned in the Heraklea leases
receive further elucidation from inscriptions found on the
sites of Thisbe (Boiotia), Olymos, Mylasa, etc.[3] For our
present purpose it is important to note that special rights
approximating to ownership were conceded to leaseholders
in order to improve cultivation. In some cases the emphyteutic condition must have originated in downright occupation by outsiders.[4]

4. *Rights and Remedies in Land Law.*

Self-help.   Certain claims were considered by the Greeks to be so
self-evident that those who asserted rights under them
could proceed to put themselves into possession by their
own private action, without any warrant or decree of
judicial or administrative authorities. Such a situation

---

[1] *I. J. G.* I, xii, 202, § 3, ll. 105–8 καὶ αἴ τινί κα ἄλλῳ παρδῶντι τὰν γᾶν, ἄν
κα αὐτοὶ μεμισθωσῶνται, ἢ ἀρτύσωντι ἢ ἀποδῶνται τὰν ἐπικαρπίαν, ἂν αὐτὰ
τὰ παρέξόνται πρωγγύως οἱ παρλαβόντες ἢ οἷς κ' ἀρτύσει ἢ οἱ πριαμένοι τὰν
ἐπικαρπίαν, ἂν ἅ καὶ ὁ ἐξ ἀρχᾶς μεμισθωμένος.
[2] *Ibid.*, pp. 213 ff.   [3] *Ibid.*, pp. 253 f.
[4] Mitteis, *Zur Geschichte der Erbpacht im Alterthum* in *Abhandl.
der k. sächs. Gesells. der Wissenschaften*, XX, no. 4 (1901).

arose in three cases. After the death of a person his sons entered (ἐμβατεύειν) into the inheritance *ipso facto*,[1] in accordance with the view that they had been joint owners with their father. They were *heredes sui* in Roman law, and in old French law the same principle was expressed by the maxim " le mort saisit le vif ". This continuation of " seisin " on the part of sons and of their male descendants extended also to sons by adoption, if the latter had been adopted in the lifetime of the father, but not in the case of adoption by testament.[2]

The second eventuality when ἐμβάτευσις was admitted by law arose from hypothecary obligations. If a debtor, who had obtained a loan under hypothecary security, had not made payment in time (ὑπερήμερος) the gage was liable to be seized without further formalities by the creditor. A case in point is that mentioned in the speech against Apaturios, where the creditor seized a ship by ἐμβάτευσις.[3] Thus by law a hypothecary mortgagee was assimilated to a *heres suus* and allowed to proceed to execution by his own hand.[4] We have to distinguish from this case the execution which might take place against any insolvent debtor, as the property of the latter might be considered as a general security for the repayment of debts. In that case execution would proceed from a judgement or the order of a magistrate, unless there was a preliminary agreement that the creditor had the right to take steps to satisfy his claim by distress.[5]

Property pledged as a security for the payment of a dowry was deemed by Greek law to be safeguarded by hypothecary right, so that the husband or, eventually, the κύριος, of a woman could seize it in satisfaction of her claim.

[1] Isaios, III, § 59 ἀκριβῶς γὰρ ἐπιστάμεθα πάντες ὅτι ἀδελφῶν μὲν κλήρων ἐπιδικασία πᾶσίν ἐστιν ἡμῖν, ὅτῳ δὲ γόνῳ γεγόνασι γνήσιοι παῖδες, οὐδενὶ ἐπιδικάζεσθαι τῶν πατρῴων προσήκει.

[2] *Ibid.*, § 60 καίτοι . . . ὅσοι μὲν ἂν καταλίπωσι γνησίους παῖδας ἐξ αὑτῶν, οὐ προσήκει τοῖς παισὶν ἐπιδικάσασθαι τῶν πατρῴων· ὅσοι δὲ διαθήκαις αὐτοὶ εἰσποιοῦνται, τούτοις ἐπιδικάζεσθαι προσήκει τῶν δοθέντων. τοῖς μὲν γὰρ, ὅτι γόνῳ γεγόνασιν, οὐδεὶς ἂν δήπου ἀμφισβητήσειε περὶ τῶν πατρῴωνι, πρὸς δὲ τοὺς εἰσποιήτους ἅπαντες οἱ κατὰ γένος προσήκοντες ἀμφισβητεῖν ἀξιοῦσιν.

[3] Dem. XXXIII, § 6.

[4] Beauchet, *op. cit.*, III, pp. 262 ff., seems right on this point against Guiraud, p. 228.

[5] Dem. XLI, § 5.

The third eventuality in which seizure by self-help was allowed arose from the execution of a judgement: procedure by distress was rendered necessary in this case because the city was altogether disinclined to use its power of administrative coercion. As regards public prosecutions it relied, as we have seen, mainly on accusations by individual citizens; in the same way, it had not the time or the means to employ bailiffs to enforce decisions of tribunals in civil cases. Usually the winning party took steps on his own account with the eventual recourse to a δίκη ἐξούλης if he was refused satisfaction by the loser. This reserve of an action against a condemned party who prevents execution was the principal means of insisting on the satisfaction of one's rightful claims. Before turning to a closer examination of this form of procedure let us first mention some other methods of asserting rights to property.

Action in vindication.

By the side of self-help by ἐμβάτευσις stood in the case of claims to inheritance the ἐπιδικασία. If there were no male heirs in the direct line and the deceased had not adopted a son during his lifetime, the succession was declared to be open to adjudication (ἐπίδικος). If a son had been adopted by the deceased by testament, his claim had to be tested in connexion with the question as to the state of mind of the testator and his freedom from corrupting influences.[1] In the absence of sons, daughters had the first claim, as ἐπίκληροι, and the adjudication bore on the recognition of their right together with a decision as to which of the agnates should receive them in marriage (ἐπιδικασία ἐπικλήρων).[2] If none of these claims could be produced, the relatives could urge their claims on the strength of comparative proximity of degree and other circumstances.[3] The adjudication was announced by a public declaration, made by a herald, calling upon all pretenders or opposers to come forward before the Archon and to state their claims or to contest the claims of others

---

[1] ISAIOS, VI, § 9. See on succession CAILLEMER, Le droit de succession à Athènes.

[2] ISAIOS, VI, § 14 ὥστ᾽ οὔτ᾽ ἐπιτροπεύεσθαι προσῆκε τὴν Καλλίππην ἔτι, τριακοντοῦτίν γε οὖσαν, οὔτε ἀνέκδοτον καὶ ἄπαιδα εἶναι, ἀλλὰ πάνυ πάλαι συνοικεῖν, ἢ ἐγγυηθεῖσαν κατὰ τὸν νόμον ἢ ἐπιδικασθεῖσαν.

[3] DEM. XLVIII, §§ 22 ff.

(ἀμφισβητεῖν).[1] The adjudication turned entirely on the
question of comparative right, and did not settle the
problem in a final and absolute manner. If a pretender
appeared on the scene who had not previously tried his
chance, or if one of the parties concerned entered a plea in
error in regard to the conduct of the ἐπιδικασία, the lists
were reopened and a διαδικασία took place. The Demos-
thenic speech against Olympiodoros gives an example of
such vicissitudes, while the speeches of Isaios on the estate
of Hagnias and Demosthenes against Makartatos and
against Leochares present a lively picture of the complicated
claims and counterclaims among which archons and tribunals had to pick their way towards solutions. The principal
feature of the procedure by ἐπιδικασία and by διαδικασία
was that there were no plaintiffs and no defendants, but
parties to a controversy seeking a judicial declaration of
right. There was, however, in so far a difference between
the two varieties of controversy that in the case of a διαδικασία after adjudication the opponents of the persons who
had obtained possession had to make a considerable deposit
(προκαταβολή) amounting to one-tenth of the inheritance in
dispute. The fairness of this requirement was obvious, as
otherwise there would have been no limit to the attempts
to get hold of profitable estates.

The διαδικασία of inheritance is the species of adjudication most copiously illustrated in our sources, but it is only
one species of a wide genus. Caillemer defined this kind of
procedure in the following words : the attribution of a right
or of a charge to a person designated by the judge from
among two or more persons who assert that they are entitled to the right or to exemption from the charge.[2] It is
quite distinct from an action (δίκη) or from the rendering of
accounts (εὔθυνα).[3] It amounted to a declaration of better
right,[4] or relative right as between several persons ; and in
so far it established a prejudicial situation which might be
appealed to in case of any further dispute between the

---

[1] Dareste refers the expression to pretenders; Lipsius gives it a
wider meaning (p. 582).
[2] CAILLEMER, s.v. *diadikasia* in DAR. et S.
[3] DEM. XXIV, § 54; XX, § 147.
[4] Cf. the *jus merum* of the English writ of right.

parties.[1] Besides the class already discussed—the διαδικασία
as to inheritance—we have to note decisions as to citizens
liable to be charged with some public duty or payment, like
a trierarchy, the training of a chorus, or as to the inscription
of a particular person on the roll of public debtors.[2] Again,
if a premium had been offered for the denunciation or capture of a criminal and several Athenians claimed to have
offered the information required, the selection of the one
entitled to receive the premium was the result of a *diadikasia.*[3] A dispute between claimants to a priesthood or
some income connected with a sacerdotal office was conducted on similar lines of procedure.[4] One of Demosthenes'
private orations was delivered in support of a claim to the
exclusive use of a name.[5] In connexion with confiscations
any claim of third persons to some part of the property
seized by the State was similarly settled as between the
aggrieved party and the State.[6] In the speech against
Zenothemis the dispute between the two merchants Protos
and Zenothemis, each of whom claimed a hypothecary
mortgage in regard to the corn freight on Hegestratos' ship,
must have been engaged by way of a *diadikasia,* and each
of them could make out a *prima facie* case.[7] Perhaps if a
number of speeches of Lysias, Isaios, Hypereides, Deinarchos,
mentioned by the lexicographers, had survived, we might
be able to add other important classes of trials conducted
by *diadikasia,* but in the absence of this evidence we can
only endorse the supposition [8] that the *diadikasia* may have
served to settle controversies as to the right of property not
derived directly from succession or testament, but based on
other varieties of title, for example on registration, on
donation, on uncontested possession for a long time, etc.[9]

---

[1] BEAUCHET, pp. 377 f.
[2] DEM. XXIV, § 13.   [3] ANDOKIDES, I, §§ 27, 28.
[4] The subject was treated in orations which have not come down to
us. BEAUCHET, III, p. 380.
[5] DEM. XXXIX.   [6] LYSIAS, XVII.
[7] VINOGRADOFF, " On the legal background in Demosthenes' speech
in *Zenothemis v. Demon.*" *International Review of Legal History,* 1922,
pp. 202 ff.
[8] BEAUCHET, III, p. 381.
[9] On the subject of the *diadikasia* our principal authority is
G. A. LEIST, *Der attische Eigentumsstreit im System der Diadikasien.*

But such suppositions cannot form part of any systematic teaching on the subject.

What is more, there is some evidence of an entirely different course of action open to those who wanted to assert rights as to property. I mean the curious, though controversial, passages bearing on the δίκη οὐσίας. We have, to begin with, the following statement in Harpokration's Glossary, which has to be given in full, as there is a considerable difference of opinion among leading scholars as regards its translation and interpretation.[1] It may be rendered in the following way: "Claimants who go to law against those in possession of estates or houses bring the action οὐσίας in the second instance, while in the first instance they have recourse to an action ἐνοικίου in the case of houses and καρποῦ in the case of estates. In the third instance there is the action ἐξούλης. It was possible for the holders (the defendants)[2] to retain possession of the property if they were defeated in actions καρποῦ and ἐνοικίου or in the second stage as to οὐσία,[3] while, if they lost in the trial ἐξούλης it was impossible for them to hold on any longer to possession, but they had to evacuate the property adjudicated to their opponents." And the lexicographer refers in support of this summary to speeches of various orators, especially of Isaios, and to the eighteen books of Theophrastos' treatise on the laws; unfortunately none of these references can be verified from the texts which have come down to us.

The meaning of the terms designating the four actions is not difficult to make out; the passage deals with actions for the recovery of rents (καρποῦ, ἐνοικίου), for the recovery of property (οὐσίας = κτημάτων), and for the recovery of possession (ἐξούλης). Nor is the sequence in which the three stages are enumerated an unnatural one, although it does not present the same order as the one usually followed in Roman and in mediaeval procedure, in which litigants tried conclusions as to possession before coming to grips on

---

[1] For the Greek text see Appendix to this chapter, p. 228.
[2] The MSS. have ἐλοῦσι, which editors alter into ἔχουσι.
[3] TH. REINACH, in DAR. et S., s.v. *enoikiou dike*, explains οὐσίας as *l'action en revendication proprement dite*.

the question of title. In Greece evidently the first step of
a claimant asserting his rights as owner of a plot of land
or of a house was to demand from the occupier the payment
of a rent; the evidence might be easy to obtain by producing testimony as to customary or habitual payments in
former years. In a second stage the trial turned to a dispute about the title to the property in question, and this
could be termed appropriately a δίκη οὐσίας, as it concerned
the attribution of certain κτήματα and not a claim as to
rent or proceeds. A third eventuality arose when a person
who had been shown to hold as a lessee or whose title had
been proved to be inferior continued nevertheless to hold
on to the house or to the plot. This was a case of trespass
and dispossession, and the remedy open to the plaintiff was
a δίκη ἐξούλης with its increased fines.

So far the passage does not present any particular difficulty, and we are able to quote in corroboration of it extant
references in certain speeches still accessible to modern
students. In a fragment of a speech of Lysias preserved
by Harpokration the orator asks his adversary why he
does not bring an action for recovery of rent (ἐνοικίου) in
respect of a house which, he asserts, belongs to him.[1] In
Demosthenes' speech against Olympiodoros a similar argument is used.[2]

The only difficulty for the understanding of the passage
of Harpokration about οὐσίας δίκη arises out of the regular
progress from the first instance to the second, and from the
second to the third. What is the reason of this obligatory
ascent from actions as to rent to actions as to property and
ultimately as to possession ? It seems to me that too much
has been made of the systematic statement of Harpokration
as to stages of procedure. There is no reason to consider
these transitions as obligatory, and we can well imagine
that some claimants may have started right away by con-
testing the title to κτήματα (οὐσία), while others may have
brought the action of disseisin (ἐξούλης) without going
through the two previous stages. We are dealing, after

---

[1] HARPOKRATION, s.v. καρποῦ δίκη. See Appendix, p. 228.
[2] [DEM.] XLVIII, § 45 διὰ τί σὺ . . . οὐδεπώποτέ μοι ἔλαχες ἐνοικίου
δίκην τῆς οἰκίας, ἧς ἔφασκες μισθῶσαί μοι ὡς σαυτοῦ οὖσαν;

all, with a statement by a late lexicographer, who, of course, had the inestimable privilege of being able to refer to a number of speeches and treatises lost to us, but who cannot be relied upon as regards his deductions concerning the connexion to be established between various juridical rules. Even if it were established that there were practical advantages in starting litigation from the point of view of an owner claiming rent, this would not prove that such a preliminary contest was obligatory in all cases of vindication of property in land.[1]

The δίκη ἐξούλης—the action of disseisin, if we may use such a term derived from the well-known action of Mediaeval common law—took in any case a most important place in Greek procedure, and the best means of judging of its application is offered again by a statement of Harpocration.[2] Under ἐξούλης δίκη he tells us that " it is the name of an action brought by persons who assert that they are being kept out of their own property against those who are keeping them out. The term is said to come from the verb ἐξίλλειν, which means to push or thrust out. The action is used also in the case of damages by those who do not get them within the proper time-limit, when the persons convicted become defaulters. Those who succumbed in a δίκη ἐξούλης gave up to the successful litigant what they had taken from him, and paid the required penalty to the State. The action was used also by a creditor who tried to obtain possession of some property of his debtor, and who was prevented by some one. Also if a person is deprived of the products of his labour in cultivating land, the law gives an action ἐξούλης against the depriving party. So, too, in the case of a slave and of everything in which a person claims rights. This is shown clearly by saios and by Lysias in his speech against Stratokles in a trial ἐξούλης. Deinarchos, however, in the *diadikasia* of the Krokonidae employs the term in a special sense, applying

The action of disseisin.

---

[1] BEAUCHET's interpretation (III, pp. 368 ff.) tends to turn the οὐσίας δίκη into an action for the execution of a decision. Against this see LIPSIUS, p. 680.
[2] HARPOKR. s.v. ἐξούλης δίκη. Cf. above, chap. III, p. 60. See appendix to this chapter, p. 229.

it to the priestess who refused to perform sacrifices. Tha
the action is applicable in every case of ejectment fro
private property, and not only, as Caecilius thinks, in tl
case of losers in a trial who owe a fine, is made clea
by Phrynichos in his *Proastriae* (as well as by othe
evidence)."

The statement is somewhat obscured by the intermixtu
of general propositions and of references to special case
This may be the result of the fact that the lexicograph
used heterogeneous materials without much skill in sortir
them.   But apart from this juxtaposition of general rul
and particular applications there is nothing contradictor
or unreasonable in Harpokration's enumeration. He lay
down repeatedly and emphatically that the action ἐξούλ
was used as a remedy against all kinds of disseisin o
eviction, and states specifically that the opinion of Caeciliu
who confined the range of the action to the enforcement o
rights recognized by judicial decision, but neverthele
withheld by the defendants, is wrong.   Two of the speci
cases in which the action was used—the recovery of slav
and the recovery of products of one's labour—are covere
distinctly by the general principle of the security of posse
sion.   In two other cases the possession of things withhe
is guaranteed by judicial sentences—these are the cases o
unpaid fines and unpaid debts. Lastly, there is the referen
to the refusal of a priestess to perform certain duties co
nected with her office.   We do not know the circumstanc
of this last case, but it seems probable that the action w
brought by persons or by a corporation interested in tl
regular performance of certain religious rites and damage
by their interruption; perhaps the priestess had refused
pay a fine inflicted by a judgement.

Even if there were nothing else in the way of materi
we should be justified in rejecting Beauchet's contention
that the δίκη ἐξούλης was restricted to cases when
judicial sentence had been passed, and presented therefo
an exact parallel to the Roman *actio judicati*. But the
is additional evidence to show that the action in questi
had a much wider range.   There is, for instance, the app

---

[1] BEAUCHET, III, 395.

cation of an action which could hardly be anything else but a δίκη ἐξούλης in connexion with the ejectment of a man in possession of a bath-house.[1] In this instance the δίκη ἐξούλης appears as the counterpart of an ἐξαγωγή—an eviction or ejectment—and it is probable that a contest following on an ejectment led normally to an action of ἐξούλης on the part of the disseised. In Demosthenes' speech against Zenothemis,[2] the ἐξαγωγή is spoken of as a form of simulated self-help which could have been converted easily into actual violence, and called for a reaction by δίκη ἐξούλης. Altogether the action in question appears to be closely connected with the maintenance of possessory rights against infringement by lawless self-help. In this sense it is a necessary step in the substitution of orderly methods for private self-defence and for execution by private force. No distinction is made between possessory and petitory remedies—both sides are equally covered by the proceedings against illegal intrusion and illegal obstruction of rightful claims.[3] At the same time it must be said that although the action resembles the Roman procedure by interdicts, it is entirely devoid of the preliminary character imparted to the latter by the Romans and imitated by Norman lawyers. There is no cogent reason why possession should be regarded as a kind of outwork to property and strictly distinguished in procedure from trials of right and title. As in the cases of the German *Gewere,* procedural methods admitted of a good deal of intermixture between claims based on possession and claims based on title, because title itself was treated not as an absolute, but as a relative qualification.

When all this has been said, it is hardly necessary to point expressly to the fact that the Greeks were not indifferent to the juridical value of possession. Inasmuch as all orderly trials require a proper start from some determined situation of the parties, Greek law prohibited arbitrary seizure of subjects of litigation—chattels as well as plots of land. The law of Gortyn lays down definite rules

Posses-
sion.

---

[1] ISAIOS, V, 22.
[2] DEM. XXXII. Philippi was the first to recognize the fact. See article by VINOGRADOFF as above, p. 222, n. 7.
[3] Cf. LIPSIUS, p. 667.

about the party who should hold in his possession a slave a
to whose ownership there was trial between two claimants
A law of Zaleukos is reported to have settled the matte
definitely among the Epizephyrian Lokrians, and Polybio
has inserted in his history an account of a complicate
case in which one of the claimants had tried to secur
for himself the benefit of actual possession by seizing th
subject of litigation a short time before the trial.[2] Thes
instances show conclusively that a kind of *uti possideti*
rule was recognized by Greek jurisprudence. But it re
mains characteristic of the Greeks that the contrast betwee
possession and ownership was not developed into anythin,
like the elaborate doctrine which obtained in Roman law
Their treatment of the problems connected with individua
appropriation may be characterized as fluid and dependen
on varying circumstances. Their doctrine of property wa
indeed governed by the idea of providing safeguards fo
possessions guaranteed by the city, but it was liable at an
moment to be curtailed for the sake of public safety o
public service.

APPENDIX TO CHAPTER X

HARPOKRATION, *Lexicon* (ed. *Dindorf*, 1853), p. 229.
οὐσίας δίκη.

Οἱ δικαζόμενοι περὶ χωρίων ἢ οἰκιῶν πρὸς τοὺς ἔχοντα
οὐσίας ἐδικάζοντο τὴν δευτέραν δίκην. ἡ δὲ προτέρα ἦν τῶ
μὲν οἰκιῶν ἐνοικίου, τῶν δὲ χωρίων καρποῦ, τρίτη δὲ ἐπ
τούτοις ἐξούλης. καὶ ἐξῆν τοῖς ἑλοῦσι κρατεῖν τῶν κτημάτω
καὶ εἰ τὴν δίκην τὴν τοῦ καρποῦ ἢ τοῦ ἐνοικίου καὶ εἰ τὴ
δευτέραν ἡττηθεῖεν τὴν τῆς οὐσίας· εἰ δὲ καὶ ἐξούλης ἁλοῖε
οὐκέτι ἐξῆν ἐπικρατεῖν, ἀλλ' ἐξίστασθαι ἔδει ἤδη τῶ
κτημάτων τοῖς καταδικασαμένοις.

Ibid., p. 169.
καρποῦ δίκη.

Λυσίας ἐν τῷ κατὰ Δημοσθένους ἐπιτροπῆς " εἰ γάρ ᵗ
ἐγκαλεῖς τῷδε τῷ μειρακίῳ καὶ τῶν σῶν τι ἔχει, δικάσι

---

[1] *I. J. G.* I, xvii, §§ 1 ff., pp. 354 ff.
[2] POLYBIOS, XII, 16. Cf. LIPSIUS, p. 170, n. 120.

αὐτῷ κατὰ τοὺς νόμους, εἰ μὲν χωρίου ἀμφισβητεῖς, καρποῦ,
εἰ δὲ οἰκίας, ἐνοικίου, ὥσπερ οὗτος σοὶ νῦν ἐπιτροπῆς
δικάζεται."

Ibid., p. 117.

ἐξούλης δίκη.

"Ονομα δίκης ἣν ἐπάγουσιν οἱ φάσκοντες ἐξείργεσθαι τῶν
ἰδίων κατὰ τῶν ἐξειργόντων. εἴρηται μὲν οὖν τοὔνομα ἀπὸ
τοῦ ἐξίλλειν, ὅ ἐστιν ἐξωθεῖν καὶ ἐκβάλλειν. δικάζονται δὲ
ἐξούλης, κἀπὶ τοῖς ἐπιτιμίοις οἱ μὴ ἀπολαμβάνοντες ἐν τῇ
προσηκούσῃ προθεσμίᾳ, ὑπερημέρων γενομένων τῶν καταδι-
κασθέντων. οἱ δὲ ἀλόντες ἐξούλης καὶ τῷ ἑλόντι ἐδίδοσαν ἃ
ἀφῃροῦντο αὐτόν, καὶ τῷ δημοσίῳ κατετίθεσαν τὰ τιμηθέντα.
ἐδικάζετο δὲ ἐξούλης καὶ ὁ χρήστης κατέχειν ἐπιχειρῶν
χρῆμα τοῦ χρεωστοῦντος καὶ κωλυόμενος ὑπό τινος. καὶ
ἐπεργασίας δέ τις εἰ εἴργοιτο, δίδωσιν ὁ νόμος δικάζεσθαι
πρὸς τὸν εἴργοντα ἐξούλης. καὶ περὶ ἀνδραπόδου δὲ καὶ
παντὸς οὗ φησι τίς αὐτῷ μετεῖναι. ταῦτα δὲ σαφῶς Ἰσαῖος
διδάσκει καὶ Λυσίας ἐν τῷ κατὰ Στρατοκλέους ἐξούλης.
Δείναρχος μέντοι ἐν τῇ Κροκωνιδῶν διαδικασίᾳ ἰδίως κέχρη-
ται τῷ τῆς ἐξούλης ὀνόματι ἐπὶ τῆς μὴ βουλομένης τὰ ἴδια
δρᾶν. ὅτι δὲ ἐπὶ παντὸς τοῦ ἐκ τῶν ἰδίων ἐκβαλλομένου
τάττεται τοὔνομα καὶ οὐχ ὡς οἴεται Καικίλιος μόνων τῶν ἐκ
καταδίκης ὀφειλόντων καὶ Φρύνιχος ἐν Προαστρίαις δῆλον
ποιεῖ.

POLLUX, VIII. 59.

Ἡ δὲ τῆς ἐξούλης δίκη γίνεται, ὅταν τις τὸν ἐκ δημοσίου
πριάμενον μὴ ἐᾷ καρποῦσθαι ἃ ἐπρίατο, ἢ τὸν νικήσαντα ἃ
ἐνίκησεν, ἀλλ' ἢ ἔχοντα ἐκβάλλῃ ἢ σχεῖν κωλύσῃ, ἢ αὐτὸς
ὁ ὀφλὼν ἢ ἄλλος ὑπὲρ αὐτοῦ. καὶ μὴν καὶ εἰ ὁ μὲν ὡς ἐωνημένος ἀμφισβητεῖ κτήματος, ὁ δὲ ὡς ὑποθήκην ἔχων ἐξούλης
ἡ δίκη.

CHAPTER XI

CONVENTIONS AND TRANSACTIONS

1. *Form and Substance in Conventions.*

Philo-
sophic
view of
conven-
tions.

ARISTOTLE treats in several places of the conventions entered into by individuals and juridical persons. We have already had occasion to speak of his statement in the *Ethics* about voluntarily and involuntarily imposed obligations (συναλλάγματα ἑκούσια καὶ ἀκούσια) which correspond to the obligations *ex contractu* and *ex delicto* of Roman and of modern law. In the *Rhetoric*[1] he explains the great importance of conventions for social intercourse and describes them as a kind of law established by private agreement. At the same time he lays stress on the fact that their validity and practical application depend ultimately on the general legal order adopted by the Commonwealth. This close connexion between private agreements and public rules reminds us of the saying of Demosthenes previously quoted,[2] according to which law (νόμος) may be defined as universal convention (συνθήκη κοινή). Two important consequences may be deduced from this view of the matter. To begin with, private conventions can only be recognized and enforced if they do not contravene the laws of the city. This should be self-evident, and yet the point must be insisted upon, because there are one or two passages which seem to be in contradiction to it. In Demosthenes' speech against Lakritos[3] a convention is mentioned as

---

[1] *Rhet.* I, 15, § 21 ἡ γὰρ συνθήκη νόμος ἐστὶν ἴδιος καὶ κατὰ μέρος, καὶ αἱ μὲν συνθῆκαι οὐ ποιοῦσι τὸν νόμον κύριον, οἱ δὲ νόμοι τὰς κατὰ τὸν νόμον συνθήκας. καὶ ὅλως αὐτὸς ὁ νόμος συνθήκη τις ἐστίν, ὥστε ὅς τις ἀπιστεῖ ἢ ἀναιρεῖ συνθήκην, τοὺς νόμους ἀναιρεῖ. ἔτι δὲ πράττεται τὰ πολλὰ τῶν συναλλαγμάτων καὶ τὰ ἑκούσια κατὰ συνθήκας, ὥστε ἀκύρων γιγνομένων ἀφαιρεῖται ἡ πρὸς ἀλλήλους χρεία τῶν ἀνθρώπων.
[2] Cf. above, p. 18.
[3] [DEM.] XXXV, § 13 συγγραφή· ... κυριώτερον δὲ περὶ τούτων ἄλλο μηδὲν εἶναι τῆς συγγραφῆς.

expressly free from objection on the ground of any
existing law. It is not admissible, however, that an infringement of any specific command or prohibition was
meant. The contracting party signified by this clause
that he would not avail himself against the other side of
legal rules which might otherwise have been appealed to
in favour of the promisor. We frequently find instances of
such " renunciations " in mediaeval legal practice.[1] Again
in the Arkesine contracts preserved in certain inscriptions
found in the island of Amorgos [2] there is an emphatic
declaration that no law or decree shall be deemed stronger
($\kappa\nu\rho\iota\acute{\omega}\tau\epsilon\rho\alpha$) than the agreement in question. Here again
the literal sense of the words cannot obscure their intended
meaning. The contract was made on behalf of a sovereign
city, and the declaration referred to amounts to a promise
that no legislative or administrative measures will ever be
taken that might invalidate or curtail the contractual
obligations specified.

A second inference to be drawn from the close connexion
recognized between the social contract constituting the
Commonwealth and private agreements may be expressed
in the words that all transactions are recognized as conventions which are enforceable at law. This principle is
not devoid of technical meaning and specific application.
So-called *natural* obligations are not considered as a
separate class, or rather, we should say, Greek law gives an
equal force to all varieties of convention established by
mutual consent, so-called " nude pacts " being also included.
There is, however, an exception which strengthens the rule
by its explicit opposition. We are told [3] that Charondas
declared that in the case of sale the money had to be paid
on the delivery of the goods, so that credit agreements were
not actionable. Plato develops a similar rule in the *Laws*,
and justifies it by the consideration that those who have
consented to forgo the receipt of the price for a certain
time have implicitly admitted that they are willing to

---

[1] Cf. MEYNIAL, *Les Renonciations*, in *Nouvelle Revue de droit français
et étranger* (1900–1902).
[2] *I. J. G.* I, xv a, 11, 43 ff., p. 316.
[3] THEOPHRASTOS, *ap.* STOB. *Florileg.* XLIV, 22.

abide by the decision of the other parties to the agreement.
These remarks may seem to suggest that friendly arrangements in the nature of non-actionable transactions were
not unusual in the Greek world, and it may have occurred
sometimes that a so-called ἔρανος loan assumed the
form of a gift[1]; but we find in that very case of ἔρανοι
that they gave occasion to frequent litigation and were
treated in accordance with special methods of procedure, so
that the immunity from action cannot have had a lasting
effect on the law of the subject. The existence of certain
unprotected transactions can be dismissed therefore as a
peculiarity of local custom and the product of certain
special doctrines.

Early
traces of
formal-
ism.

Students of ancient law are accustomed to regard the
early history of legal transactions as dominated by more or
less rigid formalism. It is not only the well-known features
of the *jus Quiritium*—the *mancipatio*, the *nexum*, the
manus injectio, the *sponsio*, the *stipulatio*—that are characterized by ceremonial acts and solemn words without
which the transaction remains imperfect and void.[2] The
same recourse to sacramental acts and words is to be
observed in Germanic, Celtic, and Slavonic custom. I will
cite as an example the dramatic procedure of *affatomia*[3] in
Salic law—the ceremony of throwing a stick as a symbol
of possession into the lap of a middleman, who had to pass
the ownership of a house to an intended donee after having
performed certain acts of hospitality as master of the house.
Everywhere we come across certain forms prescribed by
traditional custom in the case of binding acts in law. Quite
apart from any particular tendency of the Roman mind to
clothe transactions in certain set forms of act and word
there was evidently a cogent reason that induced these
various peoples to work out juridical forms and to hold on

---

[1] [Dem.] LIII, 8 f. ἀπεκρινάμην ὅτι . . . τάς τε τριακοσίας, ἃς τῷ ἀδελφῷ
ἔδωκα ἐφόδιον ὅτε ἐπορεύετο ἐπὶ τοῦτον, ἀφιείην αὐτῷ, χιλίας τε δραχμὰς
ἔρανον αὐτῷ εἰς τὰ λύτρα εἰσοίσοιμι. . . . ἐπειδὴ οὐκ ηὐπόρουν ἀργυρίου, . .
κομίσας ὡς Θεοκλέα τὸν τότε τραπεζιτεύοντα ἐκπώματα καὶ στέφανον χρυσοῦ
. . . ἐκέλευσα δοῦναι τούτῳ χιλίας δραχμάς, καὶ τοῦτο ἔδωκα δωρειὰν αὐτῷ τ
ἀργύριον.
[2] Girard, *Manuel*, pp. 284 ff.
[3] Grimm, *Deutsche Rechtsalterthümer*, I⁴, 662.

tenaciously to them even in epochs of more advanced intercourse. Nor is it impossible to unravel the reason of such
formalistic treatment. It may be explained to some extent
by the wish to ensure the observation of the agreement by
a quasi-religious sanction, and to give a sharp and marked
manifestation to certain important acts of the parties concerned, and of impressing them on the surrounding public.
One might go further and interpret the curious combinations of formal acts and solemn words—like the joining of
hands (*dextrarum prehensio, paumée*, handfasting, ἐγγύη,
related to γυῖα),[1] the solemn declaration in set formulas,
the swearing of oaths, and the ceremonial steps (the *hepto-
pada* of the Brahmanic marriage) as traditional remnants
of religious rituals of alliance or pacification.[2] In any case
it is evident that archaic formalism goes back to much
deeper roots than mere superstition or magic practices
suggested by individual devices. The reasonable explanation
for these universally recurring usages has to be sought in
tribal custom and relations between kindreds which necessarily assumed the character of international treaties,[3]
although it would be hazardous to try to account for every
detail by reference to a system of religious law. Let us
see whether definite traces of this archaic formalism may
not be discovered in Greek tradition. At first sight it seems
that nothing similar to the elaborate rules of Roman or
Germanic custom obtained in Greece. There is nothing
so picturesque and concrete in the legal custom of the Greeks
in spite of their well-known sensitiveness to outside impressions. All the authorities agree that the binding force of
Greek contracts did not depend on the strict adherence to
any particular form. All that we know about them suggests
again and again that the obligation in voluntary agreements
depended on consent, on the mutual concurrence of wills.
There was, however, in reality no irreconcilable contrast
between the development of Greek law and that of other
national systems in this respect. There are some traces of

---

[1] Prof. J. A. Smith suggests that the term may be interpreted as
ἐκγυίη, *emancipatio*.
[2] L. GERNET, in *Revue des études grecques*, see below, p. 235 note.
[3] Cf. *Outlines of Hist. Jur.* I, 364 ff.

formalism in ancient Greek custom, while, on the other
hand, Roman law in the course of its evolution arrived
eventually at the recognition of intention and consent as the
constitutive factors in contract; this result was achieved
at a late stage by means of the *jus honorarium* and the
jus gentium. The archaic methods of the *jus civile* stood
out in consequence in sharper outlines. What we are
concerned with now, however, is to show that in spite of
the early prevalence of the consensual contract conditioned
by the lively commercial intercourse of the Greek cities
and the sensitiveness of the nation as regards psychological aspects of jurisprudence, there are distinct traces
of archaic formalism in the treatment of transactions at an
early stage of Greek civilization.

A starting-point is afforded by the Homeric tale of the
capture of Ares and Aphrodite by the jealous Hephaistos.[1]
The culprits are entangled in the net cunningly laid for
them by the lame husband. The assembled gods enjoy
the sight and laugh at the comical situation. Poseidon,
however, takes the part of Ares and entreats Hephaistos to
free Ares from the bonds, assuring him that the ransom
required by the offended husband would be paid by the
adulterer. Hephaistos refuses on the ground that if Ares
takes to flight instead of paying, he will not be able to
exact anything from Poseidon : δειλαί τοι δειλῶν γε καὶ
ἐγγύαι ἐγγυάασθαι. Thereupon Poseidon pledges himself
to pay the fine himself if Ares escapes without paying it,
and Hephaistos agrees to accept that second promise.
There has been a good deal of controversy in connexion
with this passage. Partsch[2] has explained it as an assumption of liability on the part of Poseidon, who acts as an
ἐγγύης, that is, a surety for Ares, and offers himself as
a hostage to Hephaistos in the place of the culprit. Esmein
and Glotz have translated ἐγγύαι as promises, and have
explained the whole transaction as the substitution of
a convention with Poseidon for the convention with Ares,
as originally proposed by Poseidon.[3] M. L. Gernet has

---

[1] *Odyssey*, VIII. 305 ff.
[2] *Griechisches Bürgschaftsrecht*, I, 11 ff.
[3] ESMEIN, *Mélanges de Rome*, VIII, 436.   GLOTZ, *Solidarité*, p. 132.

recently developed their thesis further in a very subtle and interesting disquisition,[1] assuming that Poseidon's action in the matter was a manifestation of solidarity between kinsmen. The enigmatic verse 351 quoted above in Greek is translated from this point of view as follows: "the promises of the weak (*impuissants*) are weak promises." A decisive turn is supposed to have been given to events by this reply of Hephaistos: he refused to enter into a convention with the powerless Ares, and in consequence Poseidon pledged himself to pay the fine himself.

I may say that the interpretation defended by the French scholars seems convincing in a general way. Partsch's theory, built up on the analogy with the German submission of hostages as sureties (*zur Hand gehen*), leaves unexplained the curious subdivision of the narrative into two distinct parts—the first dealing with a promise by Poseidon on behalf of a third person, which Hephaistos does not accept; the second indicating that Poseidon steps in himself as a party to a convention, which Hephaistos does accept. What is more, a translation which refers the δειλία to Hephaistos, and renders ἐγγύαι by *sureties* and ἐγγυάασθαι by *accepting sureties* seems misleading, because there is no likelihood that the speaker would disparage himself, while in reference to Ares the expression δειλῶν would apply naturally, as he was bound and therefore would have acted under duress. Besides, Partsch's interpretation makes it impossible to connect the two accepted meanings of ἐγγυᾶν —*to stand as surety* and *to give in marriage*—by any reasonable transitional link similar to the Latin triad— *sponsor, sponsio, sponsalia.*

We shall have occasion to come back to the question of sureties. What we are concerned with now is the fact that the passage in question treats of two kinds of conventions practised in ancient Greek law, and calls them ἐγγύαι. Now this leads directly to the consideration of the Greek betrothal as a contract originating in the tribal stage of Greek civilization, but enduring with characteristic modifications in the classical period of the city. The Greek

[1] L. GERNET, *Revue des études grecques*, XXX (1917), pp. 254 ff.

ἐγγύη appears as a characteristic formal contract like the
Old English wedding and the Scandinavian *máldagi*.[1] The
requirement of a formal betrothal stated in an old law
quoted by Demosthenes laid stress on the performance of
rites established by law. In order to breed legitimate
children a man has to marry a wife in accordance with
legal custom (ἐπὶ δικαίοις). By a piece of luck even the
formulae employed in the Greek wedding have been preserved for us by Herodotos in the story of Megakles'
marriage with Agariste.[2] Kleisthenes, the father of the
bride, pronounces the sacramental formula of betrothal—
ἐγγυῶ παῖδα τὴν ἐμὴν Ἀγαρίστην, νόμοισι τοῖσι Ἀθηναίων—
and the bridegroom confirms the contract by his acceptance
φαμένου δὲ ἐγγυᾶσθαι Μεγακλέος, ἐκεκύρωτο ὁ γάμος
Κλεισθένεϊ. There can be no doubt that the juridical basis
of marriage was provided in ancient law by a formal contract of betrothal (*verbis*) concluded between the father or
curator (κύριος) of the bride, on behalf of her family or
kindred, and the bridegroom, behind whom stood his family
or kindred, as we may infer from the analogy of the
wedding.[3] Even at a later epoch the ἐγγύησις ἐπὶ δικαίοις
remained the legal foundation of legitimate descent and
consequently of legitimate marriage.   The institution was
materially modified by later practice, and the consummation
of marriage came to be recognized as a second element in
the formation of the contract.[4] We are, however, not concerned at present with these later developments, but with
the evidence afforded by ancient custom as to the verbal
formalism of an important contract in early Greek law.

Coming back to Demodokos' story in the *Odyssey*, let us
notice that the term characteristic for the wedding of
a betrothed bride was applied by the rhapsode to a convention as to compensation for adultery. If the interpretation accepted by Esmein, Glotz, and Gernet is right
Poseidon suggested first a convention between Ares and

---

[1] Cf. AMIRA, *Nordgermanisches Obligationenrecht*, II, 282 ff., and
Grundriss des germanischen Rechts, 181 ff.
[2] HERODOTOS, VI, 130.
[3] *Outlines of Hist. Jurispr.* I, p. 319.
[4] Demosthenes' mother and sister were ἐγγυηταί, but not married
see his speech against Aphobos A (XXVII). Cf. DEM. XLI.

Hephaistos, and subsequently offered to conclude a convention himself with the aggrieved husband of Aphrodite. No sacramental words were pronounced, and no solemn acts were performed on the occasion, but it has been pointed out with considerable probability [1] that the repeated reference to the presence of the gods, who witness the transaction, lends it validity. Publicity is one of the requirements of a formal convention; the dramatic performance which gives a concrete expression to the concurrence of wills must take place before the public; its proper public is originally the assembly of the people in arms or in its civil capacity. Legal history presents curious examples of the gradual symbolization of this civic public—the substitution of skeleton *comitia* for the real *comitia* in the Roman procedure of adoption and testament-making, the probable substitution of the ten witnesses in the *confarreatio* ceremony. In Greek law the formal requirements of archaic contracts made way for two modern institutions— registration, which was currently employed, for instance, in the matter of constitution of dower, and the calling in of witnesses, which was, however, not required as a necessary element of the convention, though it was considered the best means for proving facts.

Another set of comparisons that is suggested by the study of Greek contracts bears on the question whether certain conventions might be void or voidable on account of a substantial flaw. It need hardly be said that there are no indications of the doctrine of consideration, dear to the hearts of Common lawyers. French lawyers with their staunch adherence to the necessity of an adequate *cause* to justify a convention also look with disappointment on the attitude of Greek courts of the classical period in this respect. There was no definite limit to the capacity of an Athenian to enter into any kind of convention that he desired, provided it was not made in defiance of the laws of the City.[2] Sometimes agreements were made for immoral purposes, for example, for entering into or continuing

Requirements of substance.

---

[1] GERNET, *loc. cit.*
[2] BEAUCHET, *Droit privé*, IV, p. 42.

immoral intercourse, but these were obviously supporte
rather by bad customs than by judicial authority: at an
rate there is no evidence as to actions brought before th
courts in connexion with them.   On the other han
Athenian litigants did not scruple to press home agreement
intended to achieve some result which could not be describe
as straightforward or even honest.   The dispute betwee
Kallistratos and Olympiodoros presents a case in poin
A convention had been made between them for the acquisi
tion of an inheritance that could only be obtained by on
of the parties concerned if the claim of the other party wa
wrong.   Nothing prevented Kallistratos from trying t
get the agreed advantage from the *suppressio veri* an
suggestio falsi which had been arranged between th
partners.[1]   This, however, is rather a reflection on th
state of current Greek morality than a characteristic o
the legal system.

On the whole, it may be said without fear of contradiction
that conventions in Greece in the classical period wer
formed by simple consent, ὅσα τις ἂν ἕκων ἕτερος ἑτέρ
ὁμολογήσῃ, ταῦτα κύρια εἶναι.[2]   In keeping with thi
absence of formal requirements stands the absence o
definite terms or rather the occurrence of several term
designating conventions.   Συνθήκη, συνάλλαγμα, ὁμολογία
are used more or less indiscriminately.   Συγγραφή has a
somewhat more special connotation because it applies a
well as χειρόγραφον to written instruments.   The writing
is not, however, of the essence of the convention in the
classical period in the same sense as the *verba* of the *stipulatio* are of the essence of the Roman verbal contract.   An
important modification of this statement will have to be
noticed in course of time.   At present we are considering
the principles of the classical period, and it is clear that
writing was not an obligatory condition for the validity of
any kind of convention at that time, although it was commonly used by business-like persons in order to secure

[1] DEM. XLVIII, *passim.*   Cf. DARESTE, *Plaidoyers civils de Démosthène,* II, p. 2.
[2] DEM. LVI, § 2; XLVIII, § 54.   HYPER VI, §§ 7, 8.
[3] BEAUCHET, *op. cit.,* IV, 15, 53 ff.

convenient proofs of the transaction.   In Plato's *Krito*
stress is laid on the purely consensual essence of conventions,[1] while in the pseudo-Demosthenic speech against
Timotheos [2] a convention is mentioned which had not been
secured either by a written instrument or by witnesses.
Yet it is not treated as invalid for that reason, but as
incapable of being ascertained in its details.   It was therefore possible for an Athenian pleader to build up an argument on circumstantial evidence that made a convention
probable, although no instrument or deposition could be
produced in Court.[3]

All this is true, and it would be wrong to judge of Greek
contractual law from the point of view of the rigid rubrica-
tion of forms and requirements of contract with which we
are familiar in Roman and in modern law.   The Greeks
treated conventions as they treated delictual obligations in
the light of utility (τὰ συμφέροντα) and of equity (τὸ
ἐπιεικές).   The centre of interest lay for them in the intentions of the parties, but this did not exclude the advisa-
bility of taking precautions for the proper and effective
carrying out of these intentions.   Registration, witnesses,
and instruments were not strictly obligatory: even in their
absence a party to a convention could claim an *equitable
remedy*, and was allowed to argue for its recognition,
but the usual method of claim was legal, and based on
some tangible kind of proof—registration, witness, instrument [4]

The necessities of business intercourse led gradually to
a use of instruments (συγγραφαί) that amounted to the

(marginal note: Equity in conventions.)

(marginal note: The literal contract.)

---

[1] PLATO, *Krito*, 51 e ὃς δ' ἂν ὑμῶν παραμείνῃ . . . ἤδη φαμὲν τοῦτον
ὡμολογηκέναι ἔργῳ ἡμῖν ἃ ἂν ἡμεῖς κελεύωμεν ποιήσειν ταῦτα, καὶ τὸν μὴ
πειθόμενον τριχῇ φαμὲν ἀδικεῖν, . . . καὶ ὅτι ὁμολογήσας ἡμῖν πείσεσθαι οὔτε
πείθεται οὔτε πείθει ἡμᾶς, εἰ μὴ καλῶς τι ποιοῦμεν.

[2] [DEM.] XLIX, § 2 λαβὼν ἀργύριον . . . οὐ μόνον οὐκ ἀπέδωκε χάριν,
ἀλλὰ καὶ τὸ δοθὲν ἀποστερεῖ με.   καίτοι σφαλέντος μὲν τούτου ἀπώλλυτο . . .
τὸ συμβόλαιον· οὔτε γὰρ ἐπ' ἐνεχύρῳ οὔτε μετὰ μαρτύρων ἔδωκε (ὁ πατήρ).

[3] BEAUCHET, IV, 23.

[4] DEM. XXXIII, § 36 πάντες ἄνθρωποι, ὅταν πρὸς ἀλλήλους ποιῶνται
συγγραφάς, τούτου ἕνεκα σημηνάμενοι τίθενται παρ' οἷς ἂν πιστεύσωσιν, ἵν',
ἐάν τι ἀντιλέγωσιν, ᾗ αὐτοῖς ἐπανελθοῦσιν ἐπὶ τὰ γράμματα, ἐντεῦθεν τὸν
ἔλεγχον ποιήσασθαι περὶ τοῦ ἀμφισβητουμένου.   Cf. BEAUCHET, *op. cit.*,
IV, 19 ff.

recognition of a species of formal convention, the contract
litteris, as conclusive in itself and not merely accessory as a
proof of the existence of a consensual agreement.   This process appears most distinctly in documents of the Hellenistic
and of the Roman epoch, but there can be no doubt that the
later evidence only summarizes a development which proceeded from the practice of the classical age.   As this subject has been discussed controversially since the publication
of a famous monograph by Gneist,[1] it might not be amiss
to point to certain determining considerations in the treatment of the question.   The problem arises from the fact
that a certain kind of Greek contracts, namely the bilateral
συγγραφαί, are mentioned by Roman writers as constituting an obligation in themselves, apart from and even in
contradiction to the actual transactions which underlay
them.   Two passages are usually quoted in this connexion.
Gaius[2] tells us that foreigners in the provinces—evidently
Greeks or Hellenized Orientals—were using instruments of
their own (συγγραφαί) to conclude obligatory conventions
instead of the usual Roman contracts.   A scholiast of the
fifth century, pseudo-Asconius, has an even more explicit
statement on the subject.[3]   He makes a distinction between
chirographa, written documents, and συγγραφαί, inasmuch
as the first merely report what has actually taken place,
while in the latter a convention arises even if the statement
does not correspond truly with what has happened.   In the
syngrapha sums of money are commonly mentioned which
have not been paid or have only been paid in part as the
persons concerned expressed their wish at that time.   This
is in accordance with the customs and rules of the Greeks.

---

[1] GNEIST, *Die formellen Verträge des neueren römischen Obligationenrechts in Vergleichung mit den Geschichtsformen des griechischen Rechts.*
[2] GAIUS, III, § 134 Praeterea litterarum obligatio fieri uidetur
chirographis et syngraphis, id est si quis debere se aut daturum se
scribat; ita scilicet si eo nomine stipulatio non fiat.   quod genus
obligationis proprium peregrinorum est.
[3] PSEUDO-ASCONIUS *in Verr.* II, 1, 36 Inter syngraphas et cetera
chirographa hoc interest, quod in ceteris tantum quae gesta sunt
scribi solent, in syngraphis etiam contra fidem veritatis pactio venit
et non numerata quidem pecunia aut non integre numerata pro
temporaria voluntate hominum scribi solent more institutoque
Graecorum ; et ceterae tabulae ab una parte servari solent, syngraphae
signatae utriusque manu utrique parti servandae traduntur.

Besides, other instruments are kept by one of the parties only, while the συγγραφαί are executed by both parties, and copies are in the keeping of both.

Gneist does not acknowledge that these references to binding contractual forms of Greek origin testified to the existence of a specific literal contract used in the Eastern provinces of the Empire concurrently with the usual Roman forms. Lately Professor Brandileone has come forward with a renewed defence of Gneist's conclusions, arguing that the Greeks never recognized anything but conventions by consent, and that, in so far as there can be any talk of alteration of the law of contracts in the Imperial period, it amounted to the gradual spread of a modified form of the Roman verbal contract—the *stipulatio*, which was largely adopted by foreigners, especially after the publication of Caracalla's constitution of A. D. 212 by which Roman citizenship was granted to the provincial subjects of the Empire.[1] He contests the value of the passages of Gaius and pseudo-Asconius for the solution of the problem. Gaius is supposed to be stating certain reflections on Greek practices from the point of view of the Roman classification, while the evidence of the scholiast is brushed aside as a confused statement of a late writer, incapable of grasping nice distinctions or of giving an exact account of them. As far as Brandileone allows he finds it a positive significance to this notice in the reference to a "temporary" intention of the parties which does not modify the fundamental grounds of contracts concluded either *re* or *verbis*. Such special pleading can hardly remove the impression conveyed by Gaius and the scholiast that a species of literal contract had found a home in the Eastern provinces, and had struck firm roots there in spite of the extensive diffusion of Roman citizenship and Roman rules in the beginning of the third century B.C.

The epoch-making investigations of Mitteis bearing on the vitality of Hellenistic vulgar law in the East have led to a revision of Gneist's doctrine. In a chapter of his

The doctrine of Mitteis.

---

[1] BRANDILEONE, *Sulla supposita obligatio litterarum nell' antico iritto greco.* Bologna. 1920.

Reichsrecht und Volksrecht Mitteis called attention not only
to the weighty import of the passages just quoted, but to
the rich harvest of contractual instruments in the inscriptions of Greece and Asia Minor, as well as in the papyri of
Egypt.[1] He saw in them examples of a mode of concluding
conventions that had taken shape in the East, under the
influence of the common use of writing, for the sake of
securing adequate proof of agreements of all kinds.
Gradually the literal form of the contract had hardened,
as it were, and had become a constitutive factor of the
agreement. In consequence various obligations were apt
to assume the outward form of a contract (συγγραφή) of
debt, and to obtain execution on the strength of formal
though fictitious instruments independently of the actual
transactions which had taken place under their cover.
Mitteis pointed to a signal instance in the inscription
reciting the dealings of the woman banker, Nikarete of
Thespiae, with the city of Orchomenos in Boiotia.[2] She
had lent money to the city on several occasions, but the
city was unable to pay on the expiration of the term. A
respite was granted in the guise of a fictitious loan to the
three polemarchs, the treasurer, and ten persons selected by
Nikarete from among the citizens, with powers for the
creditor to proceed to execution against these persons, and
with the proviso that the new συγγραφή could be made
payable to bearer. When the time came for the substitutes
to make the agreed payment, it was delayed again for a
short time and a convention (ὁμολογία) was made with the
city itself that the sum due should be paid in the course
of two months. In this convention the story of the previous
transactions was briefly recited as a preamble to the promise
of payment. This time the city acquitted its debts, and
ordered the various instruments bearing on them to be
engraved on a stone slab. It is evident, as Mitteis points
out, that the loan contract (συγγραφή) concluded with the
fourteen select citizens of Orchomenos was a fictitious
instrument representing an entirely different transaction

---

[1] *Reichsrecht*, p. 479 ff.
[2] *I. J. G.* I, xiv, pp. 276 ff.   Cf. pp. 333 ff.

rom those which had actually taken place. It asserted
contra fidem veritatis " that 18,833 drachmae had been
aid by the lady at Thespiae to the fourteen persons in
uestion, while in reality these 18,833 drachmae represented
he sum total of a number of loans made to the city. Thus
he formal device of a loan was used to cover a contract of
uretyship, and the meaning of the transaction was obviously
o make it possible for the creditor to recover his money
y execution against representative citizens instead of
roceeding to a cumbersome and uncertain execution against
he city at large. The practice of directing an execution
gainst private citizens for the satisfaction of a debt in-
urred by a city was by no means unusual in Greece, and
s illustrated on a large scale by contracts as to loans con-
luded by the city of Arkesine in the island of Amorgos.
While insisting on the formal character of the title obtained
y the creditor in the συγγραφή under discussion, Mitteis
lid not assert that in all cases when a συγγραφή or *cautio*
was presented the existence of the writing made it impos-
ible to plead for the nullity of the contract on the ground
f fraudulent misrepresentation. The practice of Imperial
escripts mentioned in Justinian's *Codex* shows that the
Roman authorities did not renounce the right of verifying
he good faith of parties to a transaction.[1] But the exercise
f such an eminent control does not alter the fact that for
rdinary purposes the statement of a duly executed συγγραφή was taken as conclusive without reference to the
ontents of the actual transaction. It is difficult to meet
he evidence adduced by Mitteis from the point of view of
Gneist's theory. The most recent follower of this theory,
Professor Brandileone, is constrained to urge that the
Nikarete transactions are based on a real contract in so far
s the money had been actually paid by the banker, and
hat a reference to this *causa* of the obligation is to be
ound in the last convention (ὁμολογία) which preceded the
ayment of the debt by the city. But this cannot explain
way the συγγραφή conditioning the original respite and
omposed in the style of an independent and fictitious loan

---

[1] RICCOBONO in the *Z. SS. Rom. Abth.* XXXV, 214 ff.

to the fourteen Orchomenians. The desperate expedient of treating the two documents as one connected whole, and looking for the material cause of both in the later one of the two, will hardly satisfy unprejudiced readers. One may well ask what *causa* there was in the earlier συγγραφή apart from the fiction of a loan received by the fourteen sureties.

To sum up this rather lengthy disquisition : we have to admit, I think, that although Greek law laid chief stress on the concurrence of the wills of parties to a convention, the constant recourse to written instruments for the sake of proof led gradually to the development of literal contracts in which the form of the instrument came to be considered as establishing a contractual obligation, and it was not easy, though not impossible, to rebut the presumption by direct proof of fraudulent misrepresentation. This process had gone so far in the course of the Roman period that the codification of Justinian and the mediaeval gloss derived from it assumed the literal contract to be one of the recognized species of contractual obligation, and the pseudo-Asconius gloss is interesting in so far as it traces that class of conventions definitely to Greek sources. But the notice in Gaius III, 128–34, shows that the instruments of the Greeks were already regarded as specimens of literal obligation in the beginning of the second century. Egyptian papyri and the Orchomenos inscription help to trace the connexion with earlier Greek practice. It is not far from a συγγραφή of 230 B. C. to the συνθῆκαι of which Demosthenes speaks in the speech against Apaturios or Hypereides in the speech against Athenogenes.[1] Even though a wide latitude must be assumed as regards pleadings based on the equity

---

[1] DEM. XXXIII, § 15 καὶ συνέθεντο ἐν ταῖς συνθήκαις, εἰ μὲν τρεῖς ὄντες ὁμογνώμονες γενοίμεθα, ταῦτα κύρια εἶναι αὐτοῖς, εἰ δὲ μή, οἷς οἱ δύο γνοίησαν τούτοις ἐπάναγκες εἶναι ἐμμένειν.   συνθέμενοι δὲ ταῦτα, ἐγγυητὰς τούτων ἀλλήλοις κατέστησαν.   Cf. § 19.

HYPER. III (V), § 8 ὡς γὰρ εἰπόντος αὐτοῦ ταῦτα ἐγὼ προσωμολόγησα εὐθὺς ἐκ τῶν γονάτων λαβὼν τῶν αὐτοῦ γραμματεῖον τὸ ἐγγεγραμμένο. ἀνεγίγνωσκεν.   ἦσαν δὲ αὗται συνθῆκαι πρὸς ἐμέ· ὧν ἐγὼ ἀναγιγνωσκομένω μὲν ἤκουον, ἔσπευδον μέντοι ἐφ' ὃ ἧκον τοῦτο διοικήσασθαι, καὶ σημαίνετο τὰς συνθήκας εὐθὺς ἐν τῇ αὐτῇ οἰκίᾳ ἵνα μηδεὶς τῶν εὖ φρονούντων ἀκούσαι τ. ἐγγεγραμμένα, προσεγγράψας μετ' ἐμοῦ Νίκωνα τὸν Κηφισιέα.

f mutual consent, the influence of the prevailing practice
s to proof did gradually pave the way for the recognition
f the force of properly drawn-up instruments.

2. *The Enforcement of Obligations.*

The most characteristic contract of early law is *debt*, and
he means of execution against a party who does not fulfil
is obligations are chiefly manifested in the case of non-
ayment of loans.   The simplest way of coercing an in-
olvent debtor was to seize him personally and to hold him
aptive so long as the loan had not been repaid.   There is
lenty of evidence to show that the Roman *nexum* had its
arallels in Greek law.   In the archaic period it was pre-
alent everywhere, as we can judge, for example, from the
ccount of the state of Attika before Solon, when the
reater part of the population was burdened with debts
nd many were imprisoned or even sold into slavery over
he border.   One of the chief measures of Solon's reform
ut an end to this disastrous condition by prohibiting the
eizing of debtors in their persons,[1] and we are told that in
this matter the Athenian legislation followed a precedent
et by Bokchoris in Egypt [2]: it was held that although
property belonged to private individuals and could therefore by right be attached for their debts, the persons of
the debtors belonged to the city, which ought not to lose
its subjects on account of their private liabilities.   However, even after Solon, personal imprisonment of debtors
took place in Athens on some occasions in the case of
lebtors who could not fulfil their obligations to the State [3]
nd in execution of commercial debts.[4]   The latter case is
noteworthy because it must have occurred very often: the
remedy was evidently suggested by the necessities of lively
commercial intercourse regulated by summary decisions in
monthly trials ' (ἔμμηνοι δίκαι).

In the rest of Greece the arrest and imprisonment of

Personal
arrest.

---

[1] PLUTARCH, *Solon*, c. 13.   AR. *Ath. Const.* c. 6.
[2] DIODORUS SICULUS, I, 79, 4 ; 94, 5.
[3] HERMANN-THUMSER, *Griech. Alterth.* I, 568.
[4] DEM. XXXIII, § 1.

insolvent debtors was universally practised and obviously much favoured by creditors as a likely means of obtaining payment either from the debtor himself or from his relatives and friends. We find it specifically mentioned in Halikarnassos,[1] in the Orchomenos contracts in regard to sureties,[2] and in the contracts of Arkesine, as one of the ordinary forms of execution.[3]

Distress.

By the side of personal arrest corresponding to the *manus injectio* of Roman law stood the seizure of goods belonging to the insolvent debtor or to the party that had broken some convention—for example, had failed to pay rent within an agreed term. The seizure might be only directed towards securing a gage like the *pignoris capio*, or it might be an actual execution (πρᾶξις) intended to give satisfaction to the full to the creditor or claimant. Originally it was not possible to draw careful distinctions between these two varieties. Distress took the form of forceful self-help (συλᾶν) and was used in the enforcement of compensation for delicts as well as in the execution of conventions.[4] It was based on a claim of right, the enforcement of which had to be justified if necessary before the Courts of the city. Distress preceded the judicial trial as a rule, and the proper means of defending oneself against unjust distress was to oppose it by force, always with the proviso of subsequent justification. An illustration of this kind of authorized private action may be found as late as in the Makedonian period (second century) in the documents relating to the establishment of the franchise sacred to Dionysos in Teos.[5] The Arkadians join in the declarations of immunity from distress of the territory in question and concede the right to the Teians to seize the persons and the goods of any Arkadians who should commit injustice within the precincts of the franchise. The right to oppose unjust incursions takes the shape of a counter-distress as to the

---

[1] *I. J. G.* I, i, pp. 2 ff.
[2] *Ibid.*, xiv, pp. 376 ff.   [3] *Ibid.*, xv, pp. 313 ff.
[4] See above, Chaps. VIII and IX.
[5] MICHEL, 58, p. 68, ll. 31 ff. l. 35 αἴ τινες τῶν ὁρμωμένων Ἀρκάδων ἀδικήσωντί τινα Τηΐων ἢ κοινᾶι ἢ ἰδίαι πὰρ τὸ γραφὲν δόγμα περὶ τᾶς ἀσυλίας ὑπὸ τᾶς πόλιος τᾶς Ἀρκάδων, ἐξέστω τῶι παραγενομένωι Τηΐων ἐπιλαβέσθαι καὶ τῶν σωμάτων καὶ χρημάτων, αἴ τίς κα ἄγηι.

persons and the property of the offenders. It is obvious
that the people using such reflected distress did not wait
until they had obtained a condemnation, but acted on their
private responsibility in the hope of justifying their conduct eventually before a tribunal if it was impugned by
any one.

The tendency to avoid judicial trials is manifested in an
orderly form in a number of conventions which mention
specifically that the non-fulfilment of conditions agreed upon
by one party will give the other party the right to proceed
to execution without having recourse to the formalities of
judicial procedure. A clause in point is quoted by Demosthenes in his speech against Lakritos.[1] It occurs twice in
the Arkesine contracts—once in the form of a reference to
the treaty between Naxos and Arkesine, and the second
time in the shape of an express statement that if the
debtors are remiss in paying off the capital, the city and
all its inhabitants should be subjected to execution καθάπερ
δίκην ὠφληκότων ἐξούλης ἐν τῆι ἐκκλήτωι καὶ ὄντων ὑπερημέρων ἀζημίωι ὄντι πάσης ζημίας.[2] The reference to the
δίκη ἐξούλης shows that the creditors had the right to
proceed without further delay to execution, but that the
judgement which might have been an equivalent to their
direct action would have been a judgement in disseisin,
implying a penal element. It seems that this highly
threatening wording of the contract was intended to
emphasize in every way the stringent character of the
obligations to which the debtors had to submit. It presents in this regard a marked contrast with the lenient
treatment of Orchomenos by Nikarete. But these are
distinctions of fact; as for the law it amounted substantially to the right of the creditor to take immediate

---

[1] [DEM.] XXXV, § 12 ἐὰν δὲ μὴ ἀποδῶσιν ἐν τῷ συγκειμένῳ χρόνῳ, τὰ
ὑποκείμενα τοῖς δανείσασιν ἐξέστω ὑποθεῖναι καὶ ἀποδόσθαι τῆς ὑπαρχούσης
τιμῆς· καὶ ἐάν τι ἐλλείπῃ τοῦ ἀργυρίου, οὗ δεῖ γενέσθαι τοῖς δανείσασι κατὰ
τὴν συγγραφήν, παρὰ ᾽Αρτέμωνος καὶ ᾽Απολλοδώρου ἔστω ἡ πρᾶξις τοῖς δανείσασι καὶ ἐκ τῶν τούτων ἁπάντων, καὶ ἐγγείων καὶ ναυτικῶν, πανταχοῦ ὅπου ἂν
ὦσι, καθάπερ δίκην ὠφληκότων καὶ ὑπερημέρων ὄντων, καὶ ἑνὶ ἑκατέρῳ
τῶν δανεισάντων καὶ ἀμφοτέροις.
[2] I. J. G. I, xv, p. 318, § 6. Cf. the commentary of the editors,
pp. 333 ff.

action (ἐμβάτευσις) without attending to any cumbersome technicalities of judicial procedure. The care taken in certain cases to give notice that execution will follow without any reference to the decision of a Court implies that usually the procedure was not so simple and the aggrieved party had to apply for redress to a tribunal. The result would be eventually reached by a roundabout way, but would be the same in substance as one by πρᾶξις directed against the property of the defaulter *ex causa judicati*.[1] In general it may be taken for granted that goods were seized or plots of land and houses occupied by the creditors themselves, without intervention of officers of the City,[2] although by way of exception, magistrates might have to lend their assistance for the execution of the judgement; in Athens the demarchs acted in this capacity.[3]

Sureties.   Greek law was exceedingly prolific in the matter of securing the fulfilment of obligations by providing guarantees from third persons. Looking back for a moment at Demodokos' story in the *Odyssey*,[4] let us notice that the intervention of Poseidon has a decisive influence in persuading Hephaistos to conclude a convention as to the payment of the fine (μοιχάγρια) incurred by Ares, and that the convention is concluded directly between the offended party and the intervener, while not a word is pronounced by the culprit. This is characteristic of the attitude of a surety in ancient law. Poseidon's obligation is not an accessory to that of a principal, but a substitute for the latter. Although there is nothing to indicate that Poseidon assumes the part of a hostage,[5] his responsibility in regard to the payment of the fine is placed in the foreground, a *vinculum* binds him to Hephaistos, while it remains for him to seek satisfaction from Ares, whose release he has procured. This tallies well with the position of a chieftain or an influential relative of the offender. In later law, we

---

[1] BEAUCHET, IV, 446 f.
[2] DEM. XLVII, 35.
[3] HAUSSOULLIER, *La vie municipale à Athènes*, pp. 104 ff.
[4] Above, p. 234.
[5] This is the view held by Partsch, *op. cit.*, pp. 23 f.

come across a conception of suretyship derived from these
archaic antecedents. Sureties appear in all kinds of conventions—as to voluntary agreements as well as in delictual
obligations. In the speech of Demosthenes against Pantainetos,[1] for instance, an arrangement to abide by the
deposition of a slave is guaranteed by sureties on both
sides. In the speech against Apaturios a similar convention is made between two adversaries to abide by the
decision of a board of arbitration. Every lease, every
loan, is corroborated by sureties. In the case of criminal
responsibility, sureties were personally liable for the
appearance of the accused and for the fulfilment of the
sentence, so that in case of his absconding they might be
subjected to the punishment incurred by him. When
Agoratos took to flight his sureties also escaped,[2] and Andokides even talks of unfortunate men put to death in the
course of the Hermakopidae affair, because the persons for
whom they had stood surety had fled.[3] This extreme
instance may, however, be explained by the state of
panic which prevailed in Athens at that time. In any
case the fact that sureties were made liable to the full
extent of the principal obligation and were proceeded
against without delay or excuse is characteristic of the
social tendency of the institution—the lack of confidence
in the credit and good faith of single individuals and the
spreading of the circle of responsibilities to the friends or
relatives of the principals.

A curious modification arose when a convention was made
secure by the setting aside of a certain sum in the keeping
of a reliable third person in order that it should be paid to

---

[1] DEM. XXXVII, § 40 ἀναγιγνώσκει μοι πρόκλησιν μακράν, ἀξιῶν ὅν φησιν
οἰκέτην ταῦτα συνειδέναι, βασανίζεσθαι, κἂν μὲν ᾖ ταῦτ' ἀληθῆ, τὴν δίκην
ἀτίμητον ὀφλεῖν αὐτῷ, ἐὰν δὲ ψευδῆ, τὸν βασανιστὴν Μνησικλέα ἐπιγνώμον'
εἶναι τῆς τιμῆς τοῦ παιδός. λαβὼν δ' ἐγγυητὰς τούτων παρ' ἐμοῦ κτλ.

[2] LYSIAS, XIII, §§ 24 ff. ὁ δὲ Ἀγόρατος καὶ οἱ ἐγγυηταὶ καθίζουσιν ἐπὶ
τὸν βωμὸν Μουνιχίασιν· ἐπειδὴ δὲ ἐκάθισαν, ἐβουλεύοντο τί χρὴ ποιεῖν·
ἐδόκει οὖν τοῖς ἐγγυηταῖς καὶ τοῖς ἄλλοις ἅπασιν ἐκποδὼν ποιήσασθαι τὸν
Ἀγόρατον ὡς τάχιστα, . . . καὶ αὐτοὶ ἔφασαν συνεκπλευσεῖσθαι.

[3] ANDOK. I, § 44 ἀκούσαντες δὲ ταῦτα Μαντίθεος καὶ Ἀψεφίων ἐπὶ τὴν
ἑστίαν ἐκαθέζοντο, ἱκετεύοντες μὴ στρεβλωθῆναι ἀλλ' ἐξεγγυηθέντες κριθῆναι.
μόλις δὲ τούτων τυχόντες, ἐπειδὴ τοὺς ἐγγυητὰς κατέστησαν, ἐπὶ τοὺς ἵππους
ἀναβάντες ᾤχοντο . . . καταλιπόντες τοὺς ἐγγυητάς, οὓς ἔδει (ἐν) τοῖς αὐτοῖς
ἐνέχεσθαι ἐν οἷσπερ οὓς ἠγγυήσαντο.

the promisee in case the convention was not carried out or some condition remained unfulfilled. This is the so-called μεσεγγύη practised chiefly in cases when a recourse to justice would have been impossible or beset with difficulties. Lysias tells, for instance, that Ergokles deposited three talents with a " middleman " (μεσέγγυος) on condition that they should be paid to certain pleaders in the case of his acquittal.[1]

Gage and mortgage.

Another way of ensuring the fulfilment of obligations is the pledging of goods or landed estate as a security. The gage (ἐνέχυρον) in Greek law was used approximately in the same way as the *pignus* in Rome. It was pledged usually as a material equivalent of a debt. The delivery of symbolic objects, chararacteristic of the German *wed*, did not develop in a corresponding manner in Greece. The juridical consequences of the taking of a gage are derived by necessity from the transfer of the object from the debtor to the creditor: its possession passes to the latter, while property remains with the debtor so long as he has not transgressed the term set for repayment.[2]

A much more interesting situation arises when the material security consists in the delivery of a landed estate, or when chattels are pledged on the same conditions as are usually operative in the case of landed estates. Greek law developed in this direction two interesting institutions—the πρᾶσις ἐπὶ λύσει and the ὑποθήκη. These forms differ from the ordinary gage (ἐνέχυρον) in two respects: in the case of the sale conditioned by possible repayment the property of the plot or of the goods passed to the creditor and the loan assumed the aspect of a sale in which the risks attending the transaction were borne by the creditor, who on the other hand obtained provisional possession and exercised the rights of an owner. This meant, for instance, that if a ship was sold in this manner, as happened in the case treated by Demosthenes in his speech against Apaturios,[3] and this ship suffered shipwreck while held by the creditor, the debtor would be absolved from

---

[1] LYSIAS, XXIX, § 6.
[2] BEAUCHET, IV, p. 177.
[3] [DEM.] XXXIII.

the payment of the debt. Nothing indicates, however, that he might claim compensation for the loss of surplus value, unless a special clause of the convention guaranteed such compensation.[1] The estate sold in this way could be sold further by the purchaser, who exercised in this case his right of free disposal, and the debtor could not prevent the sale, which did not, however, affect the condition of possible resumption within the agreed term.[2]

The ὑποθήκη is based, on the contrary, on the retention of ownership and possession by the debtor, so that the right of the mortgagee comes into operation only when the mortgagor has infringed the stipulations of the loan, e. g. when he has failed to make the payment within the agreed term (ὑπερημερία). Very commonly the ὑποθήκη was employed in order to secure to the wife the restitution of dowry in case of divorce,[3] and sometimes, on the contrary, the payment to the husband of the *dos profecticia*, the dower settled on a bride by her parents. Another common case arose from the obligation imposed on the guardians of orphans to secure the property rights of their wards by a corresponding mortgage.[4] In these eventualities the economic background of the transaction is sufficiently apparent. It was not in the interest of the obligees to liquidate abruptly the obligation, which would on many occasions remain as it were in suspense while the parties concerned lived and worked in good harmony. At the same time the imposition of the mortgage served as a guarantee in case of a disruption or disturbance of harmonious co-operation. In the same way hypothecary liability arose naturally in the case of leaseholders and lodgers, who were not deprived of the use of their chattels by the City or by landlords, but had generally to submit to the liability of the effects introduced by them into the farm or the lodging for the punctual carrying out of the conditions as to rent, terms, improvements, &c. Altogether the ὑποθήκη arose, as its name indicates, from the imposition of certain burdens on a constituted economic organization.

---

[1] LIPSIUS, pp. 703 ff. [2] *Ibid.*, pp. 692 ff.
[3] *I. J. G.*, I, vi, *Register of Mykonos*, pp. 49 ff.
[4] LIPSIUS, 520 ff.

Origins of
ὑποθήκη.

This being so, if seems to me that the much debated question as to the origins of the law of mortgage [1] and the relative priority of the ὑποθήκη or the πρᾶσις ἐπὶ λύσει has to be decided in favour of the former. It is impossible, of course, to maintain dogmatically that both methods could not have been used at the same time independently of each other. But the hypothecary mortgage agrees better with the historical evidence bearing on indebtedness in the early period. The most detailed account we possess in this respect is derived from the story of Attika before Solon and of the reforms which put an end to the "enslavement of the Attic land".[2] It is stated specifically that the holdings of the peasantry were crushed by the weight of the stone slabs bearing record of the debts, and it is difficult not to recognize in these ὅροι the hypothecary muniments familiar to epigraphists.[3] The σεισάχθεια cannot have consisted in the redemption (λύσις) of estates sold to satisfy creditors, because one of the main reasons of the crisis consisted in the fact that holdings could not be alienated by sale. This legal obstacle was removed by Solon's legislation, and land was henceforth mobilized, but the plots crushed by the ὅροι had never been sold, and could therefore not be redeemed.[4] We are driven to infer that the debts imposed on them had accumulated in the form of increasing rents and arrears, and that the liberation consisted both in the annulment of part of these rents, and in the possibility of treating land for purposes of securing loans in a manner similar to chattels, as an ordinary ἐνέχυρον, or by the expedient of a sale on condition of redemption (πρᾶσις ἐπὶ λύσει = mancipatio fiduciae causa).[5]

[1] HITZIG, Griechisches Pfandrecht; SZANTO, Wiener Studien, IX; BEAUCHET, op. cit., III, 187; LIPSIUS, pp. 696 ff.

[2] SOLON, Poetae lyrici Graeci (Bergk), II, Fr. 36. PLUTARCH, Solon, c. 15.

[3] Cf. I. J. G. I, viii, pp. 107 ff.

[4] What is one to make of the anecdote related by Aristotle, Ath. Const. c. 6, about the παλαιόπλουτοι—Solon's friends who invested money in loans because they knew about the coming reform in land-law? Such stories do not inspire much confidence as a rule. As the term παλαιόπλουτοι is well established, however, it may have been used to designate a group of families which derived their wealth from the acquisition of estates burdened with hypothecary obligations.

[5] So far I agree with BEAUCHET (III, p. 185), who, however, denies the existence of all kinds of hypothecary securities before Solon.

Certain considerations appear to militate against such an interpretation.   Hypothecary arrangements of the kind just mentioned would be devoid of the principal and final guarantee stipulated on behalf of the creditor—namely his right to foreclose : as the holding engaged was inalienable it could not be passed on to the lender in the event of the insolvency of the debtor. The argument against alienation by sale seems to tell equally against alienation by foreclosure. The inference is unavoidable as regards mortgage in its well-known later form. But the corresponding consequence was only drawn exceptionally in ancient law, as we can gather from a notice of Aristotle,[1] who ascribed a special prohibition of the kind to Oxylos, the legendary companion of the Heracleidae. But the argument would not apply against the admission of an earlier transitional use of the *hypotheca* in the sense of a real burden engrafted on the holding. The existence of some arrangement of that kind seems required by the juridical and economic conditions attributed to the epoch before Solon and to his reformatory action. There can hardly be a doubt that the land was distributed in inalienable family holdings ($\kappa\lambda\hat{\eta}\rho o\iota$). If so, the Aristotelian saying $\dot{\eta}$ $\delta\grave{\epsilon}$ $\gamma\hat{\eta}$ $\pi\hat{a}\sigma a$ $\delta\iota$' $\dot{o}\lambda\acute{\iota}\gamma\omega\nu$ $\hat{\eta}\nu$ meant simply that the soil was in the control of a few.   It can be reconciled with the existence of inalienable family holdings by the assumption of a semi-servile condition into which a large part of the owners of $\kappa\lambda\hat{\eta}\rho o\iota$ had lapsed in consequence of indebtedness.   And here the notion of a dependence based on a kind of predial servitude, inherent to the soil, involving heavy rent, and secured by inscriptions on $\ddot{o}\rho o\iota$, appears as the only compromise fitting the situation and corresponding in its various parts with well attested facts. The regulations of Solon as to a timocratic distribution into four classes are in no way opposed to the view advocated in the above paragraphs. Solon never attempted to start from a clean slate. He had to reckon with a society in which social inequalities had come to play a great part, although the differences could not be estimated properly by the size of estates. He graduated the classes according to standards of income

[1] *Pol.* VIII (VI), 1319 a, 12.

which, at the outside, were calculated on a very modest scale. How many of the πεντακοσιοιμέδιμνοι were really large landowners, and how many only ranked on an equal footing with them we cannot say, nor is it possible to make out how far the division into classes was prepared in the previous social order by an unequal distribution of shares among the πολύκληροι and ordinary ζευγῖται. The sixth chapter of Aristotle's *Athenian Constitution* inspires confidence in no one. I should like to suggest that the divergent development of *fiducia* and *pignus* in Roman law may have been connected with the early expansion of Rome on Italian soil. The social struggle between patricians and plebeians reflected originally in the institution of *nexum* did not lead to the imposition of hypothecary ὅροι, but was turned off into the channel of conflicts as to the occupation of *ager publicus*.

Modern writers familiar with the definite and complex institutions of lease and mortgage have failed to describe with sufficient precision the rudimentary and transitional species of security found in Greece, but they have supplied us with all the component elements of the combination.[1]

A second difficulty concerns the diffusion of the hypothecary mortgage through Greece. It was of course by no means restricted to Attika. We get glimpses of it at Delphi, in Naxos, in Lemnos, in Halikarnassos, in Delos, in Kos, in Thera, in Cumae, etc.[2] How is it to be explained that an institution of general application should have had a development so closely conditioned by events of Athenian history? The answer to this should be, I think, that apart from the immense influence of Athens in shaping later Greek law—an influence that would go far to account for many late developments—there was a similarity of circumstances and social requirements in the Greek world at large which suggested similar juridical devices. Solon's

---

[1] Szanto, *Wiener Studien*, IX, came near the solution indicated in the text: he regarded the ὑποθήκη and the πρᾶσις ἐπὶ λύσει as independent of each other, and derived the first from the earlier form of personal liability. In my opinion the liability became predial before Solon.

[2] *I. J. G.* I, viii, pp. 107 ff.

reform of land law, for example, appears to have been preceded by the similar legislation of Charondas in Magna
Graecia.[1] The struggle of the Demos against landed aristocracy was, of course, by no means peculiar to Athens, and
presented obvious points of analogy in all cities where the
geomoroi tried to defend the position against the oncoming
tide of the Demos.

The problems of agrarian indebtedness and of the securities obtained by landed capitalists were certainly to the
fore in most States that had a considerable rural population.
The solutions of these problems, without being identical,
must have moved very much on similar lines, and the provision of securities based on real estate without dis-
possessing the peasant population was obviously one of the
most convenient expedients. The generalization of legal
rules as to hypothecary mortgage must have taken place at
a later period.[2] As in the case of transfer of landed property, the establishment of mortgages and fiduciary sales
(πρᾶσις ἐπὶ λύσει) of all kinds was commonly safeguarded
against abuses and infringements by public proclamations
and registration.[3]

It lies outside the scope of this survey to consider the
much-debated subject of the influence of the Greek law of
mortgage on Roman law.[4] The only remark which I should
like to make in this connexion refers to the evidence supplied by the use of the term *hypotheca* for the continuity
of Greek customs under Roman rule. The statements of
Gaius and of Marcian prove, if nothing else, that the practice of securing interests by obligations imposed on estates
rather than on persons using them had its popular roots in
the economy of the Hellenized East.

3. *Lease and Sale.*

It would be out of the question to discuss the details of
the Greek law of contract, as embodied in the various
species of conventions. The rules inserted in the speeches

[1] AR. *Pol.* II, 1274 a.
[2] Beauchet's theory requires a similar surmise.
[3] E. g. the *Register of dowers at Mykonos, I. J. G.* I. vi.
[4] *R.-Enc.* X, 343 ff.

of orators and commented on by them are to a great extent
technical and suggested by various political and economic
conditions rather than by considerations of juridical doctrine.   They are discussed with much learning in the
leading works on Greek law, such as those of Caillemer,
Beauchet, Meier and Schömann, Lipsius, Hitzig, &c., but it
would be impossible to fit these details into a scheme of
jurisprudence.   I do not attempt, therefore, to pass in
review all the known classes of conventions—debt, deposit,
mandate, partnership, contract of service (*locatio operarum*),
and I may perhaps plead in extenuation of this omission
that the Greeks themselves did not differentiate much between the various conventions in their organization of
procedure.   The main action was common to all: it was
the δίκη συνθηκῶν παραβάσεως.   But it will help us to
grasp the leading ideas of the law of contract if we look
somewhat more closely to the working of two important
varieties of that department—the law as to leases and the
law of sale.

Ordinary
leases.

The transfer of the use of houses, land, or chattels by
their owner to other persons was widely practised in Greece,
and the rules governing such transactions were very similar
to those obtaining in Roman law.   When the surrender of
the right of usage was compensated for by payments in
money or in kind, there arose the contract of lease and hire
(*locatio conductio*), of which we have many illustrations in
epigraphic documents and some in forensic speeches.   Almost
all the extant examples deal with the property of cities, of
demes, of phratries, and other associations, or with estates
belonging to temples, but this is only accidental and depends
on the fact that juridical persons were bound to manage
business in a more circumstantial and formal way than
private persons.   The conventions of the former were
generally engraved on stone, while the agreements between
private persons were usually written on tablets and therefore had not the same chance of surviving.   The care with
which conveyances as to temple property or public property were formulated and recorded shows that the formal
side of such conventions was by no means overlooked or
neglected.   In spite of the fact that there were no specific

requirements as to the conclusion of a lease and that the contract was formed by the agreement between the parties and the concurrence of their wills, there were two aspects of such a transaction which involved definite conformity to certain rules and requirements. To begin with, it was necessary to determine with precision the capacity of the lessors to act in the matter as well as the extent of their right of making a valid agreement. The question did not arise in this form in the case of private owners, but it recurs over and over again in the inscriptions recording conventions in which one of the parties was a moral person. A city, a deme, a temple were abstractions unless represented by definite plenipotentiaries, and such plenipotentiaries were either certain magistrates or specially designated commissioners,[1] or even the people of the city or association in their lawfully constituted assembly.[2] Apart from that the conventions are often framed in such a way as to refer for authority to some general regulations passed on the subject.[3] These features do not affect the freedom of agreement between bailor and bailee, but they put into a strong light a point which is sometimes slurred over in the usual treatment of contractual relations in Greek law. Whatever stress we may lay on the consensual character of Greek conventions, we must not forget that the Greeks were very much alive to the necessity of clothing their agreements in definite forms and providing them with conclusive proofs so as to preclude as much as possible misinterpretation and misunderstandings. They did not labour the problem of the *causa* in contract, but they attached a great deal of importance to practical measures devised to safeguard a strict fulfilment of obligations. For this reason, although there is ample evidence as to the consensual essence of the contract of lease, there are also occasions when oaths [4] or the testimony of witnesses [5] are mentioned

---

[1] BEAUCHET, *op. cit.*, IV, 163 f.
[2] For instance, *I. J. G.* I, xiii², p. 238. *Leases of the deme of Aixone.*
[3] HOMOLLE, *Les archives de l'intendance sacrée à Délos*, p. 1194; *Bull. de correspondance hellénique*, VI, 63 ff.; XIV, 421 ff.
[4] HAUSSOULLIER, *Bull. de corr. hell.* III, 253.
[5] See above, p. 237.

as important for the conclusion of a proper agreement of
this kind : while, on the other hand, the drawing up of an
instrument is considered to be so important that the parties,[1]
especially the lessors, take elaborate and costly measures to
ensure publicity by inscriptions.

Turning to the contents of Greek leases, it is to be
observed that the rule expressed by the German proverb
" Kauf bricht Miete ", " sale prevails over lease ", seems to
have obtained in Greece as well as in Rome in the absence
of a specific agreement to the contrary. This may be
inferred *e contrario* from occasional prohibitions to the
lessor to alienate while the lease was running.[2] The obligation of the lessor to warrant the possession of the lessee
against third persons was, naturally, admitted. But it
depended on the lessee to decide whether he preferred for
the sake of an expeditious settlement to assume himself
the position of defendant ($\alpha\dot{v}\tau o\mu\alpha\chi\epsilon\hat{i}v$)[3] or to call on the
lessor to enter the lists against eventual claimants. If the
estate was damaged by *vis major*, as for example by an
incursion of enemies, the lessor had to bear part of the
ensuing loss : in the Aixone lease, e.g., half the rent is remitted in such circumstances.[4] On the other hand the
cultivation of the plots is not only to be carried on in
accordance with customary standards of efficiency, but is
often regulated by special and minute rules[5] and super-
vised by representatives of the lessor.[6] It may be surmised
that at the conclusion of the lease the owner could claim
compensation from the lessee for any deterioration or loss
caused by the latter's negligence. No evidence is extant as
to a possible counter-claim on the part of the tenant on the
ground of improvements brought about by his industry and
care.

Varieties of leases.   Leases may assume forms varying with the prevailing
economic and social conditions. It is easy to distinguish four
principal varieties in this respect : leases at rack rents to be

---

[1] DEM. XLV, § 31.
[2] BEAUCHET, *op. cit.*, IV, 168 f.
[3] *Ibid.*, IV, 136 ff.
[4] *I. J. G.* I, xii, p. 204, § 8.   [5] *Ibid.*, xiii[2], p. 238, § 3.
[6] *C. I. A.* II, 600 ; *I. J. G.* I, xii, p. 204 ; I, 120 ff.

paid either in money or in kind, stock and farm leases
(*bail à chaptel*), leases for part profit (*métayage, colonia
partiaria*), and emphyteutic tenancies. Greek evidence is
chiefly concerned with the first and the last varieties.
Apart from archaic cases like that of the Attic ἐκτήμοροι,
who may have been partly tenants and partly heavily
indebted peasant owners, or that of customary tenants of
the type of the Kretan Ϝοικῆες or the Thessalian πενέσται,
we hardly ever hear of farmers receiving their outfit
from landowners or dividing the produce of their agricultural labour to acquit their rent.[1] This does not mean
that such arrangements were unknown, but that they did
not come, as a rule, under the notice of the engraved
records and of the city Courts: such as there were must
have been transacted mainly by verbal and customary
agreements. On the other hand we get plenty of information as to conventional rack rents and as to emphyteutic
long leases. The former are the natural outcome of a
lively cash intercourse produced by the commercial hus-
bandry of the cities, and it is with them that students of
inscriptions mostly have to deal. As for the third variety
of leases, their main features have been briefly considered in
the preceding chapter.[2]

In the case of the contract of sale we have the advantage
of getting a short but systematic survey of its most
important points from the work of Aristotle's pupil Theophrastos. In the XVIIIth and possibly in the XVIIth
book of his *Laws* he treated of this subject, and a few
pages of his exposition have been preserved for posterity by
Stobaeus.[3] Modern inquirers can hardly do better than
follow Theophrastos' text, supplementing with such information as may be gathered from the inscriptions and
pleadings that bear on the matter of sale.

The first point noticed is the publicity of sales and of
hypothecary conventions.[4] Theophrastos describes regis-

The fragments of Theophrastos.

---

[1] *I.J.G.* I, xii, p. 200, § 1.
[2] See above, p. 217 f.
[3] THEOPHRASTOS, Περὶ συμβολαίων ; STOBAEUS, *Florilegium*, XLIV,
22, ed. Meineke, II, 166 ff.
[4] *Ibid.*, p. 166, ll. 4 ff. οἱ μὲν οὖν ὑπὸ κήρυκος κελεύουσι πωλεῖν . . . οἱ

tration as the most perfect method of ensuring the transfer
of title, but mentions also various other devices, such as
proclamation by a herald sixty days in advance, or proclamations on five consecutive days preceding the sale, or
the payment of a small coin to three neighbouring householders in order that they should be able to testify to the
bargain.[1] These proceedings are intended to establish in
a definite manner the act of transfer, to secure for the
purchaser the possibility of a recourse to official documents
or, at least, to trustworthy witnesses. On the other hand
they call for objections and challenges if any one wants to
produce them. What is even more important, the procedure
is not a mere reflection of the wishes of the consenting
parties. It amounts to certain positive requirements which
though not distinctly stated may be easily surmised. The
officials superintending registration have the right and the
duty to refuse the performance of this act if the formalities
of the procedure have not been properly carried out;[2] and
we may add, on the strength of the Halikarnassos and
Iasos inscriptions,[3] that confirmation is not a mere question
of form: the *mnemones* mentioned in these documents are
taking a prominent part in the conclusion of the convention,
and a late example from the Roman epoch provides an
illustration of this kind of public supervision.[4] In other
words, the formalities of public proclamation and registration gave scope for the exercise of a certain public
supervision which did not amount to a denial of the fundamental doctrine of convention by consent, but made it
possible in certain cases to veto negligent or fraudulent
agreements.

It cannot be said that such interference was equally
effective in all Greek cities—it was reduced to the very

δὲ παρ' ἀρχῇ τινι . . . ἔνιοι δὲ προγράφειν παρὰ τῇ ἀρχῇ πρὸ ἡμερῶν μὴ
ἔλαττον ἢ ἑξήκοντα . . . ὅπως διαμφισβητῆσαί τε ἐξῇ καὶ διαμαρτύρασθαι τῷ
βουλομένῳ, καὶ ὁ δικαίως ἐωνημένος φανερὸς ᾖ τῷ τέλει.

[1] THEOPHR., *loc. cit.*, l. 16 Οἱ δὲ Θουριακοί . . . κελεύουσι κοινῇ τῶν
γειτόνων τῶν ἐγγυτάτω τρισὶ νόμισμά τι βραχὺ μνήμης ἕνεκα καὶ μαρτυρίας.

[2] *Ibid.*, p. 167, l. 13. After enumerating various regulations, he
says ἄνευ δὲ τούτων μὴ ἐγγράφειν τὴν ἀρχήν.

[3] *I. J. G.* I, i, 1 ff ; DITT. *Syll*[3] I, 169.

[4] CICERO, *Pro Flacco*, cc. 29-32.

attenuated expedient of proclamation in Athens—but it
must have been sufficiently general and useful, as Theophrastos has given it so large a place in his treatise.

Another guarantee of good faith was sought in an oath
imposed on the contracting parties in affirmation of the
genuineness of the transaction and the absence of collusion
or fictitious pretence.[1]

A strong light is thrown on the importance of the official
confirmation of transfers by the Tenos registration list.[2]
It is not by any means a mere enumeration of concluded
agreements. Under cover of a register of sales it confirms
varied transactions cast in this form on account of its convenience for establishing title and discouraging claims by
third parties.[3] Some of the sales mentioned in it are in
reality redemption instruments consequent on the πρᾶσις
ἐπὶ λύσει. Others are disguised constitutions of dower.
A third variety, represented by § 13, arises from execution
of a judgement by the defeated party : a certain Anaxikles
is said to have bought a plot of land from Philothea, who,
it is explained, had lost the above-mentioned plot in a suit
against the purchaser.[4] The entry nevertheless mentions
a πράτωρ as guarantor. In ordinary cases the πράτωρ is
a previous owner from whom the estate had been acquired
by the actual vendor; in other words, transfer by purchase
is traced one step higher, greater security being sought by
calling in a second *auctor*. It is difficult to guess to whom
the designation of πράτωρ could apply in the case under
discussion ; it must have been a person who had passed
property to Philothea, so that she must have had a
transfer to rely upon in spite of the fact that she
lost in the trial : she may have forfeited her right in consequence of the foreclosure of a mortgage. Yet the transaction with Anaxikles was clothed in the form of a fictitious
contract of sale between the latter and Philothea.[5]

---

[1] THEOPHR., *loc. cit.*, p. 167, ll. 6 ff.
[2] *I. J. G.* I, vii, pp. 63 ff.
[3] *Ibid.*, pp. 89 ff.
[4] *Ibid.*, § 13, pp. 68 f. Ἀναξικλῆς . . . παρὰ Φιλοθέας . . . ἐπρίατο τὰς ἐν
Σαπήθῳ αἱμασιὰς τέτταρας (description) . . . gap in text . . . περὶ ὧν
ἐνίκησεν Ἀναξικλῆς Φιλοθέαν τὴν δίκην· πράτωρ Ἀριστοκλῆς Πολυξένου. . . .
[5] *Ibid.*, p. 91.

Another indication as to the importance of these registered transfers of title is afforded by the part assigned to the guarantors or sureties—the ἐγγυηταί or πράτωρες. They are constantly mentioned at the end of the entries on the register, and their obligation was not merely a formal or accessory one. The responsibility for the legality and firmness of the bargain [1] rested primarily on them. In case of eviction the purchaser had a recourse against them or, at least, as much against them as against the vendor himself.[2] To judge from the analogy of the guarantors of the fictitious sales of emancipated slaves at Delphi these persons were usually drawn from among the most wealthy and influential citizens of a given city. Their consent to act as patrons to the transaction presented an additional asset for the security of title, and was evidently much in demand for the conclusion of conventions.

Conclu-
sion of
sale.

The second point discussed by Theophrastos concerns the conclusion of the sale. He says that in most cities the contract was deemed perfect on the payment of the price not before. A presumption was created, however, by a preliminary agreement confirmed by the payment of earnest money.[3] If the purchaser subsequently refused to pay the price the convention was annulled and he lost the deposit.[4] In the converse case, when the vendor subsequently refused to deliver the property although the agreed price was tendered to him, there arose the question whether he was liable to restore a sum of money equivalent to the price which had been agreed on and, perhaps, also the deposit. Such a solution does not appear to be equitable, but was seemingly resorted to by some legislators, as Theophrastos describes it in some detail. It has been argued that the payment of earnest money presented a formal requirement of the contract of sale.[5] Theophrastos, however, does not

---

[1] *I. J. G.* I, vii, § 41, cf. p. 100.

[2] PLATO, *Laws*, XII, 7, *init.*

[3] THEOPHR., *loc. cit.*, p. 167, ll. 17 ff. κυρία δὲ ἡ ὠνὴ καὶ ἡ πρᾶσις εἰ μὲν κτῆσιν ὅταν ἡ τιμὴ δοθῇ καὶ τὰκ τῶν νόμων ποιήσωσιν, οἷον ἀναγραφὴν ἢ ὅρκον ἢ τοῖς γείτοσι τὸ γιγνόμενον· εἰς δὲ τὴν παράδοσιν καὶ εἰς αὐτὸ τὸ πωλεῖν ὅταν ἀρραβῶνα λάβῃ· σχεδὸν γὰρ οὕτως οἱ πολλοὶ νομοθετοῦσιν.

[4] *Ibid.*, pp. 167 f., l. 30 ἐὰν δὲ λαβὼν ἀρραβῶνα μὴ δέχηται κτλ.

[5] BEAUCHET, IV, 426.

indicate anything of the sort. His statement is chiefly directed towards establishing the consequences of an eventual renunciation of the agreement.

A third point consists in the requirement that the consent given by each of the parties should be given in sound mind; a convention concluded in anger, in jealousy, or in a state of insanity is declared to be invalid.[1] This necessary provision opened the way to many disputes in the Courts, and we have an excellent illustration of the way in which it could be used by a skilful pleader in Hypereides' speech against Athenogenes. The validity of the sale of a perfumery shop was impugned in spite of the fact that the vendor had carefully secured witnesses of the transaction and a sealed instrument to confirm it. The arguments of Hypereides are derived from observations as to the psychology of amorous persons of weak character under the influence of deceitful women charmers:[2] they are strengthened by an express reference to one of Solon's restrictions on the freedom of testamentary disposition, by which the γυναικὶ πειθόμενος is regarded as incapable of a reasonable decision. There was no assertion of *laesio enormis* in the Roman sense, but of a flaw as regards the free consent (ὅσα τις ἕκων ὁμολογήσῃ). We may think what we like about Hypereides' arguments, but the fact of his using them before the Court proves that the validity of conventions could be attacked from the point of view of lack of sound mind, shown in an unreasonable resolve.

A last question put by Theophrastos is whether the property remains with the vendor until the full price has been paid. He notes the radical solution laid down by Charondas and recommended by Plato in the *Laws*. According to these legislators an actionable sale was only effected when the price had been paid, so that if some one sold on credit he had to rely exclusively on the good faith of the purchaser.[3] There can be no doubt, however, that in

Credit.

---

[1] THEOPHR., p. 167, ll. 23 ff., ending l. 27 ἔοικε γὰρ ἐκ καιροῦ τὰ τοιαῦτα καὶ πάθους γίγνεσθαι· δεῖ δὲ ἐκ προαιρέσεως· οὕτω γὰρ ἔσται τὸ δίκαιον.

[2] HYPER. III (V), § 17.

[3] THEOPHR., *loc. cit.*, p. 168 παρ' ἐνίοις δεδικάσθαι κελεύουσι τῷ μὴ δεχομένῳ τὴν τιμήν. πότερον δὲ ἕως ἂν κομίσηται κύριον εἶναι τοῦ κτήματος ;

most of the Greek States credit was recognized and practised to a large extent. Commercial intercourse on the
scale on which it was carried on in Athens or Syrakuse
could not have existed without it.[1] It must have been
extensively used in the sale of goods; as to landed estate,
it was easy to protect it by bonds, and all considerable
transactions in this branch must have been carried on by
means of instruments of some kind. The chief means of
providing against bad faith and fraud in connexion with
goods was to transact sales in the open market under the
supervision of the city's officers. The administrative organization of Athens was much developed in this respect.
Chapter LI of Aristotle's *Athenian Constitution* gives
many details on the functions of the ἀγορανόμοι, the
μετρονόμοι, and the σιτοφύλακες. They exercised a very
close supervision over the quality of the products sold, the
exactitude of the weights and measures used, and the fulfilment of conditions imposed by laws and regulations in
regard to trade.[2]

It may be said in conclusion that the treatment of conventions is highly characteristic of the general tendencies
of Greek jurisprudence. It combines in a striking manner
the fullest possible development of private initiative and
freedom of decision with the constant intervention of the
City. Archaic formalism disappeared at an early stage, but
the practices of instruments in writing and of registration
by magistrates developed steadily, and came to provide the
common foundation of title. Nevertheless, even after the
spread of these practices of literal evidence, conveyances
and conventions were considered and adjudicated upon in
the last resort by tribunals which were always disposed to

οὕτω γὰρ οἱ πολλοὶ νομοθετοῦσιν, ἢ ὥσπερ Χαρώνδας καὶ Πλάτων; οὗτοι γὰρ
παραχρῆμα κελεύουσι διδόναι καὶ λαμβάνειν· ἐὰν δέ τις πιστεύσῃ μὴ εἶναι
δίκην, αὐτὸν γὰρ αἴτιον εἶναι τῆς ἀδικίας.

[1] BUECHSENSCHUETZ, *Besitz und Erwerb im Alterthum.*

[2] *Ath. Const.*, c. 51 Κληροῦνται δὲ καὶ ἀγορανόμοι, . . . τούτοις δὲ ὑπὸ τῶν
νόμων προστέτακται τῶν ὠνίων ἐπιμελεῖσθαι πάντων, ὅπως καθαρὰ καὶ ἀκίβδηλα
πωλήσεται. κληροῦνται δὲ καὶ μετρονόμοι, . . . καὶ οὗτοι τῶν μέτρων καὶ τῶν
σταθμῶν ἐπιμελοῦνται πάντων, ὅπως οἱ πωλοῦντες χρήσονται δικαίοις. ἦσαι
δὲ καὶ σιτοφύλακες κληρωτοί. . . . οὗτοι δ᾽ ἐπιμελοῦνται πρῶτον μὲν ὅπως ὁ
ἐν ἀγορᾷ σῖτος ἀργὸς ὤνιος ἔσται δικαίως, ἔπειθ᾽ ὅπως οἵ τε μυλωθροὶ πρὸς
τὰς τιμὰς τῶν κριθῶν τὰ ἄλφιτα πωλήσουσιν κτλ.

take into consideration the spirit rather than the letter of
laws, the equity and utility of business transactions rather
than their technical requirements.   Public opinion in the
city—the δόξα τῆς πόλεως—was in the last resort the
decisive authority in the application of rules of private as
well as of public law.

At the close of this survey of the methods of Greek Summing up.
juridical thought it may not be amiss to sum up certain
points of comparison between the jurisprudence of our own
days and that of classical Greece.   Rules of law are rules
of conduct, and therefore they are necessarily surrounded
by an atmosphere of morality: with the Greeks the connexion between ethics and the administration of justice
was especially close and productive of direct results.   The
distinction between external acts and inward intention
could not fail to express itself in practice, but it was not
prominent in theory, and the spiritual aspects of human
conduct—forethought, motive, character—were insisted
upon whenever possible in estimating actions.   Compulsion
was regarded as a natural outcome of social life—the most
advanced thinkers felt as little hesitation in chastizing
or crushing a malefactor as they felt in fighting a
wolf or training a dog.   Combines for the achievement
of common purposes—both transient and enduring—grew
up in exuberant profusion and commonly developed mystic
elements as expressions of superindividual aspirations.
Corporate life was represented in all kinds of varieties—
in political intercourse as well as in business and culture.
But in all corporations or quasi-corporations the opposition
between the individuals and the collective body uniting
them was not insisted upon: on the contrary, the city and
any gild or group of worshippers were considered as identical with the members which constituted them for the
time being.   The concentration of the State within the
narrow limits of a city made it possible to attempt government by direct action of the people.   Actual democracy
was, however, restricted to a comparatively small number
of privileged citizens, selected on the basis of descent.
While rules of expediency and agreement governed the

relations between members of different cities, a rule of law was consistently applied to the relations between citizens. In apportioning rights and duties, in delimiting interests, in enforcing obligations, Greek law strove not only to maintain order and to redress grievances, but also to guarantee a just distribution of advantages and burdens. The public character of property and possession was manifested in various legal requirements, while private acquisition and rights of disposal were chiefly developed in the course of business practice and did not give rise to rigid doctrinal distinctions. In keeping with this fluid state of the law of things, transactions and conventions came at an early stage to be established by formless consent. This did not prevent the growth of customary usages as to evidence, in which written instruments were assigned a most important part, and in this way a new kind of literal contract was gradually evolved. In all departments of law stress was laid on public opinion, express or implied. All kinds of devices were used in order to secure preponderance to enacted law, but as a matter of fact in many cases government and the administration of justice depended on more or less spontaneous decrees and on equitable estimates of circumstances. There was as yet no call for natural law as opposed to professional legality, but there was ample room for speculations as to a common law of reason rising above the precepts of single cities.

BOOKS REFERRED TO IN VOL. II

A. *Abbreviated Titles used in footnotes: see list* B *for
details.*

Beauchet. Droit privé.
C. I. A. Corpus Inscr. Att.
C. I. G. Corpus Inscr. Gr.
Dar. et S. Dictionnaire des antiquités gr. et rom.
Diels. Fragm. der Vorsokr.
Ditt. Syll. Inscr. Gr.
Gercke und **Norden.** Einleitung.
Glotz. Solidarité.
**Hermann-Swoboda, Hermann-Thalheim, Hermann-Thum-
   ser.** *See* **Hermann**, Lehrbuch.
Hicks. Gr. hist. inscr.
I. J. G. Rec. des inscr. jurid. gr. **Dareste.**
Lipsius. Att. Recht.
Michel. Rec. des inscr. gr.
R.-Enc. **Pauly-Wissowa.**
Schömann-Lipsius. Griech. Alterth.
Z. SS. Zeitschrift der Sav.-Stift.

B. *Full Titles.*

Abhandlungen der . . . K. sächs. Gesellschaft der Wissen-
   schaften. See **Mitteis.**
Aischines. Speeches. Blass. Teubner.
Aischylos. Plays. Sidgwick. Script. Class. Bibl. Oxon.
American Journal of Archaeology. *See* **Dennison Rogers**
   and **Wheeler.**
American Journal of Philology. *See* **Morris.**
Amira (K. von). Nordgermanisches Obligationenrecht,
   Bd. III. Strassburg. 1897. Grundriss der ger-
   manischen Philologie. 1913.
Andokides. Speeches. Blass. Teubner.
Antiphon. Speeches. Blass. Teubner.
Antiphon the Sophist. *In* Oxyrhynchus Papyri, XI. Ed.
   B. P. Grenfell and A. S. Hunt. Egypt Exploration
   Fund. London. 1915.

Aristotle. Atheniensium Respublica. F. G. Kenyon. Oxford. 1920.

———— Πολιτεία Ἀθηναίων. G. Kaibel et U. de Wilamowitz-Moellendorff. Berlin. 1898.

———— Ethics (Nik.). I. Bywater. Oxford. 1890.

———— Politics. W. L. Newman. Oxford. 1887–1902.

———— Rhetoric. E. M. Cope. Camb. 1877.

———— Other works. Bekker.

Beauchet (L.). Histoire du droit privé de la République athénienne. Paris. 1897.

Beloch (K. J.). Griechische Geschichte. Strassburg. 1893.

Boeckh (A.). Die Staatshaushaltung der Athener. 3te Aufl., M. Fränkel. Berlin. 1886.

Brandileone (F.). Sulla supposita obligatio litterarum nell' antico diritto greco. Bologna. 1920.

Büchsenschütz (—). Besitz und Erwerb im Alterthum. Halle, 1869.

Buckland, W. W. A Text-Book of Roman Law. Cambridge. 1921.

Bürgel. Die pyläisch-delphische Amphiktyonie. München. 1877.

Bulletin de correspondance hellénique. *See* **Haussoullier, Homolle.**

Burnet (J.). Ethics of Aristotle. London. 1900.

Busolt (G.). Der zweite attische Bund. Jahrbücher für Philologie, Suppl.-B.VII, 665 ff.

Bywater (I.). Heracliti Reliquiae. Oxford. 1877.

Caillemer (E.). La prescription à Athènes : études sur les antiquités juridiques d'Athènes, No. 7. Paris. 1869.

———————— Le droit de succession légitime à Athènes : études sur les ant. jur., etc. Paris, 1879.

———————— *In* **Dar.** et **S.**, s.v. *diadikasia*.

Calhoun (G. M.). The early history of crime and criminal law in Greece, *in* Proceedings of the Classical Association, vol. XVIII (1921). London. 1922.

———————— Oral and written pleadings in Athenian Courts, *in* Transactions of the American Philological Association, vol. I (1919), pp. 177 ff.

Cloché (P.). Le conseil athénien des cinq cents et la peine de mort, *in* Revue des études grecques, XXXIII. 1920.

Cope (E. M.). Commentary on Aristotle's Rhetoric. Ed. J. E. Sandys. Cambridge. 1887.

Corpus Inscriptionum Atticarum. I. A. Kirchhoff. Berlin. 1873. II. U. Köhler. Berlin. 1877.

Corpus Inscriptionum Graecarum. A. Boeckh, etc. Berlin. 1828-77.

Corpus juris civilis. P. Krüger and Th. Mommsen. Berlin. 1893.

Cuq (É.). Les institutions juridiques des Romains. Paris. 1904.

Daremberg (C.) et Saglio (E.). Dictionnaire des antiquités grecques et romaines. Paris. 1873-1917.

Dareste (R.). Plaidoyers civils de Démosthène. 1875.

———————— Du droit de représailles, *in* Revue des études grecques, II, p. 305. Paris. 1889.

———————— **Haussoullier (B.)** and **Reinach (Th.).** Recueil des inscriptions juridiques grecques. Paris. 1891-.

Demosthenes. Speeches. Blass. Teubner.

———————— ———————— Butcher. Script. Class. Bibl. Oxon. *See also* **Weil.**

Dennison Rogers (J.). Fragment of an Argive Inscription, *in* American Journal of Archaeology, New Series, V, p. 159. 1901.

Dictionnaire des antiquités gr. et rom. *See* **Daremberg,** etc.

Diels (H.). Die Fragmente der Vorsokratiker. 3te Aufl. Berlin. 1912.

Digest. *See* Corpus juris civilis.

Dikaiarchos. *In* Fragmenta Historicorum Graecorum.

Dikaiomata herausg. von der Graeca Halensis. Berlin. 1913.

Diodorus Siculus. Histories. Dindorf. Teubner.

Dittenberger (G.). Sylloge Inscriptionum Graecarum. 3te Aufl. Leipzig. 1915-.

Esmein (J. P.). Mélanges d'archéologie et d'histoire, VIII, p. 426. Rome, Paris. 1888.

Euripides. Plays. Murray. Script. Class. Bibl. Oxon.

Foucart (P.). Des associations religieuses chez les Grecs. Paris. 1873.

Fränkel (M.). Die attischen Geschworenengerichte. Berlin. 1877. *See also* **Boeckh.**

Fragmenta Historicorum Graecorum. C. and Th. Muller. Paris. 1841.

Francotte (H). La polis grecque. Studien zur Geschichte und Kultur des Altertums, I. Paderborn, 1907.

Gai Institutiones; with translation and commentary by Ed. Poste. 4th ed. E. A. Whittuck. Oxford. 1904.

Gellius, Aulus. Noctes Atticae. Hosius. Teubner.

Gercke (A.) und Norden (E.). Einleitung in die Altertums-wissenschaft. Leipzig. 1910.

Gernet (L.). Hypothèses sur le contrat primitif en Grèce, *in* Revue des études grecques, XXX, p. 249. Paris, 1917.

Gilbert (G.). Handbuch der griechischen Staatsaltertümer. Leipzig. 1893.

Girard (P. F.). Manuel élémentaire de droit romain. Paris. 1910.

Glotz (G.). La solidarité de la famille dans le droit criminel en Grèce. Paris. 1904.

——————— Le travail dans la Grèce ancienne. Paris. 1920.

Gneist. Die formellen Verträge des neueren römischen Obligationenrechts in Vergleichung mit den Geschichts-formen des griechischen Rechts. 1844.

Gomperz (Th.). Greek Thinkers. Translated by L. Magnus. London. 1901–12.

Griechischen Dialekt-Inschriften, Sammlung der. H. Collitz. Göttingen. 1884.

Grimm (J.). Deutsche Rechtsalterthümer. 4te Ausg. Leipzig. 1899.

Guiraud (P.). La propriété foncière en Grèce jusqu'à la conquête romaine. Paris. 1893.

Harpokration. Lexicon in decem oratores Atticos. Ed. G. Dindorf. Oxford. 1853.

Haussoullier (B.). La vie municipale en Attique. Biblio-thèque des écoles françaises d'Athènes et de Rome. Fasc. 38. Paris. 1884.

——————— Inscriptions de Chio : *in* Bulletin de corr. hell., III, p. 230. *See also* Rec. des inscr. jurid.

Hellenica Oxyrhynchia. Grenfell and Hunt. Script. Cl. Bibl. Oxon.

Hermann (K. F.). Lehrbuch der griechischen Antiquitäten;

neu herausg. von H. Blümer und W. Dittenberger.
I. Abt. 1, 2, V. Thumser. Abt. 3, H. Swoboda.
II. Abt. 1, H. Thalheim. Freiburg. 1889–.

Herodotos. Histories. Dietsch-Kallenberg. Teubner.

Hicks (E. L.) and **Hill (G. F.).** Manual of Greek Historical
Inscriptions. Oxford. 1901.

Hildenbrand (K.). Geschichte und System der Rechts- und
Staatsphilosophie. Leipzig. 1860.

Hillier von Gaertringen (F.). Inschriften von Priene.
Berlin. 1906.

Hinneberg (P.). See **Wilamowitz-Moellendorff.**

Hirzel (R.). Themis, Dike und Verwandtes. Leipzig. 1907.

Hitzig (H. F.). Altgriechische Staatsverträge über Rechtshilfe. Zürich. 1907.

——————— Das griechische Pfandrecht. München. 1895.

Hogarth (J. G.). Naukratis, 1903. *In* Journal of Hellenic
Studies. London. 1905.

Homer. Odyssey. Allen. Script. Class. Bibl. Oxon.

Homolle (T.). Les archives de l'intendance sacrée à Délos.
Bibliothèque des écoles françaises d'Athènes et de Rome.
Fasc. 49, p. 1194. Paris. 1887.

——————— Comptes des temples déliens, *in* Bulletin de
corr. hell., VI, p. 1, and XIV, p. 389. Paris. 1882, 1890.

——————— *In* **Dar.** et **S.,** s. v. *donarium.*

Hypereides. Speeches. Kenyon. Script. Class. Bibl. Oxon.

Isaios. Speeches. Thalheim. Teubner.

Isokrates. Speeches. Blass. Teubner.

Jebb (R. C.). The Rhetoric of Aristotle translated. Cambridge. 1909.

Journal of Hellenic Studies. See **Hogarth.**

Keil (B.). *In* **Gercke** und **Norden,** Einleitung.

Kenny (C. S.). Outlines of Criminal Law. Cambridge.
1909.

Laurent (F.). Histoire du droit des gens et des relations
internationales. Gand et Paris. 1850–70.

Lécrivain (C.). *In* **Dar.** et **S.,** s. v. *ephesis.*

Leist (G. A.). Der attische Eigentumsstreit im System der
Diadikasien. Jena. 1886.

Lexica Segueriana, Immanuelis Bekkeri anecdota Graeca,
Vol. I. Berol. 1814.

Lipsius (J. H.). Das attische Recht und Rechtsverfahren. Meier und Schömann. Leipzig. 1905–15.

———————— Griechische Alterthümer. G. F. Schömann. 4te Aufl. 1897–1902.

———————— In Z. SS. Roman. Abth., XXXVII, p. 1 (1916), and XXXIX, p. 36 (1918).

Lykurgos. Speeches. Blass. Teubner.

Lysias. Speeches. Hude. Script. Class. Bibl. Oxon.

Meier. *See* **Lipsius.**

Meyer (Ed.). Geschichte des Alterthums. Stuttgart. 1893.

———————— Forschungen zur alten Geschichte. Halle. 1892–99.

Meynial (E.). Des renonciations, *in* Nouvelle revue historique de droit français et étranger. 1900, 1901, 1902, 1904. Paris.

Michel (C.). Recueil d'inscriptions grecques. Bruxelles. 1897–1912.

Mitteis (L.). Römisches Privatrecht, *in* Systematisches Handbuch der deutschen Rechtswissenschaft. Ed. K. Binding. Leipzig. 1908.

———————— Reichsrecht und Volksrecht in den östlichen Provinzen des römischen Kaiserreichs. Leipzig. 1891.

———————— Zur Geschichte der Erbpacht im Alterthum, *in* Abhandl. der phil.-hist. Cl. der K. sächs. Gesellschaft der Wissenschaften, XX, no. 4. Leipzig. 1901.

———————— Romanistische Papyrusstudien, *in* Z. SS., Roman. Abth., XXIII, p. 274 (1902).

Morris (C. D.). The jurisdiction of the Athenians over their allies, *in* American Journal of Philology, V, p. 298. Baltimore. 1884.

Muller (C. and T.). Fragmenta Historicorum Graecorum. Paris. 1848.

Nettleship (R. L.). Lectures on the Republic of Plato. London. 1910.

Newman (W. L.). The Politics of Aristotle. Oxford. 1887–1902.

Nouvelle revue de droit. *See* **Meynial.**

Ott (L.). Beiträge zur Kenntniss des griechischen Eides. Leipzig. 1896.

Oxyrhynchus Papyri XI. Ed. B. P. Grenfell and A. S. Hunt. London. 1915.

Partsch (J.). Griechisches Bürgschaftsrecht. Leipzig.
1909.

Pauly (A. F. von). Real-Encyclopädie der classischen
Altertumswissenschaft. Ed. G. Wissowa. Stuttgart.
1893–.

Perrot (G.). Essai sur le droit public d'Athènes. Paris.
1867.

Philippi (A.). Der Areopag und die Epheten. Berlin. 1874.

Phillipson (Coleman). The international law and custom
of ancient Greece and Rome. London. 1911.

Philochoros. In Fragm. Hist. Graec.

Plato. Dialogues. Burnet. Script. Class. Bibl. Oxon.

Plutarch. Parallel Lives. Sintenis. Teubner.

Pöhlmann (R. von). Geschichte der sozialen Frage und
des Sozialismus in der antiken Welt. München. 1912.

Poland (F.). Geschichte des griechischen Vereinswesens,
in Preisschriften . . . von der . . . Jablonowski'schen
Gesellschaft, XXXVIII. Leipzig. 1909.

Pollux (Julius). Onomasticon. Bekker. Berlin. 1846.

Polybios. Histories. Büttner-Dindorf. Teubner.

Preisschriften . . . von der fürstlich Jablonowski'schen
Gesellschaft zu Leipzig. See Poland and Ziebarth.

Prinz (H.). Funde aus Naukratis, in Beiträge zur alten
Geschichte (Klio), 7tes Beiheft. Leipzig. 1908.

Proceedings of the Classical Association. See Calhoun.

Rabel (E.). Δίκη ἐξούλης, in Z. SS., Roman. Abth.,
XXXVI, p. 340 (1915), and XXXVIII, p. 296 (1917).

Real-Encyclopädie. See Pauly.

Recueil des inscriptions juridiques grecques. See Dareste.

Reinach (Th.). In Dar. et S., s. v. enoikiou dike.

Revue des études grecques. See Cloché, Dareste, Gernet.

Riccobono (S.). Stipulatio ed instrumentum, etc. In Z. SS.,
Roman. Abth., XXXV, p. 214 (1914).

Rikkert (H.). System der Philosophie. 1920.

Röhl (H.). Inscriptiones graecae antiquissimae. Berlin.
1882.

Rose (Valentin). Aristoteles Pseudepigraphus. Lips. 1863.

Salomon (M.). Der Begriff des Naturrechts bei den Sophi-
sten, in Z. SS., Roman. Abth. XXXII, p. 129 (1911).

Schmidt (L. V.). Ethik der alten Griechen. 1882.

Schömann (G. F.). *See* **Lipsius.**

Schulthess. *In* Real-Encycl., s.v. γραμματεῖς.

Solon. Fragm., *in* Poetae Lyrici Graeci, Bergk. Leipzig. 1866.

Sophokles. Plays. Ed. R. C. Jebb. Cambridge. 1883-.

Stobaeus (Joannes). Florilegium, ed. A. Meineke. Lips. 1855–7.

Studien zur Geschichte und Kultur des Altertums. *See* **Francotte** and **Weber.**

Swoboda (H.). *See* **Hermann.**

Szanto (E.). Das griechische Bürgerrecht. Freiburg. 1892.

———————— Anleihen griechischer Staaten, *in* Wiener Studien, VII. Zeitschrift für die österreichischen Gymnasien. Wien. 1885.

———————— Hypothek und Scheinkauf im griechischen Rechte, *in* Wiener Studien, IX.

———————— *In* Real-Encycl., s.v. ἐκεχειρία.

Thalheim (Th.). *In* Real-Encycl., s.v. ἀτιμία and βλάβης δίκη. *See also* **Hermann.**

Theophrastos *apud* **Stobaeum,** q.v.

Thonissen (J. J.). Le droit pénal de la République Athénienne. Bruxelles. 1875.

Thukydides. Histories. Stuart Jones. Script. Cl. Bibl Oxon.

Thumser (V.). *See* **Hermann.**

Tod (M. N.). International Arbitration amongst the Greeks Oxford. 1913.

Toepffer (J.). Attische Genealogie. Berlin. 1889.

Vinogradoff (P.). Outlines of Historical Jurisprudence, I Oxford. 1920.

———————————— The legal background of Demosthenes speech in Zenothemis *v.* Demon. Offprint from the Revue d'histoire du droit. Haarlem. 1921.

Weber (H.). Attisches Prozessrecht in den attischen Seebundstaaten. Studien zur Geschichte und Kultur des Altertums, I, 5. Paderborn. 1908.

Weil (H.). Les plaidoyers politiques de Démosthène. Paris 1883.

Weiss (E.). Recitatio und Responsum, etc., *in* Z. SS., Roman. Abth. XXXIII, p. 215 (1912).

Wheeler (J. R.). Some inscriptions from the Argive Heraeum, *in* American Journal of Archaeology, First Series, IX, p. 351. Baltimore. 1894.

Wide (S.). Griechische und römische Religion. *In* Gercke und Norden, Einleitung, Bd. 2. Leipzig. 1910.

Wiener Studien. *See* **Szanto.**

Wilamowitz-Moellendorff (U. von). Aristoteles und Athen. Berlin. 1893.

———————————————————— Zum ältesten Strafrecht der Kulturvölker. Leipzig. 1905.

———————————————————— *In* Kultur der Gegenwart, II. P. Hinneberg. Berlin. 1909.

Wundt, M. Geschichte der griechischen Ethik, I. Leipzig. 1908.

Wyse, W. The Speeches of Isaeus. Cambridge. 1904.

Xenophon. Hellenika *and* Memorabilia. Marchant. Script. Cl. Bibl. Oxon.

——————— Respublica Atheniensium. Teubner.

Zeitschrift der Savigny-Stiftung für Rechtsgeschichte, Romanistische Abtheilung. Weimar. 1880–. *See* **Lipsius, Mitteis, Rabel, Riccobono, Salomon, Weiss.**

Zeller (E.). Outlines of the history of Greek Philosophy, translated by S. F. Alleyne and E. Abbott. London. 1901.

——————— Socrates and the Socratic Schools, translated by O. J. Reichel. London. 1868.

Ziebarth (E.). Das griechische Vereinswesen, *in* Preisschriften . . . von der . . . Jablonowski'schen Gesellschaft, XXXIV. Leipzig. 1896.

Zimmern (A. E.). The Greek Commonwealth. Oxford. 1911.

INDEX TO VOLUME II

Philokrates, accusation of, by
  Hypereides, 169.
Philothea, case of, 261.
Phoinissai of Euripides, 24.
Phoinix of Thera, shrine in
  memory of, 123.
φονικαὶ δίκαι, 177.
φόνος ἀκούσιος, 177 ff., 182.
— ἑκούσιος, 179, 182.
φωρά, 176.
φόροι, 112.
φράτορες, 120.
phratriarch, 89, 124.
phratries, 85, 121, 124.
phratry, constitution of, 86 f.
  duty of, in homicide, 178.
φρόνησις, τὸ φρονεῖν, 41.
Phrynichos, reference to, of Harpokration, 226.
  slayer of, 95.
φύσις and νόμος, 26 f., 40.
phylae, 85.
pignoris capio, 59, 246.
pignus, 250, 254.
Plato, caricatures of, 29.
  condemnation of juries by, 11.
  on αἰδώς and ἀναισχυντία, 33.
  on consent in convention, 239.
  on continuity of Athenian
    State, 104.
  on credit sales, 231, 263.
  on cult of Hestia, 100.
  on damages, 195.
  on death from blows, 183.
  and death penalty, 188.
  on Dorian customs, 8.
  on δόξα τῆς πόλεως, 38.
  on duties to State, 39 f.
  on education of citizen, 16.
  on equity, 64.
  on jurisprudence and justice,
    38.
  on land law, 9.
  on numbers in State, 85 f.
  on religious obligation, 98.
  on the sophistic doctrine, 25.
  on tribal lordships, 1.
Platonic classes in the State,
  39.

Platonic dialogue of *Minos* on
  custom, 21.
"ideas", 41.
plea of self-defence, 186.
pleas of land, 214.
"plebeians" in phratry, 86.
πλῆθος = complex of citizens,
  113.
πλωτῆρες, 119.
plots (of land) with slaves,
  200.
Plutarch, on accusation of Perikles, 132.
  on colonies in time of Perikles,
    203.
  on procedure against homi-
    cides, 177.
  on Solon's law of abuse,
    194.
ποινή, 188.
poisoning, 47, 167, 181 f., 184.
Poland on associations, 123,
  126 f.
polianomoi, 218.
police, interference of, 147.
policy of tyrants at Athens, 148 f.
polis, the Greek, 2, 12 ff.
— execution on, 108.
— as moral personality, 104.
πόλις ἔκκλητος, 160.
πολιτεία, relation of, to the State,
  98, 106.
— = citizenship, 117 f.
political accusation, 166. *See
  also* προβολή.
political allegiance of colony to
  mother city, 158.
  crimes, 169 f.
  education, Protagoras on, 188.
  privileges, loss of, 189 f.
  psychology of Protagoras, 31 f.
  trial, 62, *see also* εἰσαγγελία.
Politics, 97, 105 f., 129 f., 143 f.,
  212, *and see* Aristotle.
πολιτικὸν δίκαιον, 44.
pollution, 75, 185.
πολύκληροι, 254.
Polybios, on case of seizure,
  228.